Desserts
BY
Nancy Silverton

Desserts

BY

Nancy Silverton

IN COLLABORATION WITH HEIDI YORKSHIRE

RECIPES TESTED BY ELISE DI DONATO
DECORATIVE PAINTINGS BY DEBORAH HEALY
TECHNIQUE DRAWINGS BY WENDY WRAY

HARPER & ROW, PUBLISHERS, NEW YORK
CAMBRIDGE, PHILADELPHIA, SAN FRANCISCO, WASHINGTON
LONDON, MEXICO CITY, SAO PAULO, SINGAPORE, SYDNEY

FIRST EDITION

DESIGNED BY JOEL AVIROM

———————————————————————————————

Library of Congress Cataloging-in-Publication
Data
Silverton, Nancy.
    Desserts by Nancy Silverton.

    Includes index.
    1. Desserts.   I. Title.
TX773.S52   1986   641.8′6   86-45148
ISBN 0-06-181770-8

———————————————————————————————

86 87 88 89 90 MPC 10 9 8 7 6 5 4 3 2 1

To my parents, Larry and Doris Silverton, who have supported
me with encouragement, and occasionally cash,
in my formative years of cooking.

I've long believed that the two most important parts of a menu are the desserts and the appetizers. Think about your impressions when you visit someone's house for the first time. Your two strongest memories are usually your first impressions, as you arrive, and your last impressions, when you leave. The same can be true for a restaurant meal; for some, the dessert is the grand finale of the entire evening.

That's why, from the very beginning, I was lucky to have Nancy Silverton making desserts for me at Spago. When we first opened the restaurant, things were chaotic, to say the least. I was so worried about money that we were working with a skeleton crew. I was alone at the grill, Mark Peel was doing the pasta, we had one man on salad and another for the pizza, and frankly, there were moments when we were really overwhelmed.

A new restaurant has its ups and downs for a while, but our customers always left happy after we sent them a complimentary assortment of Nancy's desserts, a big platter of cookies, tarts, cakes and ice creams that showed off what she could do. We sent so many of those platters on the house that the dessert assortment unexpectedly became a specialty of ours, and people would come back and ask for it again and again. Few restaurants serve as large a selection of desserts as we do, but few restaurants have ever had a dessert chef as talented, energetic, ambitious, and dedicated as Nancy Silverton.

Before we opened Spago, Mark Peel, my chef (and Nancy's future husband), came to me, blushing, and said that we just had to hire her. I teased him a lot, because I knew he was attracted to her, but I also trusted his judgment. As it turned out, Nancy's desserts suited my cooking so well that working with her was easy. Most pastry chefs make things too complicated, but Nancy has the instinct for just making them better. For instance, when I suggested that we serve small apple pies, she didn't start thinking of ways to make them fancier; instead, she simply worked at making them as good as possible. She succeeded so well that, from the very beginning, Individual Apple Tarts with a scoop of caramel ice cream have been one of our best-selling desserts. When we first opened, I was crazy about her Pecan Tartlettes; during one period of time, I ate so much of her Prune-Armagnac Ice Cream that I couldn't look at it for weeks afterward. I continue to love the taste and texture of her Lemon-Lime Tart.

I've often felt that Nancy could have been my sister, because we think almost the same way. We didn't have to talk for an hour before she understood what I wanted; sometimes she seemed to know what I wanted before I did myself. Not to say that we never argued. When Nancy wanted something important—more help in the kitchen, an expensive new ice-cream machine, anything she felt she needed to make her work better—she didn't let up until she got it.

In a profession where difficult personalities and temper tantrums are not uncommon, Nancy has a quiet professionalism that sets her apart. I remember her in a chocolate-smudged apron, keeping an eye on the egg whites beating in the mixer as she constructed a truffle cake, then suddenly, in response to the unerring clock in her head, pulling a perfectly baked sheet of cookies out of the oven—all the while watching her assistants going about their work. A good pastry chef has to be exact and to have patience—both qualities Nancy has in abundance. And she really loves what she does. She used to come in to the restaurant even on her days off. And when she was working hard on a new recipe, she could forget everything, including the discomfort of working ten-to-twelve-hour days in her ninth month of pregnancy, in her quest to get something right. In fact, I'm still amazed remembering how Nancy managed to give birth to her first child, Vanessa, on her day off. She was in great spirits and energetically back at work, with Vanessa assisting her, only two weeks later.

From your standpoint, as the reader of this cookbook, Nancy's best quality is her unusual ability to teach people well. So many chefs are secretive, guarding their recipes and their expertise, but Nancy is generous with her knowledge. Her attitude has always been that other people—her assistants in the restaurant, her cooking-school students—should be able to make desserts as well as she can, and the recipes in this book reflect that attitude, too.

Nancy's generosity with her knowledge also means that these recipes are long, but don't be put off by their length. Some cookbook writers will leave important steps out of a recipe in order to create an illusion of simplicity.

Nancy doesn't leave you guessing. Her desire in writing down these recipes was to give you the benefit of her experience, as if you were standing in the kitchen looking over her shoulder. Whether or not you're an experienced dessert maker, you'll be able to approach these recipes with the same self-possessed calm that Nancy has in the kitchen, and the results will surely please you.

Wolfgang Puck
April, 1986

INTRODUCTION

*I*was a late bloomer when it came to food. As a child I always opted for my neighbor's creamed tuna on toast over my mother's Boeuf Bourguignon. On family vacations, while my father, mother, and sister would be searching out ethnic food, I'd be on the lookout for a twenty-four-hour coffee shop. I did like to putter around the kitchen, though. My childhood friend, Margy Rochlin, loves to remind me of how, at age eight, I called her into my mother's kitchen to give her step-by-step instructions on my newly developed recipe: sautéed canned potatoes with paprika.

My turning point came when I was a freshman at college in northern California, an English major, with no particular career plans. The first week in the dormitory, I met Bill, who ran the natural foods section of the dormitory kitchen. I promptly purchased my first cookbook (*Cooking Creatively with Natural Foods*), became a vegetarian, and convinced him to hire me. At the time I had no idea that mastering the perfect lentil loaf would someday turn into an obsession for baking.

A few restaurant kitchens and three years later, I fell into baking by fluke. Michael McCarty of Michael's Restaurant in Santa Monica offered me a job as assistant pastry chef. (A rule of thumb in the restaurant business is to take what you are offered.) Initially I was apprehensive. I shared the fear that most people have, that baking is a rigid and absolute art. True, dessert making turned out to be precise in that it is bound by certain chemical factors, but after some familiarity with ingredients and technique, I was surprised at how wide those boundaries really are.

Nothing replaces a hands-on approach to cooking. The only way to improve is to experiment and make mistakes. Practically every time I pick up a whisk or crack an egg I learn something new.

I prefer desserts to be intense in flavor, which is not to be confused with being heavy or overly sweet. Chocolate desserts should taste chocolatey, lemon desserts should taste tart. Before I start to work on a new recipe, I close my eyes, scrunch my face, and try to conjure up exactly what the end result should look and taste like. I'm not satisfied until the dessert I've made measures up to the one I'd imagined.

What I have to offer to you is a wide collection of recipes that I have worked on over the past few years. They will give you an idea of the enormous possibilities in dessert making. I've tried to achieve a balance between French- and American-style desserts. Some are a hybrid of the two. All of them fulfill what is to me the most important requirement of dessert making—flavor, texture, and presentation —and all of them have their roots in desserts I have eaten, desserts that have been taught to me, and desserts I have read about. Some recipes are more time-consuming than others, but if they are broken up into component parts, which can be made well in advance, the final assemblage can be done quickly and with relative ease.

The challenge in creating a good dessert, and the pleasure it brings to its recipient, is unmatched by any other type of cooking. There is something that is associated with a homemade dessert that evokes among all of us a sense of comfort and well-being—it is a gift of love.

*T*here is no way to quantify the amount of help others have given me in completing this book. Writing a cookbook, like cooking in a restaurant, is a collective effort. This is my opportunity to thank those whose help was immeasurable.

Wolfgang Puck and Barbara Lazaroff offered advice and push. They created Spago Restaurant, to which I owe my professional success. They remain friends, mentors, and examples of perfectionism and hard work.

Many times able assistants become lost in the shadows of the so-called limelight; however, without them, little can be accomplished. Therefore I wish to thank my dedicated and long-suffering assistants at Spago—Mary Bergin, Melinda Bulgarin, Lissa Doumani, Alan Gross, Beatrice Keech, and Kevin Ripley. Special thanks must go to Dana Farkas, who struggled with me over the development of many of the recipes, and to Amy Pressman who provided inspiration at key points.

Jimmy Brinkley was my pastry chef at Michael's Restaurant (I was his assistant). Working with him was an eye-opening and horizon-expanding experience. He taught me the basics and that it's not necessary to make "name" desserts. If it's great, that's enough.

I must mention the people who have influenced and taught me over the years, people without whom I would still be making lentil loaf: Bob Miller, Michael Goldblatt, Michael Goldstein, Jonathan Waxman, Billy Pflug, Michael McCarty, Mark Miller, Gaston Lenôtre, and, of course, Jean Bertanou.

I have emphasized throughout this book the importance of using only the best ingredients and equipment, so I fondly remember those who have supplied those essential things: Alan Weiss of West Central Produce in Los Angeles has always tried to send the best and freshest products and has supplied seasonal information.

Tom, Frank, and Kay Chino of Chino Ranch in Del Mar, California, raise the finest, sweetest fruits I have tasted. Paula Kaplan, my Rykoff sales representative, was my unfailing supplier of equipment, dry goods, and local restaurant gossip.

A special thanks to Wendi Matthews, who attended the birth of this book and my two children and has gone on to become their second mother; to my sister and brother-in-law, Gail and Manfred Krankl, and my husband's parents, Cheryl and Fred Peel, for their loving support.

I could never forget my collaborator, Heidi Yorkshire, who took over two hundred recipes and produced a coherent book. My literary agents, Maureen and Eric Lasher, convinced me that this could be done and stuck by me throughout. Ann Bramson, my editor, offered invaluable help and advice. Elise di Donato assisted in testing these recipes with patience. My friend and collaborator Joan Hoien is dearly missed.

And finally, most important, my husband Mark and my children, Vanessa and Benjamin, put up with all the chaos, and to them I'm always grateful.

Nancy Silverton
New York
June, 1986

Thanks to Analee and Boris Yorkshire, for loving support; Maureen and Eric Lasher; Anne Sprecher, Loren MacArthur, Neil Feineman, Arlene Feldman, Paddy Calistro, Lucinda Dyer; Elise, Peter, and Francesca di Donato; Ann Holbrook; Ann Bramson; Sallie Coolidge; the NWU, L.A. local; my loving sister, Wendy Yorkshire; and the steadfast Michael Balter. And to Nancy Silverton, who has made me forever a perfectionist—about desserts.

H.Y.

TRADE SECRETS

Contrary to what most professional chefs would like you to think—there's no such thing as a list of secrets for successful dessert making. A secret implies something that's hidden, but the goal of this chapter, and of all the recipes in this book, is to take the mystery and the fear out of making desserts.

The big advantage that a professional chef has over a typical home cook is familiarity with the ingredients and processes that together make up any given dessert. You need to be familiar with the products so you're able to select the best, and familiar with the basic techniques so that you can recognize when you have arrived at the proper results.

My colleague Beatrice Keech tells the story of how she once worked for a well-known French pastry chef who kept his book of recipes under lock and key. He would give out, at most, only half of each recipe to the people who worked for him, so that no one would ever be able to duplicate his desserts. He didn't realize that it's not only the quantity of sugar, chocolate, or whatever ingredient that makes a perfect dessert, but also using good-quality ingredients and making each stage of the recipe perfectly that's the key. The accumulation of impeccably executed steps along the way—egg whites beaten to silky smoothness; a cake just springy to the touch when it's taken out of the oven; chocolate truffle cream glossy before it's chilled—guarantees professional results.

As Julia Child says, long recipes are teaching recipes. I've made every recipe in this book over and over, some of them hundreds of times. To turn my experience to your advantage, I've written all the recipes in some detail, giving you as many watch points as possible regarding the colors, textures, aromas, flavors, and temperatures.

Every time you make one of these desserts, following the detailed instructions, you'll be perfecting your knowledge of each of the techniques. Also, since it's unrealistic to expect that every time you make a given dessert the conditions will be exactly the same—the temperature outside could be different, or the thickness of the pan, or the intensity of the flame on the stove—having some guidelines for judging the success of each step will help you succeed no matter what the conditions.

Some processes are called for so often, in so many recipes, that they merit a more detailed explanation than I've included in the recipes themselves. You'll find those expanded explanations in this chapter, as well as information on frequently used ingredients. I've explained specific techniques and special ingredients used in only one or two dishes in the recipes themselves.

INGREDIENTS AND TECHNIQUES

ALCOHOLS AND LIQUEURS: The most commonly used alcohols in desserts are probably Cognac and rum, because they complement so many different flavors. If you want to invest in only a couple of bottles, these are the ones to keep on hand. Many recipes call for other flavored alcohols and liqueurs, such as crème de menthe, poire Williams (French pear alcohol), Calvados (French apple brandy), or various fruit and nut liqueurs like orange, apricot, tangerine, or hazelnut. These liqueurs are added to intensify special flavors. (If you've had a liqueur stashed away for a long time, taste it; it will lose its flavor after a time.)

To substitute other liquids for alcohols: If you want to eliminate alcohol from a recipe, substitute an equal amount of water, fruit juice, or strong coffee, depending on the flavors in the dessert. Add the liquid at the same point in the recipe that the alcohol would be added, and at the same temperature. (Alcohols and liqueurs can also be substituted for each other in the same amounts, as long as the flavors are complementary.)

ALMOND MEAL: Many recipes call for almond meal (finely ground almonds), which is now available in specialty shops and some health food stores. Don't confuse it with almond powder or almond flour, which have too fine a texture. I prefer to use blanched almond meal, made of almonds without skins. The unblanched meal has little specks of brown in it from the almond skins, which are unattractive in a finished dessert.

To make almond meal: For each cup of almond meal, grind ⅔ cup blanched almonds in a nut grinder or Mouli grater until they reach the consistency of fine cornmeal. In a food processor, grind the almonds with a bit of the sugar called for in the recipe. The sugar will prevent the nuts from getting too gummy. Stop grinding while the nuts still have their fluffy texture; do not grind to a paste.

BAKING POWDER AND BAKING SODA: Both are frequently used leavening agents. They assure that a heavy cake batter will rise. When there is not enough leavening in a recipe, the finished cake will be too compact; when there is too much, the cake will rise too high, crack on the top, fall quickly when removed from the oven, and be dense on the bottom when cut.

Baking soda, an alkaline, reacts with acidic ingredients (like buttermilk or fruit juice) and the carbon dioxide formed in that reaction makes the cake rise. The alkaline also stabilizes an acidic batter and keeps it from separating. Baking soda will keep indefinitely if it remains dry.

Baking powder, which has baking soda in it, is acidic, and is therefore used in batters that don't have acidic ingredients. Baking powder has a limited shelf life; check the expiration date on the container.

To activate baking soda: In most of my recipes, I have chosen to activate the baking soda first, by mixing it with an equal amount of boiling water. In many recipes, this makes the final product rise better than sifting it into the dry ingredients. If the water you use to activate it is truly boiling, the baking soda will sizzle and bubble.

BEATING TO A RIBBON: When eggs and sugar are beaten long enough so that when the beater is lifted, the mixture that falls back into the bowl will hold its shape for a few seconds.

BUTTER: All recipes in this book call for unsalted butter. It is generally fresher than salted butter when you buy it, and should be stored frozen.

In cold weather, the butter can usually be left at room temperature to soften before it is beaten. In hot weather, however, butter that's too warm tends to get greasy and will separate. It is better to use it straight from the refrigerator and to beat it longer than the recipe calls for, if necessary, to get the right consistency.

To cream butter: This basic operation for making butter-based cakes and cookies beats air into the butter, adding volume and making it creamy so that other ingredients will then mix in smoothly. If a recipe includes lemon or orange zest, I always add the zest to the butter while it is creaming, because the beating releases the flavor in the zest.

Cut the butter into small pieces and beat on low speed in an electric mixer, using the paddle attachment, until it starts to soften. In cold weather, you can hold the mixing bowl with the butter in it over a burner for a few seconds until the bottom of the bowl warms and the butter just starts to melt. Increase speed to medium-high and beat for 3–5 minutes, until the butter whitens, holds soft peaks, and makes a slapping sound when it hits the sides of the bowl. (By hand, use a wooden spoon and slap the butter from side to side in a large bowl.)

If the butter becomes runny in hot weather (rather than light and fluffy), put the bowl into the refrigerator and chill it until firm, then begin again. Adding the sugar just after the butter breaks up, instead of after it is completely beaten, is another way to avoid runny butter in hot weather.

BUTTER, CLARIFIED: When butter is clarified—that is, when the milk solids in it are separated and discarded—it does not burn as easily as unclarified butter and therefore can be used at much higher temperatures. Also, in recipes where lightness is important, like the Popovers, clarified butter is called for because you want the taste of pure butter without the weight of the milk solids.

To make clarified butter, melt unsalted butter in a saucepan over low heat. Turn off heat and let the butter settle for a few minutes. With a spoon, skim off and discard all the foam that has risen to the surface. Then pour or spoon out the clear butter into a bowl, being careful not to disturb the solids that have sunk to the bottom of the saucepan. Discard the solids.

Clarified butter keeps longer than regular butter in the refrigerator.

For recipes that list clarified butter as an ingredient, measure half again the quantity of butter and then clarify as directed above. For example, if a recipe calls for ½ cup clarified butter, start with ¾ cup unclarified. If a very small amount of clarified butter is called for, it is probably easiest to clarify no less than ½ cup, keeping the rest frozen or refrigerated for another use.

CHOCOLATE: Unless you use an excellent chocolate, there is no point in making a chocolate dessert. Before you buy any quantity, taste a sample first. You should be able to close your eyes and know that you're eating chocolate, not wax, or worse.

Unfortunately, most domestic chocolate is simply not up to the standards of the imported brands. Among the best are Suchard, Lindt, Tobler, Calabaut, L'Abbaye, and Cadbury. Cookware shops like Williams-Sonoma and some fine supermarkets are now selling high-quality chocolate in large quantities, which were once available only to restaurant kitchens.

For dark chocolate, I always use bittersweet chocolate. American semisweet chocolate is not the same (it is too sweet), nor is unsweetened chocolate, which contains no sugar. One of the advantages of using European chocolates is that the law requires them to be labeled with the percentage of cacao, or pure chocolate, they contain. The taste of a chocolate depends on its percentage of pure chocolate and cocoa butter.

The chocolates I use are all *couverture* quality, which means that they contain between 31 and 38 percent cocoa butter (average 34 percent) and between 38 and 61 percent pure chocolate (average 40 percent). The taste and texture of a finished dessert is based as much on the amount of fat (cocoa butter) in the chocolate as on the amount of pure chocolate.

Milk chocolate is made from lightly roasted cocoa beans, contains more cocoa butter than dark chocolate, and has powdered milk mixed in. Brands of milk chocolate vary considerably in sweetness, and, as with bittersweet chocolate, imported brands are far superior to domestic.

White chocolate is also made from lightly roasted beans mixed with cocoa butter and powdered milk. It is technically not a chocolate at all, because it does not contain the pure chocolate that comes from the center of the cocoa bean and gives darker chocolate its color. When buying white chocolate, be sure that it contains cocoa butter, not vegetable oil.

To store chocolate: Store chocolate well wrapped, in a cool place. If too warm, the cocoa butter will separate and rise to the surface in light streaks. The chocolate can still be used, however, despite its looks. If it is refrigerated, chocolate will "sweat" when it warms to room temperature, and the moisture will prevent it from melting smoothly.

Dark chocolate will keep for years. Milk and white chocolate, because of the milk in them, can become rancid in six to nine months. You'll be able to tell by tasting it.

To melt chocolate: Cut or break chocolate into 2-inch pieces and place in a heatproof bowl. Place the bowl over a pot of barely simmering water to melt. Make sure the bowl is several inches larger than the pot so no steam gets into the chocolate, or the chocolate will seize up. (The water should not touch the bottom of the bowl or the chocolate will burn.) When chocolate is melted, turn off heat and let stand over warm water until ready to use. Use chocolate warm, because as it starts to cool it will harden around the edges of the bowl. Chocolate can be remelted any number of times.

Milk chocolate and white chocolate burn more easily than dark chocolate. Watch them carefully while melting, being sure that the flame under the pot is low and that the heat is turned off as soon as they are melted. White chocolate will cara-melize and turn brown if overheated, which makes it unusable.

If a few drops of water get into the chocolate as it melts, it will stiffen. (On the other hand, a large quantity of liquid can easily be mixed into melted chocolate with no problem.) To soften stiffened chocolate, stir in vegetable oil by teaspoon-fuls until it smooths out.

Untempered melted chocolate loses its gloss when it hardens. However, this is important only for certain candies. For this reason I have decided not to include the method for tempering chocolate.

COCONUT: I use only unsweetened coconut, preferably the long-shred variety, which is available at health food stores. I like the look of the long strands, but if it is unavailable you can substitute the shorter shred. Never substitute sweetened coconut for unsweetened.

CREAM: Recipes call for heavy cream, also known as whipping cream. (Do not confuse with light cream or half-and-half, which is half milk, half cream.) Try to find a heavy cream without preservatives or additives; don't use ultra-pasteurized cream if you can avoid it. If you live near a dairy, you can buy manufacturer's cream, which has no stabilizers or whipping additives, and a higher butterfat content than supermarket cream. It will produce a smoother, creamier product.

To whip cream: Cream must be very cold to whip properly. Whip it straight from the refrigerator, using chilled utensils. I often add about 2 tablespoons of sour cream to each cup of heavy cream, because it smooths out the texture of the cream and adds a slightly sour taste that I like, reminiscent of French crème fraîche.

I whip cream to fold into desserts or to serve on the side. For those purposes, the cream should be whipped only to soft peaks that barely hold their shape. Whipped cream should not be so thin that it won't hold its shape, as it will thin out whatever it is being combined with. Nor should it be so stiff that it becomes rocky and curdled-looking, as it will not blend smoothly and easily into the preparation. Over-whipped cream turns quickly into butter.

If you're energetic, it is best to whip cream by hand, because there's no chance of overbeating and losing the smooth texture.

To whip cream in an electric mixer, use the whisk attachment and beat the cream on low speed (with the sour cream, if specified), until it thickens enough not to spatter. Increase speed to medium-high and beat just until the cream is thick and mousselike, no stiffer. Remove from mixer and whisk a few times by hand to form soft peaks. Refrigerate until needed.

Cream can be whipped in advance and stored in the refrigerator. Whisk it briefly by hand to stiffen if it separates during storage.

To fold whipped cream into another preparation: When any two preparations are folded together, they should have the same texture. When adding whipped cream to a heavier batter or mousse, for instance, whisk one third to one half the whipped cream into the batter until combined to lighten its texture, then fold and stir in the rest of the whipped cream with a rubber spatula.

CRÈME ANGLAISE: Crème anglaise is a custard, a mixture of milk or cream or a mixture of the two, gently cooked with egg yolks and flavored with sugar and other flavorings like vanilla, liqueurs, or mint. Gently cooking the egg yolks thickens the custard until it will just coat the back of a spoon, still pourable. Crème anglaise is the base for all ice cream recipes in this book, as well as custard sauces and a number of other desserts.

Fear of curdling the egg yolks has made many cooks avoid custard making, but the process is not as tricky as you might think, and nothing will develop your confidence as much as simply doing it a few times. The more experience you have, the more you'll develop a feeling for this simple operation.

To make a crème anglaise: In a saucepan, scald cream or milk with vanilla bean or other flavorings, such as lemon zest or mint leaves. Turn off heat, cover pan, and let flavorings infuse for 30 minutes.

In a mixing bowl, whisk together the egg yolks and sugar for a few minutes until the sugar has dissolved. It is best to do this by hand, rather than using an electric mixer, because if too much air is beaten into the eggs it becomes difficult to cook them properly or to tell if the custard has thickened enough.

Reheat the cream mixture, infused with the flavorings, to scalding. Pour about one fourth of the hot cream into the egg yolks, whisking continuously. Return mixture to saucepan and whisk together with remaining cream. Cook, stirring slowly but constantly with a wooden spoon, covering the entire bottom of the pan as you stir. The mixture will turn slightly yellow in color, the tiny bubbles on the surface will disappear, and it will thicken slightly, enough to lightly coat the back of a spoon. When you run your finger across the back of the spoon, the trail of your finger should remain, and the custard should not flow together again. Immediately strain the crème anglaise through a fine-mesh strainer into a bowl and whisk it for a few seconds to release the heat, stopping the cooking.

The heat on the stove can be as high as you dare; the lower the temperature, the longer the custard will take to thicken, but the more remote the possibility of curdling. There are also a few ways to stop the custard from curdling: (1) Cook it over a pot of simmering water rather than over direct heat; (2) Keep a couple of tablespoons of cold cream (measured from the total needed in the recipe) in the bowl into which you plan to strain the custard. When the cooked custard is stirred into the cold cream, the temperature will lower immediately, stopping it from cooking further; (3) Set the bowl in a bed of ice cubes when thickened to cool the custard immediately.

To salvage a curdled custard: Crème anglaise curdles when the temperature of the mixture goes too high and the eggs scramble rather than thickening smoothly. To tell if a custard has curdled, slip a metal spoon into it; if tiny dots of cooked egg show up on the metal, it has curdled. You can't use it in that condition, because you'll be able to feel the bits of egg on your tongue when you eat it. It can be salvaged by whizzing it immediately in a blender—it should smooth out perfectly. If large pieces of egg show up on the spoon, it has overcurdled. In that case, throw it away and start over.

EGGS: All recipes in this book were tested with extra large eggs. In general, I have no preference about whether eggs are at room temperature or refrigerated for use in most desserts. I do find, however, that cold eggs are easier to separate because the yolks are firmer. (Also, fresh eggs are easier to separate than older eggs because the membrane surrounding the yolk is firmer and less likely to break.) Custards made with cold eggs will, of course, take longer to heat and thicken than custards made with room-temperature eggs.

Measuring broken eggs: 1 liquid ounce = 1 egg white; 1 tablespoon stirred egg yolk = 1 yolk; 3 tablespoons mixed whites and yolks = 1 whole egg.

To beat egg whites: Smoothly whipped egg whites are easy to achieve, and they're an essential step in making beautiful desserts. If the whites aren't smooth and firm, cakes won't rise well, batters will be thin, and mousses will have the wrong texture.

To start with, be sure the mixing bowl and beater are clean and completely dry, and that there is not a speck of egg yolk in the whites.

It may sound strange, but egg whites get better with age. With age, the proteins in the whites develop and become thicker, which makes the whites beat to greater volume and silkier smoothness than fresh egg whites. If you do keep a container of egg whites, stir them before measuring to mix in the thick proteins that rise to the top. As long as there are no yolks mixed in, the whites will keep refrigerated, covered, for quite a long time. Don't freeze the egg whites, as this retards the aging process. You will be able to tell when the egg whites are no longer good, because they will become thin and watery. Don't be put off if they have a slight odor; they are still quite usable.

Sugar acts as an emulsifier to beaten egg whites, smoothing out the texture. Too little sugar will result in whites that separate and look rough and rocky. The formula I use is 1 egg white to 1½ teaspoons sugar. Very fresh egg whites might need a touch more sugar—add a pinch or two before you start beating to help them mount.

Egg whites are best when a large amount of air is beaten into them gradually. To beat eggs in an electric mixer, use the whisk attachment and beat the egg whites on low speed for a few minutes until foamy. Increase speed to medium and beat until soft peaks form. Increase speed to high and very gradually beat in the sugar until stiff, glossy peaks form.

To beat by hand, use an unlined copper bowl (always clean and dry) and a large balloon whisk. Add the sugar at the beginning and beat in steady strokes.

Beaten egg whites must be used immediately; they cannot sit. Always beat them at the last possible minute before using, with everything else ready. Don't wash your hands, don't answer the phone, use them!

To salvage overbeaten egg whites: Overbeaten egg whites are no longer smooth. To correct the texture, add a raw egg white or a few teaspoons more sugar—one or the other, not both—and beat again briefly until smooth. It is better to slightly underbeat whites than to overbeat them, because overbeaten ones are very difficult, and take longer, to combine smoothly into a batter. Instead of just lightening a batter, overbeaten whites will thin it out, and the batter will be speckled with little white dots of egg white.

To incorporate egg whites into other preparations: Most people are far too careful when combining beaten egg whites with other preparations, handling them much too gingerly. Time is the most important factor here, and if you pussyfoot around they can curdle and become impossible to incorporate into your mixture.

For any two mixtures to be incorporated, they must be of a similar consistency. Whether you're adding egg whites to a thick, sticky batter to lighten its texture, or adding them to a thin batter to thicken it, in either case you need to create a similar consistency in both mixtures before the egg whites can be successfully folded in.

Start by whisking one third to one half the beaten whites into the batter to combine. Don't be afraid of deflating the egg whites. Fast and fearlessly whisk the first portion in with a wire whisk or your fingertips. Then, fold and stir in the rest with a rubber spatula or your cupped hand, breaking up the egg whites, giving a few folds and a few stirs, mixing from the bottom to the top of the bowl. The mixture should be totally homogeneous, without any chunks of unincorporated white. When totally incorporated, fill the cake pans or mold.

Now, you can stop for a moment and take a deep breath—filled cake pans don't have to go into the oven immediately.

FLOUR: Desserts in this book are made with unbleached pastry flour, unless otherwise specified. Cake flour is an acceptable substitute. Both these flours are made of "soft" wheat, which contains little gluten, the protein that can make a pastry tough. Cake flour contains even less gluten than pastry flour. Products made with soft flour will be more tender than if they are made from all-purpose flour, which is made from "harder" wheat, containing more gluten. If you aren't sure what kind of flour is in an unmarked bag or jar, just squeeze a handful—cake flour and pastry flour will hold their shape.

To measure flour, scoop it out of the container in a dry measuring cup, level it with the back of a knife, and then sift it, if sifting is called for. (If the flour is lumpy, break it up with your hands before measuring.) Never tap a measuring cup to level flour, as it will pack down. Store flour in the freezer to keep it dry and free of bugs.

FROSTING A CAKE: Most of the cakes in this book are decorated with a pourable chocolate glaze rather than frosted with a heavier mixture. To frost a cake with two or more layers sandwiched together, do not begin to frost the outside until the filling is firm enough to prevent the layers from sliding around. (On a warm day you may have to refrigerate frosting until you're ready to use it. Make sure it's smooth and spreadable before continuing.) When firm, hold the cake in the palm of your hand, and with a long-bladed metal spatula frost the side of the cake, rotating your hand as you go, with a smooth even layer about ¼ inch thick. Return the cake to the refrigerator or freezer until the frosting is firm again. Set the cake on a flat surface and scrape the remaining frosting onto the top of the cake with a spatula. Spread the frosting over the surface of the cake. To ensure that the coating is thin and even, lay the flat side of the spatula across the middle of the cake and, holding the handle of the spatula in one hand and lightly pressing the top side of the blade with your other hand, rock the spatula back and forth from one edge of the cake to the other a couple of times, allowing the excess frosting to fall over the edge of the cake. Pick the cake up in the palm of your hand again and, while rotating the cake, bring the spatula downward from top to bottom along the edge of the cake at a 30-degree angle to redistribute the excess frosting and smooth the sides of the cake.

FRUIT, POACHING: There are two reasons to poach fruit: to infuse a flavor, such as pears poached in ginger, or to improve the flavor and softness of fruit that doesn't seem quite ripe enough, or flavorful enough. Peaches, plums, apricots, nectarines, and pears—all take well to poaching.

Fruit that needs to be poached is usually lacking in sugar content, so I poach it in sugar syrup and usually add a flavoring, like a few tablespoons of lemon juice or an appropriate alcohol. Peel the fruit or leave the skins on, according to the recipe.

To poach fruit halves, place them in a saucepan or high-sided sauté pan and cover with sugar syrup mixed with flavoring. Heat to boiling, reduce heat to a simmer, and cook gently until the fruit is tender but not mushy. The amount of time needed varies with the type and ripeness of the fruit. Almost-ripe peaches, for instance, are just heated to the boil and then drained immediately or left to cool in the poaching liquid. Firm pears, on the other hand, are usually poached for close to an hour.

Ideally, let the fruit cool in the syrup, to absorb as much flavor as possible, but if it seems too soft, drain immediately and spread the fruit out on a baking sheet to cool as fast as possible and stop the cooking.

If a recipe calls for sliced fruit, place the slices in the bottom of a large heatproof bowl, heat the syrup and flavoring to a boil, and pour it over the fruit. If the fruit is almost soft, drain immediately and spread the slices out on a baking sheet to cool. Otherwise, let the fruit cool in the syrup until it reaches the desired softness.

Sugar syrup can be reused a number of times. If, after a couple of uses, it becomes too thick, thin it with water.

GELATIN: Gelatin is available in two forms: granulated and in sheets. Sheet gelatin is preferred by many professional cooks because it is flavorless and less likely than granulated gelatin to lump. The recipes in this book, however, call for granulated gelatin because it is more widely available. Remember to remelt the gelatin over simmering water if it has hardened before you have gotten a chance to use it.

To use sheet gelatin, figure 5 sheets to 1 tablespoon granulated. Soak the sheets for a few minutes in ice water until soft, squeeze out the water, and then follow instructions for using granulated gelatin.

GINGER: Fresh ginger is widely available year-round in the produce section of supermarkets, and it keeps well in the refrigerator. Unless otherwise specified, peel it with a vegetable peeler before using. "Young" ginger, which is available seasonally, is much less fibrous, and does not need to be peeled before use.

Because ginger contains quite a bit of acid, it has to be blanched before it is added to dairy products to keep them from curdling, as described in the recipes for Ginger Ice Cream and Ginger Parfait, for example. To blanch, place the peeled and sliced ginger in a saucepan and cover with water. Bring the water to a boil and boil for 30 seconds. Drain well and proceed with the recipe.

Candied ginger: Sold in supermarkets. It is usually coated with sugar, and has a peppery, spicy flavor. For most recipes, the sugar coating is rinsed off to eliminate the extra sweetness.

INFUSING FLAVORS: Infusing is a method of adding an intense, concentrated flavor to a dessert, especially one made with milk or cream. The milk or cream is placed in a saucepan with a flavoring like lemon or orange zest, vanilla beans, ginger, or fresh herbs, and is heated to scalding. The saucepan is then removed from the heat, covered, and allowed to stand for at least one hour, until the liquid is completely infused with the flavor. The flavoring is usually strained out and discarded.

NUTS: Several varieties of nuts are used in these recipes, mainly hazelnuts (also called filberts), almonds, and walnuts. For long storage, refrigerate or freeze to keep them from getting rancid.

Almonds can be bought blanched (with the skins taken off) or unblanched (with the skins on). For almond meal, I prefer blanched almonds. For ice cream, unblanched almonds are preferable because they don't get soft. Hazelnuts are used with the skins removed after toasting.

Toasting nuts: Toasted nuts get stale faster than raw nuts, so always toast them just before you're going to use them. Preheat oven to 325 degrees. Spread the nuts on a baking sheet and toast for 8–10 minutes. Test for doneness by breaking a nut in half. The interior should be lightly brown with no burnt aftertaste. Rub with a clean dish towel when cool to remove skins.

PASTRY: Handling pastry isn't hard, but it does take practice. It's simply a matter of touch, of knowing when the pastry is the right temperature and pliability to be rolled out easily. If you give yourself the chance to work with pastry often, you'll soon be comfortable enough to manipulate it like a pro.

To roll out pastry: The most important factor when rolling out pastry is the temperature of the room you're in—the cooler, the better. Try to work with the dough before turning on the oven, which heats the kitchen.

You'll need a large clear countertop, smooth and solid, giving you plenty of room to work, preferably one that's low enough to give your arms some leverage as you roll. (If the counter is too high, stand on a phone book or work on a tabletop to get the right angle.) A refrigerated slab of marble is ideal for rolling pastry because it retains cold. You can get a similar effect by chilling any surface—cover it briefly with ice packs, boxes of frozen foods, or a baking sheet covered with ice.

In warm weather, take the pastry directly from the refrigerator, cut it into fourths or sixths, pound it with a rolling pin to soften, and then work it briefly with your hands, without kneading it, into a smooth, pliable (but not sticky) ball. No matter what the weather, always use your fingertips to work the dough, because they're cooler than your palms.

In cold weather, take chilled pastry out of the refrigerator and let it stand at room temperature until it's almost soft enough to roll out. Then beat it for a moment or two with a rolling pin to soften.

Before you begin to roll out your dough, brush your pan or flan ring with melted butter. Keep a small bowl of flour nearby as you roll. Some flour on the work surface is absolutely necessary to keep the pastry from sticking, but use as little as possible. The softer the dough and the warmer the weather, the more flour you will end up using. If the dough cracks when you begin to roll it, let it stand a bit more to soften; if it is greasy or sticking too much to the work surface, refrigerate it again until firm. (Remember that working pastry with your hands too much will develop the gluten in the flour, which will make it elastic and difficult to roll out, and result in a tough crust.)

To roll, place a ball of pastry in the center of a floured surface. Pound the ball with a rolling pin to flatten it into a disk about 1 inch thick. Begin rolling the dough from the center of the disk, turning it slightly clockwise after each stroke to make an even circle. (Dust both the surface of the dough and the underside as necessary to avoid sticking.)

Roll dough into a circle at least 2 inches larger in diameter than the ring or pan to be lined, and to a thickness of ⅛ to ¼ inch. Roll in short strokes, stopping short of the edges of the dough so the edges don't get too thin. Lift and turn the circle every so often to keep it from sticking.

When the circle is finished, fold it gently in quarters, set the centerpoint in the center of the pan, and then unfold carefully. Or you may set the rolling pin across the top edge of the dough, and roll the rolling pin downward, rolling the dough around the pin. Unroll the dough into the mold.

If the dough is too soft to line the pan, slip it onto a baking sheet and chill for a few minutes until firm enough to handle. If it gets too firm, let it soften at room temperature so that it doesn't crack when you try to line the pan.

To fit the dough into the pan, go around the edges systematically, picking up the dough and easing it down so that it fits gently into the corners and sides of the pan. Don't stretch the dough to fit, or it will shrink later during baking. Dip the knuckle of your index finger in flour and go around the pan, pressing the dough into the corners with your knuckle. With your three middle fingers inside the pan and your thumb at the same point outside, press the dough into the sides of the pan, pinching slightly if necessary to make sure that the dough is an even thickness all around and especially that the dough is not too thick along the corners. The side pastry must be at a right angle to the bottom at this point (no sloping sides), or you'll lose the height of the shell when it shrinks during baking.

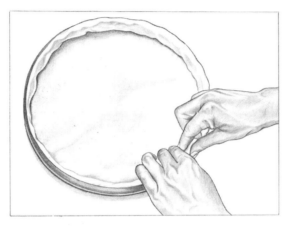

Lining a tart pan

Finally, with a sharp paring knife, trim the pastry even with the top of the pan and chill until firm.

To blind bake: After a lined flan ring or pie pan has chilled for about one hour (to allow the gluten to relax and to prevent shrinkage when the dough is cooked), completely line the bottom and sides with parchment paper, aluminum foil, or coffee filters. (I prefer the large, flat-bottomed coffee filters from automatic drip coffee makers, because they're pliable, reusable, and soft enough not to damage the unbaked pastry. If the filters aren't large enough to line the entire shell, arrange three or four of them in an overlapping pattern to completely cover the bottom and drape over the sides.)

Fill the lining, up to the top of the rim, with dried beans or metal pie weights (sold at cookware shops), both of which can be saved and reused. Make sure the beans are pressed tightly into the corners of the dough. Bake in a preheated 350-degree oven for 25 minutes, until the top of the crust is golden brown.

Cool completely. Remove beans or pie weights with a large spoon and carefully peel off paper lining. If the pastry is still moist on the bottom or not golden in color, return it unlined to the oven for a few more minutes until fully cooked.

HOW TO USE A PASTRY BAG: A pastry bag is a simple and efficient way to get batter, mousse, or filling of any sort into a mold, and to pipe shapes, like rounds of meringue or piped cookies. Reading a description of how to use a bag makes it sound a little awkward, but with some experience, it will become second nature.

Buy a soft, pliable cloth bag, at least 10 inches long, not the tiny, cake-decorating type. For piping fillings, mousses, etc., you will need the large, professional-size tips, both plain round and star tips.

To fill the bag, fit the correct tip in the bottom and then hold the bag in your left hand (or your right hand, if you're left-handed). Twist the small end of the empty bag just above the tip and stuff the bag into the tip itself to keep filling from oozing out as you fill the bag. Turn the bag down in a cuff over your hand, so there is a large, easy-to-get-to opening. Spoon the filling into the bag so it is half full, never more. Twist the bag just above the filling to close and untwist the tip end.

Before starting, squirt about the first inch or so of filling out of the bag, until you hear the air bubble pop. Then proceed with piping.

The most important principle when piping is to be as close to the work surface as possible. Position the top no less than one inch and no more than two inches above the mold you're piping into. If it is positioned too close, the filling will be squished flat; if it is too distant, it is too hard to control where the filling goes. Hold your right hand above the filling (your left if you're left-handed) and guide the bag with your other hand. Let the tip rest lightly between the second and third fingers of the guiding hand. Use the hand above the filling to provide the pressure to force the filling out. Move your hand downward as you squeeze the filling out and the bag empties.

Holding a pastry bag

If the filling flows out of the bag at a steady pace, the tip will control the thickness of the filling. If too much pressure is applied to the bag, the piped filling will be too thick.

Never refill a half-empty bag, as there will be too many air pockets. Instead, always pipe the filling out completely and refill again as directed above.

When you have finished using the pastry bag, rinse it well and turn it inside-out to dry.

TO SCALD LIQUIDS: To heat a liquid just below the boiling point. The liquid will steam and make small bubbles around the edge of the pan. When scalding alcohol, make sure the flame of your burner is low to prevent the alcohol from igniting.

SUGAR, CRYSTALLIZED: Also called pearl sugar or rock sugar, crystallized sugar has large crystals that add a crunchy texture when used to coat cookies or candied grapefruit peel. I use it only on desserts that aren't too sweet to begin with. (Use only the clear crystals rather than the artificially colored varieties.)

SUGAR SYRUP: Sugar syrup is used frequently in dessert making, to soak cakes, poach fruit, and sweeten sherbets and fruit sauces.
To make sugar syrup: Whisk together 3 cups water and 2¼ cups granulated sugar in a large saucepan to combine. Bring to a boil over medium heat, and boil until the sugar has dissolved and the mixture is clear, about 30 seconds. Cool. Keeps indefinitely in the refrigerator.

VANILLA BEANS: Vanilla beans are the seed pod of an orchid vine.
I use very large, plump Tahitian vanilla beans, which are about ½ inch wide and about 5 inches long (available by mail, see page 356). Beans should be slightly firm, packed with seeds, and not too moist. Adjust the number of vanilla beans in a recipe according to the size of your beans.
Unfortunately, the skinny, shriveled-up vanilla beans found in most supermarkets have so little flavor that they're a waste of money. A vanilla bean should have a pungent, almost overwhelming vanilla aroma. Store in the refrigerator or freezer to keep fresh.
To infuse vanilla beans into liquids: To use, vanilla beans have to be infused into a hot liquid, like milk or cream, for at least 30 minutes. Split the beans lengthwise with a paring knife, scrape out the seeds, and then put the seeds and the pod into the liquid and infuse as directed in the recipe. The pods are strained out after cooking, but the tiny black seeds remain, a sign that you've used real vanilla. Use the pods for vanilla sugar (see below).
To make vanilla sugar: Making vanilla sugar is a great way to use up every part of the expensive vanilla bean. Some cooks simply store the pods in a jar with sugar, but I find that grinding the dried pods with the sugar makes a much more flavorful mixture.
To make, rinse off the used seed pods and allow them to dry at room temperature, or dry them in the oven at a very low temperature until brittle. When you've collected about a dozen, grind them into a powder in a food processor along with 2 cups of powdered sugar (equal weight of sugar and beans). Strain through a very fine mesh strainer to remove all the crunchy vanilla bean bits. Use this concentrated vanilla sugar to flavor whipped cream, to replace a small amount of plain sugar in a cake recipe, or to dust the tops of cookies.

ZESTING CITRUS FRUIT: The zest of a lemon, lime, orange, or grapefruit is the colored part of the skin, which contains the concentrated flavor and essential oils. (The white pith is not part of the zest, and has an unpleasantly bitter taste.) This concentration of flavor is more potent than the juice itself and underlines the taste of a juice, when you use it. Zest is also useful in a recipe when you want the citrus flavor but not the added liquid of juice, as in certain cookies and ice creams.

The preferred tool for zesting is a good, sharp zester, which is easy to use because it won't go any deeper than the zest. (See Equipment, below). A zester removes zest in long threads, which then need to be chopped fine for use in most recipes.

With a grater, use the smallest holes and press down lightly, rotating the fruit to remove zest from all parts. Grated zest, of course, doesn't need to be chopped.

In all the recipes, the quantity of chopped zest is specified, as well as a suggested number of fruit to give you an idea of how many to buy. Always measure zest so that you get the proper flavor in a recipe. If the fruit is small, you will probably need more to make up the right quantity of zest.

EQUIPMENT

When it comes to buying equipment, I'm a terrible example, because I've done to my kitchen exactly what I'm going to tell you *not* to do to yours. I'm an equipment buff, a gadget nut, and I run out and buy every conceivable piece of kitchen paraphernalia as soon as I know about it—and then I let it sit on the shelf, year after year, unused. I suggest that you do as I say, not as I do, and buy equipment in a slightly more sober and systematic way. After all, it's your hands that make a dessert, not any machine or gadget. Having an ice cream machine doesn't mean that you can open your freezer and magically find a quart of homemade ice cream in there.

Having the right equipment makes any job easier, and usually makes the results better. Buy the equipment you need for the recipes that interest you. Most of these desserts can be made quite beautifully if you have a few basic tools, molds, and pans on hand.

Most important, when you buy equipment, buy quality. Buying cheap super-market equipment is a false economy—light metal pans and baking sheets will warp and can let your baked goods burn; badly constructed spatulas or knives have a tendency to break just when you need them most. When you consider the amount of valuable time you spend making a special dessert, and the cost of the ingredients, it's clear that there's no point in using less-than-first-class equipment. You don't have to spend a fortune, though—used baking sheets, pans, and molds can often be found in restaurant supply stores for reasonable prices, and they last quite a long time.

No matter how terrific your equipment, your kitchen must be efficiently arranged, or dessert making can be an exercise in frustration. Allow yourself as much clean, uncluttered counter space as you can. Be sure your equipment is easy to get to, either in handy drawers or, even better, in counter-top crocks or hanging on racks. Consider buying more than one of some inexpensive utensils—having a few rubber spatulas, for example, will save washing a spatula every time you use it.

The list that follows is divided into two parts: "Essentials," tools that are necessary for many of these recipes, and "Makes Life Easier," tools that are nice to have and simplify many procedures. The list is intended only as a guide. Acquire equipment gradually, depending on the recipes you choose. (Specialized equipment that is used for only one or two desserts, or for decoration, is described in the appropriate recipes.) All the equipment is available at cookware shops and restaurant-supply houses and by mail-order (see page 356).

E S S E N T I A L S

BAKING SHEETS: At least two heavy-duty, high-quality baking sheets, generally 11 × 17 inches, are essential for almost every type of dessert making. Cheap, light sheets will warp at high temperatures, deforming cakes and cookies and letting tarts bend and lose their filling during baking. Most versatile are baking sheets with ½-inch edges, also called jelly roll pans, which can also be used for sheet cakes.

CAKE PANS: Heavy-duty metal, straight sided; 8 inches in diameter with 1½-inch-high sides.

FLAN RINGS: Most tart recipes in this book are best made in a French straight-sided flan ring, 10 inches in diameter and 1 inch high, set on a heavy-duty baking sheet. This height is not widely available in the United States but can be ordered by mail, or you can have a metal shop make one to your specifications. Until you've seen the clean, professional look of a tart made in a flan ring (which is lifted off after baking), you won't appreciate how much more beautiful it is than an ordinary pie pan or quiche dish. Also, since the flan ring has perpendicular rather than sloping sides, more filling goes into a tart made this way, and the crust is crisper because it cooks directly on the baking sheet. Some cakes and parfaits are also molded in flan rings, so one or two are versatile additions to your kitchen.

Flan rings with ½-inch-high sides (either straight or fluted, with removable bottoms) are a bit more readily available than the 1-inch-high rings, but they hold less filling, of course. In addition, for some recipes, individually sized rings are required.

MEASURING EQUIPMENT: Dry ingredients are measured in dry measuring cups, available in graduated sets from ⅛ cup to 1 cup. Ingredients like flour and sugar can be leveled off evenly with the top of the cup using the back of a knife. Liquid measuring cups, generally Pyrex with the measurements marked on the sides, are best for liquid ingredients because they always allow a little space to top off the measure. Use metal or plastic measuring spoons for measurements smaller than ¼ cup.

OVEN THERMOMETER: Obvious as it may sound, baking at the right temperature is essential for getting good results. Not all ovens are accurate, and an oven thermometer is a very inexpensive piece of insurance.

PASTRY BRUSH: Buy a broad, soft, natural-bristle brush. Don't get ones with stiff, plastic bristles—they can melt in hot liquids or leave an ugly track behind them on top of a cake or tart.

PIE PANS: Sloping sides, 10 inches in diameter. A regular pie pan is 1 inch deep; "deep-dish" is 1¼ inches. Heavy-duty metal is generally best because metal conducts heat better. If unavoidable, Pyrex will also do.

ROLLING PIN: The style of rolling pin you use is a matter of preference. I prefer the straight, French handleless type because I feel it gives me more control than the American ball-bearing type. If you prefer the American-style pin, get one with a cylinder at least 14 inches long, so that the edges of the rolling pin don't cut into the dough.

RULER OR TAPE MEASURE: Throughout this book, I specify sizes and thicknesses of pastry, cookies, truffles, or what have you in exact measurements, so that the recipes yield the right amounts and the baking times are accurate. Unless you've got a very keen eye, use a ruler or tape measure to make sure that you're making a product the same way I did.

SPATULAS: A *corne,* a handleless plastic spatula, is really efficient for scraping mixtures out of bowls and the corners of pots. Long-bladed rubber spatulas are great for folding ingredients together and can also be used for scraping out containers, but make sure that the blade is wide and flexible; the ones with narrow, stiff, or plastic blades are useless.

Three different types of metal spatulas are invaluable as well. A 10–12 inch offset metal spatula spreads sheet cake batters flat and melted chocolate onto sheet pans without leaving the traces of your knuckles behind. A long-bladed straight spatula, at least 10 inches long, smooths glazes, frostings, and cake fillings.

My favorite spatula is not really a spatula at all, but a thin, triangular-bladed paint scraper available at any hardware store. I use it for scraping chocolate off the back of sheet pans for chocolate curls and homemade chocolate chips, and for scraping pastry dough and flour off work surfaces. Choose one that's thin enough to be flexible, about 4 inches long, with a slightly beveled edge.

SPRINGFORM PANS AND CAKE RINGS: Springform pans with 3-inch-high sides are useful for baking cakes, as well as building layered cakes and molding parfaits. Once you've constructed a layer cake in such a mold, you'll never want to try putting one together free-form again. Cakes built in springform pans will always be pleasingly symmetrical. Recipes in this book call for 10-inch and 8-inch springform pans.

A French straight-sided ring, called an *entremet* ring, set on a baking sheet, is even better than a springform pan. It's slightly lower (2½ inches high), easier to work in, and there will be no indentations in the side of the cake when the ring is removed. To use as a mold to bake a cake in, the ring does not need to be buttered or floured. When using the ring to construct a cake inside, the ring must be set on a cardboard round that is covered with aluminum foil. They are not yet widely available in the United States, but they can be ordered by mail, or you can have a metal shop make one to your specifications.

Sifters and strainers

STRAINERS, SIFTERS, AND SIEVES: When my recipes call for sifting, it's usually to combine ingredients rather than to remove lumps. Therefore, I don't like the old-fashioned, multilevel flour sifters because when you're sifting a mixture of ingredients, spices and other things tend to get caught in the sifter and can't be pushed through. For sifting ingredients together, I like a drum sieve or tamis—a round, flat strainer stretched in a wooden or metal frame, like a snare drum. You can also use a simple, hand-held metal or nylon strainer.

In many recipes, you'll find a "fine-mesh strainer" specified. This is a conical strainer with tiny holes that allow nothing but liquid to pass through and strains out undesirable bits like cooked egg in custard or seeds in fruit purées.

WHISKS: Whisks should be stainless steel so that they don't rust, and have wooden handles so you don't burn yourself while stirring hot liquids. The wires should be slightly flexible to help make the whisking motion more fluid. Most important, the whisk itself should be 10–12 inches long and 2 inches across at the balloon end, with enough crossed wires to really beat air into a mixture. The tiny kind with three or four crossed wires won't do the job.

ZESTER: To remove the zest (colored part of the peel) from citrus fruit. Buy the type of zester with the blade securely riveted into the handle, or the zester will break off as soon as you try to use it. (A grater can also be used, but you have more control with a zester.) Be sure to buy the kind with four or five small holes that removes only the colored part, not the bitter white pith.

MISCELLANEOUS

BOWLS: A selection of metal or other heatproof bowls, especially large wide ones.

PARING KNIFE: For trimming and scoring.

SAUCEPANS: Stainless steel saucepans of varying sizes—2 quarts, 4 quarts, 6 quarts will be needed.

10-INCH SAUTÉ PAN

10-INCH CHEF'S KNIFE: For chopping and slicing.

WOODEN SPOONS: The thick flat spatula-style are preferred.

MAKES LIFE EASIER

AIRTIGHT JARS: For storing praline, nougatine, nuts, etc.

BISCUIT CUTTERS: Both fluted and plain, they come in graduated sizes for cutting out cookies, shortcake, and cake rounds. You can improvise a plain biscuit cutter by using a glass of the same size.

CARDBOARD ROUNDS: Almost every cake and tart is more easily decorated and served when a corrugated cardboard round (or rectangle, for a terrine or rectangular shape) is slipped underneath it before it is transferred to a serving platter. Unlike most platters, the cardboard is flat, so the dessert can be held on the hand for decorating or be moved from refrigerator to platter without danger of breaking. Also, the decorating process won't mess up your serving platter. Cardboard bases can be bought from cake-decorating stores, or simply cut them out of corrugated cardboard cartons.

COOLING AND GLAZING RACK: An 11 x 17-inch wire rack, with legs at each corner, is more versatile than a round rack, because long terrines can also be unmolded onto it for glazing. It can also be inverted onto a sheet of puff pastry when you want to keep the pastry from rising too high while baking.

ELECTRIC MIXER: Every time I use an electric mixer, I wonder to myself how in the world bakers got along before they were invented. My KitchenAid mixer is the single most useful item in my kitchen. With a free-standing mixer, you have your hands free to add ingredients, scrape, or pour, and when a mixture has to be beaten for a long time, you can go off and do something else.

If you're buying a new mixer, I suggest the KitchenAid, made by Hobart. It's really the best designed of all the mixers available. The mixer comes with a paddle attachment, for creaming butter; a balloon whisk for beating egg batters, whipping cream, and beating egg whites; and a dough hook for kneading breads like brioche. For added convenience, buy an extra bowl or two so that you aren't always washing bowls when a recipe calls for two or more different preparations to be beaten. (Hobart also makes an unlined copper bowl, which is wonderful for beating egg whites.)

FOOD PROCESSOR: For dessert making, a food processor isn't all that important: to purée, a blender is just as useful; for grinding nuts, a coffee grinder or Mouli grater can be used; for making pastry, an electric mixer is better. Some people, however, swear by their food processors, and they certainly can be used for all these operations.

4-OUNCE LADLE: For glazing.

MARBLE PASTRY SLAB: Since marble retains cold so well, it is the ideal surface for rolling out pastry. If your refrigerator is big enough, you can chill the slab in advance; or you can ice it down before using. Choose a slab at least 16 inches square so you have plenty of space for rolling out the dough.

MELON-BALLER: A multipurpose utensil. Besides the obvious, I use it for forming chocolate truffle cream into balls, and to core apples and pears. (Cut the apple in half; the melon-baller is just the right size to scoop out the core.)

METAL GUIDES: Or stacking rulers. Use metal guides to help you roll out dough to a uniform thickness or to slice loaf caked in horizontal layers. I buy ⅛-inch-thick straight aluminum molding at the hardware store, which I cut into 14–16-inch lengths and then tape them together. Then, if I want to cut a cake ⅜ inch thick, for example, I stack three pieces on each side of the cake and cut against the guides with a knife.

NUT GRINDER: For making nuts into a fluffy meal, either a hand-cranked Mouli grater or an electric grater like Moulinex is best. Electric coffee grinders and food processors will also work, but be careful not to grind the nuts into a paste.

PARCHMENT PAPER: To line baking sheets and cake pans so that batter or doughs don't stick; also for lining all types of molds so that the contents can be released easily. It is sold in sheets or rolls in cookware stores and many markets, and can be reused. Wax paper can be a perfectly good substitute for lining molds that are going to be filled (molded terrines, for example), but it can't be used to line molds or baking sheets that are going to go into the oven.

Ordinary bond typing paper (not erasable!) holds up to the heat and works very well for lining baking sheets, cake pans, and terrines.

PASTRY BAG: Get a soft, pliable nylon or cloth bag, at least 10 inches long (not the tiny cake-decorating size), and a selection of large plain and star tips. Ateco is a very popular brand, and their numbering system for tips has been used in this book. (See "How to use a pastry bag," page 27.)

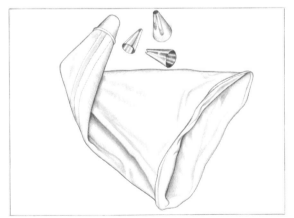

Pastry bag and pastry tips

PASTRY SCRAPER: For cleaning the work surface.

TEMPLATES: Templates are sets of round metal disks in graduated sizes that are used as guides for cutting out rounds of pastry or cake, cardboard bases, and for making decorative borders on cakes and tarts. They are much handier than trying to find a plate or a pot lid that's just the right size.

TERRINE MOLDS: The sharp corners of the French terrine molds give desserts a much cleaner, more delicate look than the round-cornered Pyrex ones. Metal loaf pans are available with straight or slanted sides in a number of different sizes. If the size you have is different than the one called for in a particular recipe, measure the volume of the pan by filling it with water and then adjust the recipe accordingly.

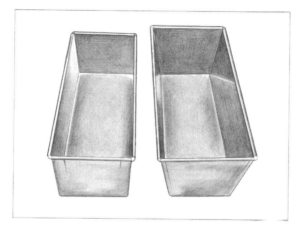

Terrine molds

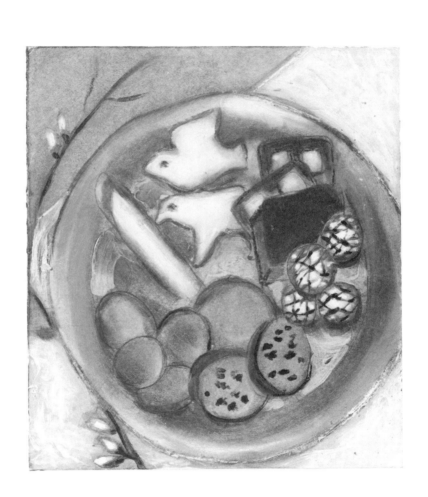

Cookies and Confections

FORMED COOKIES

White Chocolate Chip Cookies with Almonds and Fresh Mint
Peanut Butter Cookies
Chocolate Chip Lace Cookies
Chewy Ginger Cookies
Chocolate-Mint Cookies
Almond, Coconut, or Sesame Seed Tuiles
Omar's Coconut-Apple Haystacks

SLICE-AND-BAKE COOKIES

Poppy Seed–Orange Cookies
Sesame Seed Cookies
Caraway Seed Cookies
Maple-Pecan Cookies
Cinnamon-Walnut Cookies
Orange-Espresso Checkerboards

ROLLED COOKIES

Animal Crackers
Prune Pucks
Lemon Sable Cookies
Hazelnut-Chocolate Sable Cookies

PIPED COOKIES

Orange-Cardamom Cookies
Cinnamon-Raspberry Cookies
Lime-Clove Cookies

CONFECTIONS

Chocolate Fudge
Spiced Pecans
Milk Chocolate–Praline Truffles
Fresh Mint Truffles
Chocolate Truffles with Currants
Cassis Truffles
Chocolate Truffles with Candied Grapefruit Peel
Chocolate Truffles with Fresh Raspberries

To my mind, one of the most gracious desserts you can offer is a beautifully arranged platter of cookies—a light, elegant ending for a meal. Besides being interesting to the eye and pleasing to the palate, a selection of cookies is especially appropriate when people are watching their weight or concerned about eating too many sweets; your guests can feel comfortable eating just as much as they want and no more. Cookies also add a finishing touch at the side of a dish of poached fruit, homemade ice cream or sherbet, and, packaged in a pretty basket or tin, they are a much-appreciated gift.

From the cook's point of view, cookies have two other big advantages: your time and labor are only moderate, and most cookie doughs can be prepared in advance. The techniques used in cookie baking are relatively simple, which makes these recipes ideal for less-experienced bakers. I think I've found a happy medium between very time-consuming procedures and convenience-food shortcut cooking, without sacrificing good taste.

Making the Perfect Cookie: In my opinion, a good cookie doesn't simply have a particular taste, it has specific characteristics that you should look for as you sample your products. For example, a cookie should be perfectly chewy, buttery, flaky, or crisp, and never dry, doughy, or tough.

Because the techniques are simpler than for many other desserts, these cookie recipes are probably the most flexible in this book for experimenting with various flavorings. After you've mastered a recipe and are comfortable with it, use your creativity—there's small possibility for error.

For really excellent results, bake cookies at the last possible moment before serving. While all cookies can be baked ahead and stored airtight if necessary, they're so much better when they're fresh. (If you do plan to store them, wait until they're completely cool, then put them away immediately.)

Advance Preparation: Even if you're baking the cookies at the last minute, all the preparation can be done in advance. The dough or batter for most of the cookies in this chapter can be made up to a week ahead unless otherwise specified, and most preparations can be frozen unbaked up to three months, to be formed when needed.

You can "sheet up" your cookies as much as a day ahead of baking, store the sheets in the refrigerator, and then pop them in the oven at the last minute—not only will the cookies taste marvelous, but the smell of baking will perfume your home as guests arrive. (Cover sheets well with plastic wrap to protect them from moisture condensation in the refrigerator.)

Equipment and Baking: Equipment for cookie baking is basic: a couple of heavy, high-quality baking sheets are essential and they'll turn out to be one of the best investments you'll ever make for your kitchen. Cheap sheets invariably warp the first time you use them and the cookies then bake unevenly.

With only one exception (French tuiles), I never butter baking sheets; cookies will just "fry" on the baking sheet. Buttering and flouring the sheets doesn't help either—it only assures that the flour will stick to the bottom of the cookies. Instead, I line my baking sheets with parchment paper. Not only does it improve the crispness of the baked cookies, but also you can slip the entire piece of paper, cookies and all, right off the baking sheet and set one batch aside to cool while you sheet up another. (Parchment paper can be reused a few times. Do not use brown wrapping paper or wax paper to line your baking sheets, but ordinary bond typing paper will do in a pinch.)

It's a rare home oven that will bake an entire sheet of cookies evenly. Some get done before others, so don't just pull the sheets out of the oven when the timer buzzes. Test the cookies as directed in the recipes, take out those that are completely baked, and keep baking the others until they're done.

If you're not sure that your oven is reliable, you might want to try a test batch —baking two or three cookies at the recommended temperature for the specified time—before baking a whole tray. An oven thermometer is also useful to check for accuracy.

If a sheet of cookies starts to color too quickly on the bottom, you can save them by slipping a cold baking sheet underneath the hot baking sheet.

Baking one sheet of cookies at a time is the best method; however, if you're baking two sheets at once, switch their positions once halfway through the baking time. Rather than placing one sheet directly above the other in the oven, stagger their position a little so that they bake evenly. Never place baking sheets flush against the oven walls, as there should always be room for the heat to circulate.

Serving: When you're planning a cookie platter, variety is the watchword. Choose an assortment of shapes, colors, textures, and flavors. Keep the cookies all in more or less the same scale—don't mix delicate bite-size cookies with big flying saucers. A platter can be made more interesting with other additions, like chocolate truffles, candied orange or grapefruit peel, or spiced pecans.

White Chocolate Chip Cookies with Almonds and Fresh Mint

4 ounces raw almonds, unblanched

½ cup loosely packed fresh mint leaves (preferably spearmint), stems removed

10 ounces white chocolate, very cold

4 ounces unsalted butter (1 stick)

6 tablespoons granulated sugar

6 tablespoons dark brown sugar, firmly packed

1 egg

½ tablespoon almond extract

½ teaspoon baking soda

½ teaspoon boiling water

¾ cup plus 1½ tablespoons flour

Makes 7 dozen

FORMED COOKIES

This variation of America's beloved chocolate chip cookies updates the familiar formula with white chocolate, toasted almonds, and fresh mint.

MAKING THE DOUGH

Preheat oven to 325 degrees and adjust the oven rack to the middle position. Spread the almonds on a baking sheet and toast for 8–10 minutes, until they are light brown. Cool and chop coarse; set aside.

Chop the mint leaves very fine to yield approximately ⅓ cup; set aside. Chop white chocolate into pea-size pieces; set aside.

Using the paddle attachment of an electric mixer, beat the butter on medium speed until it whitens and holds soft peaks, 3–5 minutes. Add the granulated sugar and brown sugar, beating until well blended. Whisk the egg and almond extract together and beat them into the butter mixture, scraping down the sides of the bowl as necessary.

Dissolve baking soda in the boiling water.

Beat half the flour into the butter mixture, beat in the baking soda, and then add the remaining flour, beating until just combined. Beat in almonds, chopped mint, and chopped white chocolate just until combined.

Wrap dough in plastic wrap and chill at least 2 hours, or until firm.

FORMING AND BAKING THE COOKIES

Work with the dough in small batches, keeping the rest refrigerated.

With your hands, roll the dough into 1-inch balls and place 1 inch apart on paper-lined or nonstick baking sheets. Lightly flatten the cookies with the heel of your hand to keep them from rolling around on the baking sheet. Chill until firm.

Preheat oven to 325 degrees and bake 12 minutes, until golden brown. During the early stages of baking, the cookies will rise a bit into a domed shape, then, just before they are done, they will deflate, spread very slightly, and crack on top. They are done as soon as they can be lifted off the baking sheet without sticking.

Peanut Butter Cookies

4 ounces unsalted butter (1 stick)

½ cup creamy peanut butter

½ cup granulated sugar

½ cup dark brown sugar, firmly packed

1 egg

1 teaspoon baking soda

2 teaspoons boiling water

1 cup flour

1 cup currants or raisins

To Coat Cookies:
¼ cup granulated sugar

Makes 5 dozen

Currants or raisins contrast with the richness of the peanut butter in these cookies. I especially like them soft and warm, right out of the oven.

MAKING THE DOUGH

Using the paddle attachment of an electric mixer, beat together the butter and peanut butter on medium speed until smooth and well mixed, 3–5 minutes. Add the granulated sugar and brown sugar, beating until well blended. Add the egg, scraping down the sides of the bowl as necessary.

Dissolve the baking soda in the boiling water. Beat half the flour into the butter mixture, beat in the baking soda, and then add the remaining flour, beating until just combined. Beat in currants or raisins just until mixed. Wrap dough in plastic wrap and chill until firm, about 2 hours.

FORMING AND BAKING THE COOKIES

Preheat oven to 325 degrees. Adjust oven rack to the middle position.

Work with the dough in small batches, keeping the rest refrigerated.

With your hands, roll the dough into 1-inch balls and place 2 inches apart on a paper-lined or nonstick baking sheet. Chill until no longer sticky, 15–20 minutes.

Place ¼ cup granulated sugar in a saucer. Dip the bottom of a glass in the sugar and use it to slightly flatten the balls by pressing down gently. Rock the glass back and forth if necessary while pressing to avoid cracking the cookies.

Bake for 8–10 minutes, until light brown. The cookies will rise, then fall and spread into thin disks. Remove from the oven as soon as they have fallen. The cookies will be soft, but will firm up as they cool.

Chocolate Chip Lace Cookies

4 ounces unsalted butter (1 stick)

6 tablespoons granulated sugar

6 tablespoons dark brown sugar, firmly packed

1 egg

1 teaspoon vanilla extract

3/4 teaspoon baking soda

3/4 teaspoon boiling water

1/4 cup plus 3 tablespoons flour

1 cup pecans, coarsely chopped

6 ounces bittersweet chocolate chopped into pea-size pieces or 1 cup miniature chocolate chips (bittersweet chocolate is of higher quality than store-bought chocolate chips)

Makes 5 dozen

These lacy, elegant cookies—crisper and more delicate than ordinary chocolate chip cookies—were invented by happy accident when one of my colleagues, Dana Farkas, mistakenly left out half the flour in our regular chocolate chip cookie recipe.

MAKING THE DOUGH

Using the paddle attachment of an electric mixer, beat the butter on medium speed until it whitens and holds soft peaks, 3–5 minutes. Add the granulated sugar and brown sugar, beating until well blended. Whisk the egg and vanilla extract together and beat them into the butter mixture, scraping down the sides of the bowl as necessary.

Dissolve the baking soda in the boiling water.

Beat half the flour into the butter mixture, beat in the baking soda, and then add the remaining flour, beating until just combined. Beat in the chopped pecans and chocolate chips, just until mixed.

Wrap dough in plastic wrap and chill until firm, about 2 hours.

FORMING AND BAKING THE COOKIES

Work with the dough in small batches, keeping the rest refrigerated. With your hands, roll dough into ½-inch balls and place them 2 inches apart on a paper-lined or nonstick baking sheet. Press cookies down lightly with the heel of your hand to keep them from rolling around on the baking sheet. Chill until firm.

Preheat oven to 325 degrees. Adjust the oven rack to the middle position.

Bake for 9–12 minutes, until cookies are an even light brown. Cookies will rise, fall, and spread out during baking. They will be extremely soft when they come out of the oven. Because these cookies contain a lot of butter, they burn easily, so be sure to remove them from the baking sheet when they're still slightly light-colored in the center. Let cool completely before removing from baking sheet. When cooled, they will be crisp.

Chewy Ginger Cookies

6⅓ cups flour

5 teaspoons powdered ginger

4 teaspoons ground cinnamon

1 teaspoon ground nutmeg

1 teaspoon ground cloves

1 pound unsalted butter (4 sticks)

4 ounces fresh ginger root

1 cup granulated sugar

1 cup dark brown sugar, firmly packed

1 egg

1 cup molasses, preferably blackstrap

4 teaspoons baking soda

2 tablespoons boiling water

To Coat Cookies:
¼ cup granulated sugar

Makes 14 dozen

Fresh ginger root gives these cookies a wonderful naturally spicy flavor, and also makes them unusually moist.

MAKING THE DOUGH

Sift together the flour and spices through a strainer; set aside. If any spices remain in the strainer, stir them back into the flour to recombinc. Peel ginger root with a vegetable peeler, slice into rounds, and mince. (There should be about ¼ cup.)

Using the paddle attachment of an electric mixer, beat the butter and minced ginger on medium speed until it whitens and holds soft peaks, 3–5 minutes. Add the granulated sugar and brown sugar, beating until well blended. Whisk together the egg and molasses and add to the butter mixture, scraping down the sides of the bowl as necessary.

Dissolve the baking soda in the boiling water.

Beat half the dry ingredients into the butter mixture, then beat in the baking soda. Add the remaining dry ingredients, beating just until combined.

Wrap dough in plastic wrap and chill until firm, about 2 hours.

FORMING AND BAKING THE COOKIES

Preheat oven to 325 degrees. Adjust the oven rack to the middle position.

Work with the dough in small batches, keeping the rest refrigerated.

With your hands, roll the dough into 1-inch balls. Place 1½ inches apart on paper-lined or nonstick baking sheets. Chill until firm, 15–20 minutes. Put the ¼ cup sugar in a saucer. Toss the balls one at a time in the granulated sugar to lightly coat the surface; return to the baking sheet. Press cookies down lightly with the heel of your hand to keep them from rolling around on the baking sheet.

Bake for 10–12 minutes, until lightly colored. At the beginning of baking, the cookies will rise a bit into a domed shape, then, just before they are done, they will deflate, spread very slightly, and crack on top.

Remove from the oven as soon as the cookies have fallen. They will still be soft, but will firm up as they cool.

Chocolate-Mint Cookies

12 ounces bittersweet chocolate

6 tablespoons crème de menthe or peppermint schnapps

½ cup fresh mint leaves (preferably spearmint), chopped

1 cup almond meal

½ cup plus 2 tablespoons flour

¾ teaspoon baking powder

4 tablespoons unsalted butter (½ stick)

3 eggs

½ cup granulated sugar

To Coat Cookies:
¾ cup granulated sugar

¾ cup powdered sugar, sifted

Makes 3 dozen

Nostalgia for the great chocolate-mint Girl Scout cookies of my childhood inspired these, which come out of the oven dramatically white with chocolate cracks running through them. They are wonderful served with Chocolate-Mint Ice Cream or White Chocolate–Mint Ice Cream.

MAKING THE DOUGH

Cut chocolate into 2-inch pieces. In a heatproof bowl, melt chocolate with butter over barely simmering water. (The water should not touch the bottom of the bowl or the chocolate will burn.) Turn off heat and let mixture stand over warm water until ready to use.

In a small saucepan, scald the crème de menthe with chopped mint leaves. Remove from heat, cover, and let stand approximately 15 minutes. In a bowl, stir together the almond meal, flour, and baking powder. Sift through strainer to remove any lumps. If any almond meal remains in the strainer, stir it back into the flour to recombine; set aside.

Using the whisk attachment of an electric mixer, beat the eggs at high speed with ½ cup granulated sugar until the mixture is thick, pale, and forms a ribbon when the beater is lifted out of the bowl, about 5 minutes.

Pour the crème de menthe into the chocolate mixture and stir to combine. Whisk the chocolate mixture into the egg mixture until combined. Whisk in the flour mixture, combining well. The batter will be runny. Chill batter until very solid, at least 4 hours.

FORMING AND BAKING THE COOKIES

Preheat oven to 325 degrees. Adjust the oven rack to the middle position. Work with the dough in small batches, keeping the rest refrigerated.

With your hands, roll the dough into 1-inch balls and place on a baking sheet. (Your hands are bound to get a bit messy—I usually have to wash my hands several times while making these.) Chill until firm, 10–15 minutes.

The unusual white color of these cookies is achieved by rolling them first in granulated sugar and then in powdered sugar before baking. The granulated sugar acts as a barrier to prevent the butter in the cookies from melting the powdered sugar, so they stay very white.

To coat cookies, place ¾ cup granulated sugar and ¾ cup sifted powdered sugar in two small bowls. Remove cookies from refrigerator and roll one at a time in the bowl of granulated sugar to lightly coat. Then place in the bowl of powdered sugar and coat them heavily. The cookies must be completely white. If the dark chocolate color bleeds through before baking, roll again in powdered sugar. Place on paper-lined or nonstick baking sheet 1½ inches apart.

Bake for 20 minutes. Remove from the oven as soon as the cookies can be lifted off the baking sheet without sticking. Allow to cool completely. The cookies will remain soft in the center and will be white with two or three dark chocolate cracks.

Don't stack these cookies to store or you'll loosen the powdered sugar coating.

VARIATION: After you make the chocolate-mint version, experiment a bit and make this recipe your own by pairing the chocolate with different flavorings. For example, eliminate the mint leaves and replace the crème de menthe with an equal amount of rum or Cognac, or use orange liqueur and add the chopped zest of an orange to the eggs when you beat them.

Almond, Coconut, or Sesame-Seed Tuiles

2½ tablespoons unsalted
  butter

1 tablespoon grated or finely
  chopped orange zest
  (1 orange)

1 cup granulated sugar

6 egg whites

⅓ cup flour, sifted

2½ cups sliced almonds
  (blanched or unblanched),
  or 2 cups long-shred
  unsweetened coconut,
  or 1½ cups sesame seeds

2 tablespoons unsalted
  butter (if baking sheet is
  not nonstick type)

2 tablespoons milk

Makes 4 dozen

Tuiles are the epitome of crispness, so thin that they shatter when you bite into them. Traditionally these cookies imitate the curved shape of the roof tiles *(tuiles)* of the Mediterranean area of France. The hot cookies are molded over a rolling pin or a wine bottle and then crisp into a curve as they cool. The same basic batter can make three varieties with the addition of sliced almonds, coconut, or sesame seeds.

Nonstick baking sheets, without raised edges, work best for this recipe. If the baking sheet has raised edges, bake the cookies on the *back* of it—it's easier to remove the cookies.

To shape the tuiles, you will need a rolling pin or a wine bottle that is propped between two dish towels to keep it from rolling around.

MAKING THE BATTER

Using the paddle attachment of an electric mixer, beat the butter on medium speed with the orange zest until it whitens and holds soft peaks, 3–5 minutes. Beat in the sugar until well blended. Beat in egg whites gradually, scraping down the sides of the bowl as necessary. Fold in flour and *one* of the following: almonds, coconut, or sesame seeds.

❖ The batter is best made the day before, and kept refrigerated overnight.

FORMING AND BAKING THE COOKIES

Preheat oven to 325 degrees. Adjust oven rack to middle position.

If the baking sheet is *not* the nonstick type, brush it with melted butter and chill briefly. (Butter the pan again each time you use it.) Pour the milk into a saucer.

Place a teaspoonful of batter on the baking sheet. Dip a fork in milk and, using the back of the tines, tap the fork lightly up and down on the batter to spread it into a very thin circle about 3 inches in diameter. You should be able to see the baking sheet through the batter, but there must not be any holes. Spread up to six circles of batter, 2 inches apart, on the baking sheet.

(Since the cookies are removed from the baking sheet

while hot and then molded immediately into shape, you may want to try baking only two or three in the first batch, until you find out how fast you're able to work with them.)

Bake for approximately 8 minutes, until evenly golden brown. Many ovens will not bake all the cookies at the same rate, so remove only those that are done and replace the rest to cook a minute or so longer. If the cookies have raw spots, return them to the oven—uncooked areas will never become crisp.

Remove baked cookies from the sheets with a metal spatula, and immediately set them for a few moments on a rolling pin or bottle until they harden. If the cookies cool and harden before they have been removed from the baking sheet, put them back into the oven briefly and they will soften again.

Tuiles are most crisp when served the same day they are made. Store airtight, as they quickly get soggy.

Omar's Coconut-Apple Haystacks

For the Apple Purée:

2 large tart green apples, approximately 1 pound

2 tablespoons lemon juice

4 tablespoons butter (1/2 stick)

1 vanilla bean, split and scraped, optional

1/2 cup granulated sugar

For the Cookie Mixture:
2 egg whites

1/2 cup granulated sugar

4 cups long, shredded, unsweetened coconut (8 ounces)

1/2–2/3 cup Apple Purée

Makes 2 dozen

One of the most flamboyant customers at Spago was a Kuwaiti sheik known only as Omar, who had a standing reservation for the best table in the house every night. He ordered custom-made pizzas, drank only Tab, and usually picked up the check for any movie star in his vicinity. Although we offered a large and tempting selection of desserts, Omar ate only these easy-to-make coconut haystacks, crisp on the outside and moist on the inside. When he would return to Los Angeles after one of his frequent trips, we'd always get a phone call: "Omar's back—make sure you have his cookies!"

Ideally, the coconut should be the unsweetened, long-shredded type that is found in health food stores. Short-shred can be substituted, but the cookies will not look as pretty.

MAKING THE APPLE PURÉE

Peel, halve, and core the apples and slice 1/4 inch thick. Toss with lemon juice.

In a large sauté pan, melt the butter with the vanilla bean and let it bubble slightly over high heat. Add the apples and cook, stirring occasionally, until tender, 3–5 minutes. Sprinkle on the sugar and stir together with a wooden spoon. Reduce heat to medium. As the sugar melts and juice is released from the apples, a lot of liquid will collect in the pan. Continue cooking, stirring every so often to avoid scorching, until the juice and sugar have reduced to a thick syrup and the apples are translucent and completely caramelized, about 5–8 minutes. Pour into a bowl and remove the vanilla bean. Cool. Purée the mixture in a food processor, blender, or ricer. There should be 1/2 to 2/3 cup of purée.

MAKING THE COOKIES

In a large mixing bowl, combine egg whites, sugar, and coconut, using a wooden spoon or your hands. The amount of apple purée you will need will depend on how moist the coconut is, so start by adding 1/2 cup of the purée and then add a little more at a time until the batter is just moist enough to hold together in 1-inch balls formed with your hands. The batter should be sticky. The entire amount of apple purée may be needed if the coconut is very dry.

FORMING AND BAKING THE COOKIES

Preheat oven to 325 degrees. Adjust the oven rack to the middle position.

With your hands, press the mixture tightly into 1-inch balls and place 1 inch apart on a paper-lined or nonstick baking sheet. Using the first three fingers of your hand, pinch each ball into a pointed pyramid shape approximately 1 inch high. Be sure to keep each cookie tightly packed.

Bake for 20 minutes, until cookies are brown. Remove from the oven as soon as the cookies can be lifted off the baking sheet without sticking. Let cool completely before removing from baking sheet.

Poppy Seed–Orange Cookies

8 ounces unsalted butter (2 sticks)

3 tablespoons grated or finely chopped orange zest (about 3 oranges)

½ cup granulated sugar

1 egg yolk

½ teaspoon vanilla extract

2 cups minus 2 tablespoons flour

¼ cup poppy seeds

Makes 6–7 dozen

Sesame Seed Cookies

8 ounces unsalted butter (2 sticks)

2 tablespoons Oriental sesame oil

½ cup sugar

1 egg yolk

2 cups minus 2 tablespoons flour

¾ cup sesame seeds

Makes 6–7 dozen

SLICE-AND-BAKE COOKIES

A sprinkling of poppy seeds adds to the texture of these cookies, while the orange zest contributes a delicate flavor.

MAKING THE DOUGH

Using the paddle attachment of an electric mixer, beat the butter on medium speed with the orange zest until it whitens and holds soft peaks, 3–5 minutes. Beat in the sugar until well blended. Whisk together the egg yolk and vanilla extract and beat in, scraping down the sides of the bowl as necessary. Add flour and poppy seeds, mixing only enough to combine. Wrap dough in plastic wrap and chill for 30 minutes, until firm.

To form the dough into logs, slice, and bake, see directions for Maple-Pecan Cookies, page 54.

Sesame oil and sesame seeds give this cookie an Oriental touch.

MAKING THE DOUGH

Using the paddle attachment of an electric mixer, beat the butter on medium speed with sesame oil until it whitens and holds soft peaks, 3–5 minutes. Beat in sugar until well blended. Beat in egg yolk, scraping down the sides of the bowl as necessary. Add flour and sesame seeds, mixing only enough to combine. Wrap dough in plastic wrap and chill for 30 minutes, until firm.

To form the dough into logs, slice, and bake, see directions for Maple-Pecan Cookies, page 54.

Caraway Seed Cookies

8 ounces unsalted butter (2 sticks)

3 tablespoons grated or finely chopped lemon zest (3 lemons)

½ cup granulated sugar

1 egg yolk (reserve the white)

½ teaspoon vanilla extract

2 cups minus 2 tablespoons flour

6 tablespoons caraway seeds, ground or chopped fine

Sugar Coating (optional):
1 cup crystallized sugar
1 egg white (for egg wash)

Makes 6–7 dozen

Coating these cookies with crystallized sugar brings a little more sweetness to the otherwise savory caraway seed dough, and adds a crunchiness that I like very much.

The best tools for grinding the caraway seeds are a coffee grinder or a mortar and pestle. You can also chop them fine with a knife, though it's tricky to keep the seeds from flying all over.

MAKING THE DOUGH

Using the paddle attachment of an electric mixer, beat the butter on medium speed with lemon zest until it whitens and holds soft peaks, 3–5 minutes. Beat in the sugar until well blended. Whisk together the egg yolk and vanilla and beat in, scraping down sides of the bowl as necessary. Add flour and ground caraway seeds, mixing only enough to combine. Wrap dough in plastic wrap and chill for 30 minutes, until firm.

To form dough into logs, see directions for Maple-Pecan Cookies, page 54. Then proceed with coating and baking the cookies:

BAKING THE COOKIES

Preheat oven to 325 degrees. Adjust the oven rack to the middle position.

Spread the crystallized sugar evenly on a sheet of wax paper. In a small bowl, beat the egg white lightly to break it up. Brush the outside of the dough logs with beaten egg white. Roll in the crystallized sugar so that the logs are completely coated. Chill again until firm.

Using a very sharp knife, slice logs into ⅜-inch rounds and place 1 inch apart on paper-lined or nonstick baking sheets. Bake for 12–15 minutes, until firm and lightly browned.

Maple-Pecan Cookies

8 ounces unsalted butter (2 sticks)

½ cup granulated sugar

1 egg yolk

2 tablespoons pure maple syrup

½ teaspoon vanilla extract

2 cups minus 2 tablespoons flour

1¼ cups pecan halves (4 ounces)

Makes 6–7 dozen

Rolling the dough into logs

If I were allowed to make only one slice-and-bake cookie, this would be it. The real maple flavor combines so beautifully with the pecans in a tender, buttery dough that I'm tempted to call this the ultimate cookie.

MAKING THE DOUGH

Using the paddle attachment of an electric mixer, beat the butter on medium speed until it whitens and holds soft peaks, 3–5 minutes. Beat in sugar until well blended. Whisk together the egg yolk and maple syrup and beat into the butter, scraping down the sides of the bowl as necessary. Add the flour and mix only enough to combine. Beat in pecans just until combined. Wrap dough in plastic wrap and chill for 30 minutes, until firm.

FORMING THE DOUGH INTO LOGS

Divide the dough into four sections and work with one at a time, keeping the rest refrigerated. Turn one section out onto a lightly floured surface, using only enough flour to prevent the dough from sticking. With your hands, flatten the dough into a thick rectangle and then fold it over onto itself, packing it into a completely solid patty. It is important that there be no holes in the logs. Starting at the center, roll the dough with your palms into a log about 1½ inches in diameter. Place on a cookie sheet and freeze for at least 30 minutes, until firm enough to slice. Repeat with the rest of the dough.

❖ The logs should be stored well sealed in the freezer and will keep up to three months. When ready to use, slice them while still frozen.

BAKING THE COOKIES

Preheat oven to 325 degrees. Adjust the oven rack to the middle position.

Using a very sharp knife, slice logs into ⅜-inch rounds and place 1 inch apart on paper-lined or nonstick baking sheets. Bake for 12–15 minutes, until firm and lightly and evenly browned. The cookies must be cooked through to be tender.

Cinnamon-Walnut Cookies

8 ounces unsalted butter
(2 sticks)

¼ cup granulated sugar

½ cup loosely packed brown
sugar

1 egg yolk (reserve white)

1¾ cups flour

2 tablespoons cinnamon

1 heaping cup walnut
halves (4 ounces)

Walnut Coating (optional):
1 cup walnuts (4 ounces)

1 tablespoon cinnamon

¼ cup granulated sugar

1 egg white (for egg wash)

Makes 6–7 dozen

These cookies taste like a cinnamon graham cracker. Rolling them in a coating of chopped walnuts and sugar before slicing is optional, but to me they seem naked without it.

MAKING THE DOUGH

Using the paddle attachment of an electric mixer, beat the butter on high speed until it whitens and holds soft peaks, 3–5 minutes. Add the granulated sugar and brown sugar, beating until well blended. Beat in egg yolk, scraping down the sides of the bowl as necessary. Toss the flour and cinnamon together in a small bowl, then add to the butter mixture, mixing only enough to combine. Beat in walnut halves just until combined. Wrap dough in plastic wrap and chill for 30 minutes, until firm.

To form dough into logs, see direction for Maple-Pecan Cookies, page 54. Then proceed with coating and baking the cookies.

BAKING THE COOKIES

Preheat oven to 325 degrees. Adjust the oven rack to the middle position.

For the coating, chop the walnuts very fine. Mix well with cinnamon and sugar; spread the mixture evenly on a sheet of wax paper. In a small bowl, beat the egg white lightly to break it up. Brush the outside of the dough logs with beaten egg white. Roll in the walnut-cinnamon mixture so that the logs are completely coated. Chill until firm.

Using a very sharp knife, slice logs into ⅜-inch rounds and place 1 inch apart on paper-lined or nonstick baking sheets. Bake for 12–15 minutes, until firm and lightly browned.

Orange-Espresso Checkerboards

Orange Dough:

12 ounces unsalted butter (3 sticks)

9 tablespoons grated or finely chopped orange zest (9 oranges)

3/4 cup granulated sugar

1 1/2 egg yolks

3 tablespoons orange juice (1 orange)

1 1/2 tablespoons orange liqueur

3 cups flour

Espresso Dough:

12 ounces unsalted butter (3 sticks)

3/4 cup granulated sugar

1 1/2 egg yolks

1/2 tablespoon instant coffee, dissolved in 1/2 teaspoon water

1 1/2 tablespoons coffee liqueur

3 cups flour

1/4 cup freshly ground espresso coffee beans, tossed with flour

To Sandwich Doughs Together:

2 egg yolks, lightly beaten

Makes about 6 dozen checkerboard cookies and 2 dozen marble cookies

Most cookies have a casual, handmade look, but these are refined and elegant with their tiny checkerboard squares of orange and coffee butter dough. The formality of the design, and the quantity of the recipe, makes them a good choice for a wedding reception or a large party.

Frankly, this is a time-consuming project, but it can be fun to do if you're the kind of person who gets satisfaction out of straight edges and square measurements. What you need to do is actually fairly simple—just be as precise as possible and follow the illustrations. The quantity of the recipe is large enough that you can construct a number of checkerboard logs and freeze them, slicing and baking when you want the cookies.

To construct the cookies properly, the dough has to be rolled to the exact measurements specified in the recipe. I use metal guides (see page 36) alongside the dough as I roll it, so I get the perfect thickness and a sharp, clean edge. Stacking rulers or thick strips of cardboard will also do.

MAKING THE DOUGH

The method for making both doughs is the same. Lightly beat 3 egg yolks together. Divide in half; use one half for each flavor dough.

Using the paddle attachment of an electric mixer, beat the butter (with orange zest for orange dough) on medium speed until it whitens and holds soft peaks, 3–5 minutes. Beat in the sugar until well blended. In a small bowl, whisk together egg yolk and liquids. Add to dough, scraping down the sides of the bowl as necessary. Beat in flour (tossed with ground espresso for espresso dough), mixing until just combined. Wrap dough in plastic wrap and chill until firm, about 1 hour.

CONSTRUCTING THE CHECKERBOARDS

❖ The construction of the cookies can be spread out over a few days if desired.

When both the doughs are firm, remove from the refrigerator, divide each into thirds, wrap separately, and refrigerate. One at a time, on a well-floured work surface, roll the packages of dough (3 orange and 3 espresso) into 9 x 4-inch rectangles that are 3/8 inch thick. If dough becomes

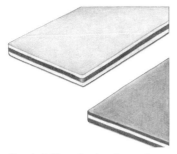

Sandwiching the dough together

Cutting the dough into strips

Stacking the strips to form checkerboard pattern

Wrapping the checkerboards in dough

too soft, refrigerate again as necessary. Refrigerate each dough rectangle until firm, about 30 minutes.

Place a rectangle of orange dough on a sheet of wax paper in the center of the work surface. Brush with lightly beaten egg yolk. Place a rectangle of espresso dough on top of it, brush with egg wash, and then top with another orange rectangle. Chill until firm. Repeat with the other three rectangles of dough (one orange rectangle sandwiched between two of espresso).

When thoroughly chilled (about 30 minutes) remove one slab of dough from the refrigerator and, using a ruler, trim to a perfect 6 x 4-inch rectangle. Using a very sharp knife and measuring carefully with a metal guide or a ruler, cut the dough crosswise into ⅜-inch-wide strips. Chill strips until firm. Repeat with remaining dough, holding one of each color aside for later use. (Also, wrap the trimmings in plastic wrap and reserve. They will be rolled into logs later.)

To assemble the checkerboards, you must line up the dough strips so that the orange and coffee colors alternate. When dough is firm, place one strip of dough on a piece of wax paper. Brush with egg wash. Now lay a strip of the other color on top of it. Brush with egg wash and put the last strip on top, alternating the colors again. The end of the strip should look like a little checkerboard. Chill. Repeat with all the strips of dough, chilling after they are assembled.

(It doesn't matter which combination of colors you start with as long as the colors alternate. You will have a checkerboard pattern 3 squares across and 3 squares down, a total of 9 squares on each cookie.)

The checkerboard strips are next wrapped in a solid sheet of dough before baking. Roll one of the reserved sections of dough into a sheet ⅛ inch thick and 6 inches wide. Place one of the checkerboard strips on the sheet of dough, lining it up with the 6-inch width, and roll the strip down the dough so that you can estimate exactly how much dough will be needed to cover it exactly. Unroll, pick up the checkerboard strip, and cut the dough to the exact length. Brush the dough with egg wash and then, starting again at the top, wrap it securely around the checkerboard strip, making sure that the dough is well-sealed onto all four sides. Carefully release any air bubbles by running the side of your finger along each side of the strip. Pinch seam gently to seal well. As each strip is rolled in dough, place on a baking sheet and chill until firm, about 30 minutes. (If the casing dough cracks, it is probably too cold—let it soften a bit and try rolling it up again.) Reserve any trimmings to make marbled logs (see below).

There will be five packets of checkerboard strips wrapped in dough. Some of the packets will be wrapped with orange dough, and some with espresso.

❖ The logs should be stored well sealed in the freezer and will keep up to three months. When ready to use, slice them while still frozen.

BAKING THE COOKIES

Preheat oven to 325 degrees. Adjust oven rack to middle position.

Slice cookies ⅜ inch thick, place 1 inch apart on a nonstick or paper-lined baking sheet, and chill until firm. Bake for 12–15 minutes, until firm and lightly browned.

Following the method for preparing slice-and-bake cookies (page 54), roll the dough trimmings into logs. They will have a marbled look. Bake as directed above.

Animal Crackers

8 ounces unsalted butter
    (2 sticks)

1½ cups granulated sugar

2 eggs

2 tablespoons cream

1 tablespoon vanilla extract

4 cups flour

2 teaspoons baking powder

To Decorate Cookie Tops:
2 egg yolks

Crystallized sugar or
    granulated sugar

Makes 8 dozen

ROLLED COOKIES

The taste and texture of these animal crackers remind me of French *petit beurre* biscuits. Use large (2–3 inch) animal cookie cutters, or 2½-inch-round French biscuit cutters.

MAKING THE DOUGH

Using the paddle attachment of an electric mixer, beat the butter on medium speed until it whitens and holds soft peaks, 3–5 minutes. Beat in sugar until well blended. Whisk together the eggs, cream, and vanilla and beat in, scraping down the sides of the bowl as necessary.

Sift together the flour and baking powder, and beat into butter mixture until just combined. Wrap dough in plastic wrap and chill about 2 hours, until firm.

ROLLING AND BAKING THE COOKIES

Work with the dough in small batches, keeping the rest refrigerated. On a lightly floured surface, roll dough out to ⅛-inch thickness. Cut dough with cutters and place on paper-lined or nonstick baking sheets. Place baking sheets in refrigerator and chill until firm, about 30 minutes. Chill any scraps and reroll when cold.

Preheat oven to 325 degrees. Adjust the oven rack to the middle position.

Whisk together the egg yolks and a few drops of water. Brush the top of each cookie with the egg mixture. Sprinkle on a light coat of crystallized or granulated sugar.

Bake for 12–15 minutes, until lightly browned.

Prune Pucks

¼ cup whole almonds (1 ounce)

8 ounces Puff Pastry trimmings (page 175)

2 egg yolks, lightly beaten

2 tablespoons granulated sugar

25–30 Poached Prunes (page 157)

¼ cup crystallized sugar

Makes 30

When Wolfgang Puck first spotted me making these crisp, luscious cookies, he asked what they were called, and immediately let me know how disappointed he was that his namesake was "only a cookie." I didn't tell him that they're called Prune Pucks because they look just like little hockey pucks to me.

FORMING THE COOKIES

Preheat oven to 325 degrees. Adjust the oven rack to the middle position. Spread the almonds on a baking sheet and toast for 8–10 minutes, until lightly browned. Cool. Chop fine and set aside. Let the puff pastry trimmings stand at room temperature until pliable but not soft.

On a lightly floured surface, roll out puff pastry to a ¼-inch-thick rectangle measuring about 7 by 18 inches. Using a ruler, trim it to 5 by 16 inches. Place on a paper-lined baking sheet and chill until firm, 15–30 minutes.

Brush the puff pastry with a thin coat of the beaten yolk. Sprinkle the surface with the granulated sugar. Line up about 11 whole poached prunes, end to end across the width of the pastry, 1 inch from the bottom edge of the long side of the pastry. Sprinkle the surface of the dough with the chopped almonds and roll up into a log around the prunes. Use more beaten egg yolks if necessary to seal the roll firmly. Chill 30 minutes, until firm.

Brush the outside of the log well with beaten egg. Spread the crystallized sugar on a piece of wax paper and roll the log in it to completely cover with sugar. Chill again until firm.

Remove the log from the baking sheet and place on a cutting board. With a sharp knife, trim the ends of the log evenly, then slice the dough into ½-inch disks. Turn the disks on their flat sides and place them 1 inch apart on a nonstick baking sheet (don't use a paper-lined sheet for this).

Cut remaining prunes in half, and press a half into the center of each cookie, so that each cookie is tightly filled. Reshape each cookie into a round with your hands. (Chill the dough briefly whenever it becomes soft.) Chill the cookies for 30 minutes before baking.

❖ The cookies can be prepared up to this point and frozen.

Preheat oven to 325 degrees and bake for 30–40 minutes. When cookies are golden brown on one side, after 15–20 minutes of baking, turn cookies over and brown on the other side, 15–20 minutes more. The pastry must be browned through. Cool completely before serving.

These cookies are best eaten the same day they are baked.

SABLE COOKIES

Meltingly tender sable cookies (pronounced SAH · blay), the French version of shortbread, have long been a favorite among cookie-lovers.

Rolling out the dough and cutting it with a French fluted-edge biscuit cutter makes a very pretty cookie, delicious whether they are filled or eaten plain.

The sable dough must be very cold to roll out, or it will stick maddeningly to the work surface. Work in small batches, keeping the rest of the dough refrigerated, and don't hesitate to return it to the refrigerator if it gets too soft to handle easily.

Use nonstick or paper-lined baking sheets and a 2-inch round cookie cutter. (For the lemon cookies, a large metal pastry tip for cutting circles out of the cookie tops.)

Lemon Sable Cookies

Cookie Dough:

¾ cup plus 2 tablespoons almond meal

¾ cup powdered sugar

5 ounces unsalted butter (1¼ sticks)

2 tablespoons grated or finely chopped lemon zest (1 lemon)

1½ teaspoons grated or finely chopped lime zest (1 lime)

¼ teaspoon ground cloves

1 egg

½ tablespoon lemon juice (1 lemon)

¾ tablespoon lime juice (½ lime)

1¼ cups flour

Although I prefer the homemade filling below, you can substitute good-quality imported English lemon curd, available where imported preserves are sold.

MAKING THE COOKIE DOUGH

In a food processor or blender, process the almond meal with the powdered sugar until it is the consistency of coarse cornmeal; set aside.

Using the paddle attachment of an electric mixer, beat the butter, lemon and lime zests, and ground cloves on medium speed until the butter whitens and holds soft peaks, 3–5 minutes. Beat in the almond meal mixture until well blended.

In a small bowl, whisk together the egg, lemon juice, and lime juice, then beat into butter mixture, scraping down the sides of the bowl as necessary. Beat in the flour, mixing just until combined. Wrap the dough in plastic wrap and refrigerate at least 8 hours.

MAKING THE FILLING

In a large metal bowl, whisk together all the filling ingredients except the butter. Set the bowl over a large pot of simmering water and whisk vigorously, incorporating as much air as possible, until the mixture resembles a thick hollandaise sauce. Remove from heat and beat in butter.

Lemon-Lime Filling:

½ cup lemon juice (3–4 lemons)

3 tablespoons grated or finely chopped lemon zest (4 lemons)

½ cup lime juice (5–6 limes)

3 tablespoons grated or finely chopped lime zest (5–6 limes)

3 eggs

3 egg yolks

¾ cup granulated sugar

4 ounces unsalted butter (1 stick), cut into 1-inch pieces

To Decorate the Cookies:

½ cup powdered sugar

Makes 60 cookies, or 30 sandwiches

Strain mixture through a fine-mesh strainer into a bowl. Refrigerate until cool.

ROLLING OUT AND BAKING THE COOKIES

Preheat oven to 300 degrees. Adjust the oven rack to the middle position.

On a floured surface, roll out dough in very small batches to ⅛-inch thickness. Use flour sparingly and touch the dough as little as possible while rolling. After each few strokes of the rolling pin, gently unstick the dough from the surface and spread a bit more flour underneath if necessary.

Using a 2½-inch-round or fluted biscuit cutter, cut out circles of dough and place on a paper-lined or nonstick baking sheet about 1 inch apart. If you will be filling the cookies with lemon-lime filling, use the wide end of a metal pastry tip (about ½ inch in diameter) and cut a circle out of the center of half the cookies (It should look like a doughnut hole.) Chill until firm, about 20 minutes.

Bake for 12–15 minutes. The cookies should color only slightly, but must be cooked through. Cool completely.

ASSEMBLING COOKIE SANDWICHES

Set aside the tops (the cookies with the holes in the center), rounded side up, on a piece of paper and cover them with a layer of powdered sugar sifted through a sieve.

Spoon or pipe ½ tablespoon of lemon-lime filling on the flat side of the sandwich bottom. Set a top on each bottom to make a sandwich. There should be enough filling in each cookie to spread out between the cookie halves and hold them together, and to make a little dome where it bulges out the hole in the top.

Don't stack these cookies to store or the filling will make them stick together.

Hazelnut-Chocolate Sable Cookies

*1 heaping cup raw
    hazelnuts (4 ounces)*

*6 ounces bittersweet
    chocolate, very cold*

1³/₄ cups powdered sugar

*10 ounces unsalted butter
    (2¹/₂ sticks)*

*1 tablespoon grated or finely
    chopped orange zest
    (1 orange)*

2 eggs

*¹/₂ tablespoon vanilla
    extract*

3 cups flour

For Filling (optional):
*2 cups Chocolate Glaze
    (page 348) or Devil's
    Food Frosting (page
    302)*

**Makes 60 cookies, or 30
sandwiches**

MAKING THE DOUGH

Preheat oven to 325 degrees. Adjust oven rack to the middle position. Spread hazelnuts on a baking sheet and toast for 8–10 minutes, until lightly browned all the way through. Cool. Rub nuts in a clean dish towel to remove skins; set aside.

Chop chocolate by hand into pieces approximately the size of a grain of rice. (A food processor tends to make the pieces too powdery. They must be big enough so they don't melt away and disappear during baking, but small enough so they don't get in your way when you roll out the dough.)

In a food processor or blender, process the toasted hazelnuts with the powdered sugar until they reach the consistency of coarse cornmeal; set aside.

Using the paddle attachment of an electric mixer, beat the butter and orange zest on medium speed until butter whitens and holds soft peaks, 3–5 minutes. Beat in the hazelnut mixture until well blended.

In a small bowl, whisk together the eggs and vanilla, then beat into butter mixture, scraping down the sides of the bowl as necessary. Beat in flour and chopped chocolate just until combined. Wrap dough in plastic wrap and refrigerate at least 8 hours.

ROLLING OUT, CUTTING, AND
BAKING THE COOKIES

Preheat oven to 300 degrees. Adjust the oven rack to the middle position.

On a floured surface, roll out dough in very small batches to ⅛-inch thickness. Use flour sparingly and touch dough as little as possible while rolling. After each few strokes of the rolling pin, gently unstick the dough from the surface and spread a bit more flour underneath if necessary.

Using a 2½-inch-round or fluted biscuit cutter, cut out circles of dough and place on a paper-lined or nonstick baking sheet about 1 inch apart. Chill until firm, about 20 minutes.

Bake for 12 minutes, until lightly browned. Cool completely.

ASSEMBLING COOKIE SANDWICHES

Stir the chocolate glaze briefly over ice to make it a spreadable consistency (not runny) so that the cookies stick together. If you are using devil's food frosting, you may need to warm it briefly over gently simmering water and whisk it until smooth to bring it to a spreadable consistency.

Spoon or pipe ½–1 tablespoon of chocolate filling on the flat side of half the cookies. Set a top (flat side touching chocolate filling) on each bottom to make a sandwich. There should be enough filling in each cookie to spread out between the halves and hold them together. Refrigerate for about 15 minutes to set chocolate filling.

Store in a cool place to keep the filling from melting.

PIPED COOKIES

Some of the prettiest butter cookies are formed by piping the dough in delicate rings from a pastry bag. This cookie dough is a very smooth one that is easily piped, not to be confused with the stiff doughs used for Christmas cookies that are forced out of mechanical metal contraptions.

Preparing the Dough: The piped cookie doughs are all based on butter, which must be beaten extremely well for the other ingredients to incorporate completely and the texture to be right for piping. It should resemble commercial whipped butter. If the butter is too soft when you start beating it, it can become greasy. Start with butter cold from the refrigerator, cut it into pieces, and beat until soft.

A perfect piped-cookie dough will be satiny smooth. If the butter wasn't beaten enough at the beginning, the dough will look like lumpy mashed potatoes. A lumpy dough is harder to pipe and makes a less attractive cookie.

In general, you'll have the most success with piped cookies on days when the temperature is moderate, so the dough is neither too stiff nor too soft.

Piping the Cookies: Using a pastry bag is a skill that improves every time you try it. For the most control, the bag should be filled less than half full. Don't handle the bag too much when piping these cookies or the dough will soften from the heat of your hands. (See "How to use a pastry bag," page 27.) If you want some guidance in forming the cookies, draw 1½-inch circles (about 1½ inches apart) on the parchment paper lining the baking sheet. Turn the paper over after you draw the circles, though, or you'll end up with pencil marks on your cookies. Then fill the still-visible circles with dough as you pipe.

Advance Preparation and Storage: If this dough stands for more than 20 minutes, it becomes stiff and difficult to pipe. Once the dough is made, pipe out all the cookies right away onto baking sheets or sheets of parchment paper and refrigerate (no more than 3 days) or freeze until ready to bake.

Orange-Cardamom Cookies

8 ounces unsalted butter (2 sticks)

4 tablespoons grated or finely chopped orange zest (3–4 oranges)

⅔ cup granulated sugar

3 tablespoons fresh orange juice (1 orange)

3 tablespoons orange liqueur

2 egg whites

2¼ cups flour

⅔ cup almond meal

2 tablespoons ground cardamom

To Fill Centers of Cookies:
1 cup apricot jam

Makes 6 dozen

Making a hole in the cookie

When I was working on desserts for the opening of Chinois on Main, I experimented quite a bit with typical Far Eastern spices like cardamom, a staple of Indian cooking. One result was this cookie combining cardamom with the flavor of fresh oranges and an apricot jam filling.

MAKING THE DOUGH

Sift together the flour, almond meal, and cardamom through a strainer; set aside. If any of the dry ingredients remain in the strainer, stir them back into the flour mixture.

Using the paddle attachment of an electric mixer, beat the butter with the orange zest on medium speed until it whitens and is extremely soft, 5–8 minutes. Beat in the sugar until well blended. Whisk together the orange juice, orange liqueur, and egg whites and add to butter mixture, scraping down the sides of the bowl as necessary. Add the flour mixture, beating until just combined.

Fill a pastry bag (No. 3 star tip) half full of cookie batter. Pipe batter onto a paper-lined or nonstick baking sheet into 1½-inch rounds, starting at the outside and spiraling inward to fill the center of the circle. The cookies should be thicker in the center than on the edges. If the weather is warm or the cookies are sticky, chill until firm.

FILLING AND BAKING THE COOKIES

In a small stainless steel saucepan, heat the apricot jam to boiling, whisking constantly. Strain through a fine-mesh strainer; set aside to cool.

Press the end of your index finger into the center of each cookie. Dip the tip of your finger in water from time to time so that it's easier to make a smooth well. Gently press an indentation into the center of each cookie and widen it to at least ½ inch in diameter by rotating your finger and pushing the dough out toward the edges of the cookie. Do not break through the bottom of the cookie. If the dough is too cold, it will crack and not widen easily when pushed; let stand at room temperature to soften. If the dough is too soft, it will be too sticky; chill until firm.

With a pastry bag fitted with a small No. 1 plain tip (or a small spoon), pipe ½ teaspoon of strained apricot jam into the well in each cookie. Chill until firm, about 30 minutes.

Continued on next page

Adjust the oven rack to the middle position. Preheat oven to 325 degrees. Bake for 20–22 minutes, until the cookies are lightly browned and lift off the baking sheet without sticking.

Cinnamon-Raspberry Cookies

2 hard-boiled eggs, yolks only

8 ounces unsalted butter (2 sticks)

1½ tablespoons grated or finely chopped lemon zest (2 lemons)

⅔ cup granulated sugar

2 teaspoons almond extract

1½ cups flour

½ cup almond meal

2 tablespoons cinnamon

1 cup raspberry jam

Makes 6 dozen

The classic Linzer torte combination of cinnamon and raspberry can be adapted to make a terrific cookie, centered with a shiny dot of raspberry jam.

Force the egg yolks through a fine-mesh strainer; set aside.

MAKING THE DOUGH AND PIPING THE COOKIES

Sift together the flour, almond meal, and cinnamon through a strainer; set aside. If any of the dry ingredients remain in the strainer, stir them back into the flour mixture.

Using the paddle attachment of an electric mixer, beat the butter on medium speed with the lemon zest and sieved egg yolk until it whitens and is extremely soft, 5–8 minutes. Beat in the sugar until well blended. Beat in almond extract, scraping down the sides of the bowl as necessary. Add the flour mixture, beating until just combined.

Fill a pastry bag (No. 3 star tip) half full of cookie batter. Pipe batter onto paper-lined or nonstick baking sheets into 1½-inch rounds, starting at the outside and spiraling inward to fill the center of the circle. The cookies should be thicker in the center than on the edges. If the weather is warm or the cookies are sticky, chill until firm.

Strain raspberry jam through a fine-mesh strainer; set aside.

Press the end of your index finger into the center of each cookie. Dip the tip of your finger in water from time to time so that it's easier to make a smooth well. Gently press an indentation into the center of each cookie and widen it to at least ½ inch in diameter by rotating your finger and pushing the dough out toward the edges of the cookie. Do not break through the bottom of the cookie. If the dough is too cold, it will crack and not widen easily when pushed; let stand at room temperature to soften. If the dough is too

Piping jam into cookie

soft, it will be too sticky; chill until firm.

With a pastry bag fitted with a small No. 1 plain tip (or a small spoon), pipe ½ teaspoon of strained raspberry jam into the well in each cookie. Chill until firm, about 30 minutes.

Adjust the oven rack to the middle position. Preheat oven to 325 degrees. Bake for 20–22 minutes, until the cookies are lightly browned and lift off the baking sheet without sticking.

Lime-Clove Cookies

7 ounces unsalted butter
    (1¾ sticks)

2½ tablespoons grated or
    finely chopped lime zest
    (5 limes)

1¾ teaspoons ground cloves

½ cup plus 2 tablespoons
    granulated sugar

1 egg yolk

1 tablespoon lime juice
    (½–1 lime)

2 cups flour

Makes 5 dozen

*Piping a cookie leaving
a hole in the center*

A spicy cookie always has an appealing aroma while baking, but this combination of lime and clove is especially seductive.

Preheat oven to 325 degrees. Adjust the oven rack to the middle position.

MAKING THE DOUGH

Using the paddle attachment of an electric mixer, beat the butter on medium speed with the lime zest and ground cloves until it whitens and is extremely soft, 5–8 minutes. Beat in the sugar until well blended. Whisk together the egg yolk and lime juice and beat them into butter mixture, scraping down the sides of the bowl as necessary. Add flour, beating until just combined.

PIPING AND BAKING THE COOKIES

Fill a pastry bag (No. 3 star tip) half full of cookie batter. Pipe batter onto a paper-lined or nonstick baking sheet into 2-inch rounds, starting at the outside edge and spiraling toward the center of the circle, leaving only a small opening in the center (rather than making a completely open ring). The ends of the circle should barely overlap where they meet or the cookie will be too thick. The cookies should be no more than ¼ inch thick.

Bake 17 minutes, until firm and lightly browned.

Chocolate Fudge

1 cup walnuts, pecans, or whole, toasted unblanched almonds

9 ounces bittersweet chocolate

2 cups heavy cream

1 cup granulated sugar in all

1 vanilla bean, split and scraped

6 tablespoons unsweetened cocoa

1/4 cup whiskey

2 tablespoons corn syrup

1 tablespoon unsalted butter

1/3 cup water

4 egg whites

1/2 cup Chocolate Glaze, optional (page 348)

Makes one 8 x 8-inch pan of very rich fudge

Fudge is a favorite of so many people, but most of the fudge that I'd tasted had an unappealingly grainy quality —until one Christmas Eve when Cheryl Peel, my husband's mother, brought over a pan of smooth, creamy, delicious-tasting fudge. This variation on her recipe calls for a stiff, shiny Italian meringue, and the condensed milk is replaced by fresh heavy cream, boiled down to thicken it. The resulting fudge has a deep chocolate flavor and a very smooth, slightly sticky texture, rather like a truffle and even easier to make. The ideal pan to use is one treated with a nonstick coating.

To toast the nuts, preheat the oven to 325 degrees. Spread the almonds on a baking sheet and toast for 8–10 minutes, until brown. Cool. Chop nuts coarse and set aside.

Cut the chocolate into 2-inch pieces. In a heatproof bowl, melt the chocolate over gently simmering water. (The water should not touch the bottom of the bowl or the chocolate will burn.) Turn off heat and let stand over warm water until ready to use.

In a medium-size saucepan, boil the cream, 3 tablespoons of the sugar, and vanilla bean until the liquid is reduced to 1 cup, about 5 minutes at a full boil. (Don't let the cream boil over.) Remove vanilla bean. Stir cream into melted chocolate.

In a small saucepan, combine the cocoa, whiskey, and corn syrup and cook over low heat, stirring constantly, until the mixture is thick and puddinglike. (The mixture can burn easily or the whiskey can ignite if the heat is too high.) Stir into chocolate-cream mixture. Stir in butter; set aside in a warm place.

MAKING THE ITALIAN MERINGUE

An Italian meringue is made by beating a hot sugar syrup into egg whites, which creates a very stiff mixture. Ideally, have the egg whites ready at the same time as the sugar syrup. If it seems that the syrup is reducing faster than the egg whites are beating up, add some water to the syrup and reduce the heat to low. Don't shut off the flame, though, or the syrup may crystallize as it stands.

(Four egg whites make almost 2 cups of Italian meringue, but only 1 cup is needed for the recipe. Because it can be tricky to make a small quantity of the meringue, and because it's not an expensive ingredient anyway, I decided that it was easier to make a larger quantity and discard some.)

In a small saucepan, whisk together the ⅓ cup water with ¾ cup of the sugar. When the water boils, it will throw sugar onto the sides of the pan. At that point, wash down the sides of the pan with a pastry brush, dipping in water as necessary to dissolve sugar. (Alternatively, place a lid on the pan for 30 seconds and the steam condensation will wash the sugar off the sides.) Boil until sugar dissolves and syrup reaches the soft crack stage (270–290 degrees on a candy thermometer).

As soon as the surface of the syrup is covered with bursting bubbles, start beating the egg whites in an electric mixer on low speed until frothy. Increase speed to medium and beat until soft peaks form. Increase speed to high and gradually beat in the remaining 1 tablespoon sugar, until stiff, glossy peaks form. Pour the sugar syrup in a very thin, steady stream into the meringue, beating at high speed for 4–5 minutes, until the meringue is shiny and stiff. Reduce speed to medium and beat until the outside of the bowl is cool to the touch. The meringue will be bright white, very smooth, and will stand in very stiff peaks.

Measure 1 cup of Italian meringue and discard the rest. Whisk meringue into chocolate mixture and combine well. Fold in nuts. Pour into an 8 x 8-inch pan and chill until hard, 2–3 hours.

GLAZING THE TOP

A layer of glaze makes a more finished-looking top.

In a heatproof bowl, warm the chocolate glaze over gently simmering water until it is just warm enough to be poured, but not hot. Pour the glaze onto the hardened fudge. Tilt pan to cover the top with a thin, even layer of glaze and pour out excess. Chill until set.

Cut into small squares with a heated knife. The fudge keeps beautifully in the refrigerator or freezer. Don't hesitate to double the recipe.

Spiced Pecans

1 egg white

1½ cups pecan halves
(4 ounces)

¼ cup granulated sugar

2 teaspoons ground
cinnamon

½ teaspoon freshly grated
nutmeg

1 teaspoon ground ginger

Makes 1½ cups

My mother's friend Sylvia Spingarn used to make these spice-coated nuts for us at Christmas. They're great plain, on a cookie platter, with ice cream, or to garnish a dessert like the Banana-Pecan Layer Cake.

Preheat oven to 325 degrees. Adjust the oven rack to the middle position.

Whisk the egg white just until frothy, about 30 seconds. In a large bowl, mix the pecan halves thoroughly with the egg white. In a small bowl, toss the sugar and spices together and then toss with the pecan halves, mixing well. Spread evenly on a nonstick baking sheet, separating the nuts, and bake for 30 minutes, until evenly browned. Cool.

Store in airtight jars or tins for up to one month, or as long as they are crisp and fresh-tasting.

CHOCOLATE TRUFFLES

Chocolate truffles may have been named because of their resemblance in shape and color to the black truffles unearthed by refined snuffling pigs in the European countryside. Or they could have been named truffles because they're as great a delicacy in the world of sweets as the rare and expensive black truffles are in savory cooking. They're also one of the easiest of all candies to make, and delicious as part of a cookie platter or served with a cup of espresso.

A truly handmade, hand-dipped truffle is not easy to find these days, even at prices up to $20 a pound. Some of the most exclusive candy shops are using preformed truffle casings of lower-quality chocolate and piping their own truffle cream inside. Since truffles keep quite a long time in the refrigerator or freezer (see individual recipes for recommended storage times), why not make your own? You'll know for sure that the ingredients you use are only the best.

When serving truffles, give them a few minutes out of the refrigerator to soften and bring out the flavor.

Hand-Forming Truffles: The basic method is to make the truffle cream, chill it until firm, form it into the desired shape, and then dip it in melted chocolate for a hard coating. Truffle cream can be formed into almost any shape, from large golf balls to small stars and logs. I prefer to make bite-size balls about 1 inch in diameter that are dipped in melted chocolate and then rolled in cocoa powder or powdered sugar. They're easy to form, don't require any special tools or molds, and they look nice on a platter of desserts or cookies. The hard coating makes a wonderful contrast with the soft interior.

The truffle cream itself is simple to make in a food processor. It should be very creamy and shiny after it has been processed; if it looks dull, whisk in a little more warmed alcohol.

Use the small scoop of a two-ended melon-baller to portion out the truffle cream. Dip the melon-baller in very hot water and shake off excess before scooping out each truffle. (You will need to replenish the hot water as it cools.)

Scoop out the truffles one by one, knock the melon-baller against the corner of the work surface to release mixture, and form them into small balls with your hands. Work quickly, because the heat of your palms will melt them. Place on a tray and refrigerate as soon as they are formed. Keep your hands cool by holding them under cold water from time to time.

Dipping the Truffles in Chocolate: Patience and organization are the keys to successful truffle-dipping.

Keep your working area organized. Arrange a partial tray of chilled truffles, the melted chocolate, the cocoa powder or powdered sugar, and a container to refrigerate the finished truffles in next to each other on the work surface. Work as close to the refrigerator as possible, keeping the balls of truffle cream chilled and refrigerating the dipped truffles as soon as they are finished.

All the recipes call for 1 pound of chocolate to dip the truffles into. You will not use the entire amount, but it's very important that the melted chocolate be deep enough that the truffles are easy to dip and cover completely. (Any leftover chocolate can be reused.) There must also be enough cocoa powder or powdered sugar, both sifted, in a deep container, so the truffles can be easily submerged.

To dip, melt 1 pound chocolate over simmering water. Test the temperature by touching a bit of chocolate to your upper lip—it should be warm to the touch but not hot. The truffles themselves have to be cold or they will melt when dipped.

Pick up a truffle with your hand and drop it into the melted chocolate. With a fork, turn it in the chocolate to cover completely and then lift it out on the tines of the fork. Tap the fork against the side of the bowl to knock any excess chocolate off the truffle, then place it in the bowl of cocoa powder or powdered sugar. Don't let truffles sit in the warm chocolate or they will melt—dip and remove them one by one. Wash your hands and the dipping fork as often as necessary to keep everything neat, and handle the truffles themselves as little as possible.

If not enough chocolate drips off the truffles after dipping, then the chocolate is too cold; if fork marks remain in the truffles after dipping, it's too hot. Depending on the temperature around you and how fast you're working, you will probably need to reheat the chocolate a few times during the dipping process. (It's foolhardy to try to make truffles on a very hot day.) *Continued on next page*

When 4–5 truffles are sitting in the bowl of cocoa or sugar, spoon the powder over them and set the whole bowl in the freezer; leave it for a minute or so until the melted chocolate coating has set. Remove the bowl from the freezer and shake a bit to ensure that the truffles are coated evenly. Placing the truffles in the freezer guarantees that the outside coating will harden separately and have a different consistency than the truffle cream filling, and that the truffles will not stick together or get the long chocolate "tails" that can form using other methods. Take them out of the bowl, place on a tray, and refrigerate. Continue dipping and coating the remaining balls of truffle cream.

The balls of truffle cream can be made in advance and kept refrigerated or frozen to be dipped at your convenience.

VARIATIONS: Truffles can be dipped in milk chocolate instead of bittersweet chocolate, or different liqueurs and flavorings can be used. Any of the dark chocolate truffles can be simply rolled in cocoa powder without being dipped in chocolate. (The white chocolate ones are so soft that they need a hard coating, however.) After you've tried some of these recipes, experiment with your own combinations.

Milk Chocolate– Praline Truffles

8 ounces milk chocolate

1 egg yolk

¾ cup Irish cream liqueur

1 cup ground Praline (page 354)

To Dip Truffles:
1 pound bittersweet chocolate

―――――――――――――

Makes 70 bite-size truffles

Of all the truffles, these are the easiest to work with. They also keep in the freezer better than any of the others.

Cut milk chocolate into 2-inch pieces. In a heatproof bowl, melt the chocolate over gently simmering water. (Watch carefully—milk chocolate burns faster than dark chocolate.) Do not let the water touch the bottom of the bowl. Turn off heat. Whisk in the egg yolk. Let stand over warm water until ready to use.

In a saucepan, scald the liqueur. Pour onto the melted chocolate and whisk together. Whisk in ground praline. Pour the mixture into one or two shallow pans in a layer about 1 inch thick and chill or freeze until set.

Form the truffles and dip in chocolate following the directions on page 73. As soon as a few of the truffles have been dipped, place them on a tray in the refrigerator. I like the contrast of a milk chocolate truffle dipped in bittersweet chocolate, but these can be dipped in milk chocolate if you prefer. If you use milk chocolate, first strain the melted chocolate through a fine-mesh strainer to remove any lumps before dipping.

Rather than rolling these truffles in cocoa powder or powdered sugar, pipe a thin zigzag of chocolate on top after the coating has hardened in the refrigerator. Use a bit of reserved dipping chocolate to fill a paper cone for piping (see "Piping chocolate decorations," page 342).

These truffles keep exceptionally well for up to three months in the freezer.

Fresh Mint Truffles

½ cup whole fresh mint leaves, stems removed, loosely packed

1 pound white chocolate

½ cup heavy cream

5 tablespoons white crème de menthe or peppermint schnapps

4 ounces unsalted butter (1 stick)

To Dip Truffles:
1 pound bittersweet chocolate

3 cups powdered sugar, sifted

Makes 80 bite-size truffles

Fresh mint cuts the sweetness of the white chocolate and gives these truffles a refreshing quality. Their flavor makes a nice contrast on a plate of assorted candies.

The crème de menthe or peppermint schnapps must be fresh to give an intense, minty taste. If desired, one tablespoon green crème de menthe can be substituted for a tablespoon of white crème de menthe to tint the white chocolate a very pale green color.

Finely chop the mint leaves. There should be about ¼ cup. Set aside.

Cut the white chocolate into 2-inch pieces. In a heatproof bowl, melt chocolate with the cream over gently simmering water. (Watch carefully—white chocolate burns more easily than dark chocolate. The water should not touch the bottom of the bowl.) Turn off heat and let stand over warm water until ready to use.

Whisk in the crème de menthe, the chopped mint leaves, and the butter. Pour the mixture into one or two shallow pans in a layer about 1 inch thick and chill or freeze until set. Form the truffles, dip in chocolate, and roll in powdered sugar following the directions on page 73.

White chocolate does not set up as firmly as dark chocolate. Keep the truffle cream as cold as possible while you're working with it, returning it to the freezer as often as necessary to keep it firm.

After the truffles are rolled in powdered sugar, they must be kept frozen, as powdered sugar tends to bead with moisture in the refrigerator.

These truffles keep exceptionally well for up to three months in the freezer.

Chocolate Truffles with Currants

½ cup plus a few extra
   tablespoons rum

½ cup currants

1 pound bittersweet
   chocolate

¾ cup heavy cream

3 ounces (6 tablespoons)
   unsalted butter

To Dip Truffles:
1 pound bittersweet
   chocolate

3 cups unsweetened cocoa
   powder

Makes 80 bite-size truffles

At last—the grown-up version of chocolate-covered raisins.

In a stainless steel saucepan over low heat, scald the rum and currants. Cool. If the alcohol ignites, blow it out. Drain the currants, reserving the rum. Measure the rum and add a few more tablespoons, if necessary, to make ½ cup; set aside.

Cut 1 pound chocolate into 2-inch pieces. In a heatproof bowl, melt chocolate over gently simmering water. (The water should not touch the bottom of the bowl or the chocolate will burn.) Turn off heat and let stand over warm water until ready to use.

In a saucepan, scald the reserved rum and heavy cream. Again, if the alcohol ignites, blow it out. Pour onto the melted chocolate and whisk together. Whisk in butter. Pour the mixture into one or two shallow pans in a layer about 1 inch thick and chill or freeze briefly until thickened and almost set, 20–30 minutes.

Sprinkle on currants and stir to distribute them evenly into the truffle mixture. Refrigerate until firm. Form truffles, dip in chocolate, and roll in cocoa powder following the directions on page 73.

Freezing these truffles harms the consistency of the currants; store in the refrigerator.

Cassis Truffles

1 pound white chocolate

1 cup black currants, fresh
   or frozen without syrup

¼ cup water

¼ cup heavy cream

¼ pound unsalted butter
   (1 stick)

¼ cup double crème de
   cassis

Black currants, called *cassis* in French, give the white chocolate in these truffles a tart, fruity flavor and a deep purple color.

Use double crème de cassis, a liqueur, rather than cassis syrup, which is too sweet and does not contain alcohol.

Cut the white chocolate into 2-inch pieces. In a heatproof bowl, melt the chocolate with the cream over gently simmering water. (Watch carefully—white chocolate burns faster than dark chocolate. Do not let the water touch the bottom of the bowl.) Turn off heat and let stand over warm water until ready to use.

In a stainless steel saucepan, cook the black currants with the water over low heat until the liquid has completely evaporated.

To Dip Truffles:
1 pound bittersweet chocolate

3 cups unsweetened cocoa powder, sifted

Makes 135 bite-size truffles

Stir the softened black currants into the melted chocolate. Cut the butter into small pieces and then stir into the chocolate mixture along with the crème de cassis. Process the mixture briefly in a food processor and strain through a fine-mesh strainer.

Pour the mixture into one or two shallow pans in a layer about 1 inch thick and chill or freeze until set. Form truffles, dip in chocolate, and roll in cocoa powder following the directions on page 73.

White chocolate does not set up as firmly as dark chocolate. Keep the truffle cream as cold as possible while you're working with it, returning it to the freezer as often as necessary to keep it firm.

These truffles keep well for up to three months in the freezer.

Candied Lemon or Grapefruit Peel

3 lemons or 1 large grapefruit

5 cups sugar syrup (page 29)

2 tablespoons orange liqueur

⅓ cup lemon or grapefruit juice (1–2 lemons or ½ grapefruit)

1½ cups crystallized or granulated sugar, optional

Makes approximately 70 pieces

Used in Chocolate Truffles with Candied Grapefruit Peel

When tossed in crystallized sugar, these bittersweet sticks of candied peel make a nice addition to an assorted cookie plate or can be served alongside a cup of espresso or a bowl of ice cream or sherbet. Because they keep indefinitely, they're also a lovely gift.

To candy citrus peel correctly, be patient and cook it slowly. If the fire is too high and the liquid reduces too fast, the syrup crystallizes and the finished product may be tough and streaked with white.

The candied peel can be tossed in granulated sugar if crystallized sugar isn't available. Either will keep the pieces from sticking together, but I prefer the crunch and texture of crystallized sugar.

With a sharp paring knife, score the fruit in quarters and peel off the rind. Trim the ends of the pieces so that they are about 2 inches long. Cut them lengthwise into ¼-inch-wide slices.

Put the sliced peel in a stainless steel saucepan, cover with water, and bring to a boil. Boil for 5 minutes, then drain well. Return the peel to the saucepan, cover with water again, bring to a boil, and boil for 5 minutes. Drain.

In a stainless steel saucepan, combine the blanched peel, sugar syrup, liqueur, and juice and bring to a boil.

Reduce the heat and cook at a low simmer for 1 to 1½ hours. The peel is done when the syrup has thickened and the surface is covered with bubbles. Test by biting into a piece of peel—it should be completely tender to the bite, soft, and jellylike (not spongy). The colored part of the peel will be almost iridescent; the pith (the white part) of the peel might look streaked when it is first removed from the syrup, but it will clear up and become translucent after about 30 seconds out of the syrup.

Drain in a colander and then spread on a piece of wax paper or parchment paper and separate to keep from sticking together. Cool.

To coat with sugar, place crystallized or granulated sugar in a small bowl and, using your hands, toss a few pieces of peel at a time in sugar until completely coated.

Chocolate Truffles with Candied Grapefruit Peel

*1 pound bittersweet
    chocolate*

¾ cup heavy cream

½ cup orange liqueur

*3 ounces (6 tablespoons)
    unsalted butter*

*½ cup coarsely chopped
    Candied Grapefruit Peel
    (page 77, uncoated
    with sugar)*

To Dip Truffles:
*1 pound bittersweet
    chocolate*

*3 cups unsweetened cocoa
    powder*

Makes 80 bite-size truffles

The contrast between the bitterness of the grapefruit peel and the sweetness of the chocolate makes an intriguing truffle.

Cut 1 pound chocolate into 2-inch pieces. In a heatproof bowl, melt chocolate over gently simmering water. (The water should not touch the bottom of the bowl or the chocolate will burn.) Turn off heat and let stand over warm water until ready to use.

In a saucepan, scald the heavy cream and orange liqueur. Pour onto the melted chocolate and whisk together. Whisk in butter. Pour the mixture into one or two shallow pans in a layer about 1 inch thick and chill or freeze briefly until thickened and almost set, 20–30 minutes.

Sprinkle on the candied grapefruit peel and stir into the truffle mixture. Refrigerate until set. Form truffles, dip in chocolate, and roll in cocoa powder following the directions on page 73.

Freezing these truffles harms the consistency of the candied grapefruit peel; store in the refrigerator.

Chocolate Truffles with Fresh Raspberries

1 pound bittersweet
    chocolate

¾ cup heavy cream

½ cup whiskey

3 ounces (6 tablespoons)
    unsalted butter

60 firm fresh raspberries
    (fresh only; frozen
    raspberries have too high
    a water content)

To Dip Truffles:
1 pound bittersweet
    chocolate

3 cups unsweetened cocoa
    powder

Makes 60 bite-size truffles

A truffle with fresh fruit is unusual, but in this case the combination of raspberries and chocolate is excellent—the fruit lightens the intensity of the chocolate and the flavors team up very well.

Cut 1 pound chocolate into 2-inch pieces. In a heatproof bowl, melt chocolate over gently simmering water. (The water should not touch the bottom of the bowl or the chocolate will burn.) Turn off heat and let stand over warm water until ready to use.

In a saucepan, scald heavy cream and whiskey. Pour onto the melted chocolate and whisk together. Whisk in butter. Pour the mixture into one or two shallow pans in a layer about 1 inch thick and chill or freeze until thickened and almost set, 20–30 minutes.

When the chocolate mixture has set until almost firm, poke 60 indentations about ⅜ inch apart into it with the handle of a melon-baller or the end of a wooden spoon. Do not press the handle all the way through to the bottom of the pan. Dip the handle in hot water as often as necessary to keep chocolate from sticking. Place a raspberry in each indentation. Refrigerate until set.

Dip the large end of a melon-baller in very hot water and scoop up 1 raspberry and the chocolate surrounding it. Knock the handle against the corner of the work surface to release the truffle. Gently form it into a ball with your hands, adding a little extra truffle mixture if necessary to completely cover the raspberry. Try not to crush the fruit.

Dip the melon-baller in hot water and shake off the excess before scooping out each truffle. (You will need to replenish the water as it cools off.) As each truffle is formed, place it on a tray and refrigerate until completely firm. Dip the truffles in chocolate and roll in cocoa powder following the directions on page 73.

Freezing these truffles harms the consistency of the raspberries; store in the refrigerator.

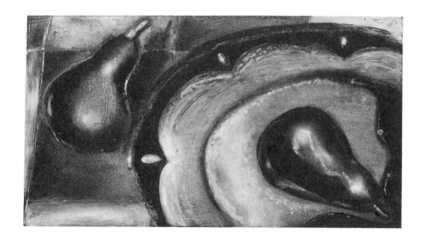

Fruit and Nut Desserts

FRESH FRUIT TARTS

Sweet Pastry
Marzipan Tart with Strawberries, Figs, or Raspberries
Berry Brown-Butter Tart
Pear and Ginger Brown-Butter Tart
Plum Tart

FRESH FRUIT CUSTARD TARTS

Lemon Lime Tart
Cherry Tart with Buttermilk Custard
Zinfandel Pear Tart
Sour Cream Custard Tart with Peaches, Apricots, or Nectarines
Rice Tart with Mango
Blackberry or Raspberry Custard Tart

INDIVIDUAL FRESH FRUIT DESSERTS

Open-Face Fruit Tarts
Caramel-Glazed Pears Poached in Riesling
Thin Apple Pancakes with Broiled Apple Slices and Apple Cider Ice Cream
Berry Dessert Pancakes
Individual Apple Calvados Tarts
Gratin of Oranges
Gratin of Fresh Berries with Lemon Curd or Vanilla Crème Brûlée
Gratin of Bananas

SIMPLE FRUIT DESSERTS

Melons in Plum Wine or Port
Fresh Berries with Crème Fraîche
Baked Pears or Apples with Crème Fraîche

AMERICAN FAVORITES UPDATED

Strawberry Shortcake
Deep-Dish Apple Pie
Huckleberry Pie
Rhubarb Pie
Pear or Apple Ginger Upside-Down Cake
Apple Cheesecake
Popovers
Blueberry Buckle
Bread Pudding

DRIED FRUIT AND NUT DESSERTS

Pecan Tartlets
Brioche Dough
Sticky Buns
Prune Tart with Brioche Crust
Caramel-Walnut Tart

Fruit and Nut Desserts

Glorious fresh fruit is one of my biggest inspirations. The variety of colors, textures, and succulent flavors has always sparked my sense of culinary invention. Whether I'm making apricot or plum tarts in the summer, or a casserole of warm baked pears and apples in cream in the winter, I always seek to bring out the intrinsic flavors of the fruit. I love changing the menu with the seasons, responding to the market and cooking with what's best and most beautiful on any given day.

I also love fruit desserts because of the wide variety of combinations possible—a tropical mango sliced into a rice custard tart, the common banana in an elegant *gratin* with rum sauce and currants, cool melon balls marinated with port and fresh mint.

Because fruit is inherently sweet, fruit desserts need relatively little sweetening. I'll often cook berries or sliced fruit into a dessert to flavor a filling or batter, then top it with more of the same fruit, but uncooked. The flavor of the fresh and cooked fruit together really permeates dishes like the Berry Dessert Pancakes and the Berry Brown-Butter Tart.

The natural beauty of fruit is another of its great qualities. A carefully arranged fruit tart or dessert is essentially self-decorated, the colors and shapes of the fruit making any other embellishment (other than a light dusting of powdered sugar, perhaps, or a highlighting with red currant jelly or apricot jam) unnecessary.

In making fruit desserts, your final product will only be as good as the ingredients you use. Luckily, fruit is usually best when it is cheapest, at the height of the season. These days, though, if you're willing to pay the price, imports from the Southern Hemisphere bring us almost any fruit year-round.

Ideally, fruit should be perfectly ripe—it should smell fruity and give a little to the touch. If it doesn't smell like anything, it won't taste like anything. Overripe fruit will break down and get mushy when cooked, whereas underripe fruit hasn't got the flavor and texture needed to make a really succulent dessert. (In some cases, slightly underripe fruit can be poached to improve its quality; see "Poaching fruit," page 24.) Berries should be juicy, not seedy, and strawberries should be red through-and-through, without the white core that is so often found.

FRESH FRUIT TARTS

Fruit tarts are light and appealing, showing off perfect fresh fruit toppings or lightly browned fillings with fruit slices peeking through. Few of the fillings are rich: even in the fruit custard tarts, the natural acidity of the fruit contrasts with the creamy filling and creates a light effect. Use only fresh fruit for these recipes, never frozen or canned.

I've found that a basic sweet pastry is ideal for tarts of all kinds. It's a tender, cookielike crust that stays crisp. Depending on the tart filling, the pastry can be varied by adding orange, lemon, or ginger.

All recipe quantities are based on tarts made in 10-inch flan rings with 1-inch-high sides. I prefer a flan ring (set on a heavy-duty baking sheet) to a pie pan because the ring can be lifted off, revealing the smooth, attractive sides of the crust, and the tart can be sliced clean rather than scooped out of a pan. If you use a flan ring, you will need to slip a cardboard round under the tart so it can be moved onto the serving platter.

A tart pan with a removable bottom also makes a nice-looking tart, and it's already on the metal bottom if you want to move it.

If you use a smaller pan than recommended, like a 10-inch ring with ½-inch-high sides, or an 8-inch tart pan, there will be filling ingredients left over, perhaps even enough to fill a second tart. A tart in a smaller pan may take less time to bake than a larger one; watch carefully while baking.

Most of the tarts are best eaten the same day they are made, although the pastry dough and some of the fillings can be prepared in advance. The recipes specify which ones will store well for a few days.

Sweet Pastry

2¾ cups flour

½ cup granulated sugar

8 ounces unsalted butter (2 sticks)

2 egg yolks

¼ cup heavy cream

Makes 1½ pounds dough (enough for two 10-inch tart shells)

An excellent tart pastry—it's sweet, short, and stays crisp under a filling. Lemon, orange, or ginger flavoring will add another dimension to the dough.

Pastry can be made in a food processor or electric mixer, but I prefer making it by hand for a tender crust. And I use cream rather than water for the color and the taste.

Sift the flour into a large bowl. Stir in the sugar. Cut the butter into ½-inch cubes and toss with the flour until the cubes are coated. Crumble the butter into the flour by rubbing it between your fingertips (the coolest part of your hand), lifting the pieces and letting them fall back down again. Continue until the mixture resembles coarse cornmeal.

In a small bowl, whisk together the egg yolks and ¼ cup heavy cream and pour onto the flour mixture. Gather the dough together with your hands. You may have to dribble on as much as 2 tablespoons extra cream to make the dough moist enough to gather together into a ball.

(In a food processor, using the metal blade, or in an electric mixer, using the paddle attachment, combine ingredients in the same order, processing the flour, sugar, and cubed butter together to a cornmeal-like consistency, and then adding the egg yolks and cream. Be sure that you stop the machine immediately when the flour reaches the cornmeal stage, and again as soon as the dough comes together after the addition of the cream. Add extra cream if necessary to make the dough come together.)

FRAISAGE (WORKING IN THE BUTTER)

This French technique of working in the butter by hand creates a light, tender, well-amalgamated crust.

Turn the dough out onto a lightly floured surface. Use flour sparingly—some of the dough will stick to the surface, but you can scrape it up and reincorporate it into the mass. Dip the heel of your hand in flour and begin smearing small sections of the dough away from you.

When the dough has been all smeared out, gather it together and form into two balls. Wrap in plastic wrap and refrigerate at least 2 hours before rolling out. Pastry should always chill after it has been made and again after rolling out to allow the gluten in the flour to relax and ensure a tender crust that will not shrink during baking.

See instructions for "Lining tart shells," page 26 and "Blind baking," page 27.

Lemon or Orange Pastry

6 tablespoons plus a few extra tablespoons heavy cream

¼ cup grated or finely chopped lemon zest (4–5 lemons) or orange zest (3–4 oranges)

2¾ cups flour

½ cup granulated sugar

8 ounces unsalted butter (2 sticks)

In a small stainless steel or enamel saucepan, scald the cream and citrus zest. Remove from the heat, cover, and let stand for 30 minutes. Strain the cream through a fine-mesh strainer, reserving the zest. If there is less than ¼ cup strained cream, add enough to make ¼ cup. Stir 1 tablespoon of the zest into the cream. Chill. Proceed as directed above, using the citrus-flavored cream in place of the heavy cream.

Ginger Pastry

2 ounces fresh ginger root

6 tablespoons plus 2 extra tablespoons heavy cream

1 egg yolk

1 tablespoon molasses, preferably blackstrap

2 cups flour

2 tablespoons ground ginger

5 ounces unsalted butter (1¼ sticks)

¼ cup plus 1 tablespoon dark brown sugar, packed

Peel the ginger root with a vegetable peeler and slice into ¼-inch rounds. Place in a small saucepan, cover with water, bring to a boil, and boil 30 seconds. Drain well.

In a small saucepan, scald the blanched ginger root and cream. Remove from heat, cover, and let stand 30 minutes. Strain, discarding the ginger. If there is less than ¼ cup cream, add enough to make ¼ cup. Chill. Whisk the egg yolk and molasses into the cream. Sift the flour and ground ginger together and proceed as directed above, adding the brown sugar in place of the granulated sugar.

Marzipan Tart with Strawberries, Figs, or Raspberries

1 Sweet Pastry tart shell (page 84), unbaked

½ tablespoon unsalted butter, melted, to butter tart ring

Marzipan Filling:
4 ounces unsalted butter (1 stick)

2 tablespoons finely chopped or grated orange zest (2 oranges)

½ cup granulated sugar

2 eggs

3 tablespoons orange liqueur

1½ teaspoons almond extract

1⅓ cups almond meal

Strawberry Topping and Glaze:
4 cups ripe strawberries, as close to the same size as possible

¼ cup red currant jelly

2 tablespoons water or brandy

Chewy almond filling is the perfect foil for the juiciness of fresh strawberries, figs, or raspberries. Although most fresh fruit desserts must be made at the last minute, the crust and filling of this tart can be baked a day ahead, ready to be topped with fruit just before serving.

Use a 10 x 1-inch or ½-inch flan ring. (If you use the lower ring, there will be enough filling for 2 tarts.)

MAKING AND BAKING THE FILLING

Preheat oven to 350 degrees. Adjust oven rack to the middle position.

Using the paddle attachment of an electric mixer, beat the butter on medium-high speed with the orange zest until it whitens and holds soft peaks, 3–5 minutes. Add the sugar, beating until well blended.

In a small bowl, lightly whisk together the eggs, orange liqueur, and almond extract. Add egg mixture and almond meal alternately to butter mixture, one third at a time, scraping down the sides of the bowl and beating well after each addition. Beat on medium-slow speed for 5–10 minutes, until the batter is very light and fluffy. Pick up a spoonful of batter and knock the spoon lightly against the side of the bowl: if the batter falls off without sticking to the spoon, the mixture is ready.

Scrape mixture into the chilled pastry shell, filling to ¼ inch from the top of the ring, and smooth evenly with an offset metal spatula or the back of a spoon. Bake for 40–50 minutes. The top edge of the pastry should be golden brown and the filling should be lightly browned and barely firm to the touch. Cool completely. Slip a 10-inch cardboard round underneath and remove flan ring.

❖ The tart can be made a day ahead up to this point. Cover with plastic wrap and refrigerate until ready to finish.

STRAWBERRY TOPPING

Stem and core strawberries. Slice about one fourth of the strawberries vertically into ¼-inch slices. You should get 3–4 slices from each strawberry. (Save the outside slices to make sauce.)

Melt the red currant jelly with the water or brandy in a small saucepan, stirring with a wire whisk or pastry brush

Fig Topping and Glaze:
8–10 ripe black Mission figs
½ cup red currant jelly
¼ cup water or brandy

Makes one 10-inch tart, serving 8–10

until it bubbles and reduces to a thick syrup, 1–2 minutes.

With a pastry brush, paint a thin layer of currant glaze over the top of the tart. Lay the sliced strawberries in a border around the outside edge of the tart, overlapping them slightly, with the points all going in the same direction. (Slice a few more strawberries, if necessary, to make the border.) Thinly paint the surface of the sliced strawberries with currant glaze to make them shine and prevent discoloration of the cut fruit.

Starting at the center of the tart, cover the entire surface with whole, cored strawberries, pointed end up, sides touching, in concentric circles. Pack in as much fruit as possible, leaving no gaps. Keep similar-size berries next to each other. Reheat the glaze until bubbly; thin with water or more liqueur if it has thickened too much to brush. Lightly brush the tops only of the whole strawberries with glaze to add highlights to the fruit, but not to coat it.

FIG TOPPING

Ripe black Mission figs are a wonderful autumn variation. The fig slices look like the petals of a flower when arranged on top of the tart.

Slice 8–10 ripe figs vertically into ¼-inch slices, discarding the end slices. You should get 3–4 slices from each fig. Heat the currant jelly as directed above. Brush the tart with currant jelly and then, starting at the edge of the tart, cover the surface with fig slices by arranging them in concentric circles in a slightly overlapping pattern, pointed ends toward the center. Paint a very thin coating of glaze over the entire surface of the tart to bring out the color of the figs.

RASPBERRY TOPPING

Use 2 cups of raspberries. Brush the tart with glaze and then arrange the raspberries on end in concentric circles to completely cover the top of the tart. Do not glaze.

Serve at room temperature, with Vanilla Sauce, Strawberry Sauce, or Raspberry Sauce.

Berry Brown-Butter Tart

1 Sweet Pastry tart shell (page 84), unbaked

Brown Butter Filling:
3 eggs

1¼ cups granulated sugar

1 tablespoon grated or finely chopped orange zest (1 orange) (for raspberry tart) or 1 tablespoon grated or finely chopped lemon zest (1 lemon) (for blueberry or blackberry tart)

½ cup flour, scant, sifted

6 ounces unsalted butter (1½ sticks)

1 vanilla bean, split and scraped

1 cup raspberries, blueberries, or blackberries

Raspberry or Blackberry Topping:
2 tablespoons red currant jelly

1 tablespoon water or brandy

2 cups raspberries or blackberries

In French, brown butter is called "beurre noisette," (hazelnut butter) because of its nutty brown color and taste. In this easy tart, raspberries, blackberries, or blueberries are cooked into the filling for flavor, and uncooked berries are arranged on top for decoration.

Use a 10 x 1-inch or ½-inch flan ring. (If you use a ½-inch-high ring, the filling recipe makes enough for 2 tarts.)

MAKING THE BROWN BUTTER FILLING

Whisk together the eggs, sugar, and zest until combined. Beat in flour until well mixed; set aside.

In a small saucepan, heat the butter and vanilla bean over high heat until brown and foamy. Continue heating until the bubbles subside and the butter is dark brown and smoking, and gives off a nutty aroma. Whisking continuously, pour hot butter in a steady stream into egg mixture, combining well. Remove vanilla bean.

❖ The brown butter can be made ahead up to this point and refrigerated for seven to ten days. Let it warm to room temperature to reach a spreadable consistency. (Cold brown butter can be piped into the tart shell using a pastry bag fitted with a No. 3 plain tip.)

ASSEMBLING THE TART

Preheat oven to 350 degrees. Adjust oven rack to the middle position.

Sprinkle bottom of the tart shell evenly with 1 cup raspberries, blackberries, or blueberries. Pour brown butter mixture over fruit, filling the shell two-thirds full, just above the fruit. To keep the sides of the pastry from falling in during baking, use your finger to seal the dough to the edges of the flan ring with a little bit of brown butter.

Bake for 45–55 minutes. When cooked, the thin smooth layer that separates from the rest of the filling will be crisp and firm to the touch. The filling underneath will be soft around the fruit and the crust golden brown. Let cool completely, at least 2 hours. Slip a cardboard round underneath, leaving the flan ring in place.

RASPBERRY OR BLACKBERRY TOPPING

Melt the red currant jelly with the water or brandy in a

Blueberry Topping:
2–3 cups blueberries

2 cups Sugar Syrup (page 29)

To Decorate Tart:
½ cup powdered sugar, optional

Makes one 10 inch tart, serving 8–10

small saucepan, stirring with a wire whisk or pastry brush until it bubbles and reduces to a thick syrup, 1–2 minutes. With a pastry brush, paint a thin layer of currant glaze on the top of the tart.

Arrange a circular row of raspberries or blackberries upright around the outside edge of the tart, placing the berries close together and just within the edge of the tart shell. Then, starting in the center of the tart, place berries in concentric circles working toward the outer edge, until the entire surface of the tart is covered with berries.

POWDERED SUGAR BORDER (OPTIONAL)

Center a 9-inch pan lid or paper round on top of the tart, leaving an even border of berries visible around the edge. Using a strainer, sift an even layer of powdered sugar over the edge of the cardboard to cover the border of berries. Carefully remove paper by lifting it straight up, so you do not spill any sugar on the center of the tart. Remove flan ring. Serve immediately because the powdered sugar will melt into the fruit if allowed to sit too long.

BLUEBERRY TOPPING

Blueberries look better on top of a tart if they're drenched briefly in hot sugar syrup to give them a shiny, dark purple color. Place the berries in a colander set over a bowl. Bring sugar syrup to a boil and pour over blueberries, allowing the syrup to run into the bowl. The berries should just be washed with the syrup; they should not sit in it and poach. If all the berries are not dark purple and shiny, remove the shiny berries from the colander, leaving the rest. Reheat the syrup and pour it over again.

Shake the colander to remove excess syrup. Mound berries on cooled tart, covering the entire surface. When you cut the tart, the berries will fall off; pile them back on to serve. Just before serving, sift powdered sugar through a strainer in random patches of white over the top. Remove flan ring.

Serve at room temperature with Vanilla Sauce, Raspberry Sauce, or Blackberry Sauce.

Keeps refrigerated for two to three days without getting soggy.

Pear and Ginger Brown-Butter Tart

1 Ginger Pastry tart shell
   (page 85), unbaked

½ tablespoon unsalted
   butter, melted, to butter
   tart ring

Ginger Brown Butter:
1½ ounces fresh ginger root
   (approximately 3 inches
   long)

7 tablespoons flour

1½ teaspoons ground ginger

2 eggs

⅔ cup granulated sugar

4 ounces unsalted butter (1
   stick)

Pears:
6 Poached Pears in Ginger
   (page 94)

1 cup liquid reserved from
   poaching pears

To Decorate Tart:
½ cup powdered sugar

**Makes one 10-inch tart,
serving 8–10**

The tastes of smooth sweet pears and sharp spicy ginger work together so well in a brown butter filling. The ginger taste is underlined by using ginger-spiked pastry for the tart shell.

Use a 10 x 1-inch flan ring set on a baking sheet. (In a ½-inch ring, this filling recipe will make 2 tarts.)

MAKING THE GINGER BROWN BUTTER

Slice the unpeeled ginger root into ¼-inch rounds; set aside. Sift together the flour and ground ginger; set aside.

Whisk together the eggs and sugar until combined. Beat in flour and ground ginger until well mixed; set aside.

In a small saucepan, heat the butter with the vanilla bean and ginger root over high heat until brown and foamy. Continue heating until the bubbles subside and the butter is dark brown and smoking, and gives off a nutty aroma. Whisking continuously, pour hot butter in a steady stream into the egg mixture, combining well. Strain; discard ginger root and vanilla bean.

❖ The ginger brown butter can be made ahead up to this point and refrigerated for seven days. Let it warm to room temperature to reach a spreadable consistency. (Cold brown butter can be piped into the tart shell using a pastry bag fitted with a No. 3 plain tip.)

ASSEMBLING THE TART

Preheat oven to 350 degrees. Adjust oven rack to middle position.

Slice four of the poached pear halves very thin and completely cover the bottom of the pastry with the slices. Pour in ginger brown butter, filling to ½ inch from the top of the shell.

Place the remaining pears cut side down on the work surface and cut them crosswise into ⅛-inch-thick slices. Keep the slices next to each other so that the pear halves remain in their original shape. Press to shingle the slices and slightly elongate the pear shape.

Slip a long-bladed knife or spatula under each sliced pear half, lifting it all at once, and place on top of the brown butter, stem end toward the center. Arrange the pear halves around the top of the tart like the spokes of a wheel.

Leave room at the center for one pear half. There should be 7 halves around the outside of the tart and 1 in the center.

To keep the sides of the pastry from falling in during baking, use your finger to seal the dough to the edges of the flan ring with a little bit of brown butter.

Bake for 1–1¼ hours, until browned. Cool. Slip a cardboard round underneath, leaving the flan ring in place.

GLAZING AND DECORATING THE TART

Just before serving, boil 1 cup of the pear poaching liquid in a small saucepan until it reduces to ¼ cup. It should be very thick and syrupy.

With a pastry brush, paint a thin layer of glaze over the pears only. Cut 7 oval pieces of wax paper and lay them over the pears. Sift powdered sugar over the tart through a fine-mesh strainer in an even layer—the paper will protect the pears from the powdered sugar and only the triangular brown butter area will be dusted with sugar. When you remove the paper ovals, pick them up carefully to avoid spilling the powdered sugar on the pears. Remove flan ring.

Serve at room temperature, with Ginger Sauce or a combination of Ginger Sauce and Pear Sauce to bring out the pear flavor. Also delicious *à la mode* with Ginger Ice Cream or Vanilla Bean Ice Cream.

Keeps refrigerated for two to three days without getting soggy.

Plum Tart

1 Sweet Pastry tart shell
(page 84), unbaked

1 pound 12 ounces elephant
heart or Anjou plums (9–
10 plums), or 2 pounds
Italian prune plums
(about 25 plums)

Brown Butter Filling:
1 egg

⅓ cup granulated sugar

3½ tablespoons flour, sifted

2 ounces unsalted butter (½
stick)

1 vanilla bean, split and
scraped

⅓ cup Vanilla Pastry
Cream (page 283)

2 teaspoons almond extract

6 tablespoons blanched
almond meal

To Decorate the Top of
the Tart:

½ cup sliced blanched
almonds

2 tablespoons red currant
jelly

1 tablespoon water or
brandy

2 tablespoons powdered
sugar

**Makes one 10-inch tart,
serving 8–10**

Plums have a summery, sweet-tart flavor that really comes to the fore when they are cooked, especially when surrounded by a chewy, almond-flavored brown butter mixed with pastry cream. The dark skins of the plum slices arranged in circles give this tart an especially beautiful hand-made look.

This recipe needs a flavorful plum that is not too juicy or overripe. Large plums such as elephant heart and Anjou work well, or choose Italian prune plums, the smallish oval plums, green inside, that are delicious when cooked. (The common Santa Rosas are too juicy.)

Use a 10 x 1-inch or ½-inch flan ring. (If you use the lower ring, there will be enough filling for 2 tarts.)

MAKING THE BROWN BUTTER FILLING

Whisk together the egg and sugar until combined. Beat in flour until well mixed; set aside.

In a small saucepan, heat the butter and vanilla bean over high heat until brown and foamy. Continue heating until the bubbles subside and the butter is dark brown and smoking, and gives off a nutty aroma. Whisking continuously, pour the hot butter in a steady stream into the egg mixture, combining well. Remove vanilla bean.

Whisk the pastry cream to soften and smooth out. (If the brown butter has been refrigerated, whisk also to soften.) Whisk pastry cream and brown butter together until combined. Stir in almond extract and almond meal, mixing well.

ASSEMBLING THE TART

Preheat oven to 350 degrees. Adjust rack to middle position.

For elephant heart or Anjou plums: spread the brown butter mixture on the bottom of the tart shell, using the back of a spoon or an offset metal spatula. Pit the plums and cut into quarters (do not peel). Starting at the outside edge of the shell, place the plums on their sides in three tight concentric circles on top of the filling, completely covering the surface. Arrange a few pieces in the center to fill in the gaps.

For prune plums: cut 7 plums in very thin slices (do not

peel) and arrange them to completely cover the bottom of the pastry. Cover with filling mixture, spreading with the back of a spoon or an offset metal spatula. Slice the remaining plums in quarters and arrange them in the same manner as the elephant heart plums, in concentric circles to completely cover the surface of the brown butter. Arrange a few pieces in the center.

Bake for 50–60 minutes, until the crust is light brown and the filling is almost set. The tart will seem a bit juicy when you take it out of the oven, but it will firm up as it cools. When cool, slip a cardboard round underneath. Leave flan ring in place.

DECORATING THE TOP

(The almonds and powdered sugar decoration should be put on just before serving.)

Preheat oven to 325 degrees. Spread the sliced almonds on a baking sheet and toast until light brown, 8–10 minutes. Cool.

Melt the red currant jelly with the water or brandy in a small saucepan, stirring with a wire whisk or pastry brush, until it bubbles and reduces to a thick syrup, 1–2 minutes. With a pastry brush, paint a thin layer of currant glaze over the top of the tart to highlight the plums without soaking them.

To make a clean border of toasted almonds and powdered sugar, center an 8-inch pan lid or paper round on top of the tart. Sprinkle the sliced almonds around the edge and sift lightly with powdered sugar. Lift the paper carefully to avoid spilling powdered sugar. Remove flan ring.

This is best eaten at room temperature the day it is made.

Poached Pears in Ginger

6–8 hard pears, preferably Bosc or Comice (slightly underripe pears will hold together better when poached)

Poaching Liquid:

6 ounces fresh ginger root

4 cups sugar syrup (page 29)

1 cup water

2 vanilla beans, split and scraped

1/4 cup lemon juice (2 lemons)

1/2 cup poire Williams (pear brandy)

Makes 8–9 poached pears

Used in Pear and Ginger Brown-Butter Tart

These ginger-perfumed pears, used for the Pear and Ginger Brown-Butter Tart, can also be served plain or with a variety of toppings: whipped cream, crème fraîche, Ginger Sauce, Vanilla Sauce flavored with pear brandy, or Ginger Ice Cream. Puréed, they make the Pear Sauce, so you may want to increase the recipe and poach a few extras.

Peel the ginger root with a vegetable peeler and slice into 1/4-inch rounds.

In a large stainless steel or enamel saucepan, combine all the poaching liquid ingredients. Peel, halve, and core pears, dropping each half as it is finished into the poaching liquid. Place a clean dish towel over the pears, on the surface of the liquid, to keep them submerged.

Bring the liquid to a boil over high heat. Reduce heat to low and cook just below simmering for 30–45 minutes, or until the pears are completely tender but not mushy. Cook the pears slowly, because the longer they cook the more they will absorb the ginger flavor. When properly poached, they will have the translucent, milky look of canned pears.

If the pears are just tender, turn off heat and let them cool in the poaching liquid. If they are a bit soft, drain immediately, spread them on a paper-lined baking sheet, and cool in the refrigerator.

Keep refrigerated three to five days, spread on a paper-lined baking sheet. Do not stack.

The poaching liquid will keep indefinitely in the freezer and can be used again for cooking pears; you will need to thin it out with water if it reduced during cooking and became too thick and sweet. This poaching liquid is also a delicious way to sweeten homemade lemonade.

FRESH FRUIT CUSTARD TARTS

Creamy custard fillings make a wonderful contrast to the light texture and acidity of fresh fruit.

In general, custard fillings contain eggs, milk or cream, flavoring, and a small amount of flour. To mix the flour in well, the fillings are best made in a blender or food processor. Most custard fillings can be made a few days in advance and refrigerated until you're ready to assemble the tart.

Eggs make custard fillings set, but if they're cooked too fast, too long, or at too high a temperature, they can curdle, making a watery, porous, separated custard. After a lot of testing, I've developed a few techniques to keep custard fillings from curdling. First, always bake a custard tart in a prebaked tart shell, because in the time that it takes to bake pastry thoroughly, the eggs are likely to curdle. Also, before filling the tart, warm the custard gently over simmering water so that it needs less time in the oven. Then, place the filled tart on a preheated baking sheet, to give it another little boost as it starts cooking.

The last five minutes of baking are a crucial period. Watch the tart carefully, jiggling it gently from time to time, so that you can remove it immediately as soon as the center has set and no longer looks liquid. Even an extra two minutes can cause curdling.

Lemon-Lime Tart

1 Lemon Pastry tart shell
(page 85), baked and set
on a cardboard round
(flan ring left on)

½ tablespoon unsalted
butter, melted, to butter
tart ring

Lemon-Lime Filling:
1 cup lemon juice (7–8
lemons)

¼–⅓ cup lemon zest (7–8
lemons)

1 cup lime juice (10–12
limes)

¼–⅓ cup lime zest
(10–12 limes)

6 eggs

6 egg yolks

1½ cups granulated sugar

8 ounces unsalted butter
(2 sticks), at room
temperature

To Caramelize Top
(optional):
2 tablespoons granulated
sugar

**Makes one 10-inch tart,
serving 8–10**

Lime adds tartness and flavor to this creamy yellow, quickly made filling, which is poured into an already-baked crust. The tart can be caramelized to add a translucent sheet of browned sugar on top.

Use a 10 x 1-inch or ½-inch flan ring. (The volume of filling depends on how much air is whipped into it during cooking. The quantity made from the recipe below could be beaten enough to fill two ½-inch rings.)

In a large metal bowl, whisk together all the filling ingredients except the butter. Set bowl over a large pot of boiling water and whisk vigorously, incorporating as much air as possible. Rotate the bowl from time to time to prevent the eggs from cooking around the sides. (If you're confident with custards, the filling may be cooked over direct heat. Whisk vigorously to avoid burning.)

Cook filling until the foam disappears and the mixture thickens to resemble an extremely thick hollandaise sauce, 5–10 minutes. This mixture will not curdle, so don't be afraid to cook it until it is very thick. Remove from heat and beat in butter bit by bit.

Strain the mixture through a fine-mesh strainer into a bowl. Scrape the filling into the baked tart shell, filling even with the top of the shell. Smooth and level with a long-bladed spatula. Refrigerate until firm and set, at least 2 hours. The tart keeps refrigerated for two days.

CARAMELIZING THE TART (OPTIONAL)

The tart must be caramelized in a salamander or with a torch (see "Caramelizing a dessert," page 339). Sprinkle the top of the tart evenly with 2 tablespoons sugar and caramelize. Cool.

Serve tart at room temperature with Raspberry Sauce. If the tart is caramelized, it must be served the same day or the caramel will get soft.

VARIATION: For a lemon-mint flavor, stir 1 cup chopped fresh mint leaves into the filling before cooking. Strain out and discard after cooking.

Cherry Tart with Buttermilk Custard

1 Sweet Pastry tart shell
   (page 84),baked

14 ounces Bing cherries

Buttermilk Custard:
1 cup buttermilk

3 egg yolks

1 tablespoon grated or finely
   chopped lemon zest
   (1 lemon)

2 tablespoons lemon juice
   (1 lemon)

2 tablespoons unsalted
   butter, melted

1 tablespoon flour, sifted

2 tablespoons granulated
   sugar

To Caramelize Tart
   (optional):
2 tablespoons granulated or
   powdered sugar

**Makes one 10-inch tart,
serving 8–10**

Tangy buttermilk contrasts with sweet, sharp cherries in this thin, fruity tart.

Use a 10 x ½-inch flan ring and 2 heavy duty baking sheets.

MAKING THE CUSTARD

Preheat oven to 350 degrees. Adjust oven rack to top third of oven and place a baking sheet on the rack.

Place all custard ingredients in a food processor or blender. Process until well combined.

(To mix by hand: In a large bowl, whisk together the buttermilk, egg yolks, lemon zest, lemon juice, and melted butter. Mix in flour and sugar until the mixture is well blended. Break up any lumps of flour with your fingers.)

❖ The custard can be made up to three days in advance and refrigerated.

ASSEMBLING AND BAKING THE TART

Pit and halve cherries. Starting at the outside edge of the baked tart shell, arrange the fruit, cut side down, in concentric circles, completely covering the bottom of the tart. Set aside.

Place the custard in a heatproof bowl and stir it over gently simmering water until it is just warm to the touch. Pour into tart shell, filling so that the top of the cherries just peek through and the filling comes to just below the edge of the tart shell.

Place in the oven on the heated baking sheet and bake for 20 minutes, until pale yellow and the tops of the cherries just peek through. During baking, the custard will set from the outside edge toward the center of the tart. Watch carefully during the last 8 minutes or so of baking, jiggling the tray occasionally, so that you can remove the tart from the oven as soon as the custard has set.

Cool. Slip a cardboard round underneath and remove the flan ring.

Serve chilled or at room temperature with Vanilla Sauce flavored with orange liqueur or Raspberry Sauce. Can be stored overnight in the refrigerator.

Zinfandel-Pear Tart

1 Sweet Pastry tart shell
   (page 84), baked

½ tablespoon unsalted
   butter, melted, to butter
   tart ring

5–7 hard pears (Bosc or
   Comice), depending on
   size

Pear Poaching Liquid:
2 bottles zinfandel (8 cups)

1 cinnamon stick

1 teaspoon whole black
   peppercorns, lightly
   crushed

1 cup lemon juice
   (6–8 lemons)

¼ cup granulated sugar

1 vanilla bean, split and
   scraped

Custard Filling:
2 eggs

¾ cup heavy cream

3 tablespoons grated or
   finely chopped lemon zest
   (2 lemons)

½ cup pear-poaching liquid

¼ cup granulated sugar

3½ tablespoons flour, sifted

**Makes one 10-inch tart,
serving 8–10**

A spicy, wintery dessert. Pears poached in zinfandel with cinnamon and black pepper—red on the outside, gradually fading to creamy pear white at the center—are sliced and arranged on a custard filling made with the spiced wine.

Use a 10 x 1-inch flan ring.

POACHING THE PEARS

In a large stainless steel or enamel saucepan, combine all the ingredients for the pear poaching liquid. Peel, halve, and core pears, dropping each half as you finish into the poaching liquid. (I place a clean dish towel over the pears, on the surface of the liquid, to keep them submerged so that they poach evenly. If you don't mind staining a dish towel with the red wine, try it.) Bring the liquid to a boil over high heat. Reduce heat to low and cook just below simmering for at least 1 hour, until pears are completely tender but not mushy. Cook the pears slowly, because the longer they cook, the more they will absorb the flavors of the wine and spices.

If the pears are just tender, turn off the heat and let cool in the poaching liquid. If they are a bit soft, drain immediately, spread them on a paper-lined baking sheet, and cool in refrigerator. Strain the poaching liquid through a fine-mesh strainer into a bowl; set aside.

❖ The pears can be poached up to three days in advance.

ASSEMBLING THE TART

Preheat oven to 350 degrees. Adjust rack to middle of oven.

Cut 4–6 pear halves crosswise into ⅛-inch-thick slices and spread evenly in one layer over the bottom of the baked pie shell.

Place all custard ingredients in a food processor or blender. Process until well combined.

(To mix by hand: In a large bowl, whisk together the eggs, cream, lemon zest, and pear-poaching liquid. Mix in sugar and sifted flour until the mixture is well combined and there are no lumps. Break up any lumps of flour with your fingers.)

❖ The custard can be made up to three days in advance and refrigerated.

Place the custard mixture in a heatproof bowl and stir it over gently simmering water until just warm to the touch. Pour into the baked pie shell, filling to ¼ inch from the top. Bake for 25 minutes, until set. Cool completely. When cool, slip a cardboard round underneath the tart. Do not remove flan ring.

GLAZING AND DECORATING THE TOP

Cut 6–8 pear halves crosswise into ⅛-inch-thick slices. Set aside. Use only the large slices to decorate the tart, reserving the small slices from the stem end of the pear for another use.

In a stainless steel or enamel saucepan, boil ½ cup poaching liquid until it measures about 1½ tablespoons and is very bubbly and sticky. It must be sticky because it will be holding the pear slices in place. Brush it over the top of the cooled tart.

Starting from the outside edge of the tart, arrange the pear slices in a circle, placing the rounded edge of the slices toward the outside. Working toward the center, cover the entire tart with a thin layer of pear slices, overlapping the slices only slightly. The pattern will look like a big chrysanthemum with petals that are red on the edges and white in the center. Remove flan ring just before serving.

MAKING THE SAUCE

In a stainless steel or enamel pan, bring the remaining poaching liquid (about 3 cups) to a boil and reduce to 1 cup to serve as a sauce. Cool.

Serve at room temperature on a plate mirrored half-and-half with the reduced wine sauce and Vanilla Sauce. Or, mirror half the plate with wine sauce and serve with crème fraîche or whipped cream on the side.

Best served the day it is made.

Sour Cream Custard Tart with Peaches, Apricots, or Nectarines

1 Sweet Pastry tart shell
   (page 84), baked

Custard Filling:
2 eggs
2 tablespoons grated or
   finely chopped orange
   zest (2 oranges)
3 tablespoons orange
   liqueur
½ cup orange juice
   (2 oranges)
¾ cup sour cream or crème
   fraîche
6 tablespoons granulated
   sugar
3½ tablespoons flour, sifted

Fruit:
1 to 1½ pounds apricots
   (9–10), peaches, or
   nectarines (3–4)

Makes one 10-inch tart,
serving 8–10

Baking peaches, apricots, or nectarines into this sour cream custard makes a beautifully colored tart with a ripe fruit taste permeating the filling.

Use a 10 x 1-inch flan ring and 2 heavy-duty baking sheets.

MAKING THE CUSTARD

Preheat oven to 350 degrees. Adjust rack to upper third of oven and place a heavy baking sheet on the rack.

Place all custard ingredients in a food processor or blender. Process until well combined.

(To mix by hand: In a large bowl, whisk together the eggs with the orange zest, orange liqueur, and orange juice. Mix in sour cream, sugar, and sifted flour until the mixture is well blended. Break up any lumps of flour with your fingers.)

❖ The custard can be made up to three days in advance and refrigerated.

ARRANGING THE FRUIT

For peaches or nectarines: Do not peel. Cut the fruit into sixths. Starting at the outside edge of the tart, lay slices on their sides, touching each other, in two concentric circles on the bottom of the baked tart shell. Arrange the few remaining pieces, skin side up, in the center to fill in the gaps.

For apricots: Do not peel. Cut the apricots into fourths. Arrange the slices on their sides, nestled together, in three concentric circles on the bottom of the baked tart shell. Place 2 or 3 slices in the center to fill in the gaps.

FILLING AND BAKING THE TART

Place the custard mixture in a heatproof bowl and stir it over gently simmering water until it is just warm to the touch. Pour approximately 2 cups of sour cream custard mixture into the tart shell. The tops of the fruit slices will be poking up through the custard.

Place the tart in the oven on the heated baking sheet and bake for 40–45 minutes. During baking, the custard will set from the outside edge toward the center of the tart. Watch carefully during the last 8 minutes or so of baking, jiggling the baking sheet occasionally, so that you can remove the tart from the oven as soon as the custard has set.

(Fruit with a high water content may give off a lot of juice when cooked, which will make the center of the tart appear very loose. Don't think that it means that the custard hasn't set; these juices will be absorbed back into the tart as it cools.)

Cool completely. Slip a cardboard round underneath and remove the flan ring.

Serve at room temperature, with Vanilla Sauce flavored with orange liqueur, or Apricot Sauce.

Rice Tart With Mango

1 Sweet Pastry tart shell (page 84), baked

¾ cup uncooked Italian arborio rice

1½ cups heavy cream in all

½ cup milk

5 tablespoons grated or finely chopped orange zest (5 oranges)

1 vanilla bean, split and scraped

¼ cup granulated sugar in all

2 ounces unsalted butter (½ stick), at room temperature

2 egg yolks

2 tablespoons sour cream

2 ripe mangoes, about 1 pound each

1 teaspoon granulated gelatin

½ cup orange liqueur

To Caramelize Top (optional):
2 tablespoons granulated sugar

Makes one 10-inch tart, serving 8–10

A creamy rice pudding filling is folded together with whipped cream and layered with slices of ripe mango into a pastry crust. A little gelatin helps the tart slice easily. The mango can be replaced with papaya, poached peaches, or apricots, as in Gaston Lenôtre's original recipe, from which this one was adapted.

Use a 10-inch flan ring. If you use a 1-inch-high flan ring, you will need two sliced mangoes and all the filling; in a ½-inch ring, use only one mango.

MAKING THE FILLING

Preheat oven to 350 degrees. Adjust the oven rack to the lower position.

In a small saucepan, cover the rice with water, bring to a boil, and boil for 30 seconds. Drain rice in a strainer and rinse well with cold water. Put the rice in a 2-quart oven-proof saucepan or casserole. Add ½ cup of the cream, milk, zest, vanilla bean, and sugar, and bring to a boil. Remove from the heat, cover, and place in the oven for 20–25 minutes, until rice is cooked and liquid is absorbed. When cooked, the rice will be soft and perhaps a bit sticky, but the grains should still retain their separate shape. (Bite into a grain of rice. You should not see an uncooked, opaque core.) If the rice is not tender but the liquid is absorbed, you can put the casserole on top of the stove, add a bit more milk or cream, and bring the mixture to a boil again before replacing in the oven. If liquid remains after the rice is tender, bring to a boil, uncovered, on top of the stove, stirring constantly until the liquid evaporates.

While the rice is baking, beat the butter on medium-high speed in an electric mixer until it whitens and holds soft peaks, 3–5 minutes. Add the egg yolks, one at a time, incorporating completely and beating until the mixture is satiny and smooth. (If you are beating by hand, beat vigorously, because this mixture tends to separate.)

In a clean saucepan or a large metal bowl, combine the egg mixture with the cooked rice mixture and reheat over medium heat until the mixture starts to bubble, whisking constantly. Remove from heat and chill. (It will cool faster if you spread it on a paper-lined baking sheet and place it in the refrigerator as soon as it stops steaming.)

❖ The filling can be made up to this point up to three days in advance. Bring back to room temperature before continuing.

ASSEMBLING THE TART

Using the whisk attachment of an electric mixer, beat the remaining 1 cup heavy cream with sour cream on low speed until it thickens enough to stop spattering. Increase speed to medium-high and beat until thick and mousselike. Remove from mixer. Whisk a few times by hand until soft peaks form. Refrigerate.

With a sharp paring knife, peel the mangoes as thin as possible. Cut the fruit away from the pit in vertical slices about ¼ inch thick. (Don't worry if the slices aren't perfect, because the fruit won't show.) Set on paper towels to drain.

When the rice mixture is cold, place the gelatin in the bottom of a large heatproof bowl and pour on orange liqueur. If all the gelatin granules do not absorb the liqueur, or if there are any lumps of gelatin, dribble on a bit more liqueur. Heat briefly over gently simmering water until the gelatin dissolves. Whisk in rice mixture to combine.

Whisk in about one third of the whipped cream to lighten the texture. (The mixture will be stiff; whisk vigorously to combine.) Fold in the rest of the whipped cream.

Arrange the fruit slices to cover the bottom of the baked tart shell. Pour rice filling over the fruit and smooth with a long-bladed spatula so that the filling is completely even with the top of the crust. Refrigerate until set, at least 1 hour.

CARAMELIZING THE TOP (OPTIONAL)

The tart must be caramelized in a salamander or with a torch (see "Caramelizing a dessert," page 339). Sprinkle the top of the tart evenly with 2 tablespoons sugar and caramelize. Refrigerate for 15–30 minutes to let the caramel harden and allow the tart to set up again. Remove ring.

Serve cold, with Mango Sauce or Apricot Sauce. If the tart is caramelized it must be served the same day or the caramel will get soft.

Blackberry or Raspberry Custard Tart

1 Sweet Pastry tart shell
   (page 84), baked
5–6 cups blackberries or
   raspberries

Custard Filling:
½ cup milk

½ cup heavy cream

2 tablespoons grated or
   finely chopped orange
   zest (2 oranges)

1 vanilla bean, split and
   scraped

2 eggs

2 egg yolks

3 tablespoons unsalted
   butter, melted

3 tablespoons orange
   liqueur

¼ cup orange juice
   (1 orange)

¼ cup sugar

½ cup flour, sifted

To Decorate Top of Tart:
Few tablespoons of
   powdered sugar

**Makes one 10-inch tart,
serving 8–10**

Plump, juicy blackberries or raspberries are cooked into this tart to flavor the custard, but the seeds keep the fruit from disintegrating as it cooks. Berries must be big and juicy, or they'll shrivel up during baking and you'll be left with a mouthful of seeds. Two cups of blueberries can also be used.

Use a 10 x 1-inch or ½-inch flan ring and 2 heavy-duty baking sheets.

MAKING THE CUSTARD

Preheat oven to 350 degrees. Adjust rack to upper third of oven and place a heavy baking sheet on the rack.

In a saucepan, scald the milk, orange zest, and scraped vanilla bean. Cover, remove from heat, and let stand 30 minutes. Remove vanilla bean and reserve for other uses.

Place all custard ingredients in a food processor or blender. Process until well combined.

(To mix by hand: In a large bowl, whisk together the milk, eggs, egg yolks, melted butter, orange liqueur, and orange juice. Mix in sugar and flour until the mixture is well blended. Break up any lumps of flour with your fingers.)

❖ The custard mixture can be made up to three days in advance and refrigerated.

ASSEMBLING AND BAKING THE TART

Cover the bottom of the tart shell with the blackberries on their sides or the raspberries standing upright in concentric circles. Pack them tight together to use as many berries as possible.

If the custard mixture has cooled, place it in a heatproof bowl and stir it over gently simmering water until just warm to the touch. Pour in the custard mixture so that it just covers the berries. Place in the oven on the heated baking sheet and bake 20–25 minutes. During baking, the custard will set from the outside edge toward the center of the tart. Watch carefully during the last 8 minutes or so of baking, jiggling the tray occasionally, so that you can remove the tart from the oven as soon as the custard has set.

Cool completely. Slip a cardboard round underneath before removing the flan ring.

Serve chilled or at room temperature, the slices dusted lightly with sifted powdered sugar. Can be served with Vanilla Sauce flavored with orange liqueur, Blackberry Sauce, or Raspberry Sauce.

This tart will keep overnight in the refrigerator.

INDIVIDUAL FRESH FRUIT DESSERTS

Composed of fruit, sauce, with perhaps a round of pastry underneath or a layer of crisp caramel on top, individual desserts, carefully arranged on oversized plates, have a custom-made charm that makes them especially appropriate at the end of a special-occasion dinner.

Although most of these desserts need to be finished at the last minute, the plates can be largely set up in advance, ready for the finishing touches. You'll be in the kitchen for only a few minutes caramelizing the top of a Gratin of Oranges, placing a scoop of ice cream on the Thin Apple Pancakes with Broiled Apple Slices, or spooning the Melons in Plum Wine into chilled crystal bowls.

Open-Face Fruit Tarts

1 pound Sweet Pastry (page 84)

4 pears, or 2–3 large green apples, or 4–6 nectarines, or 4–6 peaches, or 12 apricots, or 12 plums

3 tablespoons unsalted butter

2 tablespoons granulated sugar

½ cup granulated or powdered sugar

Extra powdered sugar for dusting tops of tarts

Makes 8 individual tarts

These lovely-looking individual tarts have a modest, uncomplicated charm—just rounds of sweet pastry topped with sliced fruit and caramelized after baking. Make them in any season, with apples, pears, apricots, peaches, plums, or nectarines. Ripe, flavorful fruit is a must, since it provides the only real taste in the tart.

The quantities of fruit given are for eight tarts of the same type, but you can also make an assortment of different types. Don't use more than one type of fruit on a single tart, however.

On a lightly floured surface, roll out pastry to ⅛-inch thickness. Using a small plate as a guide, cut eight 5-inch rounds of dough and place 1 inch apart on a nonstick baking sheet or one lined with tin foil. Chill until firm.

CUTTING THE FRUIT

It is not necessary to peel any of the fruit.

For pears and apples: Halve vertically and core. Cut off the pointed end of the pear so that the remaining fruit is more or less oval, about 2 inches long. Place the fruit cut side down on the work surface. Cut vertically (parallel to the core) in ¼-inch slices. Each pear or apple should yield 24–28 slices.

For nectarines, peaches, apricots, and plums: Halve and remove pits. Place cut side down on the cutting board and slice vertically into ¼-inch slices. Each nectarine or peach should yield 20–24 slices, and there should be 16–18 slices from each plum or apricot.

ASSEMBLING AND BAKING THE TARTS

Preheat oven to 350 degrees. Adjust oven rack to middle position.

Arrange fruit slices in a circle around the edge of the pastry, placing the rounded backs of the slices toward the outside of the circle. Working toward the center, cover the pastry with a thin layer of fruit slices, letting the slices overlap only slightly. The pattern will look like the petals of a chrysanthemum.

Covering the tartlet
with fruit

❖ The tarts can be assembled up to this point and refrigerated for a day before baking. The fruit may discolor slightly in the refrigerator, but that won't make any difference when the tarts are baked.

Dot the surface of the tarts all over with 1 teaspoon butter cut into small pieces. Sprinkle the top of each tart with ½ teaspoon granulated sugar. Bake for 40–45 minutes, until the crust is brown and the fruit is tender and slightly glazed-looking.

Before serving, preheat broiler. Just before placing each tart under the broiler, sift 1 tablespoon powdered sugar on top. Place under broiler and caramelize for about 45 seconds, watching carefully. Turn the tarts, if necessary, to keep from burning the fruit. Let cool to allow the crust to firm up.

Dust lightly with sifted powdered sugar and serve warm from the oven, topped with Vanilla Bean Ice Cream, or centered on a plate with Vanilla Mousseline Sauce on one side and a scattering of Sugared Almonds on the other.

Caramel-Glazed Pears Poached in Riesling

4 hard pears, Bosc or
   Comice

6 tablespoons poire
   Williams (pear brandy)
   in all

Poaching Liquid:
1 vanilla bean, split and
   scraped

¼ teaspoon freshly grated
   nutmeg

1 tablespoon lemon zest
   (1 lemon), in long strings

1 small cinnamon stick

4 whole cloves

6 cups Riesling or other
   fruity white wine (about
   1½ bottles)

To Glaze Pears:
2 cups sugar

1 cup water

Sauces:
2 cups sugar

1 cup water

¾ cup heavy cream

2 egg yolks

2 cups Raspberry Sauce
   (page 327)

Makes 8 servings

This dessert is a beautiful medley of flavors, colors, and textures. The pears are poached in fruity white wine and then given a hard glaze of amber-colored caramel that shatters when you cut it with your fork. They're centered on a plate mirrored half with Raspberry Sauce and half with an airy whipped cream sabayon made from the wine the pears were poached in.

POACHING THE PEARS

In a large stainless steel saucepan, combine the poaching liquid ingredients and 3 tablespoons of the pear brandy. Halve the pears and core them with a melon-baller or a sharp knife; do not peel. As you finish each one, drop it into the poaching liquid. When all four pears are cut, lay a clean dish towel on the surface of the liquid to keep the pears submerged so that they cook evenly. Bring the liquid to a boil over high heat. Reduce heat to low and cook just below simmering until tender, 40–45 minutes. Drain, reserving liquid, and set pears aside.

Return poaching liquid to the saucepan (you should have about 1¼ cups) and boil to reduce until it measures ¼ cup; set aside.

❖ The pears can be poached and the liquid reduced a few days ahead of serving.

GLAZING THE PEARS WITH CARAMEL

Arrange pears, skin side up and at least 2 inches apart, on a cooling rack set over a baking sheet. Have a shallow pan of cold water handy for cooling the caramel. In a saucepan, heat sugar and water over high heat. When the water boils, it will throw sugar onto the sides of the pan. At that point, wash down the sides of the pan with a pastry brush, dipping it in water as necessary to dissolve the sugar. (Alternatively, place a lid on the pan for 30 seconds and the steam condensation will wash the sugar off the sides.)

Cook the sugar without stirring until it turns a nice honey color. Immediately remove the pan from the heat and dip the bottom in a pan of cold water, to stop the caramel from coloring further. Then pour the hot caramel over each pear, covering completely and letting the excess drip down onto the baking sheet. If the caramel hardens, reheat briefly. Cool.

❖ The pears can be covered with caramel a few hours ahead of serving, except in very humid weather, when the caramel will not remain crisp.

MAKING THE SABAYON

Using the whisk attachment of an electric mixer, beat the heavy cream on low speed until it thickens enough not to spatter. Increase speed to medium-high and beat until thick and mousselike. Remove from mixer. Whisk a few times by hand until soft peaks form. Refrigerate.

In the bowl of an electric mixer (or a stainless steel bowl), combine egg yolks, remaining 3 tablespoons pear brandy, and ¼ cup reduced poaching liquid. Whisk over gently simmering water until the mixture is warm and mousselike, and forms a ribbon when the whisk is lifted, 3–5 minutes. Rotate the bowl as often as necessary to prevent the egg from cooking on the sides. When thickened, remove from heat. Using the whisk attachment, beat with the electric mixer at high speed until the underside of the bowl is cool, 3–5 minutes, incorporating as much air as possible. Whisk in one third of the whipped cream and then fold in the remainder until combined.

Set out eight dessert plates. Spoon ¼ cup of the sabayon mixture onto each plate and spread so it covers half the plate; spoon 1–2 tablespoons raspberry sauce on the other half of the plate, tilting plate to spread the sauce. Center a pear half, caramel side up, on each plate. Serve immediately at room temperature.

Thin Apple Pancakes with Broiled Apple Slices and Apple Cider Ice Cream

Caramelized Apple Rings:

2–3 tart green apples

2 cups dry sparkling apple
    cider (preferably
    imported French "brut"
    cider)

1/2 cup granulated sugar

1/2 teaspoon cinnamon

Pancake Batter:

1/2 cup flour

2 tablespoons granulated
    sugar

1/2 teaspoon salt

1 egg

1 egg white

1/2 cup milk, at room
    temperature

1/2 cup apple cider (from
    macerating apples)

1/4 cup clarified unsalted
    butter, melted (page 17)

Every component of this beautifully composed dessert can be eaten separately, but in this case the whole is greater than the sum of its parts. The contrasts of warm and cold, chewy and creamy, crisp and soft, make it very special.

The pancakes started out to be crepes, but I wanted a crepe that had a flavor of its own. It seemed like a simple enough project, but I worked on it off and on for about five days and the pancakes weren't getting thin enough. Finally, someone suggested that they were much more like Swedish pancakes, and changing the name solved my problem.

A 5-inch Silverstone pan is great for crepe making. Other nonstick pans are not nearly as good.

PREPARING THE APPLE SLICES

Peel and core the apples, leaving them whole. Cut crosswise into rings 3/8 inch thick, discarding the slices at the ends. There should be about 6 rings from each apple.

Place in a bowl and pour on the apple cider. Let stand 2 hours.

MAKING THE BATTER

(The milk and cider must be at room temperature before beginning or the melted butter will solidify when it is added.)

Sift the flour into a large bowl and make a well in the center. Sprinkle the sugar and salt on the flour. In a small bowl, lightly beat together the egg, egg white, milk, apple cider, and butter with a fork. Pour the liquid ingredients into the well. Using a whisk or a wooden spoon, slowly stir the liquids together, gradually drawing the dry ingredients into the liquid little by little until combined and smooth. Let stand at least 1 hour.

❖ The batter can stand refrigerated overnight. Bring it back to room temperature before cooking.

MAKING THE ICE CREAM

(The ice cream recipe is a variation on Caramel Ice Cream. The recipe is repeated here for convenience.)

In a large bowl, whisk egg yolks lightly to break them up. Set aside. In a large heavy saucepan, scald the cream

Apple Cider Ice Cream:

8 egg yolks

2 cups heavy cream

2 cups milk

1¼–1½ cups apple cider (what remains after macerating apples and measuring cider for the pancakes)

1 cup granulated sugar

2 large cinnamon sticks

Makes 18 pancakes, serving 6

and milk. Keep warm over low heat.

In a saucepan, combine the apple cider, the sugar, and cinnamon sticks. Cook over high heat until the mixture reduces and turns a dark amber color, 20–25 minutes. Immediately begin whisking it into the warm cream in three or four batches. Be careful—the cream will spatter and bubble up. The caramel must be poured into the cream as quickly as possible or it will continue to cook and burn in the pan. When all the caramel has been whisked in, reheat the cream mixture, stirring constantly, until the caramel is completely incorporated.

Pour about one fourth of the hot cream into the egg yolks, whisking continuously. Return the mixture to the saucepan and whisk together with remaining liquid. Cook over low heat, stirring constantly with a wooden spoon, until the mixture thickens enough to coat the back of the spoon. Strain through a fine-mesh strainer into a bowl. Whisk a few times to release heat. Chill.

Freeze in an ice cream freezer according to manufacturer's instructions.

COOKING THE PANCAKES

(Unless you're an experienced crepe maker, you may need a little practice getting the pan to the right temperature and making the crepes thin enough. Try doubling the batter recipe and you'll have some leeway if the first few aren't perfect.)

Preheat the pan over medium-high heat, testing the temperature by flicking a drop of water on the surface. When the pan is at the right temperature, the water will spatter and dance. If the pan is too hot, it will bubble; if it's too cold, it won't do anything.

Stir the batter each time before you measure it. Measure 1½ tablespoons batter into a small container and then pour it all at once into the pan, swirling it around to make an even coating. Each time the batter is poured into the pan it should sizzle. Cook over medium-high heat for 1 minute, until the edges are nicely browned and the pancakes lacy-looking. Run a spatula around the edges of the pancake and flip over, using your finger to help. Cook for 30 seconds more. Stack the pancakes (there should be 18) on a plate as they are finished.

❖ Pancakes can be made a day in advance and stored at room temperature, wrapped in plastic wrap.

ASSEMBLING THE DESSERT

Preheat broiler. Toss sugar and cinnamon together. Pat the macerated apple slices dry. Dip one side of each slice in cinnamon-sugar to coat. Arrange on a broiling pan sugar side up and broil 3–5 minutes, watching carefully, until the tops of the apples are caramelized and the slices are tender. They will not all take the same amount of time to caramelize; remove the apple slices that are done and reposition the others to continue cooking.

To assemble each plate: Lay one pancake flat on the plate. Lay two apple rings in a circle on the pancake and cover with two more pancakes. Place a third apple ring on top.

❖ The dessert can be assembled up to this point and held at room temperature a few hours. While the apple slices will still taste good, the caramel will lose its crispness about 30 minutes after broiling.

Preheat oven to 350 degrees. Warm 3–5 minutes. Top with a small scoop of ice cream in the center of the apple ring. Serve immediately.

Berry Dessert Pancakes

½ cup flour

¼ cup granulated sugar in all

4 tablespoons grated or finely chopped orange zest (4 oranges)

3 egg yolks

¼ cup heavy cream

2 tablespoons orange liqueur

Save this quick-and-easy dessert for a summer treat when you can find beautiful fresh berries—frozen berries are too watery to work in this recipe. Fresh sliced strawberries may be put on top, but they are too watery to cook into the pancakes.

These must be cooked in ring molds to create height and a perfect round shape. Four-inch flan rings with ½-inch sides are best, but egg poaching rings will also work. You can improvise with tuna cans that have been opened on both ends and thoroughly washed.

MAKING THE BATTER

Sift the flour in a large bowl and make a well in the center. Sprinkle 1½ tablespoons of the sugar and orange zest around the well. In a small bowl, lightly whisk together egg

5 egg whites

4 ounces unsalted clarified butter, melted (page 17)

4 cups fresh berries (blackberries, blueberries, raspberries, wild strawberries, or any combination of the four)

¼ cup powdered sugar

1 cup Vanilla Sauce or Raspberry Sauce (page 327)

Makes 8 pancakes

yolks, cream, and orange liqueur. Pour liquid ingredients into the well. With a wooden spoon or a whisk, begin stirring the liquids together, drawing in the dry ingredients bit by bit until the mixture is a smooth paste.

❖ The batter can be made up to this point several hours before cooking.

Using the whisk attachment of an electric mixer, beat egg whites on low speed until frothy. Increase speed to medium and beat until soft peaks form. Increase speed to high and very gradually beat in 2½ tablespoons of the granulated sugar until very stiff, glossy peaks form. Whisk one third of the egg whites into the flour mixture to lighten consistency, and then fold in the rest, incorporating thoroughly; set aside.

Before you start to cook the pancakes, mirror each serving plate with sauce so that the cooked pancake can be immediately inverted onto it.

COOKING AND SERVING THE PANCAKES

Pour 2 tablespoons of the clarified butter into a skillet and heat to bubbling over medium heat. Place one or two of the rings in the skillet, and spoon approximately one eighth of the batter into each one. No matter how high a ring you use, the batter should be more than ½ inch thick. Immediately scatter about 3 tablespoons berries onto each pancake. Cook until bubbles begin to break on the upper surface and the lower surface is lightly browned, 3–4 minutes.

If you are using ½-inch-high rings, leave the ring on and turn the pancake over. If you are using higher rings or tuna cans, remove the ring with a towel. Turn pancake with a spatula, and cook other side until firm to the touch, 3–4 minutes. If you have not yet removed the ring, grasp it with a dish towel and remove.

When pancakes are cooked, invert them onto the prepared plates so that the fruit side of each pancake faces up. Scatter ¼ cup mixed berries over the top of each pancake, and dust lightly with powdered sugar.

Individual Apple-Calvados Tarts

1 pound Sweet Pastry (page 84)

12 ounces Puff Pastry, fresh or trimmings (page 175)

4½ pounds tart green apples (about 12 apples)

½ cup lemon juice (2–3 lemons)

6 tablespoons unsalted butter

1 cup granulated sugar

¾ cup Calvados, apple brandy, or brandy

¾ cup heavy cream

For Top of Tarts:
2 egg yolks

2 tablespoons granulated sugar

Makes eight 4-inch tarts

What better way to satisfy apple pie lovers than to give each one his own? These have sweet pastry on the bottom, a filling of apple slices sautéed in Calvados and cream, and very crisp, brown puff pastry on top. On a buffet table, they add a nice homemade look.

I use 4-inch French nonstick tart molds, which can be found in some cookware shops or ordered by mail. Flan rings, 4 inches in diameter with ½-inch sides, will also work.

ROLLING THE PASTRY DOUGH AND LINING THE PIE SHELLS

(If you're using flan rings, brush them with melted butter and set aside. The nonstick tart shells do not need to be buttered.)

On a lightly floured surface, roll the sweet pastry to ¼–⅛-inch thickness. Using a small plate as a guide, cut into eight 5-inch circles and place, not overlapping, on a paper-lined baking sheet. Chill at least 30 minutes. When pastry is well chilled, line the tart shells or flan rings and trim excess dough with a sharp paring knife. Arrange the tart shells or flan rings 1 inch apart on a baking sheet. You may need to hold each pastry circle in your hands for a moment to soften so that it will mold easily into the shell. Chill again.

Roll out puff pastry on a floured board to ⅛-inch thickness. Roll up onto the rolling pin and unroll onto a paper-lined baking sheet. Chill 30 minutes.

Using a small plate as a guide, cut out eight 6-inch circles to fit the tops of the pie shells, lay them on wax paper so that they aren't touching, and refrigerate until needed, at least 30 minutes.

MAKING THE APPLE FILLING

Peel and core the apples and slice no smaller than ¼ inch thick. Toss slices in a bowl with lemon juice.

Depending on the size of your sauté pan, you will need to divide the apples into batches, as the mixture will not caramelize properly if the apples are crowded together. (To cook it in thirds, you need a 14-inch sauté pan; in a smaller pan, divide in fourths or even fifths.) Divide the butter, sugar, cream, and Calvados as equally as possible for the batches.

Melt the butter and let it bubble slightly over medium-high heat. Add the apples and cook, stirring occasionally, until tender, 5–8 minutes. Sprinkle on the sugar and stir together with a wooden spoon. Reduce heat to medium. As the sugar melts and the juice is released from the apples, a lot of liquid will collect in the pan. Continue cooking, stirring every so often to avoid scorching, until the juice and sugar have reduced to a thick syrup and the apples are translucent and completely caramelized, but still firm to the touch, about 15–20 minutes. Remove from heat and add Calvados and ignite, letting the alcohol burn until the flames die down on their own. Add the cream and cook 5–10 minutes, until the syrup is reduced and thick. Pour the apples into a colander set over a bowl to drain. When the apples have drained, spread them out in a wide pan or on a baking sheet so that they cool rapidly and stop cooking. Sauté the remaining apples in the same manner. Toss all the apples together in a large bowl and refrigerate until cold.

❖ The caramelized apples can be made 2–3 days in advance of baking.

FILLING THE PASTRY SHELLS

Preheat oven to 350 degrees. Adjust oven rack to lowest position.

Press the cold apple slices into firm, rounded handfuls, and then place them in the pastry-lined shells. They must be nicely rounded on top so that the tarts will look plump and full when baked.

Carefully place the puff pastry circles on top of each filled pie. Keep the rest of the puff pastry circles refrigerated until you need them. (If the tops have shrunk after cutting, you may need to gently stretch them a bit to fit the pies.) With the very tips of the tines of a fork, gently seal the edges of the pastry tops to the pie shells, being careful not to puncture the pastry. Trim overlapping pastry with a sharp paring knife. Make three slits in the top of the pies to allow steam to escape while cooking. (If the top pastry is too soft to cut cleanly, chill pies again briefly before continuing.) Chill 30 minutes, or until firm.

Continued on next page

❖ Tarts can be assembled up to three days before baking and refrigerated.

In a small bowl, lightly whisk the egg yolks. Gently brush the tops of the pies with beaten egg yolk and sprinkle lightly with granulated sugar.

Bake on the lowest rack of the oven for 45–50 minutes, until tops are brown and the visible edges of the bottom crust are golden.

Serve warm, on a plate mirrored with Caramel Sauce, topped with a small scoop of Caramel Ice Cream or Vanilla Bean Ice cream. If the tarts are not served directly from the oven, reheat them at 350 degrees for about 10 minutes.

To unmold from flan rings, let cool 15–20 minutes, then turn a sharp paring knife around the edges and remove the rings. The tarts can be easily removed from the nonstick pans; just invert them onto your hand and place on a serving dish. Unmold only the tarts you intend to use immediately; they will collapse if reheated without the pans or rings.

FRUIT GRATINS

Fruit gratins, individually arranged plates of fruit with caramelized custards, are newly popular. When you serve a dessert like this, each guest will feel that it was custom-made. On the practical side, gratins are excellent for a dinner party, because the plates can be set up in advance.

The pleasing colors and composition of gratins show up best on plates at least 6–8 inches across, not including borders. The plates must be ovenproof to withstand the heat of the broiler.

You must use a salamander or a torch (see page 339) to caramelize the top of a gratin—a home broiler is not hot enough to burn the sugar.

Gratin of Oranges

10–12 large seedless oranges in all

4 cups sugar syrup (page 29)

7 tablespoons orange liqueur in all

1 cup Bitter Orange Sauce (page 334) or Vanilla Sauce flavored with Grand Marnier (page 336)

1–2 egg whites

7 tablespoons granulated sugar in all

Makes 6 individual servings

Candied orange slices are fanned out on a plate as a base for fresh orange sections and an orange-flavored custard sauce.

CANDYING THE ORANGE SLICES

Cut 2 of the oranges crosswise, with the peel still on, into ¹⁄₁₆-inch slices. Discard the first few small slices on either end. You should have about 30 slices. (A home meat slicer is the best way to get them thin enough. If you have a friendly butcher, ask him if he'll wipe down his slicer and slice them for you.)

Put the sugar syrup and 3 tablespoons of the orange liqueur in a large stainless steel saucepan and bring to a boil. Reduce heat, add orange slices, and cook at a very low simmer for 2 hours. To test if the orange slices are properly candied, drain one slice and bite it—it should be completely tender. The orange pulp should be jellylike, the white pith very tender, not spongy, and the outside skin dark and shiny, almost iridescent. If the orange slices are overcooked, the pulp will fall out. Drain the slices on wax paper or parchment paper, as they will stick to paper towels. Reserve the orange-flavored syrup for soaking cakes or other uses.

CUTTING AND MACERATING THE ORANGE SECTIONS

Using a zester, zest long shreds of zest from 1 of the oranges. Reserve for garnish. Completely peel the other oranges with a sharp serrated knife by cutting off the ends and following the contour of the orange. Cut away the outside membrane only, and as little of the orange as possible, keeping the cut fruit round. Cut on each side of the membrane that divides each orange section and take out the section. Trim any remaining white pith off each piece.

Place sections in a bowl. Squeeze the juice out of the membrane onto the orange sections, add ¼ cup of the orange liqueur, and let oranges macerate at least 30 minutes.

❖ Drained macerating liquid can be used for making the Bitter Orange Sauce.

ASSEMBLING THE GRATIN

Pool about 1 tablespoon of sauce on each plate to keep the candied orange slices from sticking. Arrange 4–5 slices in an overlapping pattern on each plate, spreading them out so that they cover as much of the plate as possible. Divide the macerated orange sections evenly (about 10 per serving) and arrange them in a pinwheel pattern in the center of each plate.

❖ The plates can be arranged and refrigerated a few hours in advance of serving.

CARAMELIZING THE GRATIN

Just before serving, preheat the broiler. In a copper bowl, whisk the egg white until foamy. Gradually add 1½ teaspoons of sugar and beat until the white is shiny and holds stiff peaks. Fold half the beaten egg white into the remaining sauce and discard the other half.

(To beat in a free-standing mixer, it's easier to use 2 egg whites and 1 tablespoon sugar; fold one fourth into the sauce and discard the rest.)

Place 1–2 tablespoons sauce in the center of the prepared plates, on top of the orange sections.

Just before caramelizing the gratins (see "Caramelizing a dessert," page 339), sprinkle the tops with 2 teaspoons sugar. The sauce will spread out as it heats but the orange slices should still be visible. Sprinkle a few strands of reserved zest on top and serve immediately.

VARIATION: If you do not have a salamander or a torch to caramelize the sugar, assemble the dessert without the sauce and top the orange sections with a small scoop of Bitter Orange or Vanilla Bean Ice Cream.

Gratin of Fresh Berries with Vanilla Crème Brûlée or Lemon Curd

Vanilla Crème Brûlée:
one recipe Vanilla Créme Brûlée (see Individual Berry Tarts with Vanilla Crème Brûlée, page 166)

Lemon Curd:
2 egg yolks

3 whole eggs

¾ cup granulated sugar

½ cup lemon juice (3–4 lemons)

½ cup lime juice (6–8 limes)

Zest of 3–4 lemons, grated or finely chopped

Zest of 6–8 limes, grated or finely chopped

6 cups raspberries, wild strawberries, blackberries, blueberries, domestic strawberries (sliced), or any combination (about 1 cup per serving). Save a few berries to garnish the top of each plate.

1 cup Raspberry Sauce (page 327) or Strawberry Sauce (page 328)

Tart lemon curd poured over fresh berries topped with caramelized sugar makes a refreshing combination of flavors. Creamy vanilla crème brûlée is another option that gives a very different effect. Raspberry sauce or strawberry sauce underline the berry taste and provide a vibrant note of color.

MAKING THE LEMON CURD

In a large metal bowl, whisk together the lemon curd ingredients. Set bowl over a large pot of simmering water and whisk vigorously, incorporating as much air as possible. Rotate the bowl from time to time to keep the eggs from cooking on the sides.

Cook filling until the foam disappears and the mixture resembles a thick hollandaise sauce, 5–10 minutes. This mixture will not curdle, so don't be afraid to cook it until it is very thick. Remove from heat.

(If you're confident with custards, this step can be done over direct heat. Whisk vigorously to avoid burning.)

❖ Lemon curd can be made up to a week in advance and refrigerated.

ASSEMBLING AND CARAMELIZING THE DESSERT

If the lemon curd has been made in advance and has thickened, place it in a bowl and stir briefly over warm water to loosen up a bit.

Arrange the berries decoratively on each plate, in a single layer and rather close together. Pour ¼–⅓ cup lemon curd or vanilla crème brûlée over the berries to evenly cover the tops.

(For lemon curd, the plates can be caramelized immediately, if desired. For the vanilla crème brûlée, however, the plates must be refrigerated at least 30 minutes before caramelizing to allow the custard to set up.)

❖ The plates can be assembled up to two hours ahead of serving and refrigerated.

Just before caramelizing the dessert (see "Caramelizing a dessert," page 339), sprinkle it with about 1 tablespoon sugar in a thin, even layer. Scatter a few more berries on top and spoon 2 tablespoons sauce around the fruit. Serve immediately.

Continued on next page

For Caramelizing the top of
    the Gratin:
*6 tablespoons granulated
    sugar*

___

**Makes 6 individual
servings**

VARIATION: If you do not have a salamander or a torch to caramelize the sugar, you can use the same combination by pooling 2 tablespoons of sauce in the bottom of broad dessert bowls, spooning in some lemon curd, or crème brûlée, and then scattering berries on top.

Gratin of Bananas

*½ pound Sweet Pastry
    (page 84)*

*¼ cup currants or raisins
    in all*

*½ cup plus a few
    tablespoons rum in all*

*4 large ripe bananas, about
    2 pounds*

*3 tablespoons unsalted
    butter*

3 tablespoons brown sugar

*1 cup Vanilla Sauce
    (page 336)*

1–2 egg whites

*7 tablespoons granulated
    sugar in all*

___

**Makes 6 individual
servings**

Bananas, an everyday fruit, undergo a surprising transformation in a gratin, sautéed with rum and brown sugar, arranged on a round of crisp pastry, and topped with currants and rum custard sauce.

CUTTING AND BAKING THE PASTRY ROUNDS

Preheat oven to 350 degrees. Adjust oven rack to middle position. On a lightly floured surface, roll out sweet pastry to ⅛-inch thickness. Using a flan ring as a guide, cut out six 4-inch rounds of dough and place 1 inch apart on a paper-covered baking sheet. Leave the rings around the dough. Chill until firm, about 30 minutes. Bake at 350 degrees for 15 minutes, until golden brown. Cool.

MACERATING THE CURRANTS

In a small stainless steel saucepan, scald the currants and ½ cup rum. If the alcohol ignites, blow it out. Turn off heat and let currants macerate until cool.

SAUTÉING THE BANANAS

Peel the bananas and slice ⅜ inch thick; you should have about 60 slices. Drain the currants and measure the rum; add extra rum as necessary to equal ½ cup.

Divide the banana slices into three batches for sautéing. Don't crowd the pan. (If your sauté pan is big enough to hold more, divide the other ingredients accordingly.) For each batch, melt 1 tablespoon butter with 1 tablespoon brown sugar over high heat, stirring until the mixture is bubbly. Add one third of the slices. Cook for 30 seconds, then turn slices over and cook 30 seconds more, being careful not to crush or break them. Remove from heat. Add 1 tablespoon of the reserved rum. Return to heat and let cook until the alcohol evaporates. (If the rum ignites, let it burn out.) Pour the bananas onto a flat baking sheet or pan and spread them out, to disperse the heat so that they cool quickly. Sauté the other two batches in the same way.

❖ The bananas can be sautéed up to two hours in advance and reserved at room temperature.

ASSEMBLING AND CARAMELIZING THE GRATIN

Stir ¼ cup of the reserved rum into the vanilla sauce; set aside. Set a pastry round in the center of each plate, surrounded by a flan ring. Arrange 10 sautéed banana slices in an attractive overlapping pattern on top of the pastry and sprinkle each with ½ tablespoon currants.

Measure ½ cup vanilla sauce and reserve the rest. In a copper bowl, whisk the egg white until foamy. Gradually add 1½ teaspoons of the sugar and beat until the whites are shiny and hold stiff peaks. Fold half the beaten egg white into the remaining sauce and discard the other half. (In a free-standing electric mixer, it's easier to beat 2 egg whites with 1 tablespoon sugar until stiff peaks form; fold one fourth into the vanilla sauce and discard the rest.) Put about 1 tablespoon of sauce mixture inside each flan ring.

Just before caramelizing the gratins (see "Caramelizing a dessert," page 339), sprinkle the tops with 1 tablespoon sugar.

Let gratins stand for about 2 minutes to set up a little. Leaving the flan rings in place, pool 1–2 tablespoons of the remaining vanilla sauce around the rings. Divide remaining currants equally and sprinkle them on top of the sauce. Loosen the flan rings by running a sharp knife around the inside edge to release them from the custard sauce and remove. Serve warm.

VARIATION: If you do not have a salamander or a torch to caramelize the sugar, assemble the dessert without the sauce and top the bananas with a small scoop of Banana-Honey or Rum-Raisin Ice Cream.

Melons in Plum Wine or Port

1 ripe medium cantaloupe, or other orange-colored variety

1 ripe medium honeydew melon, or other green-colored variety

½ cup whole fresh mint leaves, stripped from the stems

2 cups Japanese plum wine or port

Makes ten 1-cup servings

SIMPLE FRUIT DESSERTS

A simple, summery dessert, to be served well chilled in pretty glass or ceramic bowls. At Chinois on Main, we put three tiny scoops of sherbet on top of the melon—choose from Lime-Mint Sherbet, Plum Wine Sherbet, and Grapefruit-Tequila Sherbet

Cut the melons in half and scoop out the seeds. With a melon-baller, remove the flesh from the melons and place in a large bowl. Stack the mint leaves, 4 or 5 to a stack, and cut them into thin julienne strips. Pour plum wine or port over melon balls and toss together with the mint leaves. Refrigerate for at least 2 hours, until the fruit is macerated and cold. Do not refrigerate longer than several hours because the flavor will dissipate and the melon balls will discolor.

Crème Fraîche

3 cups heavy cream or manufacturer's cream

2 tablespoons buttermilk

Makes 3 cups

In every French *crémerie* there's a big tub of thick crème fraîche, which tastes like a union between sour cream and heavy cream, but is far more heavenly than either. It makes even a simple dish wonderful, and is good on just about everything except ice cream.

If you live near a dairy, buy "manufacturer's cream" to make your crème fraîche. It has a higher butterfat content than supermarket cream and makes a thicker product.

Stir the cream and buttermilk together in a large bowl. Cover tight. Let stand at room temperature for 36 hours, until slightly thickened and mousselike, then refrigerate 24 hours more to thicken further.

Keeps up to 10 days in the refrigerator and continues to thicken as it stands.

VARIATION: For a vanilla-flavored crème fraîche, scald the cream with 1 plump vanilla bean. Let cool to room temperature. Proceed as above.

Fresh Berries with Crème Fraîche

6 cups mixed fresh berries (strawberries, raspberries, blackberries, blueberries)

1½ to 2 cups Crème Fraîche (page 122)

½ cup powdered sugar, shaved maple sugar, or dark brown sugar, optional

½ cup chopped Nougatine, optional (page 353)

1½ cups fruit sauce, optional

Makes 6 servings

It's almost silly to write a recipe for something this easy, but it's so good and it works so well that I had to include it. Remember, though, that when only two ingredients are called for in a recipe, they'd better be good—in this case, lovely thick crème fraîche and ripe, sweet berries.

Put 1 heaping cup of mixed berries on each bowl or plate. Top with 2 heaping tablespoons crème fraîche for each serving and sprinkle a few berries on top for color.

As with anything simple, there are a number of options for dressing this up. Dust a small amount of sifted powdered sugar, shaved maple sugar, or brown sugar over the berries just before serving, or sprinkle with chopped nougatine. If you like, serve with a fruit sauce (Kiwi, Raspberry, Strawberry, or Blackberry) on the side.

Baked Pears or Apples with Crème Fraîche

4 hard pears (Bosc or Comice) or hard tart green apples

¼ cup lemon juice (2 lemons)

2 tablespoons unsalted butter

1 vanilla bean, split and scraped

¼ cup granulated sugar

¼ cup Cognac or poire Williams (for pears) or Calvados (for apples)

1 cup heavy cream

2 cups Crème Fraîche (page 122)

Makes 6 servings

Browned pears or apples are baked to tenderness in liqueur-spiked cream, then served warm with rich crème fraîche on the side, or topped with a melting scoop of Vanilla Bean Ice Cream. A few nice cookies dress it up a bit more. This is an excellent winter dessert that's sophisticated but easy.

Use a 10-inch sauté pan and a large stovetop-to-oven casserole with lid.

Preheat oven to 350 degrees. Adjust oven rack to the middle position.

Peel, halve, and core fruit. Cut each half into thirds or fourths, depending on size, making slices about 1½ inches wide. Toss in a bowl with the lemon juice.

Sauté the fruit in a large sauté pan. Depending on the size of your pan, divide the fruit into two batches. If you sauté in two batches, divide the other sautéing ingredients equally between the two. Melt the butter with the vanilla bean and let it bubble slightly over medium-high heat. Add the fruit and cook, stirring occasionally, until tender, 5–8 minutes. Sprinkle on the sugar and stir together with a wooden spoon. Reduce heat to medium. As the sugar melts and the juice is released from the fruit, a lot of liquid will collect in the pan. Continue cooking, stirring every so often to avoid scorching, until the juice and sugar have reduced to a thick syrup and the fruit is translucent and completely caramelized but still firm to the touch, about 20–25 minutes. Remove from heat, add alcohol, and ignite, letting it burn until the flames die down on their own. Pour into a stovetop-to-oven casserole and set aside while you cook the other half of the fruit, following the same method.

When all the fruit is in the casserole, pour on the heavy cream, place the casserole over high heat, and bring to a boil. Cover, place in oven, and bake for 30 minutes, until fruit is tender. Strain, reserving the liquid.

Put fruit in a serving bowl. Place the reserved liquid in a small saucepan and cook until it has reduced to about ½ cup and is sticky and caramelized. Pour over fruit. Serve warm.

AMERICAN FAVORITES UPDATED

Traditional desserts like the ones in this chapter were once considered just plain home cooking, but as chefs all over the United States have embraced American cooking, old-fashioned dishes have taken on a new importance, showing up on menus in every kind of restaurant. I've taken some of my favorites and refashioned them in my own style, refining techniques according to my formal training. Many of the desserts, like the Pecan Tartlets, are less sweet than the originals, while others, like the Apple Cheesecake with sautéed apple slices, are well-loved classics with an added touch.

When you make these homey recipes, you have to see the beauty in their simplicity, because they don't have the slick presentation of more stylized desserts. But I, for one, love the way a beautifully browned cream biscuit for Strawberry Shortcake looks in a pool of bright strawberry sauce, with a generous sprinkling of sliced strawberries and a dollop of crème fraîche on top. You don't have to be fancy to eat well.

Strawberry Shortcake

Shortcake Biscuit:
2¾ cups flour

*2 tablespoons plus
1 teaspoon granulated
sugar*

*1 tablespoon plus
1 teaspoon baking
powder*

1 teaspoon salt

*7 tablespoons unsalted
butter (well softened in
cold weather)*

1 cup heavy cream

Topping:
Extra heavy cream

Extra granulated sugar

*4 cups ripe strawberries or
wild strawberries*

*2 teaspoons granulated
sugar*

*2 cups Strawberry Sauce
(page 328), optional*

*2½ to 3 cups Crème
Fraîche (page 122), or
1 cup heavy cream
whipped with
2 tablespoons sour cream*

½ cup powdered sugar

Makes 8 servings

When everyone's raving about complex, sophisticated desserts, we sometimes tend to forget basic, good-tasting things like Strawberry Shortcake. This one is the old-fashioned kind, based on a very plain and tender cream biscuit, topped with strawberries and crème fraîche.

A number of fruits, such as raspberries, or ripe peaches, nectarines or apricots can be used, but strawberries are best because they're so juicy. Wild strawberries can be used alone or mixed with domestic strawberries.

Preheat oven to 375 degrees. Adjust oven rack to upper position. Line a baking sheet with parchment paper and set aside.

Sift the flour, sugar, baking powder, and salt into the bowl of an electric mixer. Cut the butter into pieces and toss together with the dry ingredients. On low speed, using the paddle attachment, combine for 5–10 minutes, until the mixture is the consistency of a fine meal, and pale yellow in color. The tenderness of the biscuit depends on the flour and butter being thoroughly mixed. Pour in the cream and mix until the mixture just comes together in one mass.

Turn dough out onto a lightly floured surface and knead gently three or four times until it forms a smooth ball. Don't overwork it. Roll out the dough to a ¾-inch thickness. (This will seem very thick compared with pie dough, but the biscuits need the thickness—they expand as they cook but they don't rise much.)

Cut out with a 3-inch biscuit cutter. You should get about 7 biscuits the first time you roll out the dough, then gather the scraps together, roll out again, and cut 3 more. Place on the baking sheet and chill until ready to bake.

❖ Biscuits can be cut out and refrigerated up to 2 hours before baking.

Just before baking, lightly brush the tops of the biscuits with cream and sprinkle with sugar. Bake for 25–30 minutes, until they are golden brown. The biscuits may spread a little during baking; they will have a rough surface and may crack a little on top.

ASSEMBLING THE SHORTCAKES

Core the strawberries. Slice domestic strawberries lengthwise into halves or quarters depending on their size; leave wild strawberries whole. Toss strawberries with the 2 teaspoons sugar. Set aside for a few minutes until the strawberries begin to release some of their juices.

Pool 2 tablespoons strawberry sauce on each dessert plate. Split the warm biscuits horizontally with a knife and place the bottom half in the center of the dessert plate. Spoon about ¼ cup crème fraîche on top and then top with a portion of strawberries. Lean the biscuit top on an angle against the mound of strawberries. Dust with powdered sugar and serve while the biscuit is still warm.

Deep-Dish Apple Pie

Apple Filling:

6½ pounds tart green apples (about 15 apples)

2 teaspoons cinnamon

3⅓ cups granulated sugar

1 pound unsalted butter (4 sticks) plus 1 tablespoon to butter pie pan

3 cups Southern Comfort

2 cups heavy cream

Crust:

1 recipe Flaky Pastry (page 130)

3 tablespoons unsalted butter

1 tablespoon granulated sugar

Pinch of cinnamon

1 tablespoon milk

Makes one 10-inch deep-dish pie, serving 10 to 12

When it comes to making apple pie, the most hotly debated controversy is whether the apples should be cooked before they're put into the crust. Without taking sides, I will point out that Dana Farkas's recipe—with sautéed apple slices—has been called by more than one restaurant critic the best they have ever eaten.

SAUTÉING THE APPLES

Peel, halve, and core the apples and slice no thinner than ¼ inch thick. There should be about 22 cups. In a small bowl, stir together the cinnamon and sugar.

Sauté the apples in a large, high-sided sauté pan. (Depending on the size of your pan, divide them into two or three batches and divide the other sautéing ingredients more or less equally.) Melt the butter and let it bubble slightly over medium-high heat. Add the apples and cook until tender, 5–8 minutes. Sprinkle on the sugar mixture and stir together with a wooden spoon. Reduce heat to medium. As the sugar melts and juice is released from the apples, a lot of liquid will collect in the pan. Continue cooking, stirring every so often to avoid scorching, until the juice and sugar have reduced to a thick syrup and the apples are translucent and completely caramelized but still firm to the touch, about 20–25 minutes. Remove from heat. Add Southern Comfort and ignite, letting the alcohol burn until the flames die down on their own. Add the cream and cook 5–10 minutes, until it is reduced and thick.

Pour apples into a colander set over a large bowl to drain. (Reserve the juices for making a sauce to serve with the finished pie.) When the apples have drained, spread them in a wide pan or on a baking sheet so that they cool rapidly and stop cooking. Sauté the remaining apples in the same manner. Toss all the apples together in a large bowl and refrigerate until cold.

ROLLING OUT THE PASTRY AND LINING THE PIE PAN

Brush the pie pan with melted butter.

Divide the dough into two unequal parts; chill the smaller part.

On a lightly floured surface, roll the larger part into a round ⅛–¼-inch thick and large enough to overlap the edges of a 10-inch pie pan (with 1¼-inch sides) by about 1 inch. Fold the dough lightly into quarters, and place the center corner of the folded dough in the center of the pan. Unfold and arrange evenly in pan, allowing the excess to hang over the edges. Trim with a sharp knife so that about 1 inch of dough overlaps the edges of the pan. Fold the overlapping dough up onto the edge of the pie, and press the excess into the inside of the pan to make a flat thick shelf, with the edge of the dough even with the rim of the pie pan. Refrigerate for 30 minutes.

FILLING AND ASSEMBLING THE PIE

Melt 1 tablespoon of the butter; set aside.

On a lightly floured surface, roll out the rest of the dough into a ⅛- to ¼-inch-thick circle big enough to generously cover the top of the pie; set aside. Brush melted butter over the bottom crust. Fill with sautéed apples shaped into an even, rounded mound. Dot the top of the apples with 2 tablespoons butter cut into small pieces. Brush the edges of the pastry with melted butter. Cover with top crust and smooth the dough gently with your hand so that the crust adheres to the apples.

Pinch the top and bottom crust together into a sturdy, continuous wall. Be sure to press hard enough to seal the pastry so the juices won't leak. With a sharp knife, trim the excess dough around the edge of the pan.

Insert a knife in the center of the pie and turn it to make a nice-size steam hole. Cut four 1-inch slits in the top around the hole. Refrigerate or chill in freezer until firm, about 30 minutes.

❖ The pie can be made ahead up to this point and refrigerated for two to three days before baking.

BAKING THE PIE

Preheat oven to 400 degrees. Adjust oven rack to middle position. In a small bowl, stir together the granulated sugar and cinnamon. Brush the top of the pie with milk and sprinkle evenly with the sugar mixture. Place the pie on a baking sheet to protect the oven from drips and bake at 400 degrees for 30 minutes; reduce heat to 350 and bake 35 minutes longer, until the top crust is golden brown.

Continued on next page

The juices drained from sautéing the apples make an excellent sauce. Reheat before serving and thin with a little cream if too sweet or too thick. Pool a tablespoon of sauce on the dessert plate and top with a warm slice of pie and a scoop of Vanilla Bean Ice Cream or a thin slice of cheddar cheese.

Flaky Pastry

3½ cups pastry flour

¾ teaspoon salt

4 ounces unsalted butter (1 stick)

8 tablespoons chilled vegetable shortening

¾ cup water plus ice to measure 1 cup

Makes 1¾ pounds dough, enough for a 2-crust pie

Used in Deep-Dish Apple Pie

Many veteran pie makers swear that really flaky pastry is made only with vegetable shortening, while others prefer to use butter for its flavor. This recipe, developed by Dana Farkas, is a compromise—it's got shortening for flakiness and butter for flavor.

Sift together the flour and salt into a large mixing bowl. Cut the butter into ½-inch cubes and toss with the vegetable shortening and the flour until the cubes are coated. Crumble the butter into the flour by rubbing your thumbs and fingertips together, lifting the pieces and letting them fall back down again. Continue until the mixture resembles coarse cornmeal. Add the water a little at a time, starting with about ½ cup, and mix just until the mixture comes together. Add the remaining ¼ cup water if the flour is not absorbed. The amount of water the dough needs will depend on the moisture in the flour and the humidity.

Gather the dough together and knead briefly on a lightly floured board until it forms a smooth ball. Unlike the Sweet Pastry, in which the butter and flour are completely blended, you will be able to see streaks of shortening in this pastry when it's done. Chill at least 2 hours before rolling out.

(In a food processor, using the metal blade, or in an electric mixer, combine ingredients in the same order. Be sure that you stop the machine as soon as the mixture reaches the cornmeal stage and again after the addition of the liquid.)

The pastry will keep for a week in the refrigerator; up to three months frozen. Any scraps saved after rolling the dough out once can be reused for the bottom crust of a pie, but they are not flaky enough for the top crust.

Walnut–Cream Cheese Pastry

1½ cups flour

¾ cup walnuts (2 ounces)

1½ tablespoons sugar

2 tablespoons finely grated or chopped orange zest (2 oranges)

6 ounces unsalted butter, very cold (1½ sticks)

5 ounces cream cheese, very cold

1 tablespoon orange juice

Makes enough for one 10-inch 2-crust pie

Used in Rhubarb Pie

Cream cheese makes a very flaky dough, which goes well with the soft texture of rhubarb pie.

Grind the walnuts in a Mouli grater, or chop them extremely fine. Grinding them in a food processor will not make the right texture.

Sift the flour into a large bowl, and toss together with the walnuts, sugar, and orange zest. Cut the butter into ½-inch cubes and toss with the flour until the cubes are coated. Crumble the butter into the flour by rubbing it between your fingertips (the coolest part of your hand), lifting the pieces and letting them fall back down again. Continue until the mixture has the consistency of fine cornmeal. Grate in the cold cream cheese and pour on the orange juice. Gather the dough together in a ball with your hands. It will be very sticky.

(In a food processor, using the metal blade, or in an electric mixer, using the paddle attachment, combine ingredients in the same order, processing the flour, walnuts, sugar, orange zest, and butter together, and then adding the cream cheese and orange juice. Be sure that you stop the machine as soon as the flour and butter reach the cornmeal stage and again when the dough comes together after the addition of the liquid.)

Give the dough a final blending *(fraisage)* as directed in the recipe for Sweet Pastry (page 84). Wrap in plastic wrap and refrigerate at least 2 hours before rolling out.

Huckleberry Pie

Filling:

7 cups huckleberries, stemmed

4 tablespoons flour

½ cup granulated sugar

2 tablespoons grated or finely chopped orange zest (2 oranges)

¼ teaspoon ground cloves

½ teaspoon cinnamon

Crust:

1 pound Sweet Pastry (page 84), or 1 recipe Flaky Pastry (page 130)

1 tablespoon unsalted butter, melted, to butter pie pan

1 egg yolk

2 tablespoons granulated sugar

Small pinch of cinnamon

1 tablespoon milk

Makes one 10-inch pie, serving 10–12

When they're raw, huckleberries are nothing to get excited about, but once they're cooked they make a delicious, stain-your-teeth-dark-purple pie. For me, they're the berry lover's equivalent of the wine lover's "big wine"—they're a "big fruit." Huckleberries are similar to blueberries, but they are smaller, more tart, and have larger seeds.

MAKING THE FRUIT FILLING

In a large bowl, toss together the huckleberries, flour, sugar, zest, cloves, and cinnamon. Place in a strainer and let drain for 15 minutes.

ROLLING OUT THE PASTRY AND LINING THE PIE PAN

Brush the pie pan with melted butter.

Divide the dough into two unequal parts; chill the smaller part. On a lightly floured surface, roll the larger part into a round ⅛ to ¼ inch thick and large enough to overlap the edges of a 10-inch pie tin by about 1 inch. Fold the dough lightly in quarters and place the center corner of the folded dough in the center of the pan. Unfold and arrange evenly in pan, allowing the excess to hang over the edges. Trim with a sharp knife so that about 1 inch of dough overlaps the edges of the pan. Fold the overlapping dough up onto the edge of the pie tin to make a flat thick shelf, with the edge of the dough even with the rim of the pie pan. Refrigerate for 30 minutes.

FILLING AND ASSEMBLING THE PIE

Mound the fruit into the dough-lined pan. With the handle of a knife, push the fruit away from the edges so that there is a ½-inch space between the fruit and the sides of the pan. (This keeps the filling from leaking out later when you crimp the dough.)

On a lightly floured surface, roll out the remaining dough into a round ¼ inch thick and big enough to cover the top of the pie generously. In a small bowl, lightly beat the egg yolk and brush the edges of the pastry shell with it. Lay the dough round on top of the fruit, and press down well around the edges to seal.

To give the pie a nice domed shape, cup your hands around the mounded top of the pie, pressing the little-

*Crimping into a
perpendicular wall*

*Crimping into a
scalloped pattern*

finger edge of your hands firmly into the rim of the pan all the way around. This will create a slight indentation just inside the rim of the pan and a flat area about 1 inch wide around the edge.

Pinch the top and bottom crust together into a sturdy perpendicular wall, or crimp with your thumbs in a scalloped pattern to create a decorative edge. With one thumb, press the dough toward the center of the pie. Place the other thumb next to it, in the opposite direction, pressing the dough toward the outside of the pie. To keep the spacing consistent, leave one thumb in place while you move the other. Be sure to press hard enough to seal the pastry as you crimp. With a sharp knife, trim the pastry even with the edge of the pan.

Insert a knife in the center of the pie and turn it to make a nice-size steam hole. Cut four 1-inch-long slits in the pie around the hole. Refrigerate or chill in freezer until firm, about 30 minutes.

❖ Do not let the unbaked pie stand any longer than 1 hour in the refrigerator or the berry color will bleed into the pastry.

BAKING THE PIE

Preheat oven to 400 degrees. Adjust oven rack to middle position.

In a small bowl, stir together the granulated sugar and cinnamon. Brush the top of the pie with milk and sprinkle with sugar mixture. Reseal edges of pastry if they have opened. Place the pie on a baking sheet to protect the oven from drips.

Bake at 400 degrees for 30 minutes, then reduce temperature to 350 degrees and bake for 35 minutes longer, until the top crust is golden brown.

Let cool at least 1 hour before serving to let the pie set up.

Serve warm, with Huckleberry Sauce and Vanilla Bean Ice Cream.

Rhubarb Pie

Crust:

1 recipe Walnut–Cream
    Cheese Pastry (page 131)

1 tablespoon unsalted
    butter, melted, to butter
    pie pan

1 tablespoon granulated
    sugar

Filling:

1 pound rhubarb

3 tablespoons flour, sifted

1 egg

3 egg yolks

2 tablespoons finely grated
    or chopped orange zest
    (2 oranges)

1/4 cup orange juice
    (1 orange)

6 tablespoons granulated
    sugar

2/3 cup heavy cream

1/4 cup orange liqueur

**Makes one 10-inch pie,
serving 8–10**

There's no middle ground when it comes to rhubarb—you love it or hate it. If you love it, you'll want to try this custard pie, enlivened with the flavor of orange, in a very flaky walnut–cream cheese crust.

Some rhubarb pies call for steaming the rhubarb before putting it in the shell, but I prefer using it raw so that the pie has more texture to the bite. Choose crisp red or pink medium-size stalks, and avoid stringiness.

A fluted ravioli cutter is nice for cutting out the pastry strips to weave the top crust.

ROLLING THE DOUGH AND WEAVING THE
LATTICE TOP

Brush the pie pan with melted butter.

Divide the pastry into two unequal parts; chill the smaller part. On a lightly floured surface, roll the larger part into a round 1/4–1/8 inch thick and large enough to overlap the edges of a 10-inch pie pan (with 1-inch sides) by about an inch. Fold pastry gently into quarters. Lift the dough and place the center corner in the center of the tin. Unfold and arrange evenly in pan, allowing the excess to hang over the edges. Trim with a sharp knife so that about 1 inch of dough overlaps the edges of the pan. Fold the overlapping dough up onto the edge of the pie, and press the excess into the inside of the pan to make a flat thick shelf, with the edge of the dough even with the rim of the pie pan. Refrigerate for 30 minutes.

On a lightly floured surface, roll the remaining dough into a rectangle 1/4 inch thick, about 7 inches wide by 12 inches long. Slide the dough onto a piece of cardboard or the back of a baking sheet. (If the dough is very soft, refrigerate briefly to firm up.)

Using a ruler or a strip of cardboard 1/2 inch wide as a guide, cut the dough lengthwise with a sharp knife or a fluted pastry cutter into 14 strips. Chill until firm, about 20 minutes.

Lay 7 dough strips about 1/2 inch apart on a piece of cardboard or the back of a baking sheet. Peel back every other strip, lay 1 pastry strip horizontally across the strips that are lying flat, and turn the other strips back down. Lift the alternate strips, place another strip horizontally across about 1/2 inch away, and turn the strips down. Continue

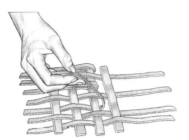

Weaving the basket design

Marking the top edge of the crust with a trussing needle

until all 14 strips are woven together. Refrigerate if necessary to firm up during weaving. When weaving is finished, chill to firm.

PREBAKING THE PIE SHELL

Preheat the oven to 350 degrees. Adjust oven rack to bottom third of oven. Remove the pie shell from the refrigerator. For a more finished look, mark the perimeter of the piecrust with the shaft of a trussing needle. Hold the needle in one hand, point the tip about two inches off center, and press almost through the dough. Rotate the pie in place; do not move the needle. Make impressions about ½ inch apart. This way it is easier to maintain the same angle with the needle. Line the pie shell with a large coffee filter or parchment paper. Fill the shell up to the rim with dried beans or metal pie weights. Bake for 30 minutes, until very light brown. When cool, remove the beans or pie weights with a large spoon and carefully peel off paper lining. Only if the pie shell is still wet on the bottom return it to the oven, unlined, for 5–10 minutes more.

MAKING THE FILLING; ASSEMBLING AND BAKING THE PIE

Preheat oven to 350 degrees. Adjust rack to top third of oven and place a baking sheet on the rack.

Wash the rhubarb, trim the ends, and cut each stalk into pieces 3 inches long and ½ inch wide. Do not peel.

Place all the filling ingredients except the rhubarb in a food processor or blender. Process until well combined.

(To mix by hand: In a large bowl, whisk egg, egg yolks, orange juice, orange zest, heavy cream, and orange liqueur together. Mix in sugar and flour until well combined and there are no lumps. Break up any lumps of flour with your fingers.)

Pack the cut rhubarb into the cooled pie shell and pour custard mixture over it. It will seem like a lot of rhubarb but it will cook down during baking.

Slide the woven top crust onto the pie, by running a long-bladed metal spatula under it to release it from the cardboard or baking sheet. Then hold the baking sheet or cardboard at an angle and ease the crust onto the top of the pie, shaking gently. Trim the ends of the strips even with the inside edge of the pan.

Sprinkle the crust evenly with 1 tablespoon granulated sugar. Place on baking sheet in preheated oven and bake for 45 minutes. The custard will be just set in the center and the top crust will be light brown and shiny where the sugar has melted.

Serve at room temperature or chilled, with Rhubarb-Raspberry Sauce and Vanilla Bean Ice Cream. Keeps well for a day or so in the refrigerator.

Pear or Apple Ginger Upside-Down Cake

Fruit Topping:

4 large pears (firm Bosc or Comice) or tart green apples (about 2 pounds)

¹⁄₄ cup lemon juice (2 lemons)

4 ounces unsalted butter (1 stick)

³⁄₄ cup granulated sugar

¹⁄₂ cup Calvados (for apples) or poire Williams (pear brandy) (for pears)

Ginger Cake:

6 tablespoons unsalted butter

2 tablespoons dark brown sugar, firmly packed

1 cup flour

1 tablespoon ground ginger

For this cake, pears or apples are caramelized in a skillet, arranged in the thick caramel on the bottom of the pan, and then baked in the same skillet under a layer of spicy ginger cake batter. When the cake is unmolded onto a platter, it has a pretty pinwheel of fruit slices on top.

TO CARAMELIZE FRUIT

Peel, halve, and core the fruit and cut into ½-inch slices. There should be about 14 slices per apple or pear. Toss in a bowl with the lemon juice.

Sauté the fruit in a large sauté pan. Depending on the size of your pan, you may need to divide the fruit into two batches. If you sauté in two batches, divide the other sautéing ingredients equally between the two.

Melt the butter and let it bubble slightly over medium-high heat. Add the fruit and cook, stirring occasionally, until tender, 3–5 minutes. Sprinkle on the sugar and stir together with a wooden spoon. Reduce heat to medium. As the sugar melts and the juice is released from the fruit, a lot of liquid will collect in the pan. Continue cooking, stirring every so often to avoid scorching, until the juice and sugar have reduced to a thick syrup and the fruit is translucent and completely caramelized but still firm to the touch, about 15–20 minutes. Remove pan from heat, add alcohol, and ignite, letting it burn until the flames die down on their own. Drain fruit in a colander set over a large bowl, saving the syrup.

When the fruit is drained, spread it out on a large baking

1 teaspoon baking soda

2 tablespoons boiling strong
   black coffee

1/2 cup molasses (preferably
   blackstrap)

1 teaspoon cinnamon

1/4 teaspoon freshly ground
   nutmeg

1/4 teaspoon ground cloves

2 eggs, separated

4 egg whites

2 tablespoons granulated
   sugar

**Makes one 10-inch cake,
serving 8–10**

sheet to stop the cooking and allow to cool. Pour the caramel drained from the fruit back into the pan and, if necessary, cook to reduce until the bottom of the pan is covered
with about 1/8 inch of thick, bubbly caramel. Remove from
heat and let cool.

PREPARING THE BATTER AND BAKING THE CAKE

Preheat oven to 350 degrees. Adjust oven rack to upper
third of oven.

Arrange the cooled fruit slices in a decorative pinwheel
pattern over the caramel in the frying pan. Start with the
outside edge and arrange the wedges in slightly overlapping, concentric circles, filling the entire bottom of the
pan. Remember: this will be the top of the finished cake.

Using the quantities specified above, make the ginger
cake batter as directed on page 173.

Spread the cake batter evenly over the fruit 3/4 inch thick
(or pipe it with a pastry bag fitted with a No. 4 plain tip).
(You may have a small amount of cake batter left over, but
it's difficult to make a butter-based cake with less than 6
tablespoons of butter.) Bake for 15–20 minutes, until
springy to the touch. Cool.

To unmold, loosen the cake from the pan by running a
knife around the edge. Place a flat heatproof serving platter
(larger in diameter than the pan) on top of the frying pan
and invert the cake onto the platter.

Serve warm, with a bowl of unsweetened whipped
cream, sour cream, or crème fraîche on the side.

Apple Cheesecake

6 ounces Sweet Pastry (page 84)

Apple Layer:
1 large, or 2 medium, tart green apples, approximately 12 ounces

1 tablespoon lemon juice

2 tablespoons unsalted butter

3 tablespoons granulated sugar

2 tablespoons apple brandy

2 tablespoons heavy cream

Cheesecake Layer:
9 ounces cream cheese

1/2 cup granulated sugar

2 eggs

1 cup sour cream

2 tablespoons lemon juice (1 lemon)

1 tablespoon grated or finely chopped lemon zest (1 lemon)

Topping (optional):
1/2 cup sour cream, or 2 tablespoons granulated sugar

Makes one 10-inch cheesecake, serving 8–10

I hate desserts that are "too much"—too high, too rich, too bland, too much of one thing—which is why I was never a big fan of cheesecake. But it's so popular that I decided to invent one that would please both myself and the cheesecake lovers. My version is a low-rise lemon-scented cheesecake set on a crisp circle of sweet pastry, with a layer of caramelized apple slices adding another interesting flavor and texture.

It is best made with gelatin-free cream cheese, available at health food stores and kosher markets, and smooth-curd sour cream.

ROLLING AND BAKING THE PASTRY ROUND

Preheat oven to 350 degrees. Adjust oven rack to middle position.

On a lightly floured surface, roll the sweet pastry into a 3/8-inch-thick round at least 10½ inches in diameter. Using the bottom of a 10-inch springform pan or a 1-inch-high flan ring as a guide, cut a round of pastry to fit the pan exactly. Place the dough round on the pan bottom (or in the flan ring set on a heavy baking sheet), and prick with a fork to prevent it from rising. Chill until firm, about 30 minutes.

Bake 20–30 minutes, until golden brown. Set aside to cool. When cool, either put sides onto springform pan or carefully set the pastry round onto a large sheet of aluminum foil. Replace the flan ring and tightly crimp the foil around the ring to prevent the filling from leaking out.

Decrease oven temperature to 275 degrees.

Peel, halve, and core the apples and cut into ¼-inch slices. Toss in a small bowl with the lemon juice.

In a large sauté pan, melt the butter and let it bubble slightly over medium-high heat. Add the apples and cook, stirring occasionally, for 3–5 minutes. Sprinkle on the sugar and stir together with a wooden spoon. Reduce heat to medium. As the sugar melts and the juice is released from the apples, a lot of liquid will collect in the pan. Continue cooking, stirring every so often to avoid scorching, until the juice and sugar have reduced to a thick syrup and the fruit is translucent and completely caramelized but still firm to the touch, about 15–20 minutes. Remove pan from heat, add alcohol, and ignite, letting it burn until the flames die down on their own. Add the cream and cook 3–5 minutes, until the syrup is reduced and thick.

Pour apples into a colander set over a large bowl to drain. When the apples have drained, spread them in a wide pan or on a baking sheet so that they cool rapidly and stop cooking.

PREPARING THE CHEESECAKE LAYER

In a large bowl, whisk the cream cheese and sugar together until smooth. Whisk in the eggs, one at a time, then stir in the sour cream and lemon juice. Strain the batter through a fine-mesh strainer (to remove lumps) into a clean bowl, and stir in the lemon zest. (Beat the batter by hand, because an electric mixer will beat in too much air and the cake won't set up well when baked.)

ASSEMBLING AND BAKING THE CHEESECAKE

Arrange a single layer of caramelized apple slices in a concentric circle on the prebaked pie crust. Place them no closer than 1 inch from the side of the pan so that they do not show through the sides of the cheesecake when it is unmolded. Pour cream cheese mixture over apple slices.

Bake at 275 degrees for 25–30 minutes, until the sides are just set and the center of the cheesecake jiggles slightly (but is not liquid) when the pan is shaken gently. It will set up further as it cools. The top should not be cracked or colored. Let cool at room temperature, then refrigerate at least 1 hour, until cold and firm.

DECORATING THE CHEESECAKE (OPTIONAL)

These options are for a more decorated look, although the cheesecake can be served as is.

Caramelizing: When the cheesecake is cold and firm, preheat broiler. Just before serving, sprinkle the top evenly with 2 tablespoons granulated sugar. Broil at high heat, watching carefully, until the sugar browns and caramelizes, no more than 30 seconds. Refrigerate 15–30 minutes to firm up.

Sour cream topping: Stir ½ cup sour cream until it becomes runny and pourable. Pour it over the top of the cheesecake and rotate the pan in your hands to spread evenly. Spread with an offset metal spatula or the back of a spoon if necessary. Chill at least 1 hour before serving.

UNMOLDING THE CHEESECAKE

Unmold by placing hot towels briefly around the pan and then releasing the sides or removing the flan ring. If edges are not perfect, smooth them with a metal spatula heated briefly in a flame.

Serve cold, with Apricot Sauce. Keeps refrigerated two to three days. If you caramelize the top of the cheesecake, it should be served within a few hours.

Apricot-Blueberry Compote

6 large, firm, ripe apricots, preferably Royal

1/3 cup granulated sugar

1 cup orange juice (3–4 oranges)

Zest of 3–4 oranges, zested with a zester in long strings

Zest of 3–4 limes, zested with a zester in long strings

1 small cinnamon stick

10 whole cloves

1/2 cup lime juice (3–4 limes)

1 cup blueberries

Makes enough to serve with 6 popovers

Used in Popovers

A combination of fruits to delight the eye and the palate. This is not a mushy stewed compote—the apricots are only halved, and keep their shape as they are cooked. Serve it warm with fresh, hot Popovers or spooned on Vanilla Bean or Caramel Ice Cream.

Choose a broad stainless steel saucepan or high-sided sauté pan big enough to hold the apricots in a single layer.

Halve the apricots and remove pits, but do not peel; set aside.

In a stainless steel saucepan, bring the sugar and orange juice to a boil. Cook over high heat until the liquid is thickened and slightly sticky, 5–10 minutes.

Add the orange zest, lime zest, cinnamon stick, cloves, and apricots, placed cut side down. Simmer slowly over low heat for 10 minutes. Add lime juice and continue cooking for another 10–15 minutes, stirring occasionally to distribute the apricots so that they cook evenly; take care not to bruise them.

When the syrup has thickened and become sticky and the apricots are completely tender (but not mushy), add the blueberries and continue cooking 5 more minutes. Remove cinnamon stick and cloves. Pour into a serving bowl. Serve warm.

Popovers

1 cup flour

¼ teaspoon salt

1 tablespoon granulated
    sugar

¼ teaspoon cinnamon

¼ teaspoon freshly grated
    nutmeg

1 cup milk

1 tablespoon vanilla extract

4 eggs

¼ cup clarified unsalted
    butter, melted, in all

Apricot-Blueberry Compote
    (page 140)

Makes 6

This is my own variation on the classic popover recipe, with sugar, cinnamon, nutmeg, and vanilla added for flavor. A good popover is light in weight, with a crisp outside and a network of custardlike webbing inside. Eggs and steam are the only things that make popovers rise—never leavening like baking powder.

Black steel popover tins, available in cookware stores, are the best for baking these light, crispy, air-filled pastries. Individual 3½-inch soufflé cups, 1½ inches deep, are also good. Don't use muffin tins as they aren't deep enough. Whichever tins you use, fill them only half full for baking.

Preheat oven to 425 degrees. Put the popover tins in the oven to heat. It is essential to bring all ingredients to room temperature before beginning.

Sift the flour into a large bowl and make a well in the center. Sprinkle the salt, sugar, cinnamon, and nutmeg on the flour. In a small bowl, lightly beat together the milk and the vanilla with a fork. Pour the liquid ingredients into the well. Using a whisk or a wooden spoon, slowly stir the liquids together, gradually drawing the dry ingredients into the liquid little by little until combined and smooth.

In a small bowl, lightly beat eggs and 2 tablespoons of the melted butter together with a fork. Add to flour mixture, combining well, but do not overbeat. Strain through a fine-mesh strainer to remove any lumps of flour.

Remove the heated tins from the oven and brush with the remaining 2 tablespoons melted butter, coating generously. Fill each tin half full of batter. Do not open the oven during the first half hour of baking. Bake at 425 for 15 minutes, then lower the temperature to 350 and bake for 15 minutes more, or until the popovers are a uniform medium brown color.

Remove popovers from oven. Using a sharp skewer, prick a hole in the top of each popover. Turn off the oven, return popovers to oven, and prop the door slightly open with a folded dish towel. Let the popovers stand in the oven for 15 minutes, to dry out the insides and keep them from getting soggy.

Remove from oven, turn popovers out of tins, and serve warm with Apricot-Blueberry Compote.

Blueberry Buckle

Crust:

½ tablespoon unsalted butter, melted

14 ounces Sweet Pastry (page 84) or Flaky Pastry (page 130)

Streusel Topping:

1⅞ cups granulated sugar

1¾ cups flour

2¼ teaspoons cinnamon

8 ounces unsalted butter, cold

Batter:

1¾ cups plus 3 tablespoons flour

6 tablespoons granulated sugar

1 tablespoon baking powder

¾ teaspoon salt

4 ounces unsalted butter, very soft (1 stick), at room temperature

4 egg yolks

2 teaspoons vanilla extract

½ cup buttermilk

The recipe for this country-style fruit cobbler, with layers of crisp pastry, blueberries, cake, and a streusel topping, was developed by Dana Farkas. Serve warm, with a generous amount of heavy cream poured over the top. The one made in the large pan is scooped out into bowls. It's easy to make and an excellent dessert for a large group.

Strawberries or peaches, among other fruits, can be used in this recipe, but I think blueberries are best; they're high in pectin so they set up well, and low in water content so the cobbler doesn't get soggy.

A 10 x 8½-inch 4-quart baking pan, 2½ inches deep, works well for this. Any dimension 4-quart capacity baking pan will work, as long as it is at least 2 inches deep; a shallow pan will not allow for the layers of fruit, cake, and streusel. Or you can use 12 soufflé cups of 1-cup capacity each.

LINING THE BAKING PAN WITH PASTRY

Brush the bottom of the baking pan or cups with melted butter. If you're using a pan, roll out the dough on a lightly floured surface, into a rectangle larger than the bottom of the pan, about ⅛ inch thick. Place the baking pan on the rolled dough and, with a sharp knife, cut a rectangle that will fit the bottom of the pan. Roll up the dough on the rolling pin and lay it in the bottom of the pan. Trim if necessary and patch any holes. For the soufflé cups, cut individual rounds of dough to fit exactly the bottom of the soufflé cups and set inside the cups. (The pastry won't show when the dessert is finished, so it needn't be picture-perfect.) Chill until firm, at least 30 minutes.

MAKING THE STREUSEL TOPPING

In the bowl of an electric mixer, combine the sugar, flour, and cinnamon. Cut the butter into chunks and toss with the dry ingredients. Using the paddle attachment, combine the ingredients on medium-low speed. The butter will gradually begin to incorporate with the dry ingredients. Once small lumps of streusel begin to form, immediately stop mixing. The mixture should be crumbly. The entire process should take about 4 minutes. Refrigerate until ready to use.

Fruit:

4½ pounds blueberries (12 cups), fresh or frozen (for individual soufflé cups, you need only 8 cups). Frozen blueberries must be thawed and drained in a colander for at least 12 hours; any retained water will cause sogginess.

Makes one 10 x 8½-inch pan, 15–20 servings, or 12 individual servings

MAKING THE BATTER

Sift together the flour, sugar, baking powder, and salt in the bowl of an electric mixer. Cut the butter into chunks and toss with the dry ingredients. Using the paddle attachment, combine the ingredients on low speed for at least 5 minutes, until the mixture has reached the consistency of a fine meal. Whisk together the egg yolks, vanilla, and buttermilk and slowly pour into the dry ingredients, beating to make a smooth, shiny batter.

ASSEMBLING THE BLUEBERRY BUCKLE

Preheat oven to 400 degrees. Adjust oven rack to middle position.

Remove pastry-lined baking pan or cups from refrigerator. Spread half the blueberries evenly over the bottom of the baking pan, or scatter one layer of blueberries into the soufflé cups. Pour (or pipe with a pastry bag and a No. 3 tip) the batter over the berries and spread it gently in an even layer, trying not to mix too much of the batter into the berries underneath. (The object is to have distinct layers of berries and cake in the finished product.) Top with remaining blueberries. Sprinkle streusel over the top, being sure to cover all the fruit.

For the large pan, bake for 30 minutes at 400 degrees. then reduce oven heat to 350 and bake for 1 hour more, or until the streusel topping is golden brown and crisp. For individual cups, bake at 350 degrees for 1 hour.

Bread Pudding

Custard:
1½ cups milk

1½ cups heavy cream

1 teaspoon freshly grated nutmeg

2 cinnamon sticks

1 vanilla bean, split and scraped

2 egg yolks

2 eggs

3 tablespoons sugar

For Cinnamon Toast:
25–28 slices of a 3½-inch-diameter French baguette or sourdough bread, sliced ⅜ inch thick (don't use stale bread as it's too crumbly)

¾ cup (6 ounces) clarified unsalted butter, melted (page 17)

5 tablespoons granulated sugar

1 teaspoon cinnamon

Caramelizing the Pan:
¼ cup plus 2 tablespoons sugar

3 tablespoons water

1½ cups Apple Purée (page 50)

Makes 10 servings

Bread pudding no doubt began as a way to use up leftover bread, a homey dish simply spooned out on a plate. This is a more dressed-up version, with a layer of caramel on the bottom, the bread transformed into cinnamon toast that's layered with custard and caramelized applesauce. It's crusty rather than eggy, and when unmolded onto a serving plate and neatly sliced into wedges, it looks like a well-browned Tarte Tatin. Serve it warm with a bowl of crème fraîche or sour cream on the side.

Use a 2-quart, straight-sided porcelain soufflé dish (3-inch-high sides, 7 inches in diameter).

For the custard, scald the milk, cream, nutmeg, cinnamon sticks, and vanilla bean in a saucepan. Remove from heat, cover, and let stand at least 30 minutes.

With a wire whisk, beat the egg yolks and the whole egg with the 2 tablespoons sugar until the sugar is dissolved. Reheat the cream mixture to scalding and pour over the beaten eggs, whisking constantly. Strain to remove bits of cinnamon stick and vanilla bean; set aside.

Preheat oven to 350 degrees. Spread bread slices on a baking sheet and toast for about 5 minutes, until the outside of the bread is slightly crisp but the inside is still soft.

Mix the clarified butter with the 5 tablespoons sugar and 1 teaspoon cinnamon. Using a pastry brush, paint a thin, even layer of butter on both sides of the bread, coating but not saturating it. (Do not use any more butter than specified—this amount must suffice for all the bread slices or the pudding will be too buttery.) Keep the sugar and cinnamon mixed with the butter by stirring with the brush before coating each bread slice.

In a small saucepan, heat the sugar and the water over high heat. When the water boils, it will throw sugar onto the sides of the pan. At that point, wash down the sides of the pan with a pastry brush, dipping in water as necessary to dissolve the sugar. (Alternatively, place a lid on the pan for 30 seconds and the steam condensation will wash the sugar off the sides.) Boil until the mixture turns a deep amber color.

Immediately pour the hot caramel into a 2-quart straight-sided soufflé dish and tilt the dish to swirl the caramel evenly over the bottom. (Don't be concerned if the caramel coating isn't even—it will remelt and redistribute itself during baking.) Set the dish aside.

ASSEMBLING THE BREAD PUDDING

Preheat oven to 350 degrees. Adjust oven rack to middle position.

Use all the bread and all the custard in assembling the pudding. It is important that the bread is entirely soaked with custard. If you're using a shallower, broad mold, you may need to make some extra custard to soak the bread completely.

Place 4–6 slices of the butter-brushed bread on the bottom of the soufflé dish. With a serrated knife, cut another slice of bread into pieces to completely fill all gaps. Pour in enough custard to just cover the bread. Press the bread with your fingertips to make sure the custard has soaked into the bread. Add more custard if the bread seems too hard. Spread with half the applesauce and moisten lightly with custard. Put on another layer of bread, again filling the gaps with small pieces of bread and covering with custard. Test again to make sure the bread is well soaked. Spread with the remaining applesauce and moisten with custard again. Finish the pudding with two layers of bread, pouring on remaining custard. Press down a bit to make sure that the custard saturates the entire pudding. Allow the pudding to sit at room temperature for about 20 minutes before baking.

Bake for 1 hour. The pudding will swell up, and when done it will be brown, crusty, and set. Cool for 30 minutes, unmold onto a serving platter, and serve warm.

Pecan Tartlets

1 tablespoon unsalted
butter, melted

1 pound Sweet Pastry (page
84) for individual
tartlets, or 12 ounces for
a 10-inch tart

6 tablespoons dark brown
sugar, loosely packed

6 tablespoons granulated
sugar

¼ cup hazelnut liqueur

¾ cup light corn syrup

2 tablespoons unsalted
butter

1 vanilla bean, split and
scraped

2 egg yolks

1 egg

8 ounces pecan halves (2
cups) for individual
tartlets, 6 ounces (1½
cups) for the 10-inch tart

**Makes 6 individual tartlets,
or one 10 x ½-inch tart,
serving 8**

DRIED FRUIT AND NUT DESSERTS

If you have preconceived notions about pecan pies, you'll be surprised by these tartlets: they're thin and chewy but not too sweet, and they have a marvelous nutty taste without the gelatinous texture of many pecan pies.

Use 4-inch flan rings with ½-inch sides, or a 10-inch ring with ½-inch side.

Preheat oven to 350 degrees. Adjust oven rack to bottom third of oven. Brush flan rings with the melted butter and place, not touching, on a paper-lined baking sheet; set aside.

On a lightly floured surface, roll the sweet pastry to ¼-inch thickness. Using a small plate as a guide, cut six 5-inch rounds and place, not overlapping, on a paper-lined baking sheet. Chill at least 30 minutes. When pastry is well chilled, use it to line the flan rings and trim excess with a sharp paring knife. You may need to hold each pastry round in your hands for a moment to soften so that it will mold easily into the ring. Chill again. (For the 10-inch tart, roll out sweet pastry to ¼-inch thickness and place in flan ring. Chill for 30 minutes.)

MAKING THE FILLING

In a large bowl, whisk together the brown sugar, granulated sugar, and liqueur. Beat in corn syrup. The mixture will be very thick and sticky.

In a small saucepan, heat the butter and vanilla bean until brown and foamy. Continue heating until the bubbles subside and the butter turns dark brown and starts to smoke. It will give off a nutty aroma. Pour immediately into the sugar mixture and whisk until combined. Remove vanilla bean. Cool.

In another bowl, whisk together the egg yolks and whole egg. Add to cooled sugar mixture and beat vigorously until combined. This filling has the best texture when beaten by hand.

For best results, make the filling the day before baking and refrigerate overnight.

ASSEMBLING THE TARTLETS

Arrange pecan halves, rounded side up, in concentric circles, slightly overlapping, to cover the bottom of the tart shells. Start from the outside and fill in toward the center.

Spoon in just enough filling to cover nuts.

(For a large tart, arrange the pecans in a sunburst pattern in a single layer, starting from the outside edge and working toward the center. Pour in 1½ cups filling.)

Bake small tarts for 30 minutes and large tart for 40 minutes, until filling rises in a small dome and is uniformly brown. The tarts will be a little soft in the middle, and the crust will be a light golden brown. To see if the pastry crust is evenly cooked, pick up the ring on one tart, check for a golden color, then replace the ring and return to the oven briefly if necessary. (If the tarts are overcooked, the filling will be hard and candylike; if undercooked, they will be mushy instead of chewy and crisp.)

Unmold as directed for Individual Apple-Calvados Tarts, page 114.

Serve warm, on a plate mirrored with Caramel Sauce, topped with a scoop of Banana Honey Ice Cream. Maple Syrup Ice Cream, Maple Sugar Ice Cream, or Vanilla Bean Ice Cream are also excellent accompaniments.

Brioche Dough

3/4 ounce cake or granulated
    yeast (1 1/4 cakes or 3
    tablespoons plus 1
    teaspoon granulated)

3/4 cup milk

3 cups all-purpose flour
    (plus a little extra if
    necessary)

4 eggs

2 egg yolks

5 tablespoons granulated
    sugar

1/2 teaspoon salt

9 ounces unsalted butter, at
    room temperature

Makes 2 pounds 4 ounces

Buttery, eggy, yeasty brioche dough is frequently used for making breads and savory dishes, but it also makes wonderful, homey desserts like Sticky Buns and Prune Tart with Brioche Crust (recipes follow). It's true that making a yeast dough is time-consuming, but you can maximize your efforts by freezing the extra brioche, formed into the shape you want, to bake on another occasion.

Brioche is made over a two-day period. The dough is made the first day and allowed to rise, then punched down and refrigerated overnight. The next day it is shaped, allowed to rise again, and baked.

Brioche should rise at about 78 degrees. Because of its high butter content and the relatively large amount of yeast in the dough, it's best not to make it in very hot weather; if the butter is too soft, it can make the dough greasy, and if the dough rises too fast, it gets a sour taste.

MAKING THE SPONGE

Place the yeast in the bowl of an electric mixer. (Break up cake yeast with your fingers.) In a small saucepan, heat the milk until tepid. The milk should be about 110 degrees, not so warm that you cannot hold your fingers in it comfortably. Pour milk onto the yeast and stir together with your fingertips to combine. Add 3/4 cup of the flour and stir again. The mixture will form a sticky dough, called the "sponge."

Pour the rest of the flour over the sponge, but do not mix it in. Cover the bowl loosely with a cloth and let stand in a warm place for 45 minutes, until the sponge begins to cause the top of the flour to crack in a kind of earthquake effect. (If the sponge doesn't bubble up, the yeast is dead and cannot be used. Discard and begin again with new yeast.)

MAKING THE DOUGH

Using the dough hook of an electric mixer, beat the flour and sponge at low speed to mix. Add the eggs, egg yolks, sugar, and salt. Continue to mix at medium-high speed until the dough is very elastic and wraps around the dough hook, about 15 minutes. You may have to help the dough come together by adding 1–2 tablespoons more flour during the mixing. Scrape the dough off the sides of the bowl as necessary. It will wrap itself in a ball around the dough hook and make a slapping sound when it has been kneaded enough. Work the dough the entire 15 minutes to develop the gluten in the flour.

Briefly knead the butter by hand on the work surface to soften it and smooth out any lumps. (Do not handle it to the point of greasiness.) With the mixer on slow speed, add the softened butter to the dough a few tablespoons at a time, waiting after each addition until the butter is absorbed. Continue mixing until the dough masses around the dough hook, about 5 minutes. The dough will be very shiny and elastic, but not oily, and will pull cleanly away from the sides of the bowl.

Cover the bowl with a large cloth or towel and let the dough rise in a warm place for 1½ to 2 hours, until triple in bulk. After dough has risen, punch it down with your hands.

Line a baking sheet with paper and sprinkle lightly with flour. Spread the dough flat on the baking sheet, dust the surface lightly with flour, and cover with paper or plastic wrap. Refrigerate overnight. Use as directed.

❖ The dough can be made in advance, but don't let it sit in the refrigerator for more than one day, as it will continue to rise. Better to freeze it for longer storage.

Sticky Buns

½ recipe Brioche Dough
(page 148)

6 ounces unsalted butter
(1½ sticks), cold but
pliable

Filling:

12 pitted prunes, preferably
soft, vacuum-packed type

7 Kadota figs

10 large dried apricots

½ cup walnuts (2 ounces),
coarsely chopped

½ cup black raisins or
currants

¼ cup granulated sugar

1 tablespoon cinnamon

To Prepare Pans:

10 tablespoons unsalted
butter

½ cup brown sugar

2 egg yolks, lightly beaten

**Makes two 8-inch round
pans of buns, each
serving 9**

Yeasty cinnamon pinwheel buns with sticky brown-sugar tops are filled with dried figs, apricots, prunes, raisins, and walnuts. Serve warm with a bowl of crème fraîche or whipped cream on the side.

INCORPORATING THE BUTTER INTO THE DOUGH (OPTIONAL)

The brioche dough will make excellent Sticky Buns just as it comes from the recipe on page 148. If you've got time to incorporate more butter into the dough, however, it will add flakiness and makes the buns extra buttery.

Place the 6 ounces of cold butter on the work surface and pound it with a rolling pin until it begins to soften. Then knead it with your fingers until it is smooth and pliable. Work quickly so that the butter doesn't melt. Form it into a ½-inch-thick rectangle that measures 5 x 8 inches.

Working as quickly as possible, roll out the brioche dough straight from the refrigerator on a lightly floured surface to a rectangle 16 x 8 inches. Handle the dough as little as possible, because when the heat of your hands warms the yeast it will start to rise and the dough will be more difficult to work with. Place the butter rectangle in the center, the 5-inch dimension lining up with the 8-inch width of the dough. Enclose the butter in dough by folding the bottom edge of the dough up and the top edge down, to meet in the middle. Fold both sides of the dough in to meet in the middle.

Using a rolling pin, press 4–5 horizontal ridges in the dough envelope at intervals across the surface, to anchor the butter in position as the dough is rolled out. Place the rolling pin in each ridge and roll back and forth a little to widen it, then, starting at the bottom, roll the dough away from you into a 16 x 8-inch rectangle. As you roll, keep reforming the rectangular shape with your hands. (See Puff Pastry, page 175, for more rolling instructions, but there is no need to handle the dough as carefully—yeast dough is more sturdy.)

Fold the bottom third of the dough up and the top third down to cover, brushing all excess flour off the dough with a pastry brush. Turn the dough so the open side of the fold is to your right. Press ridges in the dough again with the rolling pin, roll out to a 16 x 8-inch rectangle, fold in thirds, brushing off the flour, and refrigerate for at least 30 minutes. (This dough needs only two "turns.") Let dough rest 1½ to 2 hours.

PREPARING THE FILLING

Cut the prunes, figs, and apricots lengthwise into quarters. Toss together with the walnuts, raisins, sugar, and cinnamon; set aside.

PREPARING THE PANS

Using your fingers, press 5 tablespoons cold butter evenly into the bottom of each of two 8-inch round layer cake pans. Press ¼ cup brown sugar on top of the butter in each pan, distributing it evenly. Refrigerate.

ASSEMBLING THE STICKY BUNS

Divide dough in half. Refrigerate one half and roll the other into a rectangle ¼ inch thick. If the butter begins to crack under the surface of the dough, let the dough sit at room temperature for a few minutes to warm up. Trim to measure 16 x 10 inches. Brush the entire surface with beaten egg yolk.

Place the dough so that the long side of the rectangle is parallel with the bottom edge of the work surface. Sprinkle half the filling mixture on the bottom 7 inches of the dough, covering it fairly thick but leaving the top 3 inches without fruit. Roll the dough like a jelly roll from the bottom up. The roll should stick together securely. Place roll on a baking sheet and freeze or chill 30 minutes to 1 hour until firm. Repeat with the second batch of dough. With a sharp knife, evenly trim the ends of the roll.

Working quickly, cut the roll into 9 slices about 1½ inches wide. (The slices may squish and lose their shape, but you will have a chance to reshape the pinwheels when you put them in the pan.)

Turn each slice over so that the pinwheel side is up, cup it in your hands to reshape it into a circle, and gently flatten the center. Decide which side looks better and place the pinwheel in the prepared pan with the better-looking side down. (When the buns are unmolded, the bottom will show.)

Place seven buns around the perimeter of the pan, leaving about ¾-inch space between them. If there isn't enough space, cup the buns tighter in your hands so that they are smaller. Place the remaining two buns in the center.

❖ The buns can be refrigerated or frozen at this point, and the last rising will take place as they thaw or warm to room temperature. If you plan to hold them longer than one day, they should be frozen. (Cold dough, of course, takes longer to rise.)

BAKING THE BUNS

Cover pans with a towel and let rise in a warm place for about 1 hour, or until the buns have expanded enough to touch each other. Preheat oven to 350 degrees and adjust oven rack to middle position.

Bake the buns for 50–60 minutes, until crisp and brown.

When pan is cool enough to handle, unmold by placing a flat heatproof serving platter (larger in diameter than the pan) on top of the cake pan and invert the buns onto the platter.

Prune Tart with Brioche Crust

Crust:
12 ounces Brioche Dough (page 148)

½ tablespoon unsalted butter, melted, to butter tart ring

1 egg yolk

1 tablespoon sugar

½ teaspoon cinnamon

Brioche dough blends beautifully with this prune and cream filling. Lovely served warm at breakfast or brunch. Use a 10-inch flan ring with 1-inch sides set on a heavy baking sheet.

ROLLING THE BRIOCHE DOUGH

Preheat oven to 350 degrees. Adjust rack to top third of oven.

Roll out the brioche dough immediately after removing it from the refrigerator. Work quickly, handling the dough as little as possible, because when the heat of your hands warms the yeast it will start to rise and the dough will be more difficult to work with.

On a lightly floured surface, roll the dough into an 11-inch round, large enough to overlap the edges of the flan ring. Fold the dough gently into quarters, and place the center corner of the folded dough in the center of the pan. Unfold and fit the pastry into the ring. Do not trim edges.

Filling:

3 egg yolks

¾ cup heavy cream

2 tablespoons prune-poaching liquid

¼ cup sour cream or crème fraîche

6 tablespoons granulated sugar

3 tablespoons flour, sifted

¼ teaspoon freshly grated nutmeg

15–25 Poached Prunes (page 157), depending on size

To Caramelize Top of Tart:

2 tablespoons granulated sugar

Makes one 10-inch tart

Refrigerate.

MAKING THE FILLING

Place all filling ingredients (except prunes) in a food processor or blender. Process until well combined.

(To mix by hand: In a large bowl, whisk together the egg yolks, cream, and poaching liquid. Mix in sour cream, sugar, flour, and nutmeg until the mixture is well combined and there are no lumps. Break up any lumps of flour with your fingers.)

❖ The filling can be made ahead up to this point and refrigerated. Bring it to room temperature before continuing.

ASSEMBLING AND BAKING THE TART

Remove the lined flan ring from the refrigerator. Pinch the dough against the sides of the flan ring to bring it back up to full height. Trim edges evenly.

Lightly whisk the egg yolk and brush it over the inside of the crust. In a small bowl, stir together the 1 tablespoon sugar and the cinnamon and sprinkle evenly over the inside of the crust. Arrange the prunes on the bottom of the crust in a starburst pattern, leaving about ½ inch between each one. Pour in the filling mixture to within ¼ inch from the top. Bake for 35 minutes, until the custard is set. Do not remove flan ring.

CARAMELIZING THE TART (OPTIONAL)

Preheat broiler. Sprinkle the surface of the tart evenly with the 2 tablespoons sugar and place under hot broiler, watching carefully, until sugar browns. Leave the tart under the broiler no longer than 1 minute or the custard filling will curdle. Cool. Slip a cardboard round underneath before removing the flan ring. Do not refrigerate.

Serve warm from the oven or at room temperature. Refrigerating this tart doesn't do it justice.

Caramel-Walnut Tart

½ tablespoon unsalted butter, melted

1½ pounds Sweet Pastry (page 84)

1 egg yolk

Walnut Filling:
1¾ cups heavy cream

7 ounces unsalted butter (1¾ sticks)

1 vanilla bean, optional

2½ cups sugar

2¼ cups water

1 tablespoon corn syrup

4 cups walnut halves (14 ounces)

Decoration:
1½ cups Bitter Chocolate Glaze (page 348)

Makes one 10-inch tart, serving 8–10

Walnuts suspended in chewy, buttery caramel, encased in sweet pastry and covered with a glistening coating of chocolate glaze—this richly flavored tart is a real crowd pleaser. Almost any Los Angeles chef who makes this dessert has to give credit to the late Jean Bertraneau, one of the city's culinary pioneers at L'Hermitage restaurant, who made this tart so popular.

Although the recipe is long, none of the steps is at all difficult.

Unlike some of the other tarts in this book, which can use a variety of different molds, this one can be made only in a 10 x ½-inch plain flan ring set on a flat baking sheet. If the baking sheet is not of high-quality heavy metal, it will warp or bend in the oven and all the filling will run out of the tart.

PREPARING THE TART SHELL

Brush the inside of a 10-inch round flan ring with melted butter. Place the ring on a paper-lined baking sheet. On a lightly floured surface, roll the sweet pastry into a ⅛–¼-inch-thick round at least 12 inches in diameter. Fold the pastry lightly in quarters, place the center corner in the center of the flan ring, and unfold, fitting pastry into the ring. With a sharp knife, trim edges even with flan ring. Roll out another ⅛–¼-inch-thick round of dough for the top of the tart, at least 11 inches in diameter. Set pastry round flat on wax paper. Chill lined ring and pastry round until firm, at least 30 minutes.

PREPARING THE WALNUT FILLING

In a small saucepan, heat the cream, butter, and vanilla bean together until butter melts. Keep warm.

In a deep, heavy, stainless steel saucepan (at least 2-quart capacity), heat the sugar, water, and corn syrup over high heat. When the water boils, it will throw sugar onto the sides of the pan. At that point, wash down the sides of the pan with a pastry brush, dipping into water as necessary to dissolve sugar. (Alternatively, place a lid on the pan for 30 seconds and the steam condensation will wash the sugar off the sides.)

Let sugar syrup simmer over medium-high heat, without stirring, until it is thick and slowly bubbling, 20–30 minutes (268 degrees on a candy thermometer). As soon as the syrup turns an even light amber color, remove from heat and immediately pour in the warm cream. Be very careful —the mixture will foam up and spatter. Add the walnuts. Stir with a wooden spoon to mix ingredients.

Let the caramel mixture simmer slowly over low heat until it is very thick and a deep mahogany color, 25–30 minutes. When the caramel is reduced enough, a spoon will leave an empty trail behind it when it is pulled across the bottom of the pan. Stir once or twice as the mixture reduces to keep the walnuts from sticking to the bottom of the pan, or if it seems to be caramelizing unevenly; if you stir too much, however, the mixture can crystallize and become grainy. Pour into a heatproof bowl and cool at room temperature. It will be satiny smooth when rubbed between your fingers and will taste and smell nutty and buttery.

After the mixture has cooled for about 10 minutes, test it every 5 minutes or so by putting a small amount on the end of your tongue and rubbing it against the roof of your mouth. It should be satiny smooth. If it starts to feel even a little bit grainy, pour it immediately into the tart shell. (Normally I don't pour the filling into the tart shell warm because more leaks out than usual during baking; the end result, however, is still delicious.)

If the butter in the caramel mixture should separate while cooling and the mixture looks oily, bring it back together again by stirring in two tablespoons of cold cream.

FILLING THE TART

Preheat oven to 400 degrees and adjust rack to middle position.

When the caramel mixture is barely warm to the touch (about 30 minutes), pour it into the lined flan ring, gently pushing it out toward the edges of the pastry with a wooden spoon or your fingers. Fill level with the top of the tart shell—there may be some left over. Be very careful not to tear or press through the dough.

Lightly beat the egg yolk. Brush egg yolk around the outside border of the pastry. Center the dough round on top of the tart, so that it overlaps equally all the way around. Lightly pat down around the edges. Holding a rolling pin at a 45-degree angle, roll around the rim of the flan ring to cut the pastry and seal the top to the bottom. Brush a 1-inch border of egg yolk along the top edge of the crust. With the tip of a sharp knife, cut eight ¼-inch-long slits through the pastry in a random pattern to allow steam to escape. (Do not cut slits in a straight line or the tart may crack later.)

Bake for 40–50 minutes, until pastry is a rich, uniform golden brown. It is perfectly normal for some filling to leak out of tart during baking. Leave the tart on the baking sheet until you are ready to glaze it. Cool at room temperature for about 1 hour, then refrigerate at least 1 more hour until completely cold.

UNMOLDING THE TART

The tart must be completely cool before it is unmolded.

Invert the tart onto a work surface or a cooling rack set on a baking sheet, using a broad metal spatula to gently loosen it if necessary. If the tart will not come off the baking sheet easily, warm it briefly in the oven for a few minutes and try again. Cool before continuing.

Remove the flan ring by holding the tart at a 45-degree angle to the work surface and tapping the ring very firmly and sharply all around with a blunt object, then lifting it off. If the ring is hard to remove, don't give up—it will definitely come off if you bang hard enough.

GLAZING AND DECORATING THE TART

The options for decorating this tart are many, and depend only on your time and inclination. It is beautiful simply covered with chocolate glaze, or you can pipe a chocolate spiderweb pattern (page 343) on top of the glaze. The top can be bordered with Candied Walnut Halves (page 355) and the sides covered with ground Praline, Nougatine, or crushed Sugared Almonds (pages 353-4).

(If you plan to pipe a chocolate spiderweb pattern on top, you must have the chocolate melted and ready in a paper cone before you glaze the tart. See "Piping chocolate decorations," page 342.)

In a heatproof bowl, warm the chocolate glaze over gently simmering water until it is just warm enough to be poured but not hot. Letting the tart rest flat on the palm of your hand, hold it over the bowl or the cooling rack to catch the drips of glaze. Ladle all the warm glaze onto the center of the top of tart. Tilt the tart in all directions so that glaze coats the entire top and sides in an even layer. Holding the tart at an angle, shake off excess glaze. It should be covered with a very thin, shiny layer. Pipe the chocolate spiderweb decoration immediately. Chill until glaze is set, 30 minutes.

Serve chilled (the caramel is marvelously chewy when cold). Keeps up to seven days in the refrigerator.

Poached Prunes

1 pound plump pitted dried
    prunes

2 cups Armagnac or Cognac

Zest of 1 large lemon, in
    long strands

1 vanilla bean, split and
    scraped

**Makes 1 pound poached
prunes**

These poached prunes have a milder taste of alcohol than the marinated ones, because the alcohol is burned off during cooking. They are delicious eaten warm in a bowl, with a few tablespoons of heavy cream poured over them. Choose plump, pitted prunes.

Put all ingredients into a heavy stainless steel saucepan, bring to a boil, reduce heat to low, and partially cover. Simmer until prunes are tender but not mushy or broken up, about 40 minutes. It may be necessary to add more alcohol if prunes are not tender and liquid is reducing too quickly. (If you're using soft, vacuum-packed dried prunes, they will poach in much less time than 40 minutes.) Let stand until cool. Pick out strands of lemon zest. These prunes will last in their poaching liquid for several months, tightly sealed, in the refrigerator.

Continental Classics

LINZER TORTES

Linzer Torte with Blackberry-Raspberry Filling
Linzer Torte with Apricot, Peach, or Nectarine Filling

CRÈMES BRÛLÉES

Individual Berry Tarts with Vanilla or Maple Crème Brûlée
Three-Flavor Glazed Creams
Ginger Crème Brûlée Tart

PUFF PASTRY DESSERTS

Puff Pastry
Raspberry-Caramel Napoleon
Creamy Lemon Terrine with Strawberries
Marzipan Cake in a Sweet Crust
Fig Napoleon
Warm Puff Pastry Baskets with Cream and Berries
Christmas Pudding
Apple Strudel

For many years a chef wasn't considered well trained unless he or she did an apprenticeship in a European restaurant kitchen. Although Continental training isn't as strict a requirement today, the best chefs still acknowledge that learning traditional techniques is an essential base for moving on to personal expression in the kitchen.

When I studied at the school near Paris run by the famed patissier Gaston Lenôtre, I learned the classical techniques and recipes that are the foundation of fine pastry making. Then, when I returned to the United States and took over the desserts at Spago, I began to experiment with what I'd learned, using my knowledge and experience to discover new directions.

One of my favorite creative exercises has always been updating traditional recipes and giving them a new twist. Marzipan Cake in Sweet Pastry takes a flavor that's been used for centuries and turns it into a creamy cake surrounded by crisp pastry. The two Linzer tortes are filled with intensely flavored fresh fruit purée rather than preserves. In some cases I've added new flavors to classic desserts, like ginger, mint, and orange to crème brûlée.

When you tamper with tradition, you can cause an uproar. I'm certainly not advocating abandoning the old style, but as a young chef, a woman, and an American, I'm declaring my independence from the past by offering my own interpretations of these classic desserts.

LINZER TORTES

"Reminds me of my grandmother," said Wolfgang Puck when he first tasted the next two tarts. I thought he meant that they just made him think about his childhood in Austria. After more than three years of working with him, though, I finally learned to interpret his comments. "Reminds me of my grandmother" meant that a dessert was just plain good, whether or not Granny had ever made anything like it.

A traditional Linzer torte is filled with preserves, but I like these fruit purées instead for their tart fruity flavors and attractive colors. Both purées include apples to thicken the filling; you don't need any other thickeners. Because the fruit is puréed, these are a good opportunity to use up overly ripe or less attractive fruit.

When making the dough, start with very cold butter so that it will beat up well without becoming greasy. The dough can be piped into the tart ring, or patted in with moistened fingers; if you use your hands, be careful not to make the dough too thick. When made correctly, the latticework on top of the purée will not spread out during baking.

Any leftover dough can be piped into cookie shapes, as directed for the piped cookies (page 66).

The tarts must be completely cool before being unmolded or the sides can collapse. Serve them at room temperature, perhaps topped with a scoop of Vanilla Bean Ice Cream. They will store overnight in the refrigerator.

Use a 10-inch flan ring with 1-inch sides set on a paper-lined, heavy baking sheet, or a 10-inch springform pan; a pastry bag fitted with a No. 3 plain tip (optional).

Linzer Torte with Blackberry-Raspberry Filling

Filling:

2½ pounds tart green apples

1 scant teaspoon whole black peppercorns

5 cups raspberries, fresh or frozen without syrup

5 cups blackberries, fresh or frozen without syrup

¾ cup granulated sugar

Crust:

Yolks of 3 hard-boiled eggs

¾ cup blanched almond meal

2¼ cups plus 2 tablespoons flour

2 tablespoons cinnamon

¾ pound unsalted butter (3 sticks) plus ½ tablespoon, melted, to butter tart ring

3 tablespoons grated or finely chopped lemon zest (2–3 lemons)

1 cup granulated sugar

2 teaspoons almond extract

Makes one 10-inch tart, serving 8–10

PREPARING THE FILLING

Halve and core apples and cut into ¼-inch slices. There should be about 7 cups. Crush the whole peppercorns lightly against the work surface with the bottom of a pan.

Place all filling ingredients in a large stainless steel or enamel saucepan. Bring mixture to a boil over high heat and then cook uncovered over low heat, barely simmering, for 1 hour, until the mixture is extremely thick. Stir occasionally; as the fruit reduces it may burn.

Cook until no liquid remains and the fruit almost sticks to the pan. Remove from heat, process in a food processor until smooth, and strain through a fine-mesh strainer. At this point the purée should measure 3 cups. If there is more, return mixture to the pan and cook to reduce further, stirring constantly. Spread the purée onto a paper-lined baking sheet or pour into a bowl and chill. When the purée is cool, it will be firm and a skin will form on top. If the purée is at all loose, return it to the pan and cook it down again until it thickens.

❖ The purée can be prepared and refrigerated up to three days ahead at this point.

PREPARING THE CRUST

Butter the flan ring and set on a baking sheet. Preheat oven to 350 degrees. Adjust oven rack to middle position.

Press hard-boiled egg yolks through a strainer; set aside. In a small bowl, toss together the almond meal, flour, and cinnamon; set aside.

Using the paddle attachment of an electric mixer, beat the butter on medium-high speed with lemon zest until it whitens and holds soft peaks, 10–12 minutes. Beat in the sugar and egg yolks until well mixed. Add almond extract. Beat flour mixture into butter and combine well, scraping down the sides of the bowl as necessary.

ASSEMBLING THE TART

Fill a large pastry bag (No. 3 plain tip) half full of dough. Pipe the dough into the bottom of the prepared pan, piping around the circumference of the pan first and then filling in with a spiral pattern, beginning in the center. Do not overlap the lines of dough. There is no need to make a

*Piping the dough
into the tart pan*

Piping the lattice top

perfect spiral—this is simply a neat method of getting some rather sticky dough into the pan. (If you prefer, you can pat the dough into the pan in a thin layer with moistened fingers.)

Moisten your index and middle fingers in a small bowl of water, shake off excess, and pat the dough with your fingers to make a smooth, solid, even layer no more than ¼ inch thick. Holding the pastry bag at an angle, pipe two rows of dough up the side of the ring, one above the other, making a wall no higher than 1 inch. Dip your fingers in water again and press the dough into the sides of the pan to smooth and even. The dough should be no more than ¼ inch thick. Patch any holes.

(Sometimes extra dough accumulates where the sides meet the bottom. If necessary, use your index finger to scoop out dough in these "corners" to keep a right angle, rather than allowing a thick, sloping corner to form.) There may be as much as ½–¾ cup dough left after piping the shell.

Pour the purée into the shell and smooth to even with the back of a spoon or an offset metal spatula. Pipe a lattice design (5 parallel lines crossed diagonally by 5 other evenly spaced lines) on top of purée with remaining dough. Chill until dough is firm, at least 1 hour.

❖ The tart can be made ahead to this point and refrigerated overnight before baking.

BAKING AND UNMOLDING THE TART

Preheat oven to 350 degrees. Adjust oven rack to middle position. Bake for 1 hour. When done, crust will be golden brown and start to shrink away slightly from sides of pan. The filling will be shiny and set but the tart will not be firm until it is cool. Cool completely, at least 1½–2 hours.

If you used a flan ring, separate the tart gently from the baking sheet by running a long-bladed metal spatula or serrated knife underneath it. Slip a cardboard round underneath. If necessary, run a knife around the inside edge of the flan ring to loosen, and carefully lift ring off. If you used a springform pan, run a knife around the inside edge of the pan and release the sides. Allow the tart to remain on the metal bottom of the springform pan.

Linzer Torte with Apricot, Peach, or Nectarine Filling

Filling:
1¼ pounds tart apples

1 pound fresh ripe peaches, apricots, nectarines, or a combination of all three

3 large oranges

3 large lemons

1 ounce fresh ginger root

1 cup apricot jam

1 cup dried apricots (5 ounces)

1 vanilla bean, split and scraped

Crust:
½ tablespoon unsalted butter, melted, to butter flan ring

1 cup hazelnuts (4 ounces)

1 cup granulated sugar in all

Yolks of 3 hard-boiled eggs

¾ cup blanched almond meal

2¼ cups plus 2 tablespoons flour

1 tablespoon ground ginger

¾ pound unsalted butter (3 sticks)

Use apricots, peaches, nectarines, or a combination of all three to fill this ginger and hazelnut crust. Serve warm or at room temperature with Vanilla Bean or Ginger Ice Cream.

PREPARING THE FILLING

Halve and core apples and cut into ¼-inch slices. There should be about 3½ cups.

Pit peaches, apricots, or nectarines and slice into sixths. Peel oranges and lemons, cut into quarters, and remove the seeds. Slice ginger root into ¼-inch rounds and tie in a square of cheesecloth.

Place all filling ingredients in a large (5-quart) stainless steel or enamel saucepan. Bring mixture to a boil over high heat and then cook uncovered over low heat, barely simmering, for 1 hour, until the mixture is extremely thick. Stir occasionally; as the fruit reduces it may burn.

Cook until no liquid remains and the fruit is almost sticking to the pan. Remove from heat; remove vanilla bean and ginger and discard. Process briefly in a food processor until smooth. Strain through a fine-mesh strainer. At this point the purée should measure 2½ cups. If there is more, return to the pan and cook over medium heat, stirring constantly, to reduce further.

Spread the purée on a paper-lined baking sheet or pour into a bowl and chill. When purée is cool, it will be firm, shiny, and bright orange, and a skin will form on top. If it is at all loose, return it to the pan and cook it down again until it thickens.

❖ The purée can be prepared and refrigerated up to three days ahead at this point.

PREPARING THE CRUST

Preheat oven to 325 degrees. Adjust oven rack to middle position. Spread hazelnuts on a baking sheet and toast for 8–10 minutes, until light brown. Cool. Rub in a clean dish towel to remove skins.

Meanwhile, butter the flan ring or springform pan.

In a food processor or blender, grind the hazelnuts with ⅓ cup of the sugar to the consistency of coarse meal; do not grind to a paste. Press the hard-boiled egg yolks

2 tablespoons grated or finely chopped orange zest (2 oranges)

2 teaspoons almond extract

Makes one 10-inch tart, serving 8–10

through a strainer; set aside. In a small bowl, toss together the almond meal, flour, ginger, and ground hazelnuts; set aside.

Using the paddle attachment of an electric mixer, beat butter on medium-high speed with orange zest until it whitens and holds soft peaks, 10–12 minutes. Beat in remaining ⅔ cup granulated sugar and egg yolks until well mixed. Add almond extract. Beat in flour mixture and combine well, scraping down the sides of the bowl as necessary.

Assemble, bake, and unmold the tart as directed for the Linzer Torte with Blackberry-Raspberry Filling, page 162.

CRÈMES BRÛLÉES

Crème brûlée, or "burnt cream," refers to a custard that is topped with a layer of caramelized sugar before serving. I've found it to be a very versatile dessert that takes well to a number of different treatments: poured over fresh fruit, molded in tart shells, or combined with cakes as in the Three-Flavor Glazed Creams.

Many crème brûlée recipes call for baking the custard in the oven in a bain marie, but I prefer making it on top of the stove because it gives me more control over how fast the custard is cooking.

Because it is a fragile custard that can easily curdle, it is best caramelized in a salamander or with a torch (see "Caramelizing a dessert," page 339). Unlike some tarts and other desserts, I've had little success caramelizing crèmes brûlées in a home broiler. The burnt sugar adds another dimension to the dessert, but the custard is delicious whether caramelized or not.

Individual Berry Tarts with Vanilla or Maple Crème Brûlée

1¼ pounds Sweet Pastry (page 84), or 1½ pounds Puff Pastry (page 175)

1 tablespoon unsalted butter, melted, to butter flan rings

Vanilla Crème Brulée:
7 egg yolks

6 tablespoons granulated sugar or 3 ounces chopped maple sugar

3 cups heavy cream

2 vanilla beans, split and scraped

2 tablespoons unsalted butter, for large tart only

3 cups mixed fresh berries (blueberries, blackberries, raspberries, wild strawberries, or sliced domestic strawberries)

½ cup granulated sugar, optional (to caramelize tarts)

Makes eight 4-inch tarts, or one 10-inch tart, serving 8–10

I haven't found anyone who doesn't like this combination: individual flaky tart shells filled with juicy fresh berries and creamy vanilla crème brûlée, glazed with crunchy caramelized sugar.

For the 10-inch tart, the recipe calls for adding some butter to the crème brûlée to make it set up more firmly for slicing. The individual tarts don't need the butter because they aren't sliced.

Use 4 x 1-inch flan rings, or a 10-inch flan ring.

LINING THE TART SHELLS WITH PASTRY AND BAKING

Brush flan rings with the melted butter, and place, not touching, on a paper-lined baking sheet; set aside.

On a lightly floured surface, roll the pastry to ⅛–¼-inch thickness. Using a small plate as a guide, cut eight 5-inch circles and place, not overlapping, on a paper-lined baking sheet. Chill at least 30 minutes. When pastry is well chilled, line the flan rings or tart shell and trim the excess with a sharp paring knife. You may need to hold each pastry circle in your hands for a moment to soften so that it will mold easily into the shell. Place on the paper-lined baking sheet and chill again until firm, at least 1 hour.

If the pastry has fallen in, readjust it in the rings. Puff pastry tends to shrink once it is cut out, so make sure you fit it all the way into the corners of the ring.

Preheat oven to 350 degrees.

Line the tart shells with paper and fill with pie weights. Bake for 25–30 minutes, until pastry is a uniform golden brown. Remove the weights and paper liners. Return any shells that are not completely cooked to the oven to dry out. Cool. (For the 10-inch tart, see "To blind bake," page 27.)

MAKING THE VANILLA CRÈME BRÛLÉE

In a large heatproof bowl set over gently simmering water, whisk the egg yolks and sugar vigorously until mixture thickens, forms a ribbon when the whisk is lifted, and resembles a thick hollandaise sauce. You may need to take the bowl off the heat briefly a couple of times if the mixture gets too hot and starts to cook too quickly around the edges of the bowl. Leave the bowl over the heat most of the time, however, because it is essential that the egg yolks be warmed through at this point.

Meanwhile. scald the cream with the vanilla beans. Slowly whisk into yolks. Cook over a pot of warm water for 40–45 minutes, stirring occasionally, until custard is slightly thickened. The heat must be very low—check the water from time to time to make sure it stays just below simmering. The custard should never be too hot to put your finger in comfortably.

The mixture is cooked when it is thick enough to heavily coat a finger dipped into it and not to drip off. Strain through a fine-mesh strainer. If you are making the 10-inch tart, cut the butter into small pieces and whisk in; set aside.

(When you dip your finger into the crème brûlée mixture, it should be smooth. If there are any white dots in it, showing curdling, remove the vanilla beans and process the mixture briefly in a food processor before continuing.)

ASSEMBLING THE TARTS

Arrange an even layer of berries on the bottom of the baked tart shells. Fill with crème brûlée. Refrigerate until set, at least 2 hours for small tarts and 3 hours for the large tart.

CARAMELIZING

Just before caramelizing, sprinkle the top of each individual tart evenly with 1 tablespoon sugar. (Use 2 tablespoons of sugar for the large tart.) Caramelize with a torch or under a salamander until sugar browns. Return to refrigerator for 15 minutes to harden the caramel topping and let the tarts set up again.

Serve on plates mirrored half-and-half with Raspberry or Strawberry Sauce and Vanilla Sauce.

VARIATION: Scatter berries in the bottom of individual soufflé dishes, cover with crème brûlée, and refrigerate for at least 1 hour before caramelizing.

Three-Flavor Glazed Creams

Cakes:

1 recipe Orange Cake (page 171)

1 recipe Chocolate Hazelnut Cake (page 172)

1 recipe Ginger Cake (page 173)

Orange Crème Brûlée:

7 egg yolks

5 tablespoons granulated sugar

3 cups heavy cream

7 tablespoons grated or finely chopped orange zest (7 oranges)

1 cup mandarine napoleon (tangerine) liqueur

1¾ cups orange juice (7–8 oranges)

1 cup lemon juice (6–8 lemons)

Of all the desserts we served at Chinois on Main, this one got the most attention. Tiny pottery Japanese sake cups, three to a serving, each contain a different flavor of crème brûlée. The creamy custard contrasts with a soft, chewy cake round hidden at the bottom of each cup.

There's no question that making all three flavors of the glazed creams is a time-consuming project, but this is a show-stopper at a party. (Preparation time can be cut down by making the cakes in advance and freezing them.) If you'd like to make one flavor only, I'd suggest the ginger, served in individual 3-inch soufflé dishes or custard cups with cake at the bottom.

For the special occasion, use 60 straight-sided 2½-ounce sake cups (available inexpensively in Oriental import shops).

THE BASIC METHOD FOR MAKING THE CRÈME BRÛLÉE

In a large heatproof bowl set over gently simmering water, whisk the egg yolks and sugar vigorously until the mixture thickens, forms a ribbon when the whisk is lifted, and resembles a hollandaise sauce. Take the bowl off the heat briefly or rotate it from time to time during this process if the mixture gets too hot and starts to cook too quickly around the edges of the bowl. Leave the bowl over the heat most of the time, however, because the egg yolks must be warmed through at this point.

Meanwhile, scald the cream. Slowly whisk into yolks. Cook over a pot of warm water for 40–45 minutes, stirring occasionally, until custard is slightly thickened. Check the water from time to time to be sure it stays just below simmering. The custard should never be too hot to put your finger in comfortably.

The mixture is cooked when it is thick enough to heavily coat a finger dipped into it and not to drip off. Strain through a fine-mesh strainer.

(When you dip your finger into the crème brûlée mixture, it should be smooth. If there are any white dots in it, showing curdling, process the mixture briefly in a food processor before continuing.)

Ginger Crème Brûlée:
7 egg yolks

*5 tablespoons granulated
    sugar*

3 cups heavy cream

8 ounces fresh ginger root

Mint Crème Brûlée:
7 egg yolks

*7 tablespoons granulated
    sugar*

3 cups heavy cream

*4 cups fresh mint leaves,
    removed from stems and
    loosely packed*

*2 tablespoons green crème de
    menthe*

Makes 20 servings

MAKING THE ORANGE CRÈME BRÛLÉE

Before cooking egg yolks, heat the cream with the orange zest to scalding. Remove from heat, cover, and let stand 30 minutes. Reheat cream to scalding and proceed with directions above.

While crème brûlée is cooking, combine the orange juice, lemon juice, and liqueur in a stainless steel saucepan. Boil until liquid is reduced to ½ cup, about 20 minutes. It will be thick, bubbly, and just starting to turn brown and caramelize. Pour it immediately into the hot crème brûlée and continue cooking until done.

MAKING THE GINGER CRÈME BRÛLÉE

Peel fresh ginger and slice into ¼-inch rounds. Put ginger in a saucepan with water to cover generously. Bring to a boil, boil 30 seconds, and drain well in a colander. In a stainless steel saucepan, scald the cream and blanched ginger, remove from heat, cover, and let stand 30 minutes. Reheat cream to scalding and proceed with the instructions above.

MAKING THE MINT CRÈME BRÛLÉE

Roughly chop the mint leaves; you should have about 2 cups. Scald the cream and mint leaves. Remove from heat, cover, and let stand 30 minutes. Strain through a fine-mesh strainer, pressing all the liquid from the mint leaves. (The mint is removed at this stage to keep the flavor from becoming too herbaceous.) Reheat cream to scalding and proceed with instructions above, adding the crème de menthe after the crème brûlée has been strained.

ASSEMBLING THE GLAZED CREAMS

If necessary, trim the cakes horizontally with a serrated knife to ⅜-inch thickness. The cake should not take up any more than one third of the sake cup. Using a round cookie cutter the same size as the sake cup, cut out 20 rounds of each cake and place them in the bottom of the cups. For easy handling, put the cups on baking sheets, keeping the different cake flavors separated. (Leftover cake can be frozen.)

Put the crèmes brûlées into measuring cups or pitchers with narrow pouring spouts. Pour the crèmes brûlées into the cups with the appropriate type of cake: ginger with ginger, orange with orange, mint with chocolate. If the cake round floats, the crème brûlée is too thin—pour it back into a heatproof bowl and cook over gently simmering water until it thickens. Refrigerate filled cups about 2 hours, until creams are firm on top and do not jiggle.

❖ The creams can be prepared up to this point and refrigerated for three days.

GLAZING THE CREAMS

Put as many filled sake cups as will fit under the salamander on a baking sheet. Or you may caramelize them individually with a torch. Sprinkle each cup with ½ tablespoon sugar. Broil, watching carefully, for 1–2 minutes, until the sugar caramelizes and browns. Continue with all cups. Refrigerate about 15 minutes to set up again, but no more than 30 minutes or the caramel will get soggy.

Orange Cake

To Prepare Pan:
2 tablespoons butter, melted

1 tablespoon flour for dusting the pan

Cake:
5 cups flour

2 teaspoons baking powder

6 ounces unsalted butter

6 tablespoons grated or finely chopped orange zest (6 oranges)

1 cup plus 2 tablespoons plus 2 teaspoons granulated sugar in all

¾ cup almond meal

1 cup orange juice (2–3 oranges)

¼ cup sour cream

8 egg whites

Makes one 12 x 17-inch sheet cake

Used in Three-Flavor Glazed Creams

The base for the Orange-Glazed Creams. Save the extra egg yolks from the cake to use for making the crème brûlée.

Preheat oven to 350 degrees. Adjust oven rack to middle position.

Brush a sheet pan with melted butter. Line the bottom with paper and butter again. Chill briefly to set, dust with flour, knock out excess, and set aside.

Sift together the flour and baking powder; set aside.

Using the paddle attachment of an electric mixer, beat the butter on medium speed with the orange zest until it whitens and holds soft peaks, 3–5 minutes. Beat in ¾ cup plus 2 tablespoons sugar and almond meal until well combined. Add the flour to the butter alternately with the orange juice, beginning and ending with flour. Beat in sour cream.

Using the whisk attachment of an electric mixer, beat the egg whites on low speed until frothy. Increase speed to medium and beat until soft peaks form. Increase speed to high and very gradually beat in ¼ cup sugar, until very stiff, glossy peaks form.

Whisk one third of the whites into the orange mixture to lighten the texture, then fold in the rest. Pour into the prepared sheet pan, filling no fuller than ½ inch from the top, and spread evenly with an offset metal spatula. Bake for 20–25 minutes, until the cake colors slightly and is springy to the touch.

To unmold, run a knife around the edges of the cake, sprinkle the top with 2 teaspoons granulated sugar, and invert onto a work surface. Peel off paper. Leftover cake freezes well.

Chocolate Hazelnut Cake

To Prepare Pan:

2 tablespoons unsalted butter, melted

Cocoa powder or flour for dusting the cake pan

1½ cups hazelnuts (6 ounces)

½ cup plus 1 tablespoon granulated sugar in all

10 ounces bittersweet chocolate

8 ounces unsalted butter (2 sticks)

6 eggs, separated

¼ cup whiskey

Makes one 12 x 17-inch sheet cake

Used in Three-Flavor Glazed Creams

A very fudgy, brownielike cake, used as the base for the Mint-Glazed Creams. Best if made the day before you need it to allow it to set up.

Brush a sheet pan with melted butter. Line the bottom with paper and butter again. Chill briefly to set, dust with flour or cocoa powder, knock out excess, and set aside.

Preheat oven to 350 degrees. Adjust oven rack to middle position.

Spread the hazelnuts on a baking sheet and toast for 8–10 minutes, until brown. Cool. Rub in a clean dish towel to remove skins. In a food processor, grind the nuts with ¼ cup of the sugar until they are the consistency of coarse cornmeal. Do not grind to a paste. Set aside.

Cut chocolate into 2-inch pieces. In a heatproof bowl, melt chocolate with butter over barely simmering water. (The water should not touch the bottom of the bowl or the chocolate will burn.) Turn off heat and let stand over warm water until ready to use.

Using the whisk attachment of an electric mixer, beat the egg yolks with 2 tablespoons of the sugar at high speed until the mixture is thick, pale yellow, and forms a ribbon when the beater is lifted from the bowl. Add chocolate mixture and beat on medium speed until the underside of the bowl is cool to the touch. Stir in nuts and whiskey.

Beat the egg whites on low speed until frothy. Increase speed to medium and beat until soft peaks form. Increase speed to high and very gradually beat in the remaining 3 tablespoons sugar, until very stiff, glossy peaks form.

Whisk one third of the whites into the chocolate mixture to lighten the texture, then fold in the rest. Pour into the prepared sheet pan, filling no fuller than ½ inch from the top, and spread evenly with an offset metal spatula. Bake for 35–40 minutes, until the cake pulls away from the sides of the pan. The crust will be set but the cake will still be slightly soft to the touch.

Cool in the pan and refrigerate overnight. Cut out the cake rounds before removing the cake from the pan. Left-over cake freezes well.

Ginger Cake

To Prepare Pan:
2 tablespoons unsalted butter, melted

Flour for dusting the pan

Cake:
2 cups flour

6 tablespoons powdered ginger

2 tablespoons cinnamon

½ teaspoon ground nutmeg

½ teaspoon ground cloves

6 ounces unsalted butter (1½ sticks)

½ cup dark brown sugar, firmly packed

4 egg yolks

1 cup molasses (preferably blackstrap)

1½ teaspoons baking soda

1 tablespoon boiling strong black coffee or boiling water

5 tablespoons sour cream

8 egg whites

¼ cup plus 2 teaspoons granulated sugar in all

Makes one 8-inch round or square cake, or one 12 x 17-inch sheet cake

Used in Three-Flavor Glazed Creams

A soft, spicy cake, like a tender gingerbread flavored with molasses and strong coffee. Baked as a sheet cake, it's the base for Ginger Crème Brûlée and Ginger Parfait. Baked in an 8-inch round or square cake pan (adjust the cooking time accordingly), it's delicious plain, served warm with sour cream or crème fraîche.

Preheat oven to 325 degrees. Adjust oven rack to middle position.

Brush a sheet or cake pan with melted butter and line with paper. Brush with butter again, chill briefly to set the butter, and dust with flour. Shake out excess flour and set aside. Sift together flour and spices and set aside. If any of the spices don't go through the strainer, toss them back into the flour.

Using the paddle attachment of an electric mixer, beat the butter on medium speed until it whitens and holds soft peaks, 3–5 minutes. Beat in brown sugar until combined. In a small bowl, stir together egg yolks and molasses. Beating at low speed, add dry ingredients and egg yolk mixture alternately, beginning and ending with dry ingredients. Just before adding the last portion of the dry ingredients, dissolve the baking soda in the coffee or water and beat in, then beat in the last of the dry ingredients. The mixture must remain thick. Beat in sour cream and set aside.

Using the whisk attachment of an electric mixer, beat the egg whites on low speed until frothy. Increase speed to medium and beat until soft peaks form. Increase speed to high and very gradually beat in ¼ cup granulated sugar, until very stiff, glossy peaks form. Whisk one third of the egg whites into the batter to lighten texture, then fold in the rest. Turn batter into the prepared pan, filling to within ½ inch from the top, and spread evenly with an offset metal spatula.

Bake for 30 minutes, until cake is lightly browned and springy to the touch. Cool. To remove from the sheet pan, sprinkle top of cake with 2 teaspoons sugar and invert onto a work surface. Peel off paper. Leftover cake freezes well.

Ginger Crème Brûlée Tart

*1 Ginger Pastry (page 85)
or Puff Pastry (page
175) tart shell, baked in
a 10-inch flan ring*

*½ tablespoon unsalted
butter, melted, to butter
flan ring*

*½ recipe Ginger Cake (page
173), baked in a round
cake pan*

*1 recipe Ginger Crème
Brûlée (page 169)*

*2 tablespoons unsalted
butter*

*2 tablespoons granulated
sugar*

**Makes one 10-inch tart,
serving 8–10**

Spicy, smooth Ginger Crème Brûlée makes a lovely tart, poured over a layer of Ginger Cake set in a baked tart shell.

Use a 10 x 1-inch flan ring.

Set the baked tart shell on a cardboard round, leaving the flan ring on.

When the ginger cake is cool, trim it horizontally with a serrated knife so that it is about ⅜ inch thick. Trim the edges if necessary so that it fits in the baked tart shell. Center the cake round in the tart shell. Set aside.

Make the ginger crème brûlée as directed. As soon as you remove the custard from the heat, whisk in the butter until completely incorporated. Strain into the prepared tart shell. Refrigerate until set, at least 2 hours.

Caramelize, if desired, with the granulated sugar, following the directions for Three-Flavor Glazed Creams (page 168).

PUFF PASTRY DESSERTS

Puff Pastry

1¼ cups all-purpose flour

5¼ cups pastry flour

1 tablespoon salt

6 ounces unsalted butter,
    very soft

1¾ cups water

1 pound 4 ounces unsalted
    butter, cold

Extra pastry flour for
    rolling out dough

Makes 4 pounds

Puff pastry is one of the most versatile and delicious staples of pastry making. Crisp, brown, and buttery, it provides the perfect contrast to creamy fillings and juicy fruits. In French, it's called *mille-feuille,* or "thousand-layer," because all the butter that's incorporated into the dough creates many thin, crisp layers when the pastry is baked and puffs up to 4–5 times its height.

Napoleons are perhaps the best-known puff pastry dessert. The two following napoleon recipes are unusual in that they use fresh fruit and untraditional flavors—Raspberry Caramel Napoleon and Fig Napoleon. The Creamy Lemon Terrine with Fresh Strawberries is a variation on the napoleon idea, combining tart lemon filling with crisp pastry layers. Warm puff pastry "baskets" filled with cream and berries are basically an easy napoleon.

Puff pastry is not difficult if you follow some simple instructions. Also, like any other pastry-making operation, the more you do it, the better you'll become. Read the entire recipe before you start.

If you're strapped for time, you can often buy puff pastry by the pound at a good local bakery. Make sure you get an all-butter pastry. Many frozen supermarket puff pastries are made with margarine or vegetable oil instead of butter, and the taste suffers.

The trimmings from rolled-out puff pastry are called *rognures.* They won't rise or as evenly as high as fresh puff pastry, which makes them perfect for recipes that call for a flaky dough but not a high rise. They also make good tart shells, to substitute for sweet pastry. Keep trimmings in the freezer until you've collected enough to use.

A butter with a low water content is essential for making a light puff pastry. Different brands of butter have different water contents, which can be determined by squeezing the butter in your hand to see if any drops of water ooze out. Working the butter briefly with your hands will remove some of the water.

MAKING THE DÉTREMPE

When making puff pastry, you start by making a *détrempe* (dough base) of flour, water, and butter, into which you later incorporate more butter by rolling, folding, and turning the dough. The détrempe must be made at least the night before you plan to incorporate the butter, so that the gluten (protein) in the flour will relax completely and the dough will be tender and easy to roll.

Work in a cool kitchen and roll the dough on a cold surface. A marble slab that has been cooled in the refrigerator is ideal, but you can also ice your work surface by placing ice packs or even frozen foods directly on it. The work surface should be low enough that you can get some leverage when you roll out the dough.

Sift the flours and salt together into a large bowl. Cut the 6 ounces soft butter into ½-inch cubes and toss with the flour until the cubes are coated. Crumble the butter into the flour by rubbing your thumbs and fingers together, lifting the pieces and letting them fall back down again. Continue until the mixture resembles coarse cornmeal.

Make a well in the center of the mixture and pour in all the water. Draw the flour into the water little by little, mixing with the cupped fingers of your hand. The dough should be fairly sticky. If there is flour that has still not been incorporated, drip a bit more water onto the flour and stir together.

The détrempe is best made by hand, but you can use a food processor or electric mixer. In a food processor, using the metal blade, or in an electric mixer using the paddle attachment, combine flour, salt, and cubed butter and process until a coarse meal is formed. With the motor running, pour in the water in a thin stream until the mixture comes together in a ball. Turn off the machine immediately as soon as the dough comes together or it will become too elastic.

Turn the dough out onto a lightly floured surface and knead gently a few times, tucking the edges under the center, until it forms a smooth ball. With a serrated knife, make six deep slits in the dough, crossed like a tic-tac-toe board. Wrap airtight in plastic wrap and refrigerate overnight.

INCORPORATING THE BUTTER

Remove the détrempe from the refrigerator and let it sit for at least 2 hours, depending on the weather, until it is room temperature and very soft but still holds its shape. (During the winter, I let the détrempe sit out overnight rather than refrigerating it.)

To incorporate the butter properly, the consistency of the détrempe and the butter must be more or less equal. If the butter is very cold and hard, it will crack through the softened dough and seep out. If the butter is too soft, it will ooze from between the layers of dough.

Enclosing the butter

Place 1 pound 4 ounces of butter on the work surface and pound it with a rolling pin until it begins to soften. Then knead it with your fingertips until it is smooth, pliable, and about the same consistency as the détrempe. Don't handle it with the palms of your hands or it will begin to melt and become oily. Form into a 6 x 10-inch rectangle with your hands and set aside.

On a lightly floured surface, roll the dough into a rough rectangle about 16 x 8 inches. Lift and reposition the dough frequently while rolling to keep it from sticking to the work surface, and sprinkle more flour underneath it if necessary.

Place the butter in the center of the rectangle and completely enclose it in the dough by folding the bottom up, the top down, and the two sides in to meet in the middle. The edges of the dough may overlap slightly where they meet but the important thing is that the butter be completely enclosed. Stretch the dough a bit, if necessary, to cover the butter. Press the sides with your hands to reshape the dough into a rectangle.

Marking the dough with ridges

With the rolling pin, press 4 or 5 horizontal ridges down into the dough-butter package. Keeping the work surface and the rolling pin well-dusted with flour, place the rolling pin into the ridge farthest away from you and begin to roll back and forth, widening the ridge. Place the rolling pin in each successive ridge and move it back and forth until the ridges have doubled in width. Press equally in all the ridges. This process anchors the butter and starts to incorporate it.

When you reach the last ridge, continue rolling the dough away from you until it makes a rectangle of even thickness measuring about 8 x 24 inches. As you roll, keep stretching out the corners of the dough so they remain at right angles and don't round out. The dough should at no time be wider than 8 inches. If it starts to widen out as you roll, push in the sides with your hands to keep it in shape.

Rolling out the dough

Each time the dough is rolled out, it should be a homogenous, pale color; you should not be able to see any chunks of butter through it. If some butter does break through, stop rolling in that area, flour it well, and let the dough sit for a few minutes so that the butter can soften before you continue. On the other hand, if the butter is oozing out of the dough as you try to roll it, wrap the dough in plastic wrap, put the whole thing in the refrigerator, and let the butter firm up.

GIVING THE DOUGH "TURNS"

After the butter is first incorporated into the dough, each time you roll out the dough and fold it the process is called a "turn." Puff pastry needs five turns so that it will rise to its full height when baked. To remind yourself how many turns the pastry has had, mark the dough by pressing the correct number of indentations into it with your finger.

Never do more than two turns one after the other without chilling the dough and letting it relax for 30 minutes or so, or it will become elastic and hard to roll out. Ideally, the dough should not be given more than four turns in one day.

Folding the dough in thirds

Fold the dough rectangle into thirds, starting by folding the bottom third up to the center. Use a pastry brush to brush off excess flour from the bottom of the dough as you fold it. Fold down the top and brush off flour. Turn the dough so that the open flap of pastry is on your right. You have just made the first turn.

Make ridges in the dough again and roll it out to 8 x 24 inches as directed above. Fold in thirds again, brushing off excess flour. Press two indentations in the top of the dough to remind yourself that you have made two turns. Wrap tight in plastic wrap and refrigerate for at least 1½ hours, until thoroughly cold.

Remove dough from refrigerator and let it sit at room temperature for 15–30 minutes, until it is roughly the same temperature and pliability it was when you incorporated the butter. Give the dough two more turns by repeating the rolling and folding process twice more. When both turns are finished, mark the dough with four indentations, signifying four turns in all.

USING THE PUFF PASTRY

Wrap the dough in plastic wrap and refrigerate or freeze until ready to use, at least 1½ hours. For the dough to rise to its full potential, give it one more turn, for a total of five, before using. After the fifth turn, it is not necessary to chill the dough again before rolling it into the desired shape.

(If you are using fresh puff pastry in a recipe that calls for trimmings, give the dough four turns only.)

Don't store puff pastry more than five days in the refrigerator or it will begin to spot and turn gray. It will keep perfectly in the freezer for up to three months. After freezing or refrigerating, always let the dough sit at room temperature to warm to a pliable consistency before rolling.

Raspberry-Caramel Napoleon

Pastry:

1½ pounds Puff Pastry, fresh or trimmings (page 175)

2 tablespoons granulated sugar

2 tablespoons raspberry jam

Top Decoration:

1 ounce bittersweet chocolate

1 cup plus 3 tablespoons powdered sugar

1 egg white

½ teaspoon lemon juice

1½ pints fresh raspberries

Caramel-Orange Cream:

1¼ cups heavy cream

2½ teaspoons granulated gelatin

2 tablespoons orange liqueur

½ cup orange juice (2–3 oranges)

1 cup Vanilla Pastry Cream (page 283)

2 tablespoons granulated sugar

Makes 1 large napoleon, serving 10–12

This and the two following desserts are all constructed in more or less the same way: puff pastry is rolled out into a rectangle and baked as a flat sheet in a 12 x 17-inch sheet pan, then cut into pieces after baking and assembled into the dessert. You can use fresh puff pastry or trimmings, which rise less high, an advantage for these desserts. To keep the pastry flat and even as it bakes, place a large rectangular cooling rack upside-down (feet upward) directly on the unbaked pastry, and then bake as directed.

All the fillings have just a touch of gelatin in them, enough to make them set but not so much that they become rubbery.

BAKING THE PUFF PASTRY

Preheat oven to 400 degrees and adjust rack to upper third of oven. Line a 12 x 17-inch baking sheet with paper.

On a lightly floured surface, roll the puff pastry into a ⅛-inch-thick rectangle that measures 14 x 20 inches. Roll pastry onto the rolling pin and unroll onto the paper-lined pan, allowing the pastry to drape over the edges. Chill until firm, about 30 minutes. When the pastry is firm, trim it with a sharp knife along the inside perimeter of the pan.

❖ After trimming, there will be about 8 ounces of pastry left, which can be frozen for another use.

Prick the surface of the pastry all over with the tines of a fork and sprinkle evenly with 2 tablespoons granulated sugar. (If you are using a cooling rack, set it directly on top of the pastry.)

Bake for 20–30 minutes, until the layers of dough are crisp and brown all the way through. The sugar will melt and the pastry will look shiny in places. Cool. (Remove cooling rack.)

CUTTING THE PASTRY

(If you have not used a cooling rack and the pastry has risen unevenly or is more than ⅜ inch thick, trim it horizontally so that it is an even ⅜ inch thick.)

Cut pastry with a serrated knife into three long rectangles, 3½ inches wide by 15 inches long. Save all the pastry scraps to use later. Carefully turn over all three rectangles and set aside the one with the smoothest bottom to use for the top of the napoleon.

Place one of the remaining pastry rectangles, smooth side down, on a long, flat serving platter or a foil-covered cardboard rectangle. Spread on the raspberry jam in an even layer. Set aside.

DECORATING THE TOP (OPTIONAL)

❖ For a simpler way of decorating the top, see Fig Napoleon (page 188).

In a small bowl set over simmering water, melt the chocolate. Put the chocolate into a paper cone; set aside in a warm place. (See "Piping chocolate decorations," page 342.)

Sift powdered sugar through a strainer into a bowl. Whisk in egg white and lemon juice until smooth. When lifted, the mixture should fall off the whisk in a slow stream.

Place the rectangle you chose for the top of the napoleon on a cooling rack flat side up. Pour the sugar mixture down the length of the pastry and spread evenly with a long-bladed metal spatula. (Sweep the spatula only once over the pastry—if you go back and forth over the top you will pick up pastry crumbs.) Allow the excess to drip over the sides.

Pipe chocolate across the rectangle in thin horizontal lines about 1 inch apart. Pull the tip of a sharp knife through the warm chocolate toward you along the length of the pastry, making three vertical lines, equally spaced across the 3½-inch width. Turn pastry around and make three parallel lines through the chocolate, in between the first lines. Place a border of raspberries in a rectangle around the pastry top, ½ inch from the edge and about 1 inch apart (using about 22 raspberries). Refrigerate to set.

MAKING THE CARAMEL-ORANGE FILLING

Using the whisk attachment of an electric mixer, beat the heavy cream on low speed until it thickens enough not to spatter. Increase speed to medium-high and beat until thick and mousselike. Remove from mixer. Whisk a few times by hand until soft peaks form. Refrigerate.

Place the gelatin in the bottom of a large heatproof bowl and pour on the orange liqueur and orange juice. If all the gelatin granules do not absorb the liquid, or if there are any lumps of gelatin, sprinkle on a bit more juice (or water) until all the granules have absorbed the gelatin evenly. Heat briefly over gently simmering water, without stirring, until the gelatin dissolves. Turn off heat and keep warm.

In a small saucepan, heat the pastry cream to boiling, whisking constantly; set aside.

In a small heavy saucepan, melt the 2 tablespoons sugar over high heat, stirring constantly, until brown and caramelized. Immediately scrape into pastry cream and whisk to combine. Then, add the hot cream to the melted gelatin mixture and whisk together. (If the gelatin has hardened, warm it briefly to remelt before adding pastry cream.) Let cool to room temperature.

Whisk one third of the whipped cream into the caramel mixture to lighten the texture, then fold in the rest. Allow mixture to set to piping consistency. You can hasten the setting process by placing the filling over a large bowl of ice water and folding continuously until the mixture has set enough to form soft peaks when a bit is lifted with the spatula. Remove from ice water. Set aside ¾ cup of the caramel cream.

ASSEMBLING THE NAPOLEON

With a metal spatula or a pastry bag (No. 3 plain tip), spread or pipe half the remaining caramel cream on the pastry rectangle spread with raspberry jam. Smooth with a long-bladed spatula. Don't pipe too close to the outside edges of the pastry or the cream will ooze out when the napoleon is assembled. Scatter on half the remaining raspberries. Place the next pastry layer on top, press down gently, pipe on the other half of the caramel cream, and scatter on the remaining raspberries. Put on decorated top. With the reserved ¾ cup caramel cream, neatly frost the sides of the napoleon. Crush the reserved pastry trimmings in your hand and press them onto the sides. Refrigerate until set, at least 2 hours but no more than 8 hours. Trim ends with a serrated knife to expose layers.

Serve cold. Cut ½-inch slices and lay them flat on plates mirrored with Caramel Sauce, Raspberry Sauce, or Vanilla Sauce flavored with orange liqueur. Do not store overnight.

Creamy Lemon Terrine with Strawberries

1½ pounds Puff Pastry trimmings (page 175)

1½ tablespoons granulated sugar

1½ cups heavy cream

10–15 ripe strawberries

2 teaspoons granulated gelatin

¼ cup lemon juice (1–2 lemons)

1½ cups Lemon Curd (½ recipe, page 116)

2 tablespoons powdered sugar

Makes 10–12 servings

When this terrine is cut, each piece looks like a window frame of golden puff pastry filled with layers of tart pastel-yellow lemon curd and gleaming red strawberries. This is essentially a napoleon that has been molded into a slightly different shape.

Use one 10 x 4 x 3-inch slant-sided terrine mold.

Prepare a 10 x 14-inch foil-covered rectangle to unmold the cake onto.

Roll out and bake the puff pastry as directed in the recipe for Raspberry-Caramel Napoleon, page 180.

LINING THE TERRINE WITH PASTRY

You will be cutting the pastry into pieces to line the bottom, sides, and top of the terrine. You will need all the pastry to line it completely, so plan carefully with a ruler before you cut to get the maximum number of pieces from the pastry rectangle.

(If you have not used a cooling rack and the pastry has risen unevenly or is more than ⅜ inch thick, trim it horizontally so that it is an even ⅜ inch thick. If it is thicker, it will take up room in the pan needed for the filling.)

Using a serrated knife, cut a piece of pastry to fit the bottom of the mold and set in place, flat side touching the pan. Measure the long sides of the mold, taking into account the thickness of the pastry in the bottom. Cut pieces to fit the two long sides and set in place again, flat sides touching the pan. Cut a piece to fit the top of the mold and set aside. Save all the pastry scraps—they will fit together to make the middle layer. Set the mold aside.

MAKING THE FILLING

Using the whisk attachment of the electric mixer, beat the heavy cream on low speed until it thickens enough not to spatter. Increase speed to medium-high and beat until thick and mousselike. Remove from mixer. Whisk a few times by hand until soft peaks form. Refrigerate.

Stem and core the strawberries, cut in half, and set aside.

Place the gelatin in the bottom of a large heatproof bowl and pour on the lemon juice. If all the gelatin granules do not absorb the juice, or if there are any lumps of gelatin, dribble on a bit more juice (or water) until all the granules have absorbed the gelatin evenly. Heat briefly, without stirring, over gently simmering water until the gelatin dissolves. Turn off heat and keep warm.

Whisk the lemon curd into the gelatin until well mixed. Whisk one third of the whipped cream into the lemon mixture to lighten the texture, then fold in the rest of the whipped cream. Allow to set to piping consistency. You can hasten the process by placing the filling over a large bowl of ice water and folding continuously until the mixture has set enough to form soft peaks when a bit is lifted with the spatula. Remove from ice water.

ASSEMBLING THE TERRINE

Put about one fourth of the lemon mixture into the pastry bag (No. 3 plain tip) and pipe in an even layer into the bottom of the pastry-lined terrine. (The filling can also be spread with an offset spatula or the back of a spoon.) Arrange half the cut strawberries, cut side up, in an even layer and then pipe in another portion of lemon mixture to cover the strawberries. Using the reserved pastry scraps, piece together as complete a layer of pastry as possible over the lemon mixture. Pipe in another portion of the lemon mixture, arrange the remaining strawberries on top, and then finish with the rest of the lemon mixture. (There may be as much as ½ cup filling left over.) Top with reserved pastry, flat side facing up.

Chill until firm, at least 2 hours but no more than 8 hours. When firm, invert onto the cardboard rectangle and shake to release. Trim the ends with a serrated knife to expose the layers. Dust the top lightly with powdered sugar sifted through a sieve.

Serve cold. Cut ½-inch slices with a serrated knife and lay them flat on plates mirrored with Strawberry Sauce or half-and-half with Strawberry Sauce and Kiwi Sauce. Do not store overnight.

Marzipan Cake in a Sweet Crust

1 tablespoon unsalted
   butter, melted

12 ounces Sweet Pastry
   (page 84)

Cake Batter:
²/₃ cup flour

¼ cup almond meal

¾ teaspoon baking powder

14 ounces almond paste,
   well chilled

7 ounces unsalted butter
   (1¾ sticks)

4 tablespoons grated or
   finely chopped lemon zest
   (6 lemons)

¼ cup rum

½ teaspoon almond extract

5 eggs

6 ounces candied ginger, in
   all, optional

To Finish Cake:
2 tablespoons powdered
   sugar

5 ounces Puff Pastry
   trimmings (page 175),
   optional

1 egg, lightly beaten with a
   fork, optional

**Makes one 10-inch cake,
serving 12**

I love desserts with the contrasts built in—smooth and crisp, peppery and icy, acidic and creamy—which is why I wrapped this creamy, dense marzipan cake in a crunchy, cookielike crust. A slice of this cake, left over from the night before, with a good cup of morning coffee is my favorite.

The cake can be decorated with a simple dusting of powdered sugar, but there are two other possibilities: baking a puff pastry latticework on top, or folding candied ginger into the batter and pressing candied ginger on top of the cake halfway through cooking. The latticework is more for looks than for taste, but the ginger results in a crunchy, peppery-tasting topping that contrasts with the smoothness of the cake.

Use a 10-inch springform pan or a 10-inch entrement ring with 2½-inch sides. A pastry cutter for the latticework is a specialized piece of equipment you may want to buy.

LINING THE PAN WITH PASTRY

Brush the springform pan with butter; set aside. On a lightly floured surface, roll out sweet pastry into a ⅛–¼-inch-thick round at least 11 inches in diameter. Using the base of the springform pan as a guide, cut out a round of dough and place it in the bottom of the pan.

Gather the dough scraps together and roll into a long rectangle ⅛–¼ inch thick and about 3 inches wide. Cut two or three strips of dough long enough together to completely line the insides of the pan. Fit strips inside the sides of the pan so that the ends just meet, and press them together to seal. Trim dough overlapping the top of the pan with a sharp knife. Chill lined pan for at least 30 minutes.

MAKING THE CAKE

Preheat oven to 325 degrees. Adjust oven rack to middle of oven.

Sift the flour, almond meal, and baking powder together through a fine-mesh strainer into a large bowl; set aside. If any almond meal remains in the strainer, stir it back into the flour mixture. Grate the chilled almond paste through the largest holes of a grater, or chop into bits; set aside.

Using the paddle attachment of an electric mixer, beat

the butter on medium speed with the lemon zest until it whitens and holds soft peaks, 3–5 minutes. Beat in almond paste until well combined, about 5 minutes.

In a small bowl, lightly whisk together the rum, almond extract, and eggs. Add to butter mixture alternately with dry ingredients, beginning and ending with the dry ingredients. Scrape down the sides of the bowl as necessary. Continue beating for about 10 minutes, until batter is very light and fluffy. Pick up a spoonful of batter and knock the spoon lightly against the side of the bowl; if the batter falls off without sticking to the spoon, the mixture is ready.

If you are making the ginger variation, chop the 6 ounces of ginger into small pieces to make 1½ cups. Fold ½ cup of chopped ginger into the batter and set the rest aside.

Turn batter into chilled, pastry-lined springform pan. Batter should fill no more than two-thirds of the pan. Take a bit of batter on your fingertip and use it to seal the top of the pastry to the sides of the pan, so that they stay up during baking.

(For the caramelized ginger and latticework toppings, the cake will be removed from the oven briefly during baking to finish and then returned to the oven. See directions below before continuing.)

Bake at 325 degrees for 75–80 minutes, until the top is puffed, rounded, deep brown, and firm to a light touch. For this cake, better to cook it a little longer if you're unsure rather than underbake it.

Cool cake completely, about 2 hours, remove sides of pan, and dust lightly with powdered sugar.

FOR LATTICEWORK PASTRY TOPPING

Making the lattice top

While cake is baking, roll out puff pastry trimmings to ⅛-inch thickness on a lightly floured surface. Cut out a round of dough 12 inches in diameter. Chill until firm. With a sharp paring knife, make rows of 1-inch-long slits in the dough about ½ inch apart, staggering placement of the slits every row so that when the dough is stretched it will have a latticework or honeycomb effect. Be sure all the slits are parallel. Place on a baking sheet and stretch slightly and carefully to pull slits apart to achieve latticework effect. If pastry is too soft, chill it briefly on wax paper before stretching or it will sag. Chill again after stretching.

After the cake has baked for 40 minutes and is set, remove it from the oven and brush top with beaten egg. Lay puff pastry round on top of cake. It should overlap edges of pan slightly. With your thumb, press carefully around edge to cut off excess pastry and seal. Lightly brush top with beaten egg. Return cake to oven and bake 35–40 minutes more, until top is golden. Cool cake completely, about 2 hours, before removing sides of pan. Just before serving, dust with powdered sugar.

FOR CARAMELIZED GINGER TOPPING

After the cake has baked for 40 minutes and is set, remove it from the oven and brush the top with beaten egg. Press the remaining cup of chopped ginger onto the entire top and drizzle on the remaining egg to help the pieces stick. Return to oven and bake 35–40 minutes more. The ginger will harden and caramelize. Cool completely, about 2 hours, before removing the sides of the pan.

This cake tastes wonderful served with a bowl of the Plum Compote or the Apricot Blueberry Compote served on the side.

Serve at room temperature. Keeps refrigerated up to three days.

Fig Napoleon

Poached Figs:
6 ounces dried Kadota figs (8–10)

1½ cups sauvignon blanc or other dry white wine

2 large sprigs fresh thyme

2 tablespoons Pernod or other anise-flavored liqueur

1 vanilla bean, split and scraped

Pastry:
1½ pounds Puff Pastry, fresh or trimmings (page 175)

2 tablespoons granulated sugar

Fig Cream Filling:
1 cup heavy cream

¾ cup Vanilla Pastry Cream (page 283)

1 cup fig purée (made from the poached dried figs, see above)

2½ teaspoons granulated gelatin

3 tablespoons fig poaching liquid

16 ripe fresh figs, preferably Black Mission

¼ cup powdered sugar

Makes 1 large napoleon, serving 10–12

I love figs, and the idea occurred to me one day to combine them with some other late-September flavors from the Mediterranean—a grassy white wine, fresh thyme, a little Pernod. The resulting purée was heavenly, but it was too thick for a sauce, so it became the original component of this unusual napoleon. The seeds from the dried figs add an extra crunch.

POACHING THE FIGS

Preheat oven to 350 degrees.

In a stovetop-to-oven saucepan, combine the dried figs, wine, thyme, Pernod, and vanilla bean. Bring to a boil, cover, and bake for 20 minutes, until figs are completely tender. Measure out 3 tablespoons of poaching liquid and set aside. Remove thyme sprigs and vanilla bean and discard. Purée the contents of the pan in a food processor until smooth. There will be 1½ cups of thick purée. Chill.

Roll out and bake the puff pastry as directed in the recipe for Raspberry-Caramel Napoleon, page 180.

CUTTING THE PASTRY

(If you have not used a cooling rack and the pastry has risen unevenly or is more than ⅜ inch thick, trim it horizontally so that it is an even ⅜ inch thick.)

Cut pastry with a serrated knife into three long rectangles, 3½ inches wide by 15 inches long. Save all the pastry scraps to use later. Carefully turn over all three rectangles and set aside the one with the smoothest bottom to use for the top of the napoleon.

Place one of the remaining pastry rectangles, smooth side down, on a long, flat serving platter or a foil-covered cardboard rectangle. Spread about 4 tablespoons fig purée on the pastry in an even layer. Set aside.

MAKING THE FILLING

Using the whisk attachment of an electric mixer, beat the heavy cream on low speed until it thickens enough not to spatter. Increase speed to medium-high and beat until thick and mousselike. Remove from mixer. Whisk a few times by hand until soft peaks form. Refrigerate.

If the pastry cream is very cold and solid, whisk a few

times to smooth it out. Whisk together with the remaining fig purée until blended. Set aside.

Place the gelatin in the bottom of a large heatproof bowl and pour on the reserved poaching liquid. If all the gelatin granules do not absorb the liquid, or if there are any lumps of gelatin, sprinkle on a bit of Pernod (or water) until all the granules have absorbed the gelatin evenly. Heat briefly, without stirring, over gently simmering water until the gelatin dissolves. Turn off heat and keep warm.

Whisk the fig mixture into the gelatin. Whisk one third of the whipped cream into the fig mixture to lighten the texture, then fold the fig mixture into the rest of the whipped cream. Allow to set to piping consistency. You can hasten the process by placing the filling over a large bowl of ice water and folding continuously with a rubber spatula until the mixture has set enough to form soft peaks when a bit is lifted with the spatula. Remove from ice water. Set aside ¾ cup of the fig cream.

ASSEMBLING THE NAPOLEON

Slice the fresh figs vertically into 3–4 slices about ¼ inch thick. With a metal spatula or a pastry bag (No. 3 plain tip), spread or pipe half the remaining fig cream on the pastry rectangle spread with fig purée. Smooth with a long-bladed spatula. Don't pipe too close to the outside edges of the pastry or the cream will ooze out when the napoleon is assembled. Cover the cream with a single layer of sliced figs. Place the next pastry layer on top of the figs, press down gently, and repeat, covering with fig cream and the rest of the sliced figs. Top with the pastry layer you reserved to use on top, placed smooth side up. Press down gently.

With the reserved ¾ cup fig cream, neatly frost the sides of the napoleon. Crush the pastry trimmings in your hand and press them onto the sides. Refrigerate until set, at least 2 hours but no more than 8 hours. Trim the ends with a serrated knife to expose the layers.

DECORATING THE TOP (JUST BEFORE SERVING)

Cut five strips of paper 1¼ inches wide by 5 inches long. Lay them across the top layer of the napoleon on a diagonal, leaving 1¼-inch space between the strips. Sift powdered sugar evenly over the entire surface and then carefully remove the paper strips, lifting them straight up to avoid spilling the powdered sugar.

Serve cold. Cut ½-inch-thick slices and lay them flat on plates mirrored with Raspberry Sauce or Vanilla Sauce flavored with Pernod. Do not store overnight.

Warm Puff Pastry Baskets with Cream and Berries

14 ounces fresh Puff Pastry (page 175)

2 egg yolks, lightly beaten

1 cup heavy cream, or 2 cups Crème Fraîche (page 122)

2 tablespoons sour cream (with heavy cream only)

1 cup Caramel or Vanilla Sauce or Kiwi, Strawberry, Raspberry, or Blackberry Sauce, at room temperature

3 cups mixed fresh berries

Makes 6 individual tarts

This combination gives the impression of an easy napoleon—crisp rectangular baskets of puff pastry, warmed in the oven, filled with whipped cream and fresh berries, and served with caramel sauce, vanilla sauce, or a fresh fruit sauce.

Fresh puff pastry is needed for this recipe—trimmings left over from other projects will not rise high enough or easily enough to make a nice basket.

Preheat oven to 425 degrees. Adjust oven rack to the top third of the oven.

If the puff pastry is homemade, give it a fifth turn. Then, on a lightly floured surface, roll out the puff pastry into a ¼-inch-thick rectangle at least 12 x 6 inches. With a sharp knife, cut the pastry into rectangles measuring 3 x 4 inches. When cutting puff pastry, cut straight down with a sharp knife. Do not drag the knife through the dough.

Turn the rectangles over after cutting and place on a paper-lined baking sheet 1 inch apart. Chill until firm, about 30 minutes.

❖ At this point, the pastry can be refrigerated up to two days, or frozen for up to one month.

Just before baking, score a crisscross pattern on each pastry square, making shallow cuts 1/16 inch deep. Brush the tops with beaten egg yolk. Keep the yolk away from the edges of the pastry or you will seal them together and the pastry will not rise as high as possible.

Bake for 15–20 minutes, until the pastry has risen at least 1½ inches and is firm and a uniform golden brown.

When the pastry is done, break each rectangle horizontally more or less in half, so that you have a pastry basket and a top. Set the tops aside. With your fingers, remove the uncooked dough from the inside of each rectangle.

ASSEMBLING THE DESSERT

If the pastry is not fresh from the oven, it must be reheated. Just before serving, preheat oven to 425 degrees.

In an electric mixer, beat the heavy cream with the sour cream on low speed until thick enough to stop spattering. Increase speed to medium-high and beat until thick and mousselike. Remove from mixer and whisk a few times by hand to form soft peaks. Refrigerate. (Crème fraîche does not need to be beaten or prepared in any way.)

Place the pastry rectangles and tops on a baking sheet and reheat until crisp, 3–5 minutes.

Pool about 2 tablespoons Caramel Sauce, Vanilla Sauce, or fruit sauce on each dessert plate and top with the bottom half of one warm pastry basket. Using about ½ cup mixed berries for each serving, sprinkle a few berries in each basket. Fill with ¼–⅓ cup whipped cream or crème fraîche and arrange the rest of the berries on top of the cream. Scatter a few berries around the plate if desired. Place the pastry top on each basket and serve immediately.

For a more decorative look, you can pool Vanilla Sauce on half the plate and a fruit sauce on the other half.

VARIATION: Individual Tarts with Puff Pastry Trimmings. Puff pastry trimmings make nice individual tarts, topped with fresh strawberries, raspberries, or briefly poached blueberries (page 24). Roll out the trimmings ⅛ inch thick and cut into 5-inch rounds. Turn the pastry rounds over and lay out on a paper-lined baking sheet. Do not overlap. Chill. Prick with a fork, brush each with beaten egg yolk, and sprinkle evenly with about ½ teaspoon sugar. Bake at 425 degrees for 15–20 minutes, until golden brown. Cool. Just before serving, brush with a thin layer of currant jelly glaze (page 338) and arrange berries on top to cover the pastry.

(Puff pastry trimmings can also be used for the Open-Face Fruit Tarts, page 106.)

Christmas Pudding

The Fruit:

1½ cups (6 ounces) pecans, coarsely chopped

Candied peel of 1 lemon and 1 orange (page 77)

2 large, very ripe persimmons

1 cup black currants

1 cup golden raisins

1 cup dry sherry

4 ounces dried Kadota figs (6–8 figs)

2 ounces dried apricots (11 halves)

3 ounces dates (about 5 dates, preferably Medjool)

4 ounces dried prunes (about 12, preferably soft vacuum-packed)

1 cup Cognac or brandy (plus extra to flame the steamed puddings)

1 large apple, peeled, cored, and grated

The Batter:

1 cup flour

1 teaspoon baking soda

1 tablespoon cinnamon

1 teaspoon freshly grated nutmeg

1 tablespoon ground ginger

½ teaspoon ground cloves

1 cup dark brown sugar

½ teaspoon salt

A Christmas pudding is an ancient tradition in Britain—a mellow, fruity, black pudding, redolent with alcohol, steamed in the oven, and served flaming at Christmas dinner accompanied by a hard sauce made of butter, sugar, and Cognac. This dessert is so good that you shouldn't wait for Christmas, but serve it any time during cold weather. Don't let the long list of ingredients scare you off—the method itself is very simple.

Christmas pudding can be made up to a year in advance and allowed to season in the refrigerator—it's the ultimate make-ahead dessert.

The old-fashioned recipes call for suet to make the customary black color. Instead, I brown the butter and use dark-colored fruits to make a pudding that looks right but, to me, is much better tasting.

If the persimmons aren't totally soft and ripe, put them in the freezer overnight and they'll be usable in the morning. Dried fruit, by the way, should be soft rather than leathery.

The traditional shape for this dessert is a deep crockery "pudding basin," narrow at the bottom and wide at the top, but any ovenproof round bowl or pottery casserole can be used. You will also need a deep roasting pan to fill with water and set the bowls in during baking.

PREPARING THE FRUIT

Preheat oven to 325 degrees. Adjust the oven rack to the middle position. Spread the pecans on a baking sheet and toast for 6–8 minutes, until lightly browned. Cool. Mince candied lemon and orange peel; set aside. Scrape the soft persimmon pulp from the skin and mash it in a small bowl; set aside.

Place the currants and raisins in a small bowl. Gently heat the sherry to scalding and pour over. Slice the figs, apricots, dates, and prunes into fourths and toss together in a bowl. Gently heat the Cognac to scalding and pour over. If the alcohol ignites, blow it out. Allow the fruit to cool completely in the alcohol.

When the dried fruit is cool, mix together all the fruits, grated apple, pecans, candied peel, and alcohol; set aside.

1 cup dried white bread crumbs, made from stale bread or toasted fresh bread, not store-bought

4 eggs

1 cup buttermilk

½ cup molasses, preferably blackstrap

8 ounces unsalted butter (2 sticks)

1 vanilla bean, split and scraped

To Prepare Bowls:
2 tablespoons unsalted butter, melted

To Serve:
½ cup Cognac for each pudding

Hard Sauce (page 194)

Makes two 1-quart puddings, each serving 8

MAKING THE BATTER

Sift the flour with the baking soda, cinnamon, nutmeg, ginger, and cloves into a large bowl. If any of the spices remain in the sifter, toss them back into the flour. Combine with brown sugar, salt, and bread crumbs. In a small bowl, whisk together the eggs, buttermilk, and molasses. Pour onto the dry ingredients and whisk together thoroughly.

In a small saucepan, melt the butter and vanilla bean over high heat until brown and foamy. Continue heating until the bubbles subside and the butter is dark brown and smoking, and gives off a nutty aroma. Whisking constantly, pour the butter into the batter ingredients in a steady stream, and combine well. Remove vanilla bean and discard. Stir in the fruit and alcohol. The mixture will be sticky and wet.

STEAMING THE PUDDINGS

Preheat oven to 350 degrees. Adjust the oven rack to the middle position.

Brush two 1-quart bowls with melted butter and divide the pudding mixture evenly between them. Cover with a round of buttered wax paper. Put the bowls in a deep roasting pan. Pour boiling water into the pan one third of the way up the sides of the bowls. Very carefully (the water can slosh) place the roasting pan in the preheated oven and steam puddings for 3 hours. Add water to the roasting pan if necessary during cooking.

Unmold onto serving plates. Serve warm, flaming with Cognac or brandy, with a bowl of Hard Sauce on the side. If you are planning to store the puddings, don't unmold them. Cool in their bowls, cover tight with plastic, and refrigerate for up to one year. Steam for 1 hour before serving to reheat.

To flame the puddings: pour a few tablespoons of Cognac or brandy over the pudding and ignite with a match.

Hard Sauce

½ *pound unsalted butter,*
  very cold

1 *cup powdered sugar*

¾ *cup plus 2 tablespoons*
  Cognac or brandy

Enough for two 1-quart Christmas Puddings

Apple Strudel

4 *tart green apples*
  (1½ pounds)

¼ *cup lemon juice*
  (2 lemons)

2 *ounces unsalted butter*
  (½ stick)

¼ *cup granulated sugar*

¼ *cup Calvados or apple*
  brandy

¼ *cup heavy cream*

½ *pound phyllo dough*

4 *ounces clarified unsalted*
  butter (page 17)

½ *cup toasted bread crumbs*

1 *teaspoon cinnamon*

⅓ *cup currants or raisins*

⅓ *cup chopped walnuts*
  (about 1 ounce)

Makes 8 servings

Using the paddle attachment of an electric mixer, beat the butter on medium-high speed until it whitens and holds soft peaks, 3–5 minutes. Sift the powdered sugar through a fine-mesh sieve and beat into butter. Beat in the Cognac, 1 tablespoon at a time, until the mixture is very fluffy.

Hard Sauce must be served whipped-up and fluffy, so that it melts delicately onto the warm Christmas Pudding. If the sauce has been refrigerated or frozen, bring it back to room temperature or heat it gently over low heat, stirring constantly, until a few tablespoons of sauce have melted. Beat again in an electric mixer until fluffy and light. It freezes well.

In this recipe, the phyllo leaves are brushed with butter and then layered with caramelized apple slices, currants, walnuts, and cinnamon.

Store-bought bread crumbs taste like sawdust. Instead, cut white bread or French bread into cubes, toast it in the oven for 10–15 minutes (until thoroughly dried out but not brown), and crumble it in your hands to a fine meal.

Use a 9 x 3-inch loaf pan. (Pyrex is best because you can monitor the browning of the dough through the sides).

SAUTÉING THE APPLES

Peel, halve, and core the apples and slice ¼ inch thick. Toss with the lemon juice.

Depending on the size of your sauté pan, you may need to divide the apples into batches, as the mixture will not caramelize properly if they are crowded together. Divide the butter, sugar, cream, and Calvados as equally as possible for the batches.

Melt the butter and let it bubble slightly over medium-high heat. Add the apples and cook, stirring occasionally, until tender, 5–8 minutes. Sprinkle on the sugar and stir together with a wooden spoon. Reduce heat to medium. As the sugar melts and the juice is released from the apples, a lot of liquid will collect in the pan. Continue cooking, stirring every so often to avoid scorching, until the juice and sugar have reduced to a thick syrup and the apples are translucent and completely caramelized, but still firm to the touch, about 15–20 minutes. Remove from heat and add Calvados and ignite, letting the alcohol burn until the flames die down on their own. Add the cream and cook 3–5 minutes, until the syrup is reduced and thick. Pour the apples into a colander set over a bowl to drain. When the apples have drained, spread them out in a wide pan or on a baking sheet so that they cool rapidly and stop cooking. Sauté the remaining apples in the same manner. Toss all the apples together in a bowl and refrigerate until cold.

ASSEMBLING AND BAKING THE STRUDEL

Preheat oven to 350 degrees. Adjust oven rack to middle position.

When working with phyllo dough, the leaves must be kept damp or they will dry out and become brittle. Place the dough on a tray as soon as it is unwrapped and keep it covered at all times with a damp dish towel.

Unroll the phyllo dough until flat. Using a ruler or the bottom of the pan as a guide, cut a stack of phyllo leaves with a sharp knife so that they fit the loaf pan exactly.

Melt the clarified butter and brush the loaf pan evenly with butter. Lay 1 sheet of dough in the bottom of the pan, brush with a thin layer of butter, and sprinkle lightly with bread crumbs. Repeat, making 10 layers of dough and 9 layers of crumbs in all. (As you make the layers, remember that the clarified butter and bread crumbs have to last all the way through assembling the strudel.)

Arrange one third of the sautéed apple slices on top of the tenth layer, and sprinkle with a third of the cinnamon and a third of the currants or raisins and walnuts. Repeat the process twice more, ending with dough, so that you have 3 layers of apples, each topped with 10 layers of phyllo.

❖ The strudel can be assembled up to twenty-four hours in advance. Bake for 45 minutes, until it is crisp and golden brown. Cool slightly. Place a plate on top of the strudel and invert the strudel onto it. Place a second plate on top of the strudel and invert so the strudel is right side up.

Serve strudel warm, just out of the oven, with a bowl of whipped cream, crème fraîche, or vanilla or caramel ice cream on the side.

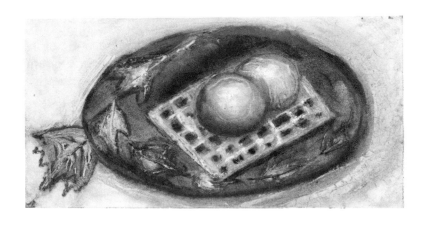

Ice Creams, Sherbets, and Their Accompaniments

ICE CREAM

Vanilla Bean Ice Cream
Honey-Almond Ice Cream
Caramel Ice Cream
Espresso Ice Cream
Maple Sugar Ice Cream
Maple Syrup Ice Cream
Ginger Ice Cream
Peppermint Tea Ice Cream
Eggnog Ice Cream
Chocolate–Jack Daniels Ice Cream
Chocolate-Mandarine Ice Cream
Chocolate-Mint Ice Cream
Milk Chocolate–Malt Ice Cream
Chocolate Truffle Ice Cream
White Chocolate–Mint Ice Cream

Banana-Honey Ice Cream
Bitter Orange Ice Cream
Rum-Raisin Ice Cream
Prune-Armagnac Ice Cream
Coconut-Nougatine Ice Cream
Black Truffle Ice Cream
Pistachio Ice Cream
Praline Ice Cream
Sesame Seed Ice Cream

SHERBETS

Concord Grape Sherbet
Plum Wine Sherbet
Tangerine Sherbet
Apricot Sherbet
Pink Grapefruit–Tequila Sherbet
Passion Fruit Sherbet
Strawberry Daiquiri Sherbet
Cassis Sherbet
Lemon-Thyme Sherbet
Mango-Coriander Sherbet
Lime-Mint Sherbet
Pink Grapefruit and Cassis Granité

ACCOMPANIMENTS

Ice Cream Sandwiches
Tulip Cups
Toffee
Oven-Baked Ice Cream Cones
Hot Fudge
Maple Dessert Waffles
Italian Ice Cream Cones
Homemade Chocolate Chips
Plum Compote

Ice Creams, Sherbets, and Their Accompaniments

Since making desserts is my profession, I'm frequently asked what my personal favorite is. People who expect me to name some exotic French creation are often surprised when I answer, "ice cream."

A good bowl of ice cream or sherbet fulfills all my requirements for a great dessert. It doesn't have to be too sweet, yet it has the intense, concentrated flavor that I love in desserts. It's creamy and rich, but it's not overwhelming because the portion size is flexible—you can have just a few spoonfuls or a giant scoop, whatever you like. The coolness adds another dimension to the flavor, intriguing in cold weather and so welcome on a hot day.

Ice creams and sherbets are simple to make. When you've made one, you've pretty much made them all. My recipes are all based on a simple crème anglaise (custard) flavored in various ways, and the sherbets are all made of flavored fruit purées or juices. They're the ideal made-in-advance dessert.

There's nothing wrong with an unadorned dish of ice cream or sherbet; add a few cookies at the side or fresh fruit, and you've got a great dessert. Two flavors of ice cream or sherbet can be better than one alone—try chocolate ice cream with espresso, pistachio, or coconut nougatine, for example, or vanilla ice cream with a fruit sherbet like cassis. Chunks of toffee or ground praline or nougatine can be sprinkled on a scoop, or a thin sheet of broken chocolate can be poked into the top (see "Making a chocolate band," page 350). With the exception of toasted unblanched almonds, I find that nuts tend to get soggy in ice cream, so I prefer to chop them and sprinkle them on top.

Because of their essential simplicity, ice creams and sherbets go beautifully with accompaniments. There's no age limit on enjoying a hot fudge sundae with thick homemade fudge, an ice cream sandwich, a crisp, freshly made ice cream cone filled with marvelously creamy ice cream. Serve one of these at a dinner party and watch your sophisticated guests' delight.

When ice cream isn't the star dessert, it makes a great supporting player, especially on top of a tart or fruit dessert. Serve Apple-Calvados Tarts crowned with a scoop of Caramel Ice Cream, for example, or Lime-Mint Sherbet on chilled melon balls marinated in plum wine.

Choosing an Ice Cream Machine: Ice cream and sherbet get their creamy consistency when air is churned into them. The air also increases their volume. Although some say that you can make ice cream without an ice cream machine (by part freezing and then whipping it), I have found that the best texture by far is created in a machine. Any machine, from the old-fashioned, hand-cranked kind to professional self-refrigerated models, will turn the ice cream so that it freezes evenly without forming ice crystals, but some do the job better than others.

A hand-cranked ice cream machine is relatively inexpensive, but it has to be packed with ice and rock salt, which can be a nuisance. The sort of machine that is placed in a home freezer is also inexpensive and effective, but will freeze only a small amount at a time.

If you're really an ice cream lover, you'll want to invest in one of the large, self-refrigerated machines that freezes ice creams and sherbets quickly and evenly, even hard-to-freeze flavors that contain alcohol. Although the machines cost several hundred dollars, they are easiest to use and create the most professional results. The recipes in this book were tested in my favorite, the Ugolini Mini-Gel, sold exclusively through the Williams-Sonoma chain.

Storing Ice Cream and Sherbet: Put an ice cream or sherbet in the freezer for at least two hours between churning and serving, to let it firm up a bit and the texture smooth out. If made more than six hours before serving, let it stand for a few minutes at room temperature or in the refrigerator for 15–30 minutes to regain its creamy texture and bring out the flavor.

The flavor of an ice cream or sherbet will dissipate after three or four days and it may start to taste like the freezer. To revive a faded ice cream or sherbet, let it melt to a liquid, correct the flavorings, and refreeze.

ICE CREAM

Once you taste homemade, naturally flavored ice cream, you'll be forever spoiled for the commercial variety. The flavors are so fresh and so immediate that they simply can't be compared to ice creams made with extracts or (even worse) artificial flavors.

In these recipes, the ice cream base is a simple crème anglaise: cream or milk is scalded and often infused (heated and allowed to steep) with flavorings like fresh mint, citrus zest, or vanilla. It is then mixed with egg yolks and sugar and cooked slowly over low heat to thicken. The base is strained and other flavorings like chocolate or alcohol are added. Let the base cool, then freeze it in an ice cream machine. Other additions, like chocolate chips, fudge swirls, crunchy toffee bits, or macerated fruit, are folded in at the very end of freezing. (See "Crème anglaise," page 20, for a complete explanation.)

The texture in an ice cream is made by balancing the amount of fat (milk, cream, egg yolks) with the sugar (and alcohol, if used). Too much sugar will keep an ice cream from freezing, but if too little is used, the ice cream will freeze rock-hard. Since alcohol doesn't freeze, enough must be added to give flavor but not so much that the ice cream will never harden.

Once you've tried the recipes my way and seen how they come out, you can improvise with the variables. More cream will make the ice cream richer, or you can reduce the fat by substituting milk, even nonfat, or cutting down on the egg yolks. You can also play with the flavorings, making the tastes sweeter or stronger, but remember that any change you make will affect the texture.

Because less air is whipped into homemade ice cream during the freezing process, and no gums or chemical stabilizers are added, it may look a bit rough as it comes out of the machine, but it will smooth out as it sits in the freezer for a few hours. The creamiest homemade ice creams are the chocolate flavors, because chocolate acts as a natural smoother.

Making the Ice Cream Base: When you make the ice cream base, beat the egg yolks and sugar by hand, never in an electric mixer. A mixer can make them so thick that they won't cook properly with the hot cream, and you may not be able to tell when the mixture is thickened.

Always taste the ice cream base before churning but after it has been chilled, and correct the flavoring. Things taste very different at room temperature than when cold.

Most of the ice creams (except the chocolate ones) will turn out more flavorful if the base is allowed to stand overnight in the refrigerator before churning. Standing lets the flavors mingle, and mellows any alcohol that's been added. The next day, taste the base, correct the flavorings to taste, and freeze. If an infused flavor is weak, you can gently reheat the base mixture, add the flavoring as directed in the recipe, and allow to infuse again.

Vanilla Bean Ice Cream

3 cups heavy cream
1 cup milk
5 vanilla beans, split and
    scraped
8 egg yolks
½ cup granulated sugar

Makes 1 to 1½ quarts

Once you've tasted a vanilla ice cream infused with the flavor of fresh, fragrant vanilla beans and speckled with their tiny black seeds, you'll never accept one made with vanilla extract again. Plump, pungent vanilla beans are essential for the taste of this ice cream.

It's lovely with fresh fruit or almost any fruit tart, or with a spoonful of Hot Fudge or warm Plum Compote on top.

In a large saucepan, scald the cream, milk, and vanilla beans. Remove from heat, cover, and let flavors infuse for 30 minutes. In a large bowl, beat together the egg yolks and sugar for a few minutes until the sugar has dissolved and the mixture is thick and pale yellow; set aside.

Reheat cream to scalding. Pour about one fourth of the hot cream into the egg yolks, whisking continuously. Return the mixture to the saucepan and whisk together with remaining cream. Cook over low heat, stirring constantly with the wooden spoon, until the mixture thickens and coats the back of the spoon. Strain through a fine-mesh strainer into a bowl and whisk a few times to release heat. Chill.

Freeze in an ice cream machine according to manufacturer's instructions.

VARIATION: For chocolate chip ice cream, add 1½ cups Homemade Chocolate Chips during the last minute of freezing. For fudge ripple, swirl in 1½ cups Hot Fudge by hand after freezing.

Honey-Almond Ice Cream

1½ cups whole almonds
    with skins (8 ounces)

3 cups heavy cream

1 cup milk

1 vanilla bean, split and
    scraped

8 egg yolks

3 tablespoons granulated
    sugar

6 tablespoons orange
    blossom or clover honey

Makes 1½ to 2 quarts

There's just enough honey in this ice cream to let you appreciate its characteristic sweetness and very pleasant aftertaste, but not enough to be cloying or overwhelming. For a delicate flavor, it's important to use a light honey like clover or orange blossom.

Preheat oven to 325 degrees. Spread the almonds on a baking sheet and toast until light brown, 8–10 minutes. Cool.

In a large saucepan, scald the cream, milk, and vanilla bean. Remove from heat, cover, and let the flavor infuse for 30 minutes. In a large bowl, beat the egg yolks with the sugar and honey for a few minutes until the sugar has dissolved; set aside.

After 30 minutes, reheat cream to scalding. Pour about one fourth of the hot cream into the egg yolks whisking continuously. Return to saucepan, and whisk together with the remaining cream. Cook over low heat, stirring constantly with a wooden spoon, until the mixture thickens enough to coat the back of the spoon. Strain through a fine-mesh strainer into a bowl. Whisk a few times to release heat. Chill.

Freeze in an ice cream machine according to manufacturer's instructions. Add toasted almonds during the last minute of freezing.

Caramel Ice Cream

8 egg yolks

2 cups heavy cream

2 cups milk

1 cup granulated sugar

1 vanilla bean, split and
    scraped

Makes 1½ to 2 quarts

The last thing this ice cream resembles is one of those sickly sweet "caramel ripple" concoctions—this is a suave, refined preparation, flavored and colored by caramelized sugar. Caramel Ice Cream is as versatile as Vanilla Bean Ice Cream, compatible with many different desserts.

The caramelized sugar must be very dark to sufficiently color and flavor this ice cream, but be careful not to burn it.

In a large bowl, whisk the egg yolks lightly to break them up. Set aside. In a large, heavy saucepan, scald the cream and milk. Keep warm over low heat.

In a small heavy saucepan or an unlined copper pan, heat the sugar and vanilla bean over medium heat until the sugar caramelizes, 5–8 minutes. Stir occasionally with a wooden spoon to ensure that the sugar colors evenly. Once one portion of the sugar begins to darken, toss it with the uncooked sugar. This will prevent the sugar from burning in one spot before the entire mixture has liquefied and turned a dark caramel color.

As soon as the mixture begins to smoke, set the bottom of the pan in a bowl of cold water to stop it from cooking and coloring further. Immediately begin whisking it into the warm cream, pouring it in in three or four batches. Be careful—the cream will spatter and bubble up. The caramel must be poured into the cream as quickly as possible or it will continue to cook and burn in the pan. When all the caramel has been whisked in, reheat the cream mixture, stirring constantly, until the caramel is completely incorporated.

Pour about one fourth of the hot cream into the egg yolks, whisking continuously. Return to the saucepan, and whisk together with remaining cream. Cook over low heat, stirring constantly with a wooden spoon, until the mixture thickens enough to coat the back of the spoon. Strain through a fine-mesh strainer into a bowl. Whisk a few times to release the heat. Chill.

Freeze in an ice cream machine according to manufacturer's instructions.

Espresso Ice Cream

1 cup decaffeinated espresso
coffee beans

3 cups heavy cream

1 cup milk

8 egg yolks

½ cup granulated sugar

2 tablespoons finely ground
fresh espresso beans

2 tablespoons coffee liqueur

Makes 1½ to 2 quarts

This espresso-flavored ice cream, speckled with bits of ground coffee, is very intense, a coffee lover's delight. Decaffeinated coffee beans are recommended because they are lower in acid than regular beans, and the resulting ice cream is smoother.

Crack and lightly crush the coffee beans by rolling lightly with a rolling pin or pressing with the bottom of a pan. Do not grind the coffee, because the fine grounds added at this point will discolor the ice cream.

In a large saucepan, scald the cream, milk, and coffee beans. Remove from heat, cover, and let flavor infuse for 30 minutes. Strain and discard coffee beans.

In a large bowl, beat together the egg yolks and sugar for a few minutes until the sugar has dissolved and the mixture is thick and pale yellow; set aside.

Reheat cream to scalding. Pour about one fourth of the hot cream into the egg yolks, whisking continuously. Return to the saucepan and whisk together with the remaining cream. Cook over low heat, stirring constantly with a wooden spoon, until the mixture thickens enough to coat the back of the spoon. Strain through a fine-mesh strainer into a bowl. Whisk a few times to release heat. Stir in ground espresso and coffee liqueur. Chill.

Freeze in an ice cream machine according to manufacturer's instructions.

VARIATION: Add 1½ cups Homemade Chocolate Chips or 1½ cups whole, unblanched, toasted almonds during the last minute of freezing. For fudge ripple, swirl in 1½ cups Hot Fudge by hand after freezing.

Maple Sugar Ice Cream

*1 cup pecans or walnuts,
    optional*

2 cups heavy cream

2 cups milk

*1 vanilla bean, split and
    scraped*

6 ounces maple sugar

8 egg yolks

Makes 1½ to 2 quarts

Maple has a distinctive, delicate sweetness that is absolutely wonderful in an ice cream. This and the following maple ice cream are flavored with different ingredients—maple sugar or maple syrup. Maple sugar, which can be difficult to find outside New England, is the color of dark brown sugar, very moist, and sold in solid lump form. (Don't confuse it with the maple sugar granules sold in health food stores.) Maple syrup is easier to find, but be sure to use pure maple syrup, not the common maple-flavored substitutes. Grade B or C maple syrup, if you can get it, is less expensive than grades A or AA, and has a stronger maple taste.

Toasted pecans or walnuts are an optional addition to either ice cream, but the nuts go so well with the maple flavor that they really add another dimension to the taste. Grinding the nuts in a Mouli grater creates the best texture. Otherwise, coarsely chop the nuts and sprinkle them on top of the ice cream when serving, rather than processing them in.

Preheat oven to 325 degrees. Spread pecans or walnuts on baking sheet and toast lightly, 8–10 minutes. When nuts are cool, grind by hand in a Mouli grater. Set aside.

In a large saucepan, scald the cream and milk with vanilla bean. Remove from heat, cover, and let flavor infuse for 30 minutes. Chop maple sugar into bite-size pieces; set aside.

In a mixing bowl, whisk the egg yolks lightly to break them up; set aside.

Reheat cream to scalding. Pour about one fourth of the hot cream into the egg yolks, whisking continuously. Return to saucepan and whisk together with remaining cream. Cook over low heat, stirring constantly with a wooden spoon, until the mixture thickens and coats the back of a spoon. Strain through a fine-mesh strainer and whisk a few times to release heat. Add the maple sugar pieces and stir, checking to make sure that all the sugar dissolves into the ice cream base. Chill. Stir in ground nuts.

Freeze in an ice cream machine according to the manufacturer's instructions.

VARIATION: 1 cup dark brown sugar can be substituted for maple sugar for a similar flavor.

Maple Syrup Ice Cream

1 cup pecans or walnuts,
    optional

3 cups heavy cream in all

2 cups milk

1 vanilla bean, split and
    scraped

2 cups pure maple syrup

8 egg yolks

Makes 1½ to 2 quarts

Preheat oven to 325 degrees. Spread pecans or walnuts on a baking sheet and toast lightly, 8–10 minutes. Cool and grind in a Mouli grater. Set aside.

In a large saucepan, scald 2 cups of the cream and the milk with the vanilla bean. Remove from heat, cover, and let flavor infuse for 30 minutes.

Place the maple syrup in a large saucepan, bring to a boil (it will boil up like cream), lower heat, and boil until it reduces to 1 cup. Let foam subside and pour into a measuring cup to measure.

In a large bowl, whisk the egg yolks lightly to break them up; set aside.

When the syrup has reduced, pour it into the cream mixture. Reheat to scalding. Pour about one fourth of the hot cream into the egg yolks, whisking continuously. Return mixture to saucepan and whisk together with remaining cream. Cook over low heat, stirring constantly with a wooden spoon, until the mixture thickens enough to coat the back of a spoon. Strain through a fine-mesh strainer and whisk a few times to release heat. Chill. Taste the ice cream base. Some maple syrups are sweeter than others, so you may want to add up to 1 cup more cream to counteract the sweetness. Stir in ground nuts.

Freeze in an ice cream machine according to manufacturer's instructions.

Ginger Ice Cream

3/4 pound fresh ginger root
1½ ounces candied ginger
2 cups heavy cream
2 cups milk
8 egg yolks
½ cup granulated sugar

Makes 1½ to 2 quarts

In an ice cream, ginger is paradoxical—hot and cool, spicy and smooth.

Peel ginger root with a vegetable peeler and slice into ¼-inch rounds. There should be about 2 cups. Blanch the ginger by placing it in a saucepan with water to cover, bringing it to a boil and boiling for 30 seconds. Drain well.

In a colander, rinse candied ginger well to remove sugar coating. Drain well, slice in half horizontally, and slice into ⅛-inch strips. Set aside.

In a large saucepan, scald the cream, milk, and blanched ginger root. Remove from heat, cover, and let flavor infuse for 1 hour. Strain; discard the ginger. Return cream to saucepan.

In a large bowl, beat the egg yolks with the sugar until sugar has dissolved and the mixture is thick and pale yellow; set aside.

Reheat cream to scalding. Pour about one fourth of the hot cream into the egg yolks, whisking continuously. Return to saucepan and whisk together with the remaining cream. Cook over low heat, stirring constantly with a wooden spoon, until the mixture thickens enough to coat the back of the spoon. Strain through a fine-mesh strainer into a bowl. Whisk a few times to release heat. Chill.

Freeze in an ice cream machine according to manufacturer's instructions. Add candied ginger during the last minute of freezing.

Make 6-inch round Sesame Seed Cookies (page 48) and roll them into free-form cone shapes. Fill each with a scoop of ice cream just before serving and set on a plate.

Peppermint Tea Ice Cream

2 cups heavy cream

2 cups milk

4 peppermint or spearmint
   tea bags

8 egg yolks

½ cup granulated sugar

½ cup peppermint schnapps
   or white crème de menthe

Makes 1½ to 2 quarts

The delicate, almost flowery taste of this uncommon ice cream is created by infusing the cream with peppermint or spearmint tea. The tea bags must be pure peppermint or spearmint "herb" tea, not black tea flavored with mint.

If you like your mint ice cream tinted green, substitute 2 tablespoons green crème de menthe for some of the white crème de menthe or peppermint schnapps.

In a large saucepan, scald the cream and milk with peppermint tea bags. Remove from heat, cover, and let flavor infuse for 1 hour. Strain; discard tea bags.

In a large bowl, beat together the egg yolks with the sugar until the sugar has dissolved and the mixture is thick and pale yellow; set aside.

Reheat cream to scalding. Pour about one fourth of the hot cream into the egg yolks, whisking continuously. Return to saucepan and whisk together with the remaining cream. Cook over low heat, stirring constantly with a wooden spoon, until the mixture thickens enough to coat the back of the spoon. Strain through a fine-mesh strainer. Whisk a few times to release heat. Stir in schnapps or crème de menthe. Chill.

Freeze in an ice cream machine according to manufacturer's instructions.

Eggnog Ice Cream

2 cups heavy cream

2 cups milk

1 scant teaspoon freshly grated nutmeg

1 vanilla bean, split and scraped

8 egg yolks

⅔ cups granulated sugar

¼ cup bourbon, preferably Wild Turkey (or less to taste)

¼ cup dark rum (or less to taste)

Makes 1½ to 2 quarts

Bourbon, rum, and the right proportion of nutmeg make this ice cream taste like a real eggnog. Excellent around Christmastime, of course. Make the ice cream base in advance and let the flavors mellow in the refrigerator overnight before freezing.

In a large saucepan, scald the cream, milk, nutmeg, and vanilla bean. Remove from heat, cover, and let flavors infuse for at least 30 minutes. In a large bowl, beat together the egg yolks and sugar for a few minutes until the sugar has dissolved and the mixture is thick and pale yellow; set aside.

Reheat cream to scalding. Pour about one fourth of the hot liquid into the egg yolks, whisking continuously. Return mixture to saucepan, and whisk together with the remaining cream. Cook over low heat, stirring constantly with a wooden spoon, until mixture thickens enough to coat the back of the spoon. Strain through a fine-mesh strainer into a bowl. Whisk a few times to release heat. Stir in bourbon and rum. Chill.

Freeze in an ice cream machine according to manufacturer's instructions.

Chocolate–Jack Daniels Ice Cream

10 ounces bittersweet
   chocolate

8 egg yolks

3 tablespoons granulated
   sugar

2 cups heavy cream

2 cups milk

6–8 tablespoons Jack
   Daniels whiskey (to taste)

Makes 1½ to 2 quarts

Chocolate and whiskey are a great grown-up combination —each flavor brings out the best qualities of the other.

Cut or break chocolate into 2-inch pieces. In a heatproof bowl, melt chocolate over gently simmering water. (The water should not touch the bottom of the bowl or the chocolate will burn.) Turn off heat and let stand over warm water until ready to use.

In a large bowl, beat the egg yolks with the sugar for a few minutes until the mixture is thick and pale yellow; set aside.

In a large saucepan, scald the cream and milk. Pour about one fourth of the hot cream into the egg yolks, whisking continuously. Return to saucepan, and whisk together with remaining cream. Cook over low heat, stirring constantly with a wooden spoon, until the mixture thickens enough to coat the back of the spoon. Strain through a fine-mesh strainer into a bowl. Whisk a few times to release heat.

Stir in melted chocolate and whiskey, until the mixture is smooth and well combined. Chill.

Freeze in an ice cream machine according to manufacturer's instructions.

Chocolate-Mandarine Ice Cream

1 pound bittersweet
    chocolate

2 cups heavy cream

2 cups milk

Zest of 3–4 tangerines,
    grated or finely chopped

8 egg yolks

½ cup granulated sugar

1 cup tangerine juice (3–4
    large tangerines)

½ cup plus 3 tablespoons
    Mandarine Napoleon
    liqueur

Makes 1½ to 2 quarts

If you like the taste of chocolate and citrus together, you'll like this variation on the usual chocolate-orange partnership. The contrast between the sweetness of the chocolate and the tartness of the citrus fruit is even more pronounced with tangerine than with orange.

Mandarine Napoleon is an imported tangerine-flavored liqueur. ("Mandarine" means "tangerine" in French.)

Cut chocolate into 2-inch pieces. In a heatproof bowl, melt chocolate over barely simmering water. (The water should not touch the bottom of the bowl or the chocolate will burn.) Turn off heat and let stand over warm water until ready to use.

In a large saucepan, scald the cream and milk with tangerine zest. Remove from heat, cover, and let flavor infuse for 30 minutes. In a large bowl, beat the egg yolks with the sugar for a few minutes until the sugar is dissolved. Set aside.

After 30 minutes, reheat cream to scalding. Pour about one fourth of the hot liquid into the egg yolks, whisking continuously. Return to saucepan, and whisk together with remaining cream. Cook over low heat, stirring constantly with a wooden spoon, until the mixture thickens enough to coat the back of the spoon. Strain through a fine-mesh strainer into a bowl. Whisk a few times to release heat.

Stir in melted chocolate, tangerine juice, and liqueur, until mixture is smooth and well combined. Chill.

Freeze in an ice cream machine according to manufacturer's instructions.

Chocolate-Mint Ice Cream

4 cups whole mint leaves,
  removed from stems,
  loosely packed

2 cups heavy cream

2 cups milk

7 ounces bittersweet
  chocolate

8 egg yolks

6 tablespoons granulated
  sugar

1½ tablespoons crème de
  menthe or peppermint
  schnapps, optional

Makes 1½ to 2 quarts

The natural taste of fresh mint brightens the flavor of the chocolate.

Coarsely chop mint leaves; there should be about 2 cups. In a large saucepan, scald the cream, milk, and chopped mint leaves. Remove from heat, cover, and let flavor infuse for 1 hour. Strain; discard mint leaves.

Cut or break chocolate into 2-inch pieces. In a heatproof bowl, melt chocolate over barely simmering water. (The water should not touch the bottom of the bowl or the chocolate will burn.) Turn off heat and let stand over warm water until ready to use.

In a large bowl, beat together the egg yolks and the sugar for a few minutes until the sugar has dissolved and the mixture is thick and pale yellow; set aside.

Reheat cream to scalding. Pour about one fourth of the hot cream into the egg yolks, whisking continuously. Return to saucepan, and whisk together with remaining cream. Cook over low heat, stirring constantly with a wooden spoon, until the mixture thickens enough to coat the back of the spoon. Strain through a fine-mesh strainer into a bowl and whisk a few times to release heat. Stir in melted chocolate until mixture is smooth and well combined. Add crème de menthe to taste if a stronger mint flavor is desired. Chill.

Freeze in an ice cream machine according to manufacturer's instructions.

Milk Chocolate-Malt Ice Cream

10 ounces milk chocolate

8 egg yolks

2 cups heavy cream

2 cups milk

¼ cup malt (preferably Horlicks brand)

2 tablespoons Irish cream liqueur

Makes 1½ to 2 quarts

The milk chocolate and the Irish cream liqueur make an extremely creamy ice cream. The milk chocolate is sweet enough that adding extra sugar isn't necessary, and mild enough in flavor that it allows the character of the malt to come through. An especially delicious filling for Ice Cream Sandwiches.

Select a good quality imported milk chocolate such as Cadbury, Lindt, or Suchard. Inferior brands lack flavor, and will make a very bland ice cream. I prefer Horlicks brand of malt because it has fewer preservatives and chemical additives than any others.

Cut chocolate into 2-inch pieces. In a heatproof bowl, melt chocolate over barely simmering water. (Keep the heat low because milk chocolate burns more easily than dark chocolate. The water should not touch the bottom of the bowl or the chocolate can burn.) Turn off heat and let stand over warm water until ready to use.

In a large bowl, whisk the egg yolks lightly to break them up; set aside.

In a large saucepan, scald the cream and milk with the malt. Pour about one fourth of the hot cream into the egg yolks, whisking continuously. Return mixture to saucepan, and whisk together with remaining cream. Cook over low heat, stirring constantly with a wooden spoon, until mixture thickens enough to coat the back of the spoon. Strain through a fine-mesh strainer into a bowl. Whisk a few times to release heat. Stir in melted chocolate and liqueur until mixture is smooth and well mixed. Chill.

Freeze in an ice cream machine according to manufacturer's instructions.

VARIATION: Add 1½ cups Homemade Chocolate Chips.

Chocolate Truffle Ice Cream

Truffle Cream:

8 ounces bittersweet chocolate

3 tablespoons butter

6 tablespoons heavy cream

5 tablespoons orange liqueur

Ice Cream:

½ pound bittersweet chocolate

8 egg yolks

¼ cup granulated sugar

2 cups heavy cream

2 cups milk

Makes 1½ to 2 quarts

This is the ultimate "chocolate–chocolate chip" ice cream —a half pound of bittersweet chocolate flavors the ice cream itself, which is then studded with bite-size bits of chocolate truffle candy. There's a nice contrast between the cold creaminess of the ice cream and the soft chewiness of the truffle bits. For a terrific plain chocolate ice cream, just leave out the truffles.

MAKING THE TRUFFLE CREAM

Cut chocolate into 2-inch pieces. In a heatproof bowl, melt chocolate with butter over barely simmering water. (The water should not touch the bottom of the bowl or the chocolate will burn.) Turn off heat and let stand over warm water until ready to use.

In a large saucepan, scald heavy cream with liqueur. If the alcohol ignites, blow it out. Stir into the chocolate mixture. Pour into a shallow baking pan. Refrigerate or freeze until firm.

There are two ways to shape the truffle cream. It can be formed into tiny balls by hand using a melon-baller, as directed in the recipe for chocolate truffles, page 72. Set the balls on a paper-lined baking sheet and keep frozen until ready to use. Alternatively, pipe the cream into logs, using a pastry bag (No. 4 plain tip). To pipe, fill the pastry bag half full of almost-set truffle cream and pipe into logs on a paper-lined baking sheet. Chill until firm. Cut with a warm knife into ½-inch-long pieces and keep frozen until ready to use.

❖ The truffles can be formed up to one month in advance and stored in the freezer.

MAKING THE ICE CREAM

Cut 1 pound chocolate into 2-inch pieces. In a heatproof bowl, melt over barely simmering water. (The water should not touch the bottom of the bowl or the chocolate will burn.) Turn off heat and let stand over warm water until ready to use.

In a large bowl, beat together the egg yolks and the sugar for a few minutes until the sugar has dissolved and the mixture has tripled in volume.

In a large saucepan, scald the cream and milk. Pour

about one fourth of the hot cream over the egg yolks, whisking continuously. Return to saucepan and whisk together with remaining cream. Cook over low heat, stirring constantly with a wooden spoon, until the mixture thickens enough to coat the back of the spoon. Strain through a fine-mesh strainer into a bowl. Whisk a few times to release heat. Stir in melted chocolate until mixture is smooth and well blended. Chill.

Freeze in ice cream machine according to manufacturer's instructions. When the ice cream is finished, fold in the chocolate truffles by hand using a rubber spatula. The truffle recipe makes enough to heavily stud the ice cream. Use fewer if you prefer.

White Chocolate–Mint Ice Cream

*2 cups whole mint leaves,
removed from stems*

2 cups heavy cream

2 cups milk

14 ounces white chocolate

8 egg yolks

*2 tablespoons green crème de
menthe*

*1½ cups Homemade
Chocolate Chips,
optional (page 244)*

Makes 1½ to 2 quarts

Mint balances the sweetness of the white chocolate in this recipe, and the green crème de menthe gives it a delicate color. It's a cooling combination that's excellent with fresh berries. If you like, stir in chocolate chips to further cut the richness and add another level of taste.

White chocolate is sweet enough that no additional sugar is needed in the recipe.

Coarsely chop the mint leaves. There should be about 1 cup. In a large saucepan, scald the cream and milk with chopped mint. Remove from heat, cover, and let flavor infuse for 1 hour. Strain; discard mint.

Cut white chocolate into 2-inch pieces. In a heatproof bowl, melt the chocolate over barely simmering water. (Keep the heat low, because white chocolate burns more easily than dark chocolate. The water should not touch the bottom of the bowl or the chocolate will burn.) Turn off heat and let stand over warm water until ready to use.

In a large bowl, whisk egg yolks lightly to break them up; set aside.

Reheat cream to scalding. Pour about one fourth of the hot cream into the egg yolks, whisking continuously. Return to saucepan and whisk together with the remaining cream. Cook over low heat, stirring constantly with a wooden spoon, until mixture thickens enough to coat the back of the spoon. Strain through a fine-mesh strainer into a bowl. Whisk a few times to release heat. Stir in melted chocolate until the mixture is smooth and well combined. Strain again if necessary. Stir in crème de menthe. Chill.

Freeze in an ice cream machine according to manufacturer's instructions. Add chocolate chips during the last minute of freezing.

Banana-Honey Ice Cream

2 cups heavy cream

2 cups milk

1 vanilla bean, split and scraped

3 large, very ripe bananas (about 1 pound)

8 egg yolks

7 tablespoons granulated sugar

½ cup sour cream

2 tablespoons orange blossom or clover honey

¼ cup dark rum

Makes 1½ to 2 quarts

Honey, rum, and sour cream each contribute their distinctive tastes to make a well-balanced banana ice cream. Only very ripe bananas, soft and brown-skinned, will produce a flavorful ice cream.

In a large saucepan, scald the cream and milk with the vanilla bean. Remove from heat, cover, and let flavor infuse for 30 minutes. Meanwhile, mash bananas well or purée briefly in a food processor; set aside.

In a large bowl, beat together the egg yolks and the sugar for a few minutes until the sugar has dissolved and the mixture is thick and pale yellow; set aside. Reheat cream mixture to scalding and pour about one fourth of it into the egg yolks, whisking continuously. Return mixture to saucepan and whisk together with remaining cream. Cook over low heat, stirring constantly with a wooden spoon, until mixture thickens enough to coat the back of the spoon. Pour into a bowl and whisk a few times to release heat. Stir in banana purée, sour cream, honey, and rum. Strain through a fine-mesh strainer. Chill.

Freeze in an ice cream machine according to manufacturer's instructions.

Bitter Orange Ice Cream

3 cups heavy cream

1 cup milk

6 tablespoons grated or finely chopped orange zest (6 oranges)

1 vanilla bean, split and scraped

3⅓ cups fresh orange juice

1¼ cups orange liqueur in all

8 egg yolks

½ cup granulated sugar

Makes 1½ to 2 quarts

The flavor of this ice cream reminds me of the 50-50 Bars, orange and cream, that I used to buy from the Good Humor man when I was a kid.

Scald the cream, milk, orange zest, and vanilla bean in a saucepan. Remove from heat, cover, and let flavors infuse for at least 30 minutes. Meanwhile, in a stainless steel saucepan, boil the orange juice and 1 cup of the orange liqueur until the mixture starts to color and has reduced to ¾ cup. Add to warm cream mixture.

In a large bowl, beat together the egg yolks and sugar for a few minutes until the sugar is dissolved and the mixture is thick and pale yellow; set aside. Reheat cream mixture to scalding and pour about one fourth of it into the egg yolks, whisking continuously. Return mixture to saucepan and whisk together with remaining cream. Cook over low heat, stirring constantly with a wooden spoon, until mixture thickens enough to coat the back of the spoon. Strain through a fine-mesh strainer into a bowl and reserve the zest. Whisk a few times to release heat. Rinse the orange zest under cold water to remove any bits of cooked egg yolks that might be clinging to it. Drain well, pressing out all water, and return zest to egg yolk mixture. Stir in remaining ¼ cup liqueur. Chill.

Freeze in an ice cream machine according to manufacturer's instructions.

Rum-Raisin Ice Cream

1 cup black currants or raisins

¾ cup dark rum (plus a little extra if necessary)

8 egg yolks

½ cup granulated sugar

2 cups heavy cream

2 cups milk

Makes 1½ to 2 quarts

Unlike commercial rum-raisin ice cream, this one is flavored with real dark rum. Since I like the flavor of rum, I've used the absolute maximum amount. You can use less, but don't add any more or the ice cream will be too soft. Currants or raisins can be used, but currants are more delicate.

In a stainless steel saucepan, over low heat, scald the rum and currants or raisins. (Keep the flame low—if the alcohol gets too hot, it will ignite.) Remove from heat and let stand until cool. Strain, setting aside the currants and reserving the rum. (Add a little extra rum if there is less than ½ cup.)

In a large bowl, beat together the egg yolks and the sugar for a few minutes until the sugar has dissolved and the mixture is thick and pale yellow; set aside.

In a large saucepan, scald the cream and milk. Pour about one fourth of the hot cream into the egg yolks, whisking continuously. Return to the saucepan and whisk into remaining cream. Cook over low heat, stirring constantly with a wooden spoon, until the mixture thickens enough to coat the back of the spoon. Strain through a fine-mesh strainer into a bowl. Whisk a few times to release heat. Stir in no more than ½ cup reserved rum. Chill.

Freeze in an ice cream machine according to manufacturer's instructions. Add currants or raisins during the last minute of freezing.

Prune-Armagnac Ice Cream

10 ounces soft pitted dried
    prunes, preferably
    vacuum-packed

1 cup Armagnac or Cognac
    (plus a few tablespoons if
    necessary)

2 cups heavy cream

1 cup milk

1 vanilla bean, split and
    scraped

8 egg yolks

½ cup granulated sugar

Makes 1½ to 2 quarts

Although this combination may seem unusual to Americans, it's a real delicacy in southwest France, near Toulouse, where Armagnac is a regional specialty and the plump local prunes are used in all kinds of pastries and desserts.

The recipe calls for soaking the prunes for 7–10 days, to soften them and to mellow the bite of the alcohol. If you're in a hurry, you can warm the Armagnac gently in a saucepan and simmer the prunes until soft. (See Poached Prunes, page 157.) Poached prunes have a less-pronounced alcohol flavor, so you may want to add a few extra tablespoons of alcohol to taste.

The Armagnac-soaked prunes are delicious all by themselves. They keep for months in the refrigerator and can be spooned over vanilla ice cream or warmed slightly and served with crème fraîche or in a bowl with heavy cream.

Place prunes in a plastic container, cover with Armagnac, and seal airtight. Refrigerate 7–10 days, until prunes are soft. Just before making the ice cream, drain prunes and reserve liquid. (Add a little extra Armagnac if there is less than ½ cup.) Cut prunes into fourths and set aside.

In a large saucepan, scald the cream and milk with the vanilla bean. Remove from heat, cover, and let the flavor infuse for 30 minutes. In a large bowl, beat the egg yolks with sugar until the sugar has dissolved and the mixture is thick and pale yellow. Reheat cream and milk to scalding. Pour about one fourth of the hot cream into the egg yolks, whisking continuously. Return to the saucepan and whisk together with the remaining cream. Cook over low heat, stirring constantly with a wooden spoon, until the mixture thickens enough to coat the back of the spoon. Strain through a fine-mesh strainer into a bowl. Whisk a few times to release heat. Stir in ½ cup of reserved Armagnac. Chill.

Freeze in an ice cream machine according to manufacturer's instructions. Add prunes during the last minute of freezing.

Coconut- Nougatine Ice Cream

2 fresh coconuts (about 4 pounds)

3 cups heavy cream in all

2 cups milk

1 vanilla bean, split and scraped

8 egg yolks

¼ cup granulated sugar

3 tablespoons hazelnut liqueur

2 tablespoons almond liqueur

1 teaspoon almond extract

1½ cups chopped Coconut Nougatine (page 353)

Makes 1½ to 2 quarts

Fresh coconut has a subtle taste, that is brought out by hazelnut and almond flavoring and crunchy chunks of coconut nougatine. I love this ice cream with Bitter Chocolate Sauce or Hot Fudge.

I tried just about every existing type of canned, bagged, and vacuum-packed coconut, but finally only the flavor of fresh coconut pleased me completely. When you buy coconuts, you can tell if they're fresh by shaking them to see if they're full of milk.

To crack open the coconuts, tap around the middle of the shell with a hammer or a heavy meat cleaver, going over the same area a couple of times; the shell will eventually split neatly in half. If the coconut meat doesn't come away from the shell easily, place the coconut halves on a baking sheet and bake at 350 degrees for 30–45 minutes, until the coconut meat begins to pull away from the shell.

Remove the coconut meat from the shell, break it into small pieces, and process it in a food processor until finely chopped. Place in a large saucepan with the heavy cream, milk, and vanilla bean, and heat to scalding. Remove from heat, cover, and let the flavor infuse for 1 hour.

Strain the cream mixture into a bowl, pressing the coconut against the strainer to squeeze out as much liquid as possible. There should be 4 cups liquid; if necessary, add additional cream to make 4 cups. Return cream to the saucepan and discard the coconut.

In a large mixing bowl, beat together the egg yolks and sugar for a few minutes until sugar is dissolved and the mixture has tripled in volume. Reheat the cream to scalding. Pour about one fourth of the hot cream into the egg yolks, whisking continuously. Return mixture to saucepan and whisk together with the remaining cream. Cook over low heat, stirring constantly with a wooden spoon, until mixture thickens enough to coat the back of the spoon. Strain through a fine-mesh strainer into a bowl and whisk a few times to release heat. Stir in liqueurs and almond extract; chill.

Freeze in an ice cream machine according to the manufacturer's instructions. Add the chopped coconut nougatine during the last minute of freezing.

VARIATION: If you don't have time to make nougatine, add 1½ cups toasted, unblanched almonds after freezing.

Black Truffle Ice Cream

8 egg yolks
1 ounce fresh black truffles
3 cups heavy cream
1 cup milk
¼ cup granulated sugar

Makes 1 quart

There is probably no bigger extravagance than fresh truffles—knobby, ugly, heavenly things that run about $20 an ounce. Fresh truffles have an entirely different taste than the slimy canned ones that are plopped on top of eggs Benedict in pretentious restaurants.

If you like the taste of fresh truffles (and if you can afford them), you will like this subtly musty, lightly perfumed ice cream. It's a dessert designed to follow an exquisite, even slightly exotic dinner, perhaps accompanied by fresh fruit.

A mandoline slicer makes it easy to slice the truffles thin.

The day before making the ice cream, place the egg yolks in a small bowl or container. Drape plastic wrap directly on top of the yolks so they don't harden. Place the whole truffle on top of the plastic wrap and cover the entire container with plastic wrap. Refrigerate 24 hours.

The next day, slice the truffle thin (¹⁄₁₆ to ⅛ inch thick) with a sharp knife or a mandoline. In a small saucepan, scald the cream, milk, and sliced truffle. Remove from heat, cover, and let the flavor infuse for 1 hour.

In a large bowl, beat together the egg yolks and the sugar for a few minutes until the sugar has dissolved and the mixture has tripled in volume; set aside.

Reheat cream to scalding. Pour about one fourth of the cream into the egg yolks, whisking continuously. Return to saucepan and combine with remaining cream. Cook over low heat, stirring constantly with a wooden spoon, until the mixture thickens enough to coat the back of the spoon. Strain through a fine-mesh strainer into a bowl, reserving the sliced truffle. Whisk a few times to release heat. Chill.

Freeze in an ice cream machine according to manufacturer's instructions. Mince the truffles by stacking a few on top of each other and slicing into thin needles, then slice crosswise into tiny chips.

When the ice cream is finished, fold the minced truffle into the ice cream by hand, so that you don't lose any valuable bits on the sides of the ice cream machine.

Because this ice cream contains very little sugar, it hardens quickly in the freezer. Your best bet is to gather a group of discerning diners and eat the whole quart the night it is made.

If you can't manage to eat it all at one sitting, return it to its original texture by refreezing it. Thaw the ice cream to a liquid (either by letting it stand at room temperature or by melting it over simmering water), strain it to take out the truffles, freeze again in the ice cream machine, and add the minced truffle.

Pistachio Ice Cream

1²⁄₃ cups shelled, unsalted, uncolored pistachio nuts (8 ounces)

2 cups heavy cream

2 cups milk

1 vanilla bean, split and scraped

8 egg yolks

½ cup granulated sugar

2 tablespoons hazelnut liqueur

1 tablespoon almond liqueur

½ teaspoon almond extract

Makes 1½ to 2 quarts

Unlike what you might guess from ice-cream-parlor pistachio ice cream, pistachio nuts are actually very mild in flavor and don't contain anything that will turn an ice cream green. This pistachio ice cream is flavored with pistachio nuts and nut liqueurs, and has a subtle and pleasantly nutty flavor.

In a small saucepan, bring 2 cups of water to the boil. Add the pistachio nuts and allow to boil for 1 minute. Drain the nuts and allow them to cool. Rub the skins off with your fingers.

Preheat oven to 325 degrees. Spread the pistachio nuts on a baking sheet and toast for 8–10 minutes. Cool and set aside. Chop 1 cup nuts very fine or grind in a food processor. Set the remainder aside.

In a large saucepan, heat the cream, milk, 1 cup chopped pistachio nuts, and vanilla bean to scalding. Remove from heat, cover, and let the flavors infuse for 30 minutes.

In a large bowl, beat together the egg yolks and sugar for a few minutes until the sugar is dissolved and the mixture is thick and pale yellow.

Reheat cream mixture to scalding. Pour about one fourth of the hot cream into the egg yolks, whisking continuously. Return mixture to saucepan and whisk together with remaining cream. Cook over low heat, stirring constantly with a wooden spoon, until the mixture thickens and coats the back of the spoon. Strain through a fine-mesh strainer into a bowl and whisk a few times to release heat. Discard nuts. Stir in hazelnut and almond liqueurs. Chill.

Freeze in an ice cream machine according to manufacturer's instructions. Add whole toasted pistachio nuts during the last minute of freezing.

VARIATION: Add 1½ cups Homemade Chocolate Chips during the last minute of freezing.

Praline Ice Cream

14 ounces (3¼ cups) whole raw hazelnuts

½ teaspoon cooking oil

¾ cup water

2½ cups granulated sugar

8 egg yolks

2 cups heavy cream

2 cups milk

¼ cup hazelnut liqueur

Makes 1½ to 2 quarts

Caramelized hazelnut praline is used two ways in this smooth, nutty ice cream—some is ground fine to flavor the cream itself, and the rest is chopped into bite-size pieces and added at the last minute for crunch.

Preheat oven to 325 degrees. Spread the hazelnuts on a baking sheet and toast 8–10 minutes. The skins will crack and the nuts will turn a light golden color. Remove from oven; cool. Rub the skins off in a clean dish towel.

Oil a baking sheet lightly with the ½ teaspoon cooking oil; set aside.

In a heavy 3-quart saucepan, heat water and sugar over high heat. When the water boils, it will throw sugar onto the sides of the pan. Wash down the sides with a pastry brush, dipping in water as necessary to dissolve sugar. (Alternatively, place a lid on the pan for 30 seconds and the steam condensation will wash the sugar off the sides.)

When the entire surface of the mixture is covered with slowly bursting bubbles but has not started to color (270–290 degrees on a candy thermometer), add all the hazelnuts at once. The mixture will turn white as the sugar solidifies and will become very hard to stir. Vigorously break it up with a wooden spoon and stir constantly to remelt the sugar and to ensure that the mixture colors evenly. If the praline starts to darken in one place, stir energetically to distribute the hot syrup. Be very careful as the nuts are extremely hot. The mixture is done just at the moment when it turns an even mahogany color and starts to smoke.

Pour quickly onto the oiled baking sheet and spread with a wooden spoon into an even layer to stop the nuts from cooking. Remove any white chunks of unmelted sugar with a spoon. Let cool and break into pieces.

In a large bowl, whisk the egg yolks lightly to break them up. In a large saucepan, scald the cream and milk. Pour about one fourth of the hot cream into the egg yolks, whisking continuously. Return mixture to saucepan and whisk together with remaining cream. Cook over low heat, stirring constantly with a wooden spoon, until the mixture thickens and coats the back of the spoon. Strain through a fine-mesh strainer into a bowl and whisk a few times to release heat.

Put half the cooled praline into a food processor and add ¼ cup of the ice cream base. Process a few minutes until a very smooth paste is formed. Stir back into the remaining custard mixture. Strain through a fine-mesh strainer or cheesecloth. You must remove all the tiny bits of nut or they will become soggy. Stir in liqueur. Chill.

Freeze in an ice cream machine according to manufacturer's instructions. While the ice cream is freezing, chop the remaining praline into coarse chunks. When the ice cream is finished, fold the praline into the ice cream by hand.

This ice cream is best eaten the same day it is made. The hazelnuts get soggy if it is stored too long.

Sesame Seed Ice Cream

Sesame Seed Brittle:
1 teaspoon toasted sesame oil

¾ cup granulated sugar

½ cup water

¾ cup sesame seeds

Ice Cream Base:
8 egg yolks

2½ tablespoons granulated sugar

2 cups heavy cream

2 cups milk

¼ cup toasted sesame oil

¼ cup hazelnut liqueur

Makes 1½ to 2 quarts

Sesame oil and a homemade sesame seed brittle flavor this unusual and delicious ice cream.

Toasted sesame oil is available in health food stores and Oriental markets. Taste the oil—some brands have an unpleasant burned taste.

PREPARING THE BRITTLE

Lightly oil a baking sheet with sesame oil. Set aside. In a heavy, 3-quart saucepan, heat sugar and water over high heat. When water boils, it will throw sugar onto the sides of the pan. At that point, wash down with a pastry brush, dipping in water as necessary to dissolve sugar. (Alternatively, place a lid on the pan for 30 seconds and the steam condensation will wash the sugar off the sides.)

When the mixture turns an even amber color, stir in sesame seeds and cook for another minute until well combined and the seeds are lightly colored. Pour quickly onto the oiled baking sheet and spread with a wooden spoon to stop the cooking. Cool. (If the mixture whitens when the sesame seeds are added, continue to stir and cook until it turns a light amber color again.)

In a food processor or blender, grind half the brittle into a powder and set aside. There should be about 1 cup. Break the remainder into bite-size pieces by chopping with a knife or crushing lightly with a rolling pin, and set aside. There should be about ½ cup.

PREPARING THE ICE CREAM

In a large bowl, beat the egg yolks and sugar for a few minutes until sugar has dissolved; set aside.

In a large saucepan, scald the cream, milk, and sesame oil. Pour about one fourth of the hot cream into the egg yolks, whisking continuously. Return mixture to saucepan and whisk together with remaining cream. Cook over low heat, stirring constantly with a wooden spoon, until the mixture thickens and coats the back of the spoon. Strain through a fine-mesh strainer into a bowl and whisk a few times to release heat. Stir in liqueur and 1 cup sesame seed powder. Chill.

Freeze in ice cream machine according to manufacturer's instructions. Add chopped brittle during the last minute of freezing.

SHERBETS

Making the perfect sherbet requires finding a balance between the acidity of a fruit and the sweetness of sugar. Because I like the true fruit flavors to shine through, I've tried to find the point at which I could use just enough sugar to ensure a smooth texture without overpowering the fruit. Without enough sugar, a sherbet tends to taste like icy fluff; without acidity, it will taste too sweet, because it lacks the characteristic pucker and tang that makes the taste come alive in your mouth.

A sherbet is simply a fruit purée or fruit juice, mixed with sugar and other flavorings, and churned in an ice cream machine to create a creamy texture without ice crystals. Fruit purées are often so thick that they need to be thinned out to freeze, but instead of thinning them with water, which dilutes the flavor, I often use sugar syrup, wine, or a complementary fruit juice to make the right consistency.

Because fruit can vary so widely in taste, I've included few sherbets that don't rely solely on the flavor of the fruit itself. Instead of a plain strawberry sherbet that requires perfectly delicious strawberries, Strawberry Daiquiri Sherbet uses lemon juice, lime juice, and rum to enhance the flavor. Pink Grapefruit-Tequila Sherbet uses the flavor of the alcohol to bring out the tart grapefruit taste. Use the flavoring quantities in the recipes as guidelines, and rely on your taste buds to make a flavorful sherbet base.

Sherbets using seasonal fruits, like tangerines or Concord grapes, can be made year-round if you purée large batches of the fruit (flavored or unflavored) and freeze them.

Concord Grape Sherbet

*¼ teaspoon whole black
    peppercorns*
1¾ pounds Concord grapes
2 cups beaujolais wine
½ cup granulated sugar

Makes 1½ quarts

Being a Californian, I'd never tasted that wonder of the Northeast, the Concord grape, until the terrific people at Chino Farms (a grower of specialty produce in southern California) started cultivating them and gave me some to try. From the first bite, it was obvious that these fragrant, richly flavored grapes would make the ultimate fruit sherbet.

The Concord grape season is only three months long (July, August, and September), but don't miss the opportunity to make this deep purple sherbet. Combined with beaujolais and spiced with black pepper, the grape flavor becomes savory and complex, which makes this sherbet a good choice to serve between courses at a meal featuring game.

The grapes freeze very well, so you can make this sherbet any time of year. Frozen grapes are also delicious to suck on, straight out of the freezer.

Crack the peppercorns in half by pressing them against the work surface with the bottom of a heavy pan. Stem the grapes.

Place all sherbet ingredients in a large enamel or stainless steel saucepan. Bring to a full boil, remove from heat, cover, and let stand for 30 minutes. Purée in a food processor. Strain through a fine-mesh strainer into a bowl. Chill.

Freeze in an ice cream machine according to manufacturer's instructions.

Plum Wine Sherbet

*1 teaspoon whole black
  peppercorns*

*2½ pounds red or purple
  plums*

*2 cups plum wine
  (available at Oriental
  groceries) or tawny port*

1 cup granulated sugar

*1 vanilla bean, split and
  scraped*

½ cup lemon juice

Zest of 2 lemons

Makes 1 quart

Each ingredient adds to the complexity of flavors in this sherbet—the sweetness and full-bodied character of the plums are brought out by the plum wine, and the tartness is enhanced by the lemon juice and zest. Black pepper introduces a hot balancing note.

Crack the peppercorns in half by pressing them against the work surface with the bottom of a heavy pan. Halve and pit the plums.

In a large stainless steel or enamel saucepan, combine all sherbet ingredients. Bring to a boil, than reduce to low heat and simmer uncovered for 30 minutes, stirring occasionally. Remove from heat and remove vanilla bean. Process in a food processor until puréed. Strain through a fine-mesh strainer into a bowl. Chill.

Freeze in an ice cream machine according to manufacturer's instructions.

VARIATION: Substitute pears for plums and zinfandel for plum wine to make another interesting fruit sherbet.

Tangerine Sherbet

3 cups tangerine juice (18–
    20 tangerines, preferably
    Setsuma variety)

¾ cup lemon juice
    (4–6 lemons)

1½ cups sugar syrup
    (see page 29)

¼ cup Mandarine
    Napoleon (tangerine)
    liqueur

Makes 1½ quarts

A simple celebration of one of winter's pleasures—tangerines—in a very pure, very tart sherbet.

In a large bowl, stir all ingredients together. Strain through a fine-mesh strainer. Chill. Freeze in an ice cream machine according to manufacturer's instructions.

Apricot Sherbet

1 pound ripe, fresh apricots
    (10–12)

6 ounces dried apricots
    (1½ cups)

½ cup water

3½ cups fresh orange juice
    (10–12 oranges)

¾ cup apricot liqueur

Makes 1½ quarts

The flavor of fresh apricots is reinforced by dried apricots, apricot liqueur, and orange juice in this intensely fruity sherbet.

Halve and pit fresh apricots. In a stainless steel saucepan, place the fresh and dried apricots, water, 2½ cups of the orange juice, and ¼ cup of the apricot liqueur. Bring to a boil. Reduce heat and simmer for about 10 minutes, until the apricots are tender. Purée in a food processor or blender until smooth. Strain through a fine-mesh strainer. There should be about 2½ cups purée. Stir in all or a portion of the remaining 1 cup orange juice to taste and ½ cup apricot liqueur. Chill.

Freeze in an ice cream machine according to manufacturer's instructions.

Pink Grapefruit– Tequila Sherbet

4 cups fresh pink grapefruit
    juice (about 5 large
    grapefruits)
½ cup tequila, preferably
    Cuervo Gold
½ cup granulated sugar

Makes 1 quart

The challenge with a grapefruit sherbet was to create a smooth consistency without adding so much sugar that the characteristic sourness of the grapefruit was camouflaged. But I finally found the right balance—tequila, which complements the grapefruit flavor beautifully, also helps keep the sherbet smooth.

Mix all ingredients together in a bowl. Strain through a fine-mesh strainer. Freeze in an ice cream machine according to manufacturer's instructions.

Passion Fruit Sherbet

3 pounds passion fruit
    (about 35)
½ cup granulated sugar
¾ cup water
1½ cups dry champagne
¾ cup fresh orange juice
    (2–3 oranges)
½ cup fresh lemon juice
    (2–3 lemons)

Makes 1 quart

Passion fruit is expensive, but this tart, tropical sherbet is worth every penny. All the characteristics of an ideal sherbet are present in this one—bright, natural color, fruity flavor, high acid content, and smooth texture. In fact, passion fruit has such a concentrated flavor that it needs to be mellowed by the addition of citrus juice and champagne.

Cut passion fruit in half and scoop out pulp and seeds directly into a large stainless steel saucepan. Bring passion fruit to a boil with sugar and water. Turn off heat and let stand 20 minutes. Strain through a fine-mesh strainer into a bowl, pressing the pulp with the back of a spoon to make sure that all the fruit comes away from the seeds and that only the seeds remain in the strainer. Stir in champagne, orange juice, and lemon juice. Chill.

Freeze in an ice cream machine according to manufacturer's instructions.

Strawberry Daiquiri Sherbet

7 cups strawberries, fresh or
  frozen without syrup

½ cup plus 2 tablespoons
  lime juice (4–5 limes)

¼ cup plus 2 tablespoons
  lemon juice (2–3 lemons)

¾ cup white rum

½ cup granulated sugar

Makes 1½ quarts

Everyone knows how much fresh strawberries can vary in flavor, from very sweet and fruity one week to watery and insipid the next. The addition of daiquiri ingredients—rum, lemon juice, and lime juice—gives this sherbet flavor, no matter how tasty the strawberries are, and also allows the use of frozen strawberries.

Stem the strawberries, Purée them in blender or food processor until smooth. Do not strain. There should be 4 cups purée. Mix all remaining ingredients together in a bowl and freeze in an ice cream machine according to manufacturer's instructions.

Cassis Sherbet

2 pounds black currants
  (8 cups), fresh or frozen
  without syrup

2 cups sugar syrup (see page
  29)

Makes 1 quart

Black currants (*cassis* in French) make a dark red, tart sherbet. The cassis berries are so flavorful that no other ingredient except sugar is necessary in this sherbet. It is wonderful on its own or layered with crisp white meringue in the Cassis Vacherin.

Stem the currants. In a large stainless steel or enamel saucepan, bring berries and sugar syrup to a boil. Remove from heat and let stand about 15 minutes, until berries have softened. Purée in a food processor. Strain through a fine-mesh strainer. Chill.

Freeze in an ice cream machine according to manufacturer's instructions.

Lemon-Thyme Sherbet

4 teaspoons grated or finely
    chopped lemon zest
    (2 lemons)

1 cup fresh lemon juice
    (5–6 lemons)

2 cups water

1/2 cup granulated sugar

1/2 cup light corn syrup

2 large branches fresh thyme

Makes 3–4 cups

Tart enough to be served as a between-course intermezzo, this sherbet also makes a light finish to a meal. Place small scoops in a champagne flute and fill the glass with ice-cold champagne.

Place all ingredients in a stainless steel or enamel saucepan and bring to a boil. Remove from heat, cover, and let steep 30 minutes. Strain through a fine-mesh strainer. Chill.

Freeze in an ice cream machine according to manufacturer's instructions.

Mango-Coriander Sherbet

3–4 large ripe mangoes
    (approximately 4
    pounds)

1/2 cup sugar syrup (see page
    29)

1/2 cup fresh lime juice (4–6
    limes)

1/2 cup fresh orange juice
    (2–3 oranges)

1–2 tablespoons ground
    coriander, to taste

Makes 1½ quarts

Because the taste of this sherbet depends entirely on the flavor of the fruit, buy soft ripe mangoes. For the freshest-tasting coriander, which adds musky sweetness, grind it yourself from coriander seeds that you buy at Indian groceries or health food stores. To get 2 tablespoons of ground coriander, start with about 4 tablespoons whole seeds, grind them in a spice grinder or small coffee grinder, and then sift through a fine-mesh strainer. Discard the husks. If you buy coriander already ground, open the container and sniff the aroma to check for freshness.

Peel the mangoes and scrape pulp out of the skin and off the large fibrous pits. If necessary, squeeze the pits in your hands to remove every last bit of fruit. In a food processor or a blender, purée pulp. Strain through a fine-mesh strainer to remove any stringiness. There should be 5 cups purée. Stir in remaining ingredients. Chill.

Freeze in an ice cream machine according to manufacturer's instructions.

Lime-Mint Sherbet

6 cups fresh mint leaves, removed from stems (about 4 large bunches)

2½ cups water

4 pure spearmint or pure peppermint tea bags (not black tea flavored with mint)

½ cup light corn syrup

2 tablespoons granulated sugar

½ cup lime juice (4–6 limes)

2 tablespoons green crème de menthe

1 tablespoon poire Williams (pear brandy)

Makes 1 quart

Serve this refreshing sherbet over melon marinated in port wine, or place small scoops in a champagne flute and fill the glass with ice-cold champagne.

Set aside 2 tablespoons whole mint leaves. Roughly chop the remaining leaves. There should be about 4 cups, loosely packed.

In a large stainless steel or enamel saucepan, bring to a boil all ingredients except the alcohols. Remove from the heat, cover, and let stand at least 1 hour. Strain through a fine-mesh strainer into a bowl, pressing out all liquid. Stir in the crème de menthe and pear brandy, combining well. Chill.

Freeze in an ice cream machine according to manufacturer's instructions. Just before freezing is finished, finely mince the reserved mint leaves. There should be about 1 tablespoon minced mint. Add to sherbet during the last minute of freezing.

Pink Grapefruit and Cassis Granité

4 cups fresh Texas pink grapefruit juice (about 5 large grapefruits)

5 tablespoons double crème de cassis (not cassis syrup)

Makes 1 quart

Unlike a sherbet, which is churned smooth in an ice cream maker, a granité is stirred by hand in the freezer, making a rough-textured frozen dessert that is not grainy or snowy but flaky, like shaved ice. This combination of pink grapefruit juice and crème de cassis makes a pinkish-purple granité that can be served for dessert or as a refreshing intermezzo between courses of a larger meal. The color contrast is beautiful when you layer the granité with peeled grapefruit sections in parfait glasses or brandy snifters.

The flavor of this dessert depends entirely on how flavorful the grapefruit juice is. Choose grapefruit that is not bitter.

Mix juice and crème de cassis and pour into a shallow pan, such as an ice cube tray without dividers. Every 20 to 30 minutes, as ice crystals form around the edge of the pan, stir them back into the mixture with a fork. This prevents the mixture from freezing into a solid block. Stir delicately, to keep from breaking up the thin sheets of frozen juice. After 2 to 2½ hours, no liquid will remain, and the entire pan will be filled with frozen grapefruit shavings. The granité is best served the day it is made.

If you wish, just before serving, layer the granité with peeled grapefruit sections (see Gratin of Oranges, page 117, for instructions on how to completely peel the grapefruit sections). This cannot be assembled in advance because the grapefruit sections freeze quickly and lose their texture.

Ice Cream Sandwiches

*4 ounces bittersweet
    chocolate*

*6 tablespoons unsweetened
    cocoa powder*

6 tablespoons water

*6 ounces unsalted butter, at
    room temperature*

*½ cup plus 3 tablespoons
    brown sugar, packed*

*½ cup plus 2 tablespoons
    granulated sugar*

2 eggs

2 teaspoons vanilla extract

1¾ cups flour

1 teaspoon baking soda

½ teaspoon boiling water

*1 cup ice cream per
    sandwich*

**Makes fourteen 4½-inch
sandwiches**

ACCOMPANIMENTS

Some people would think it's crazy to spend time making ice cream sandwiches, but I love turning my childhood favorites into grown-up desserts. If you've ever glanced at the list of ingredients on the label of a storebought ice cream sandwich, you'll know that these are in a whole different category—pure ingredients, a chocolate wafer with a subtle, Oreo-like taste, and any flavor ice cream you like to fill them.

Use one 4½-inch round biscuit cutter, baking sheet, a pastry bag fitted with a No. 4 plain tip (optional).

MAKING THE SANDWICH WAFERS

Cut chocolate into 2-inch pieces. In a heatproof bowl, melt chocolate over barely simmering water. (The water should not touch the bottom of the bowl or the chocolate will burn.) Turn off heat and let stand over warm water until ready to use.

In a small saucepan, whisk together cocoa powder and the 6 tablespoons water. Bring to a simmer over medium heat, whisking constantly, until the mixture is smooth and thick. The whisk will leave an empty trail behind it when it is drawn across the bottom of the pan. Remove from heat and whisk in melted chocolate; set aside.

Using the paddle attachment of an electric mixer, beat the butter on medium-high speed until it whitens and holds soft peaks, 3–5 minutes. Beat in brown sugar and granulated sugar until combined. In a small bowl, lightly whisk together the eggs and vanilla extract and beat gradually into butter mixture, scraping down the sides of the bowl as necessary. Beat in the chocolate mixture until combined and then add half the flour, beating until just combined. Mix baking soda with boiling water and beat in. Add remaining flour, mixing only until well combined. Do not overmix. Wrap the mixture in plastic wrap and freeze until firm, preferably overnight.

❖ The dough can be made up to this point and frozen for up to three months.

ROLLING AND BAKING THE WAFERS

Preheat oven to 325 degrees. Adjust oven rack to the middle position.

Divide dough in fourths. Place one fourth on a floured surface and keep the rest frozen. (This dough will never freeze rock-hard. It is a very sticky dough, and keeping it frozen makes it easiest to work with.) Roll out to ¼-inch thickness; cut as many rounds as possible with a 4½-inch round biscuit cutter and place on a paper-lined baking sheet. Gather scraps together and place in freezer. Continue to roll out dough until you've cut as many wafers as desired. Touch the dough as little as possible as it melts easily.

Bake for 8–10 minutes, until the wafers are slightly soft but still spring back when touched. Do not bake until hard; they will crisp as they cool.

ASSEMBLING THE ICE CREAM SANDWICHES

Using the paddle attachment of an electric mixer, beat the ice cream for about 15 seconds, to soften. Fill a pastry bag (No. 4 plain tip) with about one fourth of the ice cream; keep the rest in the freezer until ready to use. Pipe a spiral of ice cream on the flat side of one wafer; cover with another wafer, flat side toward the ice cream. Freeze. Work quickly and handle the pastry bag as little as possible to keep the ice cream from melting. (Ice cream can also be spooned onto the wafer and spread with a small metal spatula or the back of a spoon.) After sandwiches have been frozen for 30 minutes or so, smooth the edges if necessary with a metal spatula. Wrap in plastic wrap and keep frozen until ready to serve.

Tulip Cups

8 tablespoons unsalted
   clarified butter, melted
   (page 17) in all
2 egg whites
5 tablespoons granulated
   sugar
½ cup all-purpose flour
1 teaspoon vanilla

Makes 8 cups

Fill these cookie cups with ice cream, sherbet, or mousse; they're pretty, and the crunchy texture is great with a creamy dessert. They're also a lovely container for fresh berries.

You can use 4 large Pyrex custard cups, small soup bowls, or small brioche tins to shape the tulip cups. Nonstick baking sheets, without raised edges, work best for this recipe. If the baking sheet has raised edges, bake the cookies on the back of it—it's easier to remove the cookies.

Preheat oven to 325 degrees. Adjust rack to middle position. If the baking sheet is not the nonstick type, brush it with 2 tablespoons of the melted butter and chill briefly. Dip an 8-inch pot lid in flour and use it to mark two 8-inch circles on the baking sheet; set aside. (Butter and mark the pan again each time you use it.)

MAKING THE BATTER

Combine the remaining 4 tablespoons melted butter and vanilla in a small bowl; set aside in a warm place. Using the whisk attachment of an electric mixer, beat the egg whites on low speed until frothy. Increase speed to medium and beat until soft peaks form. Increase speed to high and very gradually beat in the sugar, until stiff, glossy peaks form. Alternately fold the flour and the butter mixture into the egg whites, one half at a time; set aside.

BAKING AND FORMING THE CUPS

With an offset metal spatula, spread 2 tablespoons of the batter into each marked circle, making a thin, even layer with no holes. Tilt the pan to spread the batter evenly; if there are any thick spots, they will never cook and get crisp. Bake for 5 minutes, until the circles are uniformly golden brown.

Remove the warm circles from the baking sheet with a broad metal spatula and immediately drape them over an upside-down custard cup, with the side that was against the baking sheet placed against the mold. Place another same-size cup upside down over the top to hold the cup shape. You must work quickly and gently. The cookies will harden and crisp immediately. Unmold and store airtight until ready to use. If the dough hardens on the baking sheet before you can mold it, return the baking sheet to the oven briefly to soften it. (Butter the pan again each time you use it.)

Use the cups as soon as possible after baking or they will become soggy, especially in humid weather.

Toffee

½ cup granulated sugar

¼ cup heavy cream

4 tablespoons unsalted butter

Makes 1–1½ cups

Sugar, butter, and cream combine to make a smooth caramel, which then hardens and is chopped into crunchy bits to fold into ice cream. Can be stored in the freezer, ready to chop as you need it. Use it in plainer ice creams, like vanilla, espresso, and caramel.

In a heavy saucepan, whisk together the sugar and cream. Add the butter, cut into small pieces, and cook over medium heat. Do not stir, but you will need to swirl the pan a few times to keep the mixture cooking evenly. Cook until it is a light caramel color and the bubbles popping on the surface are just starting to turn brown. Pour immediately into a shallow heatproof pan. Freeze to harden. Chop into pieces.

Oven-Baked Ice Cream Cones

6 tablespoons clarified
    unsalted butter, melted
    (page 17) in all

¼ cup maple syrup

1 teaspoon vanilla extract

2 egg whites

2 tablespoons granulated
    sugar

½ cup all-purpose flour

Makes 8 cones

Even if it takes a few tries to get them just right, these maple-flavored cones are more than worth the trouble. They are sturdy enough to be held in the hand or can be placed on a plate filled with a scoop of ice cream.

Shape the cones on cream horn molds or wooden ice-cream-cone molds, available in cookware shops. Nonstick baking sheets, without raised edges, work best for this recipe. If the baking sheet has raised edges, bake the cones on the back of it—it's easier to remove the cones.

Preheat oven to 300 degrees. Adjust the oven rack to the middle position. If the baking sheet is the nonstick type, brush it with 2 tablespoons of the melted butter. Chill briefly. Dip a 6-inch pan lid in flour and use it to mark two 6-inch circles onto the baking sheet; set aside. (Butter and mark the pan again each time you use it.)

MAKING THE BATTER

In a small bowl, mix together the maple syrup, 4 tablespoons of the clarified butter, and vanilla extract; set aside in a warm place.

Using the whisk attachment of an electric mixer, beat the egg whites on low speed until frothy. Increase speed to medium and beat until soft peaks form. Increase speed to high and very gradually beat in granulated sugar, until very stiff, glossy peaks form. Alternately fold the flour and the butter mixture into the egg whites, one half at a time; set aside.

BAKING AND FORMING THE CONES

With an offset metal spatula, spread 1½ tablespoons batter into each marked circle, making a thin, even layer with no holes. Tilt the pan to spread the batter evenly; if there are any thick spots, they will never cook and get crisp. Bake for 5 minutes, until the circles are a uniform golden brown.

The cones must be molded straight from the oven. Remove the wafer from the baking sheet with a broad spatula and turn it over onto the work surface so that the side that was against the baking sheet is facing up. If you are using a cream horn mold, wrap a small towel around your thumb to protect it from the heat and put your thumb inside the cream horn mold to hold it. Position the mold at one end of the wafer. Use your fingers to help the dough wrap around the mold. Make sure the cone is closed completely at the pointed end. If you are using a wooden ice cream cone mold, just wrap the cone around the mold. Work quickly; the dough will harden almost immediately. If it hardens on the baking sheet before you can mold it, return the baking sheet to the oven briefly to soften.

Eat the cones as soon as possible after baking or they will become soggy, especially in humid weather. Store airtight.

Hot Fudge

15 ounces bittersweet
    chocolate

1/2 cup granulated sugar

1 cup light corn syrup

1 cup plus 2 tablespoons
    water

1 1/2 cups unsweetened cocoa
    powder

1 1/2 tablespoons instant
    coffee

6 tablespoons Cognac or
    brandy

Makes 4½ cups

A shiny, black, intensely chocolate-flavored fudge sauce, velvety smooth drizzled over ice cream or added to homemade ice cream for a fudge ripple effect.

Cut chocolate into 2-inch pieces. In a heatproof bowl, melt chocolate over barely simmering water. (The water should not touch the bottom of the bowl or the chocolate will burn.) Turn off heat and let stand over warm water until ready to use.

In a large saucepan, combine the sugar, corn syrup, water, cocoa powder, and coffee and bring to a boil. Boil for 1–2 minutes, stirring constantly to prevent burning on the bottom. When the surface is covered with bubbles (and when you can no longer taste the graininess of the cocoa powder on your tongue), remove from heat and whisk in melted chocolate. Let boil a few minutes to reduce until the mixture is as thick and sticky as you like. The fudge will have a glossy shine. Stir in Cognac.

Let cool slightly before using. The fudge lasts indefinitely in the refrigerator. Again, reheat in a bowl placed over simmering water.

VARIATION: Use 1½ cups fudge for 1 quart of ice cream. Let fudge cool to room temperature. Just after the ice cream has been removed from the ice cream freezer, pick up the fudge by spoonfuls and let it fall into the ice cream, swirling it in with a rubber spatula.

Maple Dessert Waffles

1 cup plus 2 tablespoons flour

1 teaspoon baking soda

1 teaspoon salt

2 teaspoons granulated sugar

2 egg whites

½ cup buttermilk

½ cup beer

1 cup maple syrup

4 ounces unsalted butter (1 stick)

To Grease Waffle Iron:
2 tablespoons clarified unsalted butter (page 17), or spray-on nonstick pan coating

Makes 8 individual waffles

After tasting the Maple Sugar and Maple Syrup Ice Creams, I thought that an old-fashioned American waffle would go with them perfectly. After some experimentation, I came up with a maple syrup batter that turned out so good, I thought it should be boxed with a blurb on the package reading "No Syrup Necessary—It's in the Waffle!" (They're good with Vanilla Bean or Caramel Ice Cream, too.)

These waffles are crisp outside with almost a deep-fried taste, but they aren't greasy. They have a lacy quality—you can see through them when you hold them up to the light.

These were tested in an ordinary plug-in waffle iron, the kind that makes four 4½-inch-square thin waffles at once. If the waffle iron is of different dimensions, adjust the amount of batter accordingly.

Preheat waffle iron on highest temperature setting.

In a large bowl, sift together the flour and baking soda. Make a well in the center and sprinkle the salt and sugar onto the flour. In a small bowl, whisk together egg whites, buttermilk, and beer until combined. Pour the egg white mixture into the well. Using the whisk or a wooden spoon, slowly begin stirring the liquid, gradually drawing the dry ingredients in little by little until combined and smooth.

In a saucepan, bring the maple syrup to a boil and reduce until it measures ½–¾ cup. The syrup will foam up like cream as it boils. Let the foam subside and pour the syrup into a measuring cup to measure. Return it to the pan. Cut the butter into pieces and add to the syrup. Return to the boil, boiling until the butter is incorporated into the syrup. Pour the hot syrup into the flour mixture in a thin stream, stirring constantly until combined.

Brush preheated waffle iron with clarified butter or spray with nonstick coating. Be sure to grease both the top and bottom of the waffle iron and remember to grease again before cooking each batch of waffles. Pour about half the batter in an equal layer onto the bottom surface of the waffle iron. Close the top; if any batter oozes out, just scrape it off with a metal spatula. Cook until the waffle is nicely browned, 4–5 minutes. When the waffle is finished, it will be soft and lacy. It will crisp as it cools.

Using a rubber spatula and your fingers, very carefully lift one side of the waffle and gently fold it in half onto itself. Then fold the waffle in half again, bringing the top down, and lift it off the waffle iron. Unfold onto the work surface and trim any ragged edges if necessary. Cut into 4 individual waffles and place on plates. Keep warm briefly in a low-temperature oven while you wait for the second batch of waffles to cook. Don't stack the waffles on top of each other or they will get soggy.

Serve warm, topped with ice cream.

Italian Ice Cream Cones

1 cup heavy cream

1½ teaspoons vanilla extract

¾ cup powdered sugar

¾ cup flour

Pinch of freshly grated nutmeg

¼ teaspoon (rounded) cinnamon

1 tablespoon cornstarch

¼ cup unsalted clarified butter, melted (see page 17)

Makes 10 cones

An Italian *pizzelle* iron, available in cookware shops, bakes these ice cream cones over the burner of a gas stove, and embosses them with a pretty design at the same time. They come out of the iron as a flat wafer, subtly flavored with vanilla, nutmeg, and cinnamon, which can be left flat or shaped into a cone by folding it into a fluted champagne glass. These cones are too delicate to hold a scoop of ice cream—instead, they make a beautiful garnish and a crisp contrast in textures when arranged on a plate filled with homemade ice cream or sherbet.

It may take a little experimentation to get used to using the pizzelle iron, so you might want to double the recipe the first time you make them and have some extra batter to use for practice. The heat of the iron is the essential component—if the butter sizzles and burns, it's too hot; if there's no sizzling, it's too cool.

MAKING THE BATTER

In a large bowl, whisk the cream and the vanilla until it is thick and mousselike but does not form peaks. It should measure about 1¾ cups. Sift the dry ingredients through a strainer into the whipped cream and combine well. If any of the spices remain in the strainer, stir them back into the whipped cream. The batter will be thick and pastelike.

BAKING THE CONES

Heat the pizzelle iron over a medium-high flame. Brush it

Continued from previous page

lightly with butter. If the butter sizzles but does not burn or spurt, the iron is at the right temperature. Place 2 level tablespoons of batter in the center of the iron and close. If any batter oozes out, scrape it off with a knife. Let cook for 1 minute, then turn iron over and cook for 30 seconds. The wafer should be evenly brown on both sides. The uncooked parts of a wafer will never get crisp, so keep trying until you get evenly browned ones.

Carefully peel the wafer off the iron and fold it loosely in half. Drop it into a fluted champagne glass, pressing the wafer lightly with your fingers so that it takes on the shape of the flute. When crisp, remove from the glass and set aside to cool.

Remember to flip over the iron after you finish each cone, alternating the side of the iron that you first place against the flame when starting to cook each new cone. Reheat iron and repeat, using the rest of the batter.

Store airtight. These cones will keep overnight if the weather is not too humid.

Homemade Chocolate Chips

8 ounces bittersweet chocolate

Makes 1½ cups

Homemade chocolate chips have two important advantages over the commercial ones—you can use high-quality chocolate, and the chips are a much better size to use in ice cream, a real "chip" rather than a large drop.

Don't make them in hot weather; make a few batches when the weather is cool and freeze them for up to three months. I use a flexible metal paint scraper to scrape the chips off the baking sheet.

Cut chocolate into 2-inch pieces. In a heatproof bowl, melt chocolate over barely simmering water. (The water should not touch the bottom of the bowl or the chocolate will burn.) Turn off heat and let stand over warm water until ready to use.

Warm a heavy baking sheet or sheet pan slightly in the oven, until it is warm but not so hot that you can't touch it with your bare hands. Place the baking sheet upside down on a work surface.

Pour the chocolate onto the baking sheet. Using an off-set metal spatula, spread the melted chocolate evenly, covering the entire surface about ¹⁄₁₆ inch thick. Refrigerate the sheet until chocolate sets. This may take as long as 30 minutes.

Remove the sheet from the refrigerator and let chocolate soften slightly. Using a paring knife, score lines horizontally and vertically through the chocolate about ¼ inch apart, marking little squares across the surface in a graph pattern. If the chocolate cracks when you try to score it, it is too cold—let it warm up a bit more.

Using a paint scraper held at a 45-degree angle to the pan, scrape the chocolate squares off the pan, scraping away from you. Brace the edge of the sheet pan on the counter against a wall to hold it in place. As the chips come up off the pan, use the spatula to place them in a container and refrigerate or freeze. (If you touch them with your hands they will melt.) If the chocolate starts to melt or if the chips start coming up off the pan as one continuous curl of chocolate, refrigerate the sheet pan again briefly to chill. There is no limit to the number of times the chocolate can be returned to the refrigerator and then brought back to room temperature.

Removing the chips from the baking sheet

Plum Compote

4–6 red meat plums
   (1 pound)
1 tablespoon unsalted butter
2 tablespoons granulated
   sugar
¼ cup Cognac or Armagnac
2 teaspoons almond extract

Makes 2–3 cups

This compote of fresh plums is delicious warm over Vanilla Bean or Caramel Ice Cream or as an accompaniment to the Marzipan Cake in a Sweet Crust. It can also be made with nectarines, apricots, or peaches, but plums give it an appealing, puckery taste and a beautiful color.

Pit the plums and cut into eighths. In a stainless steel or enamel saucepan, cook the plums, butter, and sugar over high heat until the fruit has softened, 3–5 minutes. Remove pan from heat and add Cognac and almond extract. Return to medium-low heat and cook uncovered for 1–2 minutes, until the liquid has evaporated. (If the alcohol ignites, let it burn out.) Serve immediately.

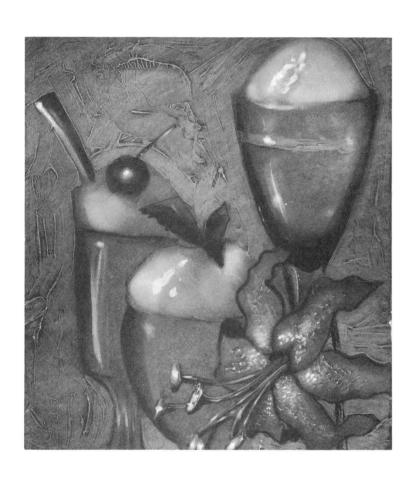

For Special Guests

MOUSSE CAKES

Chocolate Terrine with Wild Strawberries
Chocolate Mousse Cake
Chocolate-Raspberry Mousse Cake
Chocolate-Cognac Mousse Cake
Strawberry–White Chocolate Torte
Lemon Mousse Cake
Strawberry-Yogurt Mousse Cake

LAYERED CAKES

Mocha Cake
Chocolate Truffle Cake
Espresso Layer Cake
Caramel Tart
Banana-Pecan Layer Cake
Orange–Poppy Seed Cake
Marjolaine
Devil's Food Cake

FROZEN PARFAITS

Three-Chocolate Parfait with Bitter Chocolate Sauce
Poppy Seed–Caramel Parfait
Ginger Parfait
Orange, Hazelnut, and Chocolate Parfait
Coffee Parfait
Cassis Vacherin

*I*f you love to fuss over special desserts, these are the knock-'em-dead ones. I know some cooks who will spend hours making dinner and then run out and buy a dessert, but if you're like me, you'd rather buy a take-out dinner and spend your time making a show-stopping finish. These are desserts for very special people on very special occasions. The names give just an inkling of the tastes: Banana-Pecan Layer Cake, Chocolate Terrine with Wild Strawberries, Three-Chocolate Parfait with Bitter Chocolate Sauce, Strawberry–White Chocolate Torte, Poppy Seed–Caramel Parfait.

Although these recipes are generally more time-consuming than most others in the book, many of them require having two or three different preparations—like pastry cream, caramel, or sheet cakes—ready before you can begin assembling the dessert itself. These advance preparations can often be spread out over two or three days, cutting the time into manageable chunks. All of these desserts will keep at least two days stored in the refrigerator.

If some of the recipes look long, that's because all the steps are explained clearly and completely. You're spending your valuable time on these desserts, and sometimes investing in rather costly ingredients, so follow the directions carefully and you'll be sure to produce a *pièce de résistance*.

MOUSSE CAKES

Rather than just plopping a scoop of mousse into a bowl, I prefer to break up the texture with cake layers, fruit, rum-soaked currants, or other additions that make the mousse taste even creamier in contrast. A mousse molded in a flan ring or a springform pan and allowed to set until firm becomes a symmetrical, sophisticated-looking cake, decorative on its own or embellished simply with chocolate or fruit.

The mousse cakes need to be refrigerated for enough time to set up firmly in order to slice well. The mousses without chocolate may include a small amount of gelatin to help them hold their shape, but it is not enough to create a rubbery texture. Unmold mousse cakes by placing hot towels briefly around the pan and then releasing the sides or lifting off the ring.

Many of the mousse cakes can be made in advance and stored in the refrigerator for up to three days before serving.

Chocolate Charlotte Mousse

12 ounces bittersweet
   chocolate

2½ cups heavy cream

6 tablespoons sour cream

6 egg yolks

¾ cup sugar syrup
   (page 29)

Makes 6 cups

This charlotte is designed to have the density and richness that are so often lacking in mousselike fillings.

More chocolate and whipped cream are added to this charlotte mousse before it is molded into the cakes. Although this may seem like a rather roundabout method of putting together a mousse—making one preparation, letting it set up, and then adding more cream and chocolate—it's the best way to get the right texture for filling the cakes. If your electric mixer bowl is stainless steel, you'll save using two bowls by cooking the egg yolks in the mixer bowl.

Cut chocolate into 2-inch pieces. In a heatproof bowl, melt chocolate over barely simmering water. (The water should not touch the bottom of the bowl or the chocolate will burn.) Turn off heat and let stand over warm water until ready to use.

Using the whisk attachment of an electric mixer, beat the heavy cream with the sour cream on low speed until it thickens enough not to spatter. Increase speed to medium-high and beat until thick and mousselike. Remove from mixer. Whisk a few times by hand until soft peaks form. Refrigerate.

Place egg yolks in a large heatproof bowl. In a small saucepan, heat sugar syrup to boiling. Beat constantly with a wire whisk, pouring boiling syrup in a steady stream over yolks. Place bowl over gently simmering water and continue whisking until mixture is thick and forms a ribbon when the whisk is lifted, about 15 minutes. Rotate the bowl as necessary to prevent the egg from cooking around the sides. The mixture will approximately triple in volume and be hot to the touch.

Remove from heat and beat in an electric mixer on medium-high speed until the mixture has doubled in volume and the underside of the bowl is cool to the touch.

Beat in warm melted chocolate and combine well. The chocolate must be warm to incorporate smoothly into the egg yolk mixture.

Stir one third of the whipped cream into the chocolate mixture to lighten the texture, then fold in the rest. The consistency will be like very thick batter. Chill until ready to use, at least 2 hours.

Keeps refrigerated up to ten days.

Chocolate Terrine with Wild Strawberries

1 tablespoon unsalted butter, melted, to prepare pan

18 ounces bittersweet chocolate

6 ounces unsalted butter (1½ sticks)

12 egg yolks

5 tablespoons granulated sugar in all

¾ cup heavy cream

2 tablespoons sour cream

3 egg whites

1½ pints wild strawberries or raspberries (optional)

2 cups Bitter Chocolate Glaze (page 348)

Makes 10 to 12 servings

A terrine is usually a savory dish of meat, fish, or vegetables molded in a long, rectangular tin and served as a first course, but recently the terrine shape has become popular for desserts. With eighteen ounces of chocolate, this mousselike terrine is rich and exceedingly flavorful. It is studded with wild strawberries or raspberries, or a combination of both. Wild strawberries, when you can get them, are particularly delicious, as their aromatic quality perfumes the entire dessert. (Wild strawberries, also known as *fraises des bois*, are much smaller than commercial strawberries, more intense in flavor, and therefore not watery. Because of their high water content, commercial strawberries cannot be used in this dessert.) The terrine can also be made with chocolate only.

This recipe yields 6 cups of chocolate mixture, enough for a slant-sided French 10 x 4-inch terrine mold with 3-inch sides. A loaf pan, used for baking bread, can also be used, but it will hold only about 4 cups.

Prepare a 10 x 4-inch foil-covered cardboard rectangle, to unmold the terrine onto.

PREPARING THE MOLD

Using the terrine mold as a guide, cut out parchment or wax paper pieces to fit bottom, ends, and sides of pan. Brush the mold with the melted butter and line with paper. Set aside.

MAKING THE MOUSSE

Cut chocolate into 2-inch pieces. In a heatproof bowl, melt chocolate with the 6 ounces butter over barely simmering water. (The water should not touch the bottom of the bowl or the chocolate will burn.) Turn off heat and let stand over warm water until ready to use.

Using the whisk attachment of an electric mixer, beat together the egg yolks and 4 tablespoons of the sugar on high speed until the mixture is thick and mousselike. Whisk chocolate mixture into egg yolk mixture, then return it to the heatproof bowl. Over gently simmering water, whisk a few minutes until the mixture is thick, shiny, and the whisk leaves an empty trail behind it when it is drawn across the bottom of the pan. Remove from heat; set aside for a few minutes to cool.

Using the whisk attachment of an electric mixer, beat the heavy cream with the sour cream on low speed until it thickens enough not to spatter. Increase speed to medium high and beat until thick and mousselike. Remove from mixer. Whisk a few times by hand until soft peaks form. Whisk the whipped cream into the chocolate mixture.

Beat the egg whites on low speed until frothy. Increase speed to medium and beat until soft peaks form. Increase speed to high and gradually beat in remaining tablespoon of sugar, until stiff, glossy peaks form. It is important that the egg whites be beaten completely smooth before they are incorporated into the chocolate or there will be little white specks in the terrine. Whisk one third of the egg whites into the chocolate mixture, then fold in the rest.

❖ If you're using the chocolate only, simply pour the mixture into the terrine mold, smooth the top, and chill.

ASSEMBLING THE TERRINE

To layer the terrine with fruit, either pour in and spread with the back of a spoon or fill a pastry bag (No. 4 plain tip) with chocolate mixture. Pipe one fifth of the mixture into the prepared terrine mold in an even layer and tap pan on the work surface to settle it. Arrange one fourth of the wild strawberries or raspberries in the chocolate, placing them close together, but not touching, and leaving a ¼-inch border around the edges of the chocolate so that the berries will not show on the sides when the terrine is unmolded. Repeat with chocolate and berries, constructing four layers of berries and five of chocolate, ending with a layer of chocolate. Freeze up to 1½ hours, or refrigerate at least 5 hours.

❖ The freezer is the faster way to chill and firm the terrine, but don't let it stay there more than 1½ hours—if the fruit freezes, it will lose its color and becomes watery when thawed.

UNMOLDING AND GLAZING THE TERRINE

Warm the chocolate glaze over barely simmering water until it is just warm enough to be pourable, but not hot.

Before unmolding, remove terrine from freezer and spread 3–4 tablespoons warm glaze in a very thin layer on the top to form a barrier that will keep it from sticking to the serving platter. Return to freezer or refrigerator until the chocolate layer hardens.

To unmold, dip terrine briefly in hot water or wrap in hot towels, then turn it over onto a cardboard rectangle covered with foil. Holding the cardboard and the pan together, tap firmly on all sides with your hand or the handle of a spatula, and then shake vigorously to release. It will come out! Warm the sides of the terrine only briefly (maybe repeating the process once or twice) or the chocolate may melt and lose its shape. Place on a rack or a baking sheet. Peel off paper lining and smooth the sides of the terrine with a long metal spatula. Return to freezer briefly if necessary to chill and firm sides.

Pour or ladle the warm glaze over the length of the terrine, allowing the glaze to flow over the top and sides in a thin layer, making an even coating. To prevent the glaze from leaving drip marks, let the terrine sit a minute or two without moving so that the glaze can set. With a flat metal spatula, lift chocolate that has fallen off and pat it back onto areas that are not covered. Return to refrigerator or freezer for 45 minutes until the glaze is firm.

Cut terrine into ⅜-inch slices with a very hot knife, heated over a flame or in hot water in between cutting each slice. This dessert tastes best when very cold, so slice and serve immediately after taking from the refrigerator. Lay slices flat on a plate that has been mirrored with Raspberry Sauce, Strawberry Sauce, Bitter Chocolate Sauce, or Vanilla Sauce (or on a plate with half Raspberry Sauce, half Bitter Chocolate Sauce). The terrine keeps refrigerated up to 5 days, unmolded but not sliced.

Chocolate Mousse Cake

1 recipe Moist Chocolate Cake (page 255), baked in three 8-inch layers

3 cups Chocolate Charlotte Mousse (page 249)

8 ounces bittersweet chocolate

¾ cup heavy cream

1½ tablespoons sour cream

For Decoration (choose from the options below):
2–3 cups Bitter Chocolate Glaze (page 348)

1½ cups ground Praline (page 354) or Nougatine (page 353) or crushed Sugared Almonds (page 353)

Chocolate curls (page 345)

1 cake wall, made with Chocolate Almond Sheet Cake (page 267)

Cocoa powder or powdered sugar, sifted

Makes one 8-inch cake, serving 8–10

In this cake both the velvety chocolate filling and the moist cake layers are mousses, but one is baked and one isn't. There are a number of options for decorating this cake: you can glaze it with chocolate and press ground praline onto the sides, put crunchy chocolate curls on the sides and top, or finish it with a striped "wall" of chocolate cake around the bottom and a slick of chocolate glaze on top. (See "Building a cake wall," page 256.) Use an 8-inch spring-form pan or entremet ring. (If you are making a cake wall, fit it into an 8-inch springform pan before beginning. See Lemon Mousse Cake illustration, page 268.)

With a thin, serrated knife, trim the moist chocolate cake layers horizontally to an even thickness. Trim the edges so that they measure 7½ inches in diameter. Center one layer in the bottom of an 8-inch springform pan or entremet ring. Attach sides to springform pan and set aside.

Cut chocolate into 2-inch pieces. In a heatproof bowl, melt chocolate over barely simmering water. (The water should not touch the bottom of the bowl or the chocolate will burn.) Turn off heat and let stand over warm water until ready to use.

Using the whisk attachment of an electric mixer, beat the heavy cream and sour cream on low speed until it thickens enough not to spatter. Increase speed to medium-high and beat until thick and mousselike. Remove from mixer. Whisk a few strokes by hand until soft peaks form. Refrigerate.

In a large heatproof bowl, whisk the chocolate charlotte mousse vigorously over gently simmering water to soften and smooth. The mousse should be just warm to the touch but not runny. Remove bowl from heat. Whisk in the whipped cream and then add the warm melted chocolate, whisking hard to incorporate until the mixture is smooth and shiny and just barely holds soft peaks.

ASSEMBLING THE CAKE

Fill a pastry bag (No. 4 plain tip) half full of mousse. Pipe a border of mousse to fill in the space between the cake layer and the sides of the pan. Then, starting in the center, pipe an even spiral over the cake layer all the way to the sides. The mousse layers should be about ½ inch thick. (The mousse can also be spread with an offset metal spat-

Chocolate Mousse Cake
(continued)

ula or the back of a spoon.) Place a cake layer on top and press down lightly. Pipe a border of mousse and then a layer as directed above. Top with the last cake layer, press down lightly, and then pipe on mousse as directed. Smooth with a long-bladed metal spatula even with the top of the pan. Chill until firm, about 2 hours.

DECORATING THE CAKE

Option 1: Glaze and praline. In a heatproof bowl, warm the chocolate glaze over barely simmering water until it is just warm enough to be pourable, but not hot. Unmold the cake by placing hot towels briefly around the pan and then releasing the sides. Hold the cake flat on the palm of your hand over a baking sheet. Pour or ladle the warm glaze over the cake, tilting the cake and letting the glaze run down the sides to make an even layer, shaking off the excess glaze. Chill 20–30 minutes, until the glaze is completely set. Glaze again, then chill 10–15 minutes until the sides are set but still sticky. Press praline, nougatine, or sugared almonds onto the sides with fingers and palm of one hand, turning cake with the other hand.

Option 2: Unmold and glaze the cake as described in Option 1 and decorate with chocolate curls. (See "Making chocolate curls," page 345.)

Option 3: Cake wall. If you have fitted a cake wall into the pan before beginning, glaze the top of the cake before it is unmolded. Then unmold as described in Option 1. Heat ½ cup chocolate glaze as directed above. Hold the cake flat on the palm of your hand. Pour or ladle the warm glaze over the cake, tilting the pan to distribute the glaze in a thin, even layer over the top. Pour off excess. Refrigerate until set, 15–30 minutes. Unmold as directed above.

This cake takes only a total of 1 hour to set up in the refrigerator. If stored longer, the cake tastes best if allowed to sit at room temperature for 20–30 minutes to let the filling soften up a bit.

A number of sauces go well with this dessert, including Vanilla Sauce flavored with Cognac, Coffee Sauce, Bitter Chocolate Sauce, or two of the above pooled half-and-half on the dessert plate.

Moist Chocolate Cake

To Prepare Pan:
2 tablespoons unsalted butter, melted (for sheet pan or springform pans)

Cocoa powder or flour

14 ounces bittersweet chocolate

6 ounces unsalted butter (1¼ sticks)

10 eggs, separated

7 tablespoons granulated sugar (the 12 x 17-inch cake requires an extra 2 teaspoons for sprinkling) in all

1 tablespoon plus 1 teaspoon flour

Makes 3 thin 8-inch layers or one 12 x 17-inch sheet cake

Almost as light as an ordinary chocolate *génoise*, this cake has the delicious taste of real melted chocolate rather than of the milder cocoa powder that is more common in cakes. It's so moist that it doesn't need to be soaked with syrup as a génoise often does.

This cake doesn't slice easily into layers, so for a multi-layered round cake it must be baked in three separate round layers. Use three 8-inch flan rings or springform pans. For the Mocha Cake, bake it in a 12 x 17-inch sheet pan and cut out rectangles after baking.

Preheat oven to 350 degrees. Adjust rack to middle position.

If you're using flan rings, set them on two paper-lined baking sheets. For a sheet pan or springform pans, brush with melted butter and line bottom with paper. Brush again with butter, chill briefly to set and dust with cocoa powder or flour, and knock out excess. Set aside.

Cut chocolate into 2-inch pieces. In a heatproof bowl, melt chocolate with the 6 ounces of butter over barely simmering water. (The water should not touch the bottom of the bowl or the chocolate will burn.) Turn off heat and let stand over warm water until ready to use.

Using the whisk attachment of an electric mixer, beat egg yolks at high speed with 2 tablespoons of the sugar until mixture is thick, pale yellow, and triples in volume. Whisk the melted chocolate into the egg yolk mixture and return it to the heatproof bowl. Over gently simmering water, whisk a few minutes until the mixture is thick, shiny, and the whisk leaves an empty trail behind it when it is drawn across the bottom of the pan. Remove from heat; cool. Sprinkle flour over top of mixture but do not stir in.

Beat egg whites on low speed until frothy. Increase speed to medium and beat until soft peaks form. Increase speed to high and very gradually beat in remaining 5 tablespoons sugar, until very stiff, glossy peaks form. Whisk one third of the egg whites into chocolate mixture to lighten the texture, then fold in the rest.

For three round layers, divide batter evenly into flan rings or springform pans, and spread with an offset metal spatula or the back of a spoon to even. For a sheet cake, pour batter into prepared pan, making the layer no more than 2 inches thick. There may be some batter left over. Spread batter evenly with a metal spatula or the back of a spoon.

Bake for 25 minutes. For round layers, rotate the baking sheets in the oven halfway through baking. The cake will shrink slightly from sides of pan and develop a thin crust that will be medium-firm to the touch. It will fall very slightly after baking. (If the cake becomes sticky when cool, it has not been baked long enough. You can return it to the oven for 5–10 minutes to eliminate the stickiness.)

To unmold cake rounds, run a knife around the edges of the cake and remove flan rings (or release sides of spring-form pans). Turn paper over and peel it off the backs of the cake layers. To unmold sheet pan, sprinkle the top of the cake with 2 teaspoons granulated sugar. Invert onto a work surface and peel off paper.

The layers are best made the day they will be used. If made in advance, do not refrigerate or cover them as they will get sticky.

Building a Cake Wall

1 Chocolate Almond Sheet Cake (page 267) or Almond Sheet Cake (page 271)

1 to 1½ cups apricot jam or red currant jelly (for Almond Sheet Cake) or Chocolate Glaze (for Chocolate Almond Cake)

A cake wall is a stylish, professional-looking way to decorate cakes like the Chocolate Mousse Cake and the Lemon Mousse Cake. Strips of cake are sandwiched together with jam or chocolate glaze and then cut into slices. The slices are fitted around the inside of the springform pan, creating a striped wall. It is an attractive, symmetrical decoration that also serves the practical purpose of supporting the sides of the mousse when it is unmolded.

One 12 x 17-inch sheet cake will be enough to make walls for at least two cakes. The Almond Sheet Cake and the Chocolate Almond Sheet Cake work best because they are compact, moist, and sturdy. Wrap the sandwiched cake strips in plastic wrap and they will keep in the freezer for up to three months.

For the Almond Sheet Cake: In a small saucepan, heat the apricot jam or currant jelly to boiling, whisking constantly. Strain the jam through a fine-mesh strainer. Jelly does not need to be strained. Set aside.

For the Chocolate Almond Sheet Cake: The chocolate glaze should be at an easily spreadable consistency. If it is freshly made and too thin, stir it briefly over ice to thicken slightly. If it is cold and thick, heat over simmering water only enough so that when the glaze is whisked vigorously it is smooth. Do not heat enough to become runny.

To remove sheet cake from pan, sprinkle with 2 teaspoons granulated sugar and invert onto the work surface. Peel off paper. Trim about ½ inch from the edges of the cake. If you need a round piece of cake, as for the Lemon Mousse Cake, trace a 7½-inch circle in one corner of the sheet and cut out.

Cut the remainder of the sheet cake into even strips 10 inches long by 2 inches wide. Use a ruler to make the measurements as exact as possible.

Sandwiching the cake with jam

Make stacks of three strips each, sandwiching them together with a thin layer of jam or glaze spread with a metal spatula. (The jam or jelly must be spread quite thin, because it won't harden like chocolate and will ooze out later when cut.) Place the stacks on a baking sheet and freeze until firm, at least 2 hours or overnight.

When frozen, trim ¼ inch from the ends and the long sides of each stack so that it is very square. Turn the stacks so that the long striped side is up and the smooth (cake only) side is toward you. One at a time, cut crosswise into a slice ⅜ inch thick. Stand the slice against the inside of the springform pan. (In the pan, each slice will look like three vertical stripes of cake.)

Slicing the wall into pieces

Cut another slice and stand it up next to the first slice to compare the height. If it is not exactly the same size as the first slice, remove it from the pan and trim it. Replace in the pan. Repeat the same process with every slice, comparing the height and trimming each one when you put it in. This may seem like a long process, but the look of the finished cake depends on having a nice, uniform wall all around. The slices should form a wall 1½ inches high by ⅜ inch thick. Refrigerate prepared pan until ready to continue with dessert.

Chocolate-Raspberry Mousse Cake

1 Moist Chocolate Cake
  (page 255), baked in
  three 8-inch layers

3 tablespoons raspberry jam

6 ounces bittersweet
  chocolate

1/2 cup heavy cream

1 tablespoon sour cream

2 cups Chocolate Charlotte
  Mousse (page 249)

4 1/2 cups fresh raspberries

To Decorate:
1/2 cup Bitter Chocolate
  Glaze (page 348)

1 chocolate band, 3 inches
  high to wrap around 8-
  inch cake, optional (page
  350)

**Makes one 8-inch cake,
serving 8–10**

A variation of the chocolate mousse cake, with fresh raspberries scattered between the layers and covering the top. Decorate the top with chocolate glaze and add a chocolate band around the outside if you like.

Use an 8-inch springform pan or entremet ring.

With a thin serrated knife, trim the cake layers horizontally to an even thickness. Spread one layer with the raspberry jam and center it in the bottom of an 8-inch springform pan or entrement ring. Attach sides to springform pan and set aside.

Cut chocolate into 2-inch pieces. In a heatproof bowl, melt chocolate over barely simmering water. (The water should not touch the bottom of the bowl or the chocolate will burn.) Turn off heat and let stand over warm water until ready to use.

Using the whisk attachment of an electric mixer, beat the heavy cream and sour cream on low speed until it thickens enough not to spatter. Increase speed to medium-high and beat until thick and mousselike. Remove from mixer. Whisk a few strokes by hand until soft peaks form. Refrigerate.

In a large heatproof bowl, whisk the chocolate charlotte mousse vigorously over gently simmering water to soften and smooth. The mousse should be just warm to the touch but not runny. Remove bowl from heat. Whisk in the whipped cream and then add the warm melted chocolate, whisking hard to incorporate until the mixture is smooth and shiny and just barely holds soft peaks.

ASSEMBLING THE CAKE

Fill a pastry bag (No. 4 plain tip) half full of mousse. Pipe a border of mousse around the edge of the cake layer. Then, starting in the center, pipe an even spiral over the cake layer all the way to the sides. The mousse layers should be about 1/2 inch thick. (The mousse can also be spread with an offset metal spatula or the back of a spoon.) Sprinkle with 3/4 cup fresh raspberries. Place a cake layer on top and press down lightly. Pipe a border of mousse and an even layer as directed above. Sprinkle with 3/4 cup raspberries. Top with the last cake layer and press down lightly. The cake should be even with the top of the pan; trim horizontally if necessary to even.

DECORATING THE CAKE

In a heatproof bowl, warm the chocolate glaze over barely simmering water until it is just warm enough to be pourable, but not hot. Hold the cake flat on the palm of your hand over a baking sheet. Pour or ladle the warm glaze over the top of the cake, tilting the cake to distribute the glaze in a thin, even layer over the top. Pour off excess.

To cover the top with fresh raspberries, start at the outside edge of the cake and make a border of raspberries set touching each other, stem end down. Then, starting in the center and working outward in concentric circles, cover the entire top of the cake with raspberries. Chill until firm, about 1 hour.

Unmold by placing hot towels briefly around the pan and releasing the sides. Wrap the chocolate band around the cake, wax paper side out. Refrigerate. Remove paper when you take the cake out of the refrigerator to serve.

(If you are short on raspberries, or if some of the raspberries are less than perfect, the cake also looks very nice with a border of three or four circles of berries around the edge and a shiny, dark chocolate center.) If the cake has been stored for longer than 1 hour, remove the paper from the outside of the chocolate band and let the cake sit (in a cool place) for 20–30 minutes to allow the filling to soften up a bit.

Serve with Raspberry Sauce, Bitter Chocolate Sauce, or Vanilla Sauce.

Chocolate-Cognac Mousse Cake

Chocolate-Cognac Mousse:

3/4 cup Cognac

1 cup raisins, optional

14 ounces bittersweet chocolate

3 tablespoons unsalted butter

1 cup heavy cream

2 tablespoons sour cream

2 egg yolks

1/2 tablespoon instant espresso

4 egg whites

2 tablespoons granulated sugar

For Decoration (choose from the options below):

2–3 cups Chocolate Glaze (page 348)

1 1/2 cups ground Praline (page 354) or Nougatine (page 353) or crushed Sugared Almonds (page 353)

Chocolate band (page 350) and chocolate ruffles (page 346)

Cocoa powder or powdered sugar, sifted

Makes one 8-inch round cake, serving 10–12

I love the contrast in textures that's created when this very creamy chocolate mousse is molded into a casing of chocolate cake. Glaze the cake with chocolate and decorate with praline pressed onto the sides, or, if you have a little more time, wrap it in a chocolate band and top with chocolate curls dusted with cocoa powder.

If you fold Cognac-soaked raisins into the mousse, they may bring back memories of chocolate-covered raisins.

Use an 8-inch springform pan or entremet ring.

LINING THE PAN WITH CAKE

Using the bottom of a springform pan or entremet ring as a guide, cut two 8-inch rounds of chocolate-almond cake. Put one round in the bottom of the pan and set the other aside. Then, cut strips of cake 3 inches wide that, together, are long enough to line the insides of the pan. Fit the cake strips inside the mold, trimming so that the ends meet exactly and do not overlap. Trim the top edge to the exact height of the pan. (The entire cake will be glazed later, so a little patchwork with separate pieces of cake will not show.) Set aside lined pan and reserved cake circle.

MAKING THE CHOCOLATE-COGNAC MOUSSE

If you are adding raisins, scald them with the Cognac. Remove from heat and let stand until cool. If the alcohol ignites, blow it out.

Cut chocolate into 2-inch pieces. In a heatproof bowl, melt chocolate with butter over barely simmering water. (The water should not touch the bottom of the bowl or the chocolate will burn.) Turn off heat and let stand over warm water until ready to use.

Using the whisk attachment of an electric mixer, beat the heavy cream with sour cream on low speed until it thickens enough not to spatter. Increase speed to medium-high and beat until thick and mousselike. Remove from mixer. Whisk a few strokes by hand until soft peaks form. Refrigerate.

In a large mixing bowl, combine the egg yolks and melted chocolate mixture. The mixture will be thick. In a small saucepan, heat Cognac (with optional raisins) and espresso powder over low heat to steaming. Immediately pour the hot Cognac into the melted chocolate mixture and whisk together. The mixture should be smooth and very glossy. If it is dull, whisk in a few more tablespoons warmed Cognac. When chocolate has cooled to just warm to the touch, whisk in one third of the whipped cream to lighten the texture, then fold in the rest.

Using the whisk attachment of an electric mixer, beat the egg whites on low speed until frothy. Increase speed to medium and beat until soft peaks form. Increase speed to high and gradually beat in the granulated sugar, until stiff, glossy peaks form. Whisk one third of the egg whites into the chocolate mixture to lighten texture, then fold in the rest. (If the mousse isn't firm enough to keep the raisins suspended, refrigerate until it firms up. Otherwise, the raisins will sink to the bottom of the mold.)

Pour chocolate mousse into cake-lined pan. Depending on the volume of mousse, it may not fill pan to the top. Place the reserved cake round on top of the mousse. If the mousse is lower than the top of the pan, trim the edges of the cake round so that it fits inside cake walls and rests directly on the mousse. Chill until firmly set, 2 hours in the freezer or 4 hours in the refrigerator. When the cake is set, release sides of springform pan or remove entremet ring. The cake will be very solid. Before glazing, turn the cake over, so that the bottom becomes the top—this will ensure a nice level top. Place it back on the bottom of the spring-form pan or on a foil-covered cardboard round to continue.

GLAZING THE CAKE AND DECORATING THE SIDES

In a heatproof bowl, warm the chocolate glaze over barely simmering water until it is just warm enough to be poura-ble, but not hot. Hold the cake flat on the palm of your hand over a baking sheet. Pour or ladle the warm glaze over the cake, tilting the cake and letting the glaze run down the sides to make an even layer, shaking off the excess glaze. (If you are decorating the cake with chocolate ruffles, see below.) Chill 20–30 minutes, until the glaze is completely set. Glaze again, then chill 10–15 minutes, until the sides are set but still sticky. Press praline, nouga-tine, or sugared almonds onto the sides with fingers and palm of one hand, turning cake with the other hand. Return to refrigerator until glaze is completely set.

DECORATING WITH A CHOCOLATE BAND AND CHOCOLATE RUFFLES

Before glazing cake, prepare chocolate band and ruffles as described on pages 350 and 346. Glaze cake once as directed above. While glaze is still sticky, place band around cake, wax paper side out, and decorate the top with ruffles. Dust lightly with cocoa or powdered sugar sifted through a sieve.

This cake is best if eaten after it is allowed to sit at room temperature for 20 to 30 minutes so that the mousse can soften up a bit. If the cake has been decorated with ruffles, make sure it is kept out of the sunlight to prevent the chocolate from melting. Serve with Vanilla Sauce (page 336).

Three-Nut Torte

1 tablespoon unsalted butter, melted

½ cup hazelnuts (2 ounces)

½ cup walnuts (2 ounces)

½ cup almonds (2 ounces)

3 ounces bittersweet chocolate, very cold

6 eggs separated

¼ cup plus 3 tablespoons granulated sugar in all

1 tablespoon grated or finely chopped orange zest (1 orange)

½ teaspoon baking powder

Makes three 8-inch layers

Used in Strawberry–White Chocolate Torte

Neither a meringue nor a cake, this flourless torte has a delicate, almost feathery texture of its own. The wonderful taste combines chocolate, orange, and three kinds of nuts. Baked in one pan and cut into wedges, it's a simple, delicious, not-too-sweet dessert; baked in three thin layers, it's the base for the Strawberry–White Chocolate Torte.

Nut meal replaces flour in this recipe, so a light texture is essential. The texture is best if the nuts are grated by hand in a Mouli grater. If you want to use a food processor, grind the nuts with a few tablespoons of the measured granulated sugar to keep them from becoming a paste.

Use three 8-inch flan rings set on 2 heavy baking sheets (or one 8-inch round layer cake pan).

Preheat oven to 325 degrees. Adjust oven rack to the middle position. Brush the flan rings with melted butter and set on paper-lined baking sheets; set aside. (Prepare layer cake pans using parchment paper and melted butter.)

Spread the hazelnuts on a baking sheet and toast 8–10 minutes, until brown. Cool. Rub in a clean dish towel to remove skins. Cool. Grind the walnuts, almonds, and hazelnuts in a Mouli grater; set aside.

Readjust oven heat to 300 degrees. Adjust racks to upper

and lower positions of oven.

Chop chocolate by hand into pieces about the size of a grain of rice. There will be about ½ cup.

Using the whisk attachment of an electric mixer, beat egg yolks with ¼ cup sugar until the sugar has dissolved and mixture is thick, pale yellow, and forms a ribbon when beater is lifted from the bowl. Toss together the ground nuts, orange zest, baking powder, and chopped chocolate and pour on top of egg yolks; do not mix in. Set aside.

Beat egg whites on low speed until frothy. Increase speed to medium and beat until soft peaks form. Increase speed to high and very gradually beat in the 3 tablespoons sugar, until stiff, glossy peaks form.

Whisk one third of the beaten egg whites into the bowl of egg yolks to lighten the texture, then fold in the rest. Divide batter equally into prepared rings and spread evenly with an offset metal spatula or the back of a spoon. Bake for 30 minutes, just until the cake is springy to the touch. Halfway through baking, rotate the trays so that the cake layers bake evenly.

❖ If you are baking the torte in one pan, compensate for the extra thickness by letting it bake a little longer. The cake will be just springy to the touch when done.

To unmold, run a knife around the rings and remove. Turn paper over and peel it off the backs of the cake layers.

Strawberry-White Chocolate Torte

White Chocolate Mousse:

7 ounces white chocolate

1½ cups heavy cream in all

5 egg yolks

5 tablespoons lemon juice (1–2 lemons), in all

Zest of 1–2 lemons, grated or finely chopped

½ cup sugar syrup (page 29)

1 Three-Nut Torte, baked in three 8-inch layers (page 262)

2½ pints fresh strawberries

1½ teaspoons granulated gelatin

½ cup Bitter Chocolate Glaze (page 348) or White Chocolate Glaze (page 349)

Makes one 8-inch cake, serving 8–10

Although I usually find white chocolate terribly sweet, combining white chocolate mousse with sliced strawberries and chocolate-hazelnut torte creates a fresh-tasting, beautifully balanced dessert. The border of cut strawberries around the bottom of the white mousse makes the torte a look-alike for the classic French *bagatelle*, but the tastes are not at all similar.

Use an 8-inch springform pan or entremet ring.

If your electric mixer bowl is stainless steel, you'll save using two bowls by cooking the egg yolks in the mixer bowl.

MAKING THE WHITE CHOCOLATE MOUSSE

Cut chocolate into 2-inch pieces. In a heatproof bowl, melt chocolate over barely simmering water. (Watch carefully—white chocolate burns more easily than dark chocolate. The water should not touch the bottom of the bowl.) Turn off heat and let stand over warm water until ready to use.

Using the whisk attachment of an electric mixer, beat the heavy cream on low speed until it thickens enough not to spatter. Increase speed to medium-high and beat until thick and mousselike. Remove from mixer. Whisk a few times by hand until soft peaks form. Refrigerate.

Place egg yolks, 2 tablespoons of the lemon juice, and lemon zest in a large heatproof bowl. In a small saucepan, heat the sugar syrup to boiling. Beating constantly with a wire whisk, pour boiling water in a steady stream over the yolks. Place bowl over gently simmering water and continue whisking until the mixture is thick and forms a ribbon when the whisk is lifted, about 15 minutes. Rotate the bowl as necessary to prevent the egg from cooking around the sides. The mixture will approximately triple in volume and be hot to the touch.

Remove from heat and beat in an electric mixer on medium-high speed until the mixture has doubled in volume and the underside of the bowl is cool to the touch.

Beat in the warm melted chocolate and combine well. (Chocolate must be warm to incorporate smoothly into the egg yolk mixture.) Measure out 2 cups of whipped cream. Whisk 1 cup of the whipped cream into the chocolate mixture to lighten texture, then fold in 1 more cup. (Refrigerate remaining cream.) Refrigerate mousse at least 3 hours.

❖ The mousse can be made up to seven days in advance of assembling the torte.

ASSEMBLING THE TORTE

With a serrated knife, trim one of the cake layers to 6 inches in diameter and the other two to 7 inches in diameter. If the layers are thicker than ⅜ inch or uneven, trim horizontally. Trim carefully; the cake is fragile and tears easily. Center the 6-inch cake layer on the bottom of an 8-inch springform pan or entremet ring.. Put the sides on the springform pan.

Stem the strawberries and cut in half lengthwise. Pick out a number of halves that are more or less equal in size. If necessary, trim the bottoms so they are similar.

Place a border of strawberries, stem end down, and the cut side touching the insides of the pan. The strawberries should fit snugly between the cake layer and the sides of the pan.

Arranging the strawberries

Place gelatin in the bottom of a large heatproof bowl and pour on remaining 3 tablespoons lemon juice. If all the gelatin granules do not absorb the juice, or if there are any lumps of gelatin, dribble on a bit more juice or water. Heat briefly over gently simmering water until the gelatin dissolves. Turn off heat and keep warm.

Remove whipped cream from refrigerator and whisk a few times to remount, if necessary.

Whisk the mousse into the gelatin until combined. Whisk one third of the remaining whipped cream into the mousse to lighten the texture, then fold in the rest. Set bowl over ice water and fold continuously until the mixture has set enough to form soft peaks when a bit is lifted with the spatula. Remove from ice.

Piping the mousse

Fill a pastry bag (No. 4 plain tip) half-full of mousse. Pipe blobs of mousse between the strawberries in the pan, completely filling the spaces between them. Pipe a border of mousse to fill in the space between the cake layer and the strawberries. Then, starting in the center, pipe an even spiral over the cake layer and out to the sides of the pan.

Place half the remaining strawberries, cut side down, on the mousse, keeping them about ½ inch away from the edge of the pan so that they won't show when the torte is unmolded. Place a cake layer on top, press down lightly to even out the mousse, and pipe on a border and then a layer of mousse as directed above. Arrange the remaining strawberries on the mousse, cut side down and ½ inch away from the edge of the pan.

Top with the last cake layer and press down lightly. It should be just below or even with the top of the pan. If it is too high, press down a bit more or, if necessary, make it thinner by trimming it horizontally with a serrated knife. Spread the surface with a thin layer of mousse, even with the top of the pan. Refrigerate until set, at least 2 hours.

GLAZING THE TORTE

In a heatproof bowl, warm the chocolate glaze over barely simmering water until it is just warm enough to be pourable, but not hot. Hold the cake flat on the palm of your hand over a baking sheet. Pour or ladle the warm glaze over the cake, tilting the pan to distribute the glaze in a thin, even layer over the top only. Pour off excess. Refrigerate until set, 15–30 minutes.

UNMOLDING THE TORTE

Unmold by placing hot towels briefly around the pan and then releasing the sides. Refrigerate until set.

Serve with Strawberry Sauce. Store the finished torte no longer than 24 hours. The cut strawberries will lose their color if stored longer.

Chocolate-Almond Sheet Cake

To Prepare Pan:

2 tablespoons butter, melted

1 tablespoon cocoa powder or flour

4 ounces bittersweet chocolate

7 egg yolks

½ tablespoon almond extract

11 tablespoons unsalted butter

1 cup almond meal

7 egg whites

⅓ cup plus 2 teaspoons sugar in all

Makes one 12 x 17-inch sheet cake

Used in Chocolate-Cognac Mousse Cake

This light, richly flavored base for the Chocolate-Cognac Mousse Cake and all the variations of the Chocolate Truffle Cake is a sturdy one, useful for building cake "walls." (See "Building a cake wall," page 256.)

Use a 12 by 17-inch sheet pan.

Preheat oven to 325 degrees. Adjust oven rack to middle position.

Brush a 12 x 17-inch sheet pan with melted butter. Line bottom with paper and butter again. Chill briefly to set, dust with cocoa powder or flour, knock out excess, and set aside.

Cut chocolate into 2-inch pieces. In a heatproof bowl, melt chocolate over barely simmering water. (The water should not touch the bottom of the bowl or the chocolate will burn.) Turn off heat and let stand over warm water until ready to use.

In a small bowl, lightly whisk together egg yolks and almond extract. Set aside.

Using the paddle attachment of an electric mixer, beat butter at medium-high speed until it whitens and holds soft peaks, 3–5 minutes. Beat in almond meal until well mixed. Add the chocolate and egg yolks alternately, one half at a time, scraping down the sides of the bowl as necessary. Set aside.

Using the whisk attachment of an electric mixer or with a wire whisk, beat egg whites on low speed until frothy. Increase speed to medium and beat until soft peaks form. Increase speed to high and very gradually beat in the granulated sugar until stiff, glossy peaks form.

Whisk about one third of the egg whites into chocolate mixture to lighten the texture, then fold in the rest. Pour the batter into the prepared sheet pan, filling no fuller than ½ inch from the top, and spread evenly with an offset metal spatula.

Bake for 15 minutes, or until the crust is set but the cake is still slightly soft to the touch.

To unmold, run a knife around the edges of the cake. Sprinkle the top of the cake with 2 teaspoons granulated sugar and invert onto a work surface. Peel off paper. Leftover cake freezes well.

Lemon Mousse Cake

1 Almond Sheet Cake (page 271) (including wall, optional)

2 tablespoons lemon juice to soak cake (1 lemon)

Lemon Butter Cream:
6 tablespoons lemon juice (3 lemons)

4 ounces unsalted butter (1 stick)

1 tablespoon grated or finely chopped lemon zest (1–2 lemons)

3 tablespoons powdered sugar, sifted

2 tablespoons sour cream

1 cup fresh raspberries, blackberries, blueberries, or sliced strawberries, optional

Piping the buttercream

This mousse is frothy, almost weightless, but it has the definite tart flavor of lemon and lime. Fresh berries can add another dimension. An Italian meringue and a very small amount of gelatin help the mousse set up without making it rubbery.

Molding the mousse in an 8-inch springform pan or entremet ring lined with a wall of almond cake or left plain creates a pristinely symmetrical dessert.

PREPARING THE PAN

If you're making a cake wall, make a 12 x 17-inch Almond Sheet Cake, cut an 8-inch round from it for the bottom of the mousse, and use the rest to make the cake wall as directed on page 256. If you don't plan to make a cake wall, make only an 8-inch round of cake, using one third of the recipe on page 271 and baking it in a round layer cake pan. Without a wall to support the sides, the mousse cake should be no higher than 1½ inches, in which case you will need only half the above quantity of mousse (it is easier to make the Italian meringue if you make the same quantity and use only half of it).

Make the cake wall and fit it into the pan according to directions on page 256.

With a thin serrated knife, trim the cake round horizontally if necessary to ½-inch thickness. Trim the edges so that the cake measures 7½ inches in diameter and fits within the wall. (If you are not using the cake wall, still trim to 7½ inches.) Center the layer in the bottom of the springform pan. Brush cake layer with 2 tablespoons of the lemon juice. Put sides on springform pan or place entremet ring around cake; set aside.

Using the paddle attachment of an electric mixer, beat the butter with the lemon zest at medium-high speed until it whitens and holds soft peaks, 3–5 minutes. Add the powdered sugar and beat until well mixed. Stir together remaining 6 tablespoons lemon juice and the sour cream and beat in.

Using a pastry bag (No. 3 plain tip) or the back of a spoon, pipe or spread all the butter mixture on the cake, covering it completely. Scatter in berries. Refrigerate until set.

Lemon Mousse:

1 tablespoon (1 envelope) granulated gelatin

3/4 cup lemon juice (3–4 lemons) in all

4 egg yolks

1 cup plus 3 tablespoons granulated sugar

1/2 cup lime juice (3–4 limes)

1/2 cup heavy cream

1/2 cup milk

Zest of 3–4 lemons, grated or finely chopped

Zest of 3–4 limes, grated or finely chopped

1/3 cup water

4 egg whites

Makes one 8-inch cake

MAKING THE LEMON MOUSSE

Place gelatin in the bottom of a heatproof bowl and pour on 4 tablespoons of the lemon juice. If all the gelatin granules do not absorb the juice, or if there are any lumps of gelatin, dribble on a bit more juice or water. Heat briefly over gently simmering water until the gelatin dissolves. Turn off heat and keep warm.

Using the whisk attachment of an electric mixer, beat together egg yolks and 5 tablespoons of the sugar at high speed until the mixture is thick and forms a ribbon when the beater is lifted from the bowl. In a large stainless steel saucepan, scald the remaining lemon juice and the lime juice, the cream, milk, lemon zest, and lime zest. Pour about one fourth of the hot liquid into the egg yolks, whisking constantly, then return the mixture to the saucepan and whisk together. Cook over high heat, whisking constantly, until the mixture doubles in volume and just comes to a boil. Remove from heat.

Strain through a fine-mesh strainer into the bowl containing the melted gelatin and whisk together. Set aside to cool at room temperature while you make the Italian meringue. Whisk the lemon mixture from time to time to keep the gelatin from setting along the sides of the bowl. Do not refrigerate.

In a small saucepan, combine the 1/3 cup water with 3/4 cup of the sugar. When the water boils, it will throw sugar onto the sides of the pan. At that point, wash down the sides of the pan with a pastry brush, dipping in water as necessary to dissolve sugar. (Alternatively, place a lid on the pan for 30 seconds and the steam condensation will wash the sugar off the sides.)

As soon as the surface of the syrup is covered with bursting bubbles, start beating the egg whites in an electric mixer on low speed until frothy. Increase speed to medium and beat until soft peaks form. Increase speed to high and gradually beat in 2 tablespoons sugar, until stiff, glossy peaks form.

When the syrup is covered with thick, slowly bursting bubbles (soft crack stage, 270–290 degrees on a candy thermometer), pour it into the meringue in a very thin, steady stream, beating at high speed. Continue beating for 4–5 minutes, until the meringue is shiny and stiff. Reduce speed to medium and beat until the outside of the bowl is cool to the touch. The meringue will be bright white, very smooth, and will stand in very stiff peaks.

With your hands, scoop about one third of the Italian meringue into the cooled lemon mixture and incorporate it thoroughly, using your fingers as a whisk. Add remaining meringue and incorporate in the same manner. (Using your hands gives you more control over the mixing process, so that the two preparations can be incorporated more thoroughly. This is especially important because the mousse is very light in color, and it's not easy to see whether the meringue has blended in completely.)

Pour into prepared cake-lined springform pan and chill until firm, at least 3–4 hours in the refrigerator. Unmold by placing hot towels briefly around the pan and then releasing the sides. Serve with Raspberry Sauce.

If you are storing the cake overnight, allow it to sit at room temperature for 20–30 minutes before serving to let the mousse soften and lose its seemingly gelatinous texture.

Almond Sheet Cake

To Prepare Pan:

2 tablespoons unsalted
  butter, melted

Flour for pan

7 egg yolks

2 teaspoons almond extract

¾ cup pastry flour

1 cup almond meal

½ pound unsalted butter
  (2 sticks)

3 tablespoons grated or
  finely chopped lemon zest
  (3–4 lemons)

¾ cup plus 2 teaspoons
  granulated sugar in all

9 egg whites

**Makes one 12 x 17-inch
sheet cake**

Used in Lemon Mousse Cake

This cake is sturdy but moist, very well suited for building cake walls. (See "Building a cake wall," page 256.) It is the base for the Lemon Mousse Cake.

Use a 12 by 17-inch sheet pan.

Preheat oven to 325 degrees. Adjust the oven rack to the middle position.

Brush the sheet pan with the melted butter. Line the bottom of the pan with paper and butter again. Chill briefly to set. Dust with flour, knock out excess, and set aside.

In a small bowl, lightly whisk together the egg yolks and almond extract; set aside. Sift together the flour with the almond meal. If any of the almond meal remains in the strainer, toss it back into the flour.

Using the paddle attachment of an electric mixer, beat the butter with lemon zest at medium-high speed until it whitens and holds soft peaks, 3–5 minutes. Add ½ cup of the sugar and beat until well mixed. Add the dry and liquid ingredients to the butter mixture alternately in thirds, beginning and ending with dry ingredients.

Using the whisk attachment of an electric mixer, beat the egg whites on low speed until frothy. Increase speed to medium and beat until soft peaks form. Increase speed to high and very gradually beat in the remaining ¼ cup sugar, beating until stiff, glossy peaks form. Whisk about one third of the egg whites into the butter mixture to lighten the texture, then fold in the rest.

Pour batter into the prepared pan, filling to within ½ inch from the top, and spread evenly with an offset metal spatula. Bake 15–18 minutes, until cake has just started to color and is lightly springy to the touch. Cool.

To unmold, run a knife around the edges of the cake. Sprinkle the top of the cake with 2 teaspoons granulated sugar and invert onto the work surface.

Strawberry-Yogurt Mousse Cake

1 Lemon Macaroon layer
   (page 316)

Strawberry-Yogurt Mousse:
2 cups commercial
   strawberries in all

1/2 cup heavy cream

2 egg yolks

2 tablespoons sugar

2 teaspoons granulated
   gelatin

2 tablespoons lemon juice

2 teaspoons kirsch

1 cup plain, unsweetened
   yogurt

1 vanilla bean, split and
   scraped

To Fold into the Mousse:
2 cups wild strawberries or
   1 cup commercial
   strawberries

**Makes one 8 x 1-inch cake,
serving 8**

If it weren't so corny, the name "Strawberry Ambrosia" would fit this dessert perfectly—the strawberries go so well with the slightly acidic taste of the yogurt, and the chewy texture of the macaroon layer contrasts with the creaminess of the mousse.

There are eras when certain desserts are in vogue, as fruit mousses were not too long ago. Even though they tasted good, they always looked a little strange to me—somehow, folding whipped cream into dark berry purées created these garish, day-glo hues. The one exception is strawberry, which makes a delicate light-pink mousse.

If you can get wild strawberries, fold them into the mousse, but use ordinary commercial strawberries to make the purée.

Use an 8-inch springform pan, entremet ring, or an 8 x 1-inch flan ring.

PREPARING THE PAN

Trim the macaroon layer to 7½ inches in diameter and center on the bottom of the pan. If you are using an entremet ring or a flan ring set on a cardboard round (instead of a springform pan), place the ring on top of the cardboard and place both on a large square of foil. Fold the foil up, crimping it tight to the sides of the ring, even with the top. This will keep the mousse from leaking out the bottom edge of the ring before it sets.

MAKING THE MOUSSE

For the purée, stem the commercial strawberries, purée in a food processor, and set aside. Do not strain. There should be about 1 cup. If you are folding wild strawberries into the mousse, stem them and set aside. If you are using commercial strawberries, stem, quarter lengthwise, and set aside.

Using the whisk attachment of an electric mixer, beat the heavy cream at low speed until it thickens enough not to spatter. Increase speed to medium-high and beat until thick and mousselike. Remove from mixer. Whisk a few strokes by hand until soft peaks form. Refrigerate.

Using the whisk attachment, beat the egg yolks and sugar at high speed until the mixture is thick and pale yellow; set aside.

Place the gelatin in a large heatproof bowl and pour on the lemon juice and kirsch. If all the gelatin granules do not absorb the liquid, or if there are any lumps of gelatin, sprinkle on a bit more juice or water. Heat briefly over gently simmering water until the gelatin dissolves. Turn off heat and keep warm.

In a stainless steel saucepan, heat the yogurt and vanilla bean to steaming; do not allow to boil as the yogurt will curdle. Pour over the egg yolks and sugar in a slow steady stream, whisking constantly. Return to the saucepan and cook over low heat, whisking constantly, until the mixture thickens; again, do not allow it to boil. Remove from heat. Whisk a few times to release heat.

Strain the yogurt mixture onto the gelatin and whisk together. Stir in the strawberry purée. Let cool. Whisk one third of the whipped cream into the mousse to lighten the texture, then fold in the rest. Set bowl over ice water and fold continuously until the mixture has set enough to form soft peaks when lifted with the spatula. Remove from ice. Fold in the strawberries and pour into mold. Push down any strawberries that float to the top.

Chill at least 2 hours, until firm. Unmold by placing hot towels briefly around the pan and then releasing the sides or removing the ring.

Serve with Strawberry Sauce.

LAYERED CAKES

Layered cakes are architectural constructions—thin layers of cake and creamy fillings built in round pans, rings, or rectangular French terrine molds, chilled firm, and cut into thin, delicate slices. When sliced and placed flat on a plate, surrounded by sauce, the cake has a beautiful striped look and an immensely pleasing taste and texture. Mocha Cake, for example, alternates layers of chocolate and espresso cakes with coffee buttercream and dark chocolate filling, and in the Orange–Poppy Seed Cake, fluffy orange pastry cream hides slices of fresh mango between tender white cake layers.

These cakes are constructed in molds because the sides add stability and keep the layers from slipping around before the fillings have set. Once you've made a layered cake in a mold, you'll never want to do it any other way. Use a pastry bag to get fillings into a mold neatly and evenly.

Most of these cakes can be made in advance and kept refrigerated up to three days. Slice them thin—they're rich, and a little goes a long way. The cakes slice most easily when cold, but then let the slices stand at room temperature for five minutes or so before serving, to allow the flavors to come out.

Espresso Loaf Cake

Used in Espresso Cake

To Prepare Pan:
1 tablespoon unsalted butter, melted
1 tablespoon flour

Cake:
3 tablespoons unsalted butter
2/3 cup pastry flour
1/2 cup almond meal
1/2 teaspoon baking powder
3 tablespoons ground coffee
7 egg yolks

This cake is the flavorful base for the Espresso Cake and the Mocha Cake. The texture is especially designed to hold up when soaked with coffee.

Use a 12 x 3 x 3-inch straight-sided French terrine mold (8-cup capacity).

Preheat oven to 350 degrees. Adjust rack to top third of oven.

Brush the terrine mold with melted butter and line the bottom with paper. Butter again and chill briefly to set. Dust pan with flour and knock out excess; set aside.

Melt the butter in a small saucepan and set aside in a warm place. Sift together the pastry flour, almond meal, baking powder, and ground coffee; set aside. If any coffee grounds or nuts remain in the strainer, stir them back into the flour mixture.

In a heatproof bowl (preferably the bowl of an electric mixer), whisk together the egg yolks, lemon zest, 1/2 cup of the sugar, and the instant coffee. Place over a pot of gently simmering water, and lightly whisk together until

1½ tablespoons grated or finely chopped lemon zest (1 lemon)

¾ cup granulated sugar in all

2 tablespoons instant coffee

10 egg whites

Makes one 12 x 3 x 3-inch loaf cake

the mixture is warm to the touch (about 100 degrees). Place bowl on mixer. Using the whisk attachment, beat briefly on high speed to release heat, and then reduce speed to medium and beat until the mixture has tripled in volume, is thick and mousselike, and the outside of the bowl is cool to the touch. Take a few tablespoons of batter and whisk it into the melted butter. Return this small portion back to the batter and whisk together to combine; set aside.

Using the whisk attachment of an electric mixer, beat the egg whites on low speed until frothy. Increase speed to medium and beat until soft peaks form. Increase speed to high and very gradually beat in remaining ¼ cup sugar, beating until stiff, glossy peaks form.

Pour the flour mixture on top of the yolks but do not mix them in. Then, whisk about one third of the egg whites into the bowl, whisking until well mixed. Fold in the remaining egg whites, combining well. Work quickly. Once the ground coffee has been added to the batter the acid in it can break down the batter and make it runny.

Turn half the batter into each end of the prepared pan, letting it run naturally into the center of the pan. Do not level off. (Having a "valley" in the center of the loaf pan will create a cake without a hump in the center, and will discourage cracking.) Bake 15 minutes, until the surface is set, then prop open the oven door slightly and continue to bake for 35–40 minutes more, until the cake is springy to the touch and shrinks away from the sides of the pan. For a firm, solid cake that slices well, cool completely before unmolding. Leftover cake freezes well.

Mocha Cake

1 tablespoon unsalted butter, melted, to prepare pan

1 Espresso Loaf Cake (page 274)

1 Moist Chocolate Cake, baked in a 12 x 17-inch sheet pan (page 255)

½ recipe Dark Chocolate–Cognac Truffle Filling (page 278)

4 tablespoons instant espresso in all

1 cup freshly brewed coffee to soak the cake layers

2 cups Buttercream (page 299)

2 teaspoons boiling water

To Decorate Cake:
2 cups Bitter Chocolate Glaze (page 348)

1 cup ground Praline (page 354) or Nougatine (page 353) or crushed Sugared Almonds (page 353), optional

---

Makes one 12 x 3 x 3-inch cake, serving 10–12

My version of the classic French *gateau opéra* is true to the original flavor combination of chocolate and coffee, but there are some important differences. Instead of just a buttercream and a coffee-soaked sponge cake, as in the original, I use two different cakes, with a buttercream and a truffle cream filling, which gives it a more interesting texture. Also, the French version is constructed in large sheets and cut in small squares to serve, but the home cook will find it easier to build this cake in a terrine mold and cut it into thin slices.

Use a 12 x 3 x 3-inch straight-sided French terrine mold (8-cup capacity); prepare a 12 x 3-inch foil-covered cardboard rectangle to unmold the cake onto.

TO PREPARE THE PAN

Using the pan as a guide, cut out paper pieces to fit the bottom, ends, and sides of the pan. Brush the pan with melted butter. Fit paper lining into pan and set aside.

Cut two horizontal layers of espresso loaf cake ⅜ inch thick for best results. Stack metal guides or rulers ⅜ inch high next to both sides of the cake. Place the blade of a long, serrated knife on the guides and cut at a slight downward angle to make perfectly straight layers. You will be cutting each layer from the bottom of the cake. Remove each layer as it is finished and set aside, then cut the next one, again using the guides.

Cut three rectangles of moist chocolate cake 12 inches long by 3 inches wide. If the cake has risen higher than ⅜ inch, trim it horizontally with a long, serrated knife. Set aside.

❖ Unused cake can be frozen for other purposes.

Set one rectangle of Moist Chocolate Cake into the bottom of the prepared pan, smooth side down (the side that was against the pan during baking). Fill a pastry bag (No. 1 plain tip) with about half the truffle cream. Pipe a border of truffle cream around the perimeter of the pan, then pipe lines of truffle cream evenly across to cover the cake completely. Do not overlap lines, and keep the truffle cream the same thickness across the entire layer.

Dissolve 2 tablespoons espresso coffee in the brewed coffee. On the work surface, brush one side of an espresso loaf cake layer with about ¼ cup coffee. Place it, soaked side down, in the prepared terrine mold. Soak the other side with ¼ cup coffee. Be sure to saturate each cake layer completely with all the coffee indicated. It seems like a lot, but the cake texture will hold up and the resulting dessert is very moist. To check if the layer is thoroughly soaked, make a couple of slits in it and pull apart to see. When you put the cake in place, tap it with your fingers to spread the filling out evenly.

If the buttercream is not at room temperature, place it in the bowl of the electric mixer and stir it briefly over low heat, stirring constantly until a few tablespoons have melted. Remove from heat. Dissolve the remaining instant espresso in the boiling water. Using the whisk attachment, beat the buttercream with the coffee at high speed until smooth and satiny. Set aside.

Fill another pastry bag (No. 1 plain tip) with one half of the coffee-flavored buttercream. Pipe in the same manner as for the truffle cream. Repeat, alternating soaked chocolate cake, truffle cream, soaked espresso cake, and coffee buttercream, ending with a layer of chocolate cake. Each time you put on a cake layer, tap it with your fingers to spread the filling beneath it evenly. Chill until firm, at least 2 hours in the freezer or 4 hours in the refrigerator.

Unmold, decorate, and slice as directed for the Truffle Cake (page 278).

Serve with Coffee Sauce, Bitter Chocolate Sauce, or the two sauces swirled together.

Chocolate Truffle Cake

To Prepare Terrine Mold:
1 tablespoon unsalted
   butter, melted
1 Chocolate Almond Sheet
   Cake (page 267)

Dark Chocolate Truffle
   Filling:
12 ounces dark bittersweet
   chocolate
1 egg yolk
½ cup Cognac or Armagnac
½ cup heavy cream

Milk Chocolate Truffle
   Filling:
12 ounces milk chocolate
1 egg yolk
½ cup Irish cream liqueur
¼ cup heavy cream

White Chocolate–Mint
   Truffle Filling:
12 ounces white chocolate
1 egg yolk
6 tablespoons peppermint
   schnapps or white crème
   de menthe (1 tablespoon
   green crème de menthe
   can be substituted for 1
   tablespoon schnapps to
   give the filling a slight
   green tint)
¼ cup heavy cream
½ cup fresh mint leaves,
   removed from stems,
   loosely packed

If there ever was a dessert worth fussing over, this is it. Stripes of meltingly rich dark chocolate and milk chocolate truffle filling alternate with chocolate-almond cake under a shiny coating of chocolate glaze. Fresh raspberries cover the top, and the sides sparkle with ground praline.

There are three different combinations of truffle cream that you can choose: dark chocolate/milk chocolate, white chocolate–mint/dark chocolate-mint, or dark chocolate–orange/white chocolate–coffee. If you want to make only one flavor of truffle cream, double the recipe for one of the dark chocolate flavors.

The truffle cake can be made over two days' time. Make the chocolate glaze and the truffle creams the first day, then make the chocolate almond cake the day you assemble the whole thing. Use a 12 x 3 x 3-inch straight-sided French terrine mold with an 8-cup capacity; prepare a 12 x 3-inch foil-covered cardboard rectangle to unmold the cake onto.

PREPARING THE MOLD

Using the terrine mold as a guide, cut out wax paper or parchment paper to fit the bottom, sides, and ends of the mold. Brush pan with melted butter and line with paper. Set aside.

BASIC FILLING METHOD

All the fillings are made basically the same way, with a few small variations for two of them (see below).

Cut chocolate into 2-inch pieces. In a heatproof bowl, melt chocolate over barely simmering water. (The water should not touch the bottom of the bowl or the chocolate will burn. White chocolate and milk chocolate burn faster than dark chocolate.)

Stir together the melted chocolate and egg yolks; the mixture will firm up. In a small saucepan, gently heat Cognac or liqueur with cream to scalding, then stir into chocolate. Transfer mixture to a food processor or blender and process a minute or so until truffle mixture is shiny and stiff enough to pipe through a pastry bag. Dark chocolate fillings should be ready to pipe after processing; white or milk chocolate fillings may need to be stirred over ice or chilled briefly to firm up enough to pipe. If the chocolate looks

Dark Chocolate–Mint
   Truffle Filling:
*12 ounces bittersweet
   chocolate*

1 egg yolk

*½ cup peppermint schnapps
   or crème de menthe*

½ cup heavy cream

Dark Chocolate–Orange
   Truffle Filling:
*12 ounces bittersweet
   chocolate*

1 egg yolk

½ cup orange liqueur

½ cup heavy cream

White Chocolate–Coffee
   Truffle Filling:
12 ounces white chocolate

2 egg yolks

¼ cup heavy cream

3 tablespoons coffee liqueur

3 tablespoons instant coffee

1 tablespoon lemon juice

*1½ tablespoons freshly
   ground coffee*

Decoration:
*2 cups Bitter Chocolate
   Glaze (page 348)*

*1 cup ground Praline (page
   354) or Nougatine (page
   353) or crushed Sugared
   Almonds (page 353),
   optional*

*1 pint fresh raspberries (for
   dark chocolate/milk
   chocolate version only)*

**Makes one 12 x 3-inch
cake, serving 10–12**

dull or grainy, add more heated alcohol and process again until shiny.

FOR WHITE CHOCOLATE–MINT FILLING

Chop the mint leaves fine. There should be about 2 tablespoons. Stir in the chopped mint leaves after the mixture has been processed; do not strain.

FOR THE WHITE CHOCOLATE–COFFEE FILLING

Heat the cream with the coffee liqueur, instant coffee, and lemon juice; proceed as directed. After the mixture has been processed, stir in the ground coffee.

❖ Truffle creams can be made in advance and refrigerated or frozen. Reheat them gently over simmering water until melted, then process in a food processor until shiny, smooth, and of piping consistency.

CONSTRUCTING THE TRUFFLE CAKE

Cut the Chocolate Almond Cake into five strips to fit the terrine mold, approximately 12 inches by 3 inches each. Using two pastry bags (No. 1 plain tips), fill each one half-full of a different flavor truffle filling.

Place one cake strip on bottom of pan. Pipe a border of truffle filling around perimeter of cake, then pipe lines of chocolate mixture across to cover the cake completely. Do not overlap lines, and keep filling the same depth across the entire layer. Top with another cake layer and tap the surface lightly with your fingers to ensure that the truffle cream spreads out evenly. Cover with the other flavor filling in same manner. Alternate layers of cake and filling flavors, ending with cake. There will be five cake layers and four filling layers. Refrigerate at least 4 hours or freeze at least 2 hours, until firm.

UNMOLDING, GLAZING, AND DECORATING THE
CAKE

In a heatproof bowl, warm the chocolate glaze over barely simmering water until it is just warm enough to be pourable, but not hot. Keep warm.

To unmold cake, wrap the terrine mold briefly in hot dish towels or dip carefully in a hot water bath for a few seconds to loosen from pan. Place the foil-covered cardboard rectangle on top of the pan and invert the cake onto it. Hit the bottom of the pan firmly with a blunt object, and then, holding the cardboard and the pan together, shake firmly to release. It will come out of the mold! Peel off paper lining. When unmolding, use just enough heat to loosen the cake. It is better to heat the cake twice briefly than to melt the chocolate filling by heating too much.

Place the cake on a cooling rack set on a baking sheet and pour or ladle the warm glaze over the length of it. With a long metal spatula, smooth once across the top of the cake to remove excess glaze without actually touching the cake itself. Pick up one end of the rack and tap it firmly on baking sheet to allow the glaze to cover the sides of the cake.

With a metal spatula, pick up the glaze that dripped off the cake and patch any holes on the sides, if necessary. Run a spatula along the sides to smooth. The sides should have only a very thin layer of glaze so the praline or almonds will adhere. On the dark chocolate/milk chocolate version, immediately arrange fresh raspberries on top, stem side down, in three straight rows down the length of the cake.

Chill 10–15 minutes, until the sides are almost set but still a bit sticky. Remove from the refrigerator and press the praline, nougatine, or almonds onto the sides only with the palm of your hand. Chill for at least 30 minutes before serving. If you are not going to be coating the sides with nuts, chill the cake until the glaze is firm and glaze again.

SERVING

With a very sharp, heated knife, trim ¼ inch from each end of cake to expose the chocolate layers.

To serve, cut into ½-inch-thick slices with a heated knife. The knife must be reheated before each cut, or the cake will tear rather than slice. Lay slices flat on a plate that has been mirrored with Vanilla Sauce or Raspberry Sauce (milk chocolate/dark chocolate version), Mint Sauce (mint version), Bitter Orange Sauce or Coffee Sauce (with the coffee/orange version). If two sauces are suggested, you can pool them half-and-half on the plate.

Before serving, let slices soften on the plates for a few minutes to bring out the flavor.

Espresso Layer Cake

1 tablespoon unsalted
   butter, melted

1 Espresso Loaf Cake
   (page 274)

To Soak Cake:
5 tablespoons instant coffee
2½ cups freshly brewed
   coffee

Coffee Buttercream:
4 cups Buttercream (page
   299)
¼ cup instant coffee
1 tablespoon boiling water

To Decorate Cake:
2 cups Bitter Chocolate
   Glaze (page 348)
1 cup ground Praline
   (page 354) or Nougatine
   (page 353) or crushed
   Sugared Almonds
   (page 353), optional

**Makes one 12 x 3 x 3-inch
cake, serving 10–12**

This cake is pure coffee—layers of espresso loaf cake soaked in coffee, sandwiched with coffee buttercream, covered with chocolate glaze, and served with coffee sauce.

Use a 12 x 3 x 3-inch straight-sided French terrine mold (8-cup capacity); prepare a 12x3-inch foil-covered cardboard rectangle to unmold the cake onto.

PREPARING THE PAN

Using the pan as a guide, cut out paper pieces to fit the bottom, ends, and sides of the pan. Brush the pan with melted butter. Fit paper lining into pan and set aside.

Cut the cake horizontally into four layers ⅜ inch thick. For best results, stack metal guides or rulers ⅜ inch high next to both sides of the cake. Place the blade of a long, serrated knife on the guides and cut at a slight downward angle to make perfectly straight layers. You will be cutting each layer from the bottom of the cake. Remove each layer as it is finished and set aside, then cut the next one, again using the guides.

Dissolve the 5 tablespoons instant coffee in the brewed coffee. On the work surface, brush one side of a cake layer with about ¼ cup coffee. Place the layer, soaked side down, in the paper-lined terrine mold. Soak the other side with ¼ cup coffee. (Be sure to saturate each cake layer completely with all the coffee indicated. It seems like a lot, but the cake texture will hold up and the resulting dessert is very moist. To check if a layer is thoroughly soaked, make a couple of slits in it and pull apart to see.)

If the buttercream is not at room temperature, place it in the metal bowl of the electric mixer and stir it briefly over low heat, stirring constantly until a few tablespoons have melted. Remove from heat. Dissolve ¼ cup instant coffee in the boiling water. Using the whisk attachment, beat the buttercream with the coffee at high speed until satiny and smooth. Set aside.

Fill a pastry bag (No. 1 plain tip) with about one fourth of the coffee-flavored buttercream. Pipe a border of buttercream around the perimeter of the cake layer, then pipe lines of buttercream across to cover the cake completely. Do not overlap lines, and keep buttercream the same thickness across the entire layer. Top with another cake layer (soaked with coffee as directed above) and tap the surface lightly with your fingers to ensure that the buttercream spreads out evenly. Cover with buttercream in the same manner. Repeat, soaking layers and piping buttercream, using the rest of the ingredients, ending with a layer of coffee-soaked cake. Chill until firm, at least 2 hours in the freezer or 4 hours in the refrigerator.

UNMOLDING, GLAZING, AND SERVING THE CAKE

In a heatproof bowl, warm the chocolate glaze over barely simmering water until it is just warm enough to be pourable, but not hot. Before unmolding the cake, spread about 2 tablespoons of glaze on the top with a metal spatula. This will keep the moist cake from sticking to the serving platter when it is inverted. Chill to harden, 15 minutes.

To unmold cake, wrap the terrine mold briefly in hot dish towels or dip carefully in a hot water bath for a few seconds to loosen from pan. Place the foil-covered rectangle on top of the pan and invert the cake onto it. Hit the bottom of the pan a few times with a blunt instrument. Holding the cardboard and the pan together, shake firmly to release. It will come out of the mold! Peel off paper lining. When unmolding, use just enough heat to loosen the cake. It is better to heat the cake briefly twice than to melt the cake by heating too much.

Place the cake on a cooling rack set on a baking sheet and pour or ladle the warm glaze over the length of it. With a long metal spatula, smooth once across the top to remove excess glaze, without actually touching the cake itself. Pick up one end of the rack and tap it firmly on the baking sheet to allow the glaze to cover the sides of the cake.

With a metal spatula, pick up the glaze that dripped off the cake and patch any holes on the sides, if necessary. Run a metal spatula along the sides to smooth. The sides should have only a very thin layer of glaze so the praline or almonds will adhere.

Chill 10–15 minutes, until the sides are almost set but still a bit sticky, and then press the praline, nougatine, or crushed almonds onto the sides with the palm of your hand. If you are not going to be coating the sides with nuts, chill the cake until the glaze is firm and glaze again. Chill for at least 30 minutes before serving.

With a very sharp heated knife, trim ¼ inch from each end of the cake to expose the layers.

The cake must be very cold to slice well. To serve, cut into ½-inch-thick slices with a heated knife. The knife must be reheated before each cut, or the cake will tear rather than slice.

Lay slices flat on a plate that has been mirrored with Coffee Sauce. Sprinkle instant coffee granules lightly on the sauce, and with the tip of a knife, swirl random decorations. Let the slices soften at room temperature for 9 minutes to bring out flavor.

Vanilla Pastry Cream

6 egg yolks

⅔ cup granulated sugar

2 tablespoons flour, sifted

2 cups milk

1 vanilla bean, split and
    scraped

Makes 3 cups

Used in Caramel Tart

Besides being a versatile component in a number of different recipes, you can use vanilla pastry cream as a simple filling for a baked tart shell, which can then be decorated with fresh fruit. Always fill the tart at the last possible moment to keep the crust from getting soggy.

Do not use an aluminum saucepan. Aluminum is such a soft metal that it can be scraped up into the pastry cream during the vigorous whisking required and discolor the pastry cream.

Using the whisk attachment of an electric mixer, beat egg yolks with sugar on high speed until the mixture is very thick, pale yellow, and forms a ribbon when the beater is lifted from the bowl. Whisk in flour.

In a 2-quart stainless steel saucepan, scald the milk with the vanilla bean. Pour about one fourth of the hot milk into the egg yolk mixture, whisking continuously. Return to saucepan and combine with remaining milk. Cook over medium heat, whisking constantly, until the mixture thickens and bubbles in the center. Let it bubble for a few seconds to cook out the flour taste. Strain into a bowl and cover immediately with plastic wrap pressed down on the surface to prevent a skin from forming. Cool.

Keeps refrigerated for seven to ten days.

Caramel Tart

½ tablespoon unsalted
butter, melted, to butter
tart ring

1 Sweet Pastry tart shell
(page 84), baked (leave
the tart shell on the
baking sheet and do not
remove the flan ring)

3 egg yolks

1 egg

2 cups Caramel (page 333)
in all

2¾ cups heavy cream in all

1 vanilla bean, split and
scraped

1 tablespoon grated or finely
chopped orange zest
(1 orange)

⅓ cup Bitter Chocolate
Glaze (page 348)

1 Chocolate Band, 1¼
inches high, to circle a
10-inch tart, optional
(page 350)

5 tablespoons sour cream

2½ teaspoons granulated
gelatin

¼ cup orange juice

1 cup Vanilla Pastry Cream
(page 283)

1 cup Buttercream, tightly
packed (page 299)

**Makes one 10-inch tart,
serving 8–10**

The original recipe for this melt-in-your-mouth construction of caramel custard, caramel, chocolate, and a caramel cream topping, layered in a buttery, flaky crust, came from the first pastry chef I worked with, Jimmy Brinkley, then at Michael's in Santa Monica. It was christened the Heath Bar, because, surrounded by a chocolate band, it reminded us of that crunchy, creamy candy bar. A number of operations are necessary to put this together, but the final product—rich but not sweet, with an unctuously creamy texture—is worth it.

Four made-ahead preparations are required for this recipe—caramel, pastry cream, buttercream, and chocolate glaze. They can all be made up to ten days in advance. Or you can make extra amounts of these preparations when you make other desserts, store them in the freezer, and then put it all together when you have everything on hand.

Use a 10-inch plain flan ring, set on a 10-inch cardboard round. The finished tart is about 1 inch high. If you use a flan ring with 1-inch-high sides, the chocolate band is optional because the ring is high enough to contain all the filling layers. If you use a lower ring (½ inch) the chocolate band will be necessary to contain all the filling.

After baking the tart shell, allow to cool. Leave it on the baking sheet, and do not remove the flan ring.

MAKING THE CARAMEL CUSTARD

Preheat oven to 325 degrees. Adjust oven rack to lower third of oven. Place a heavy baking sheet on the rack.

In a large bowl, lightly whisk the egg yolks and whole egg to break them up. In a small saucepan, heat 1 cup of the caramel, stirring until melted. Whisk the caramel into the eggs.

In a small saucepan, scald 1¼ cups of the cream, vanilla bean, and orange zest. Pour into the egg mixture, whisking continuously until well combined. Remove vanilla bean. Pour into the baked tart shell.

Set the filled tart shell on the heated baking sheet in the oven and bake for 25 minutes, just until set. The custard sets from the outside in. If it looks as if one side is setting faster than the other, turn it around in the oven to even it out. If any air bubbles come to the top when the custard has started to set, lift the baking sheet up and let it fall back down on the oven rack to break them.

During the last 5 minutes of baking, keep a careful eye on the tart as the custard can curdle. Jiggle the tray to check how fast the custard is setting, and remove it from the oven when the custard still wiggles when shaken but is not liquid. Refrigerate until cold, about 45 minutes. When cold, slip a cardboard round underneath. Do not remove flan ring.

THE CARAMEL LAYER

In a small saucepan, heat ½ cup of the caramel, stirring, until it is warm enough to be pourable but not hot. Pour caramel onto cooled custard layer and, with an offset spatula or the back of a spoon, smooth gently to spread a thin, even layer of caramel. Refrigerate until caramel is firm, about 20 minutes.

THE CHOCOLATE LAYER

In a heatproof bowl, warm the chocolate glaze over barely simmering water until it is just warm enough to be pourable, but not hot. Using the same technique as for the caramel layer, pour warm glaze onto tart and spread. Make a thin layer. Refrigerate until set, about 20 minutes.

PUTTING ON THE CHOCOLATE BAND

Lift off the flan ring. Place the prepared chocolate band around the tart, wax paper side out, following the directions on page 350. Chill until you are ready to pipe the caramel cream, then place tart on a serving platter.

PREPARING THE CARAMEL CREAM

Using the whisk attachment of an electric mixer, beat the remaining 1½ cups heavy cream and 5 tablespoons sour cream on low speed until thick enough not to spatter. Increase speed to medium-high and beat until thick and mousselike. Remove from mixer and whisk a few times to form very soft peaks. Refrigerate.

Place gelatin in the bottom of a very large (5-quart) heatproof bowl and pour on orange juice. If all the gelatin granules do not absorb the juice, or if there are any lumps of gelatin, dribble on a bit more orange juice or water. Heat briefly over gently simmering water until the gelatin dissolves. Turn off heat and keep warm.

In a saucepan, combine ½ cup of the caramel and the pastry cream and heat to boiling, whisking constantly. Pour over melted gelatin and whisk until completely blended.

If buttercream is not at room temperature, place it in the metal bowl of the electric mixer and stir it briefly over low heat, stirring constantly, until a few tablespoons have melted. Remove from heat. Using the whisk attachment, beat the buttercream at high speed until satiny and smooth. Set aside.

Whisk one third of the whipped cream into the caramel mixture to lighten the texture, then fold in the rest. Place bowl in a larger bowl filled with ice and fold with a rubber spatula to set the gelatin. Make sure to move the mixture away from the sides of the bowl so all of it is cooled by the ice at some point and the gelatin doesn't lump. As soon as a bit of cream folded over with the spatula holds its shape, it is ready to pipe onto the tart. Remove the bowl from the ice. The cream should be completely smooth and shiny, not rough or separated. If at any time the mixture starts to stiffen, or it is not completely smooth in texture when piped, whisk vigorously and it will smooth out again.

PIPING THE CARAMEL CREAM

Remove the tart from the refrigerator and place on a serving platter. If the chocolate band has not adhered to the pastry, fill a parchment paper cone with melted chocolate and pipe it around the edge where the pastry meets the chocolate band to attach it. (See "Piping chocolate decorations," page 342.) Chill briefly to set. (Set the piping bag with the melted chocolate aside in a warm place.)

Fill a pastry bag (No. 4 star tip) half full of caramel cream. Starting at the edge of the tart, pipe three concentric circles of rounded waves of cream (about 1½ inches long) to cover the top of the tart. The waves should be arranged like the spokes of a wheel. The topping should be about ½ inch thick. (If you overlap the waves too much or make them too high, the caramel cream will be too thick.)

When the top is covered, pipe a rosette in the center, and finish with a low border of waves around the circumference of the tart, just inside the chocolate band. (Use the

Piping the caramel cream

reserved chocolate in the piping bag to pipe a crisscross pattern of thin chocolate lines on top of the caramel cream, if desired.)

Chill to firm, at least 1 hour.

When ready to serve, remove from the refrigerator and peel the wax paper from the chocolate band.

Banana-Pecan Layer Cake

To Prepare Pan:
2 tablespoons unsalted
   butter, melted

1 tablespoon flour

Banana Cake:
¼ cup pecans or walnuts
   (1 ounce)

¼ cup hazelnuts (1 ounce)

1 ounce bittersweet
   chocolate, very cold

1 very ripe banana

2 egg yolks

1 tablespoon maple syrup
   or walnut extract

2 teaspoons vanilla extract

3 tablespoons sour cream

6 tablespoons unsalted
   butter (3 ounces)

½ cup dark brown sugar

1 cup flour

1 teaspoon baking soda

1 teaspoon boiling water

6 egg whites

3 tablespoons granulated
   sugar

Filling the Cake:
1½ cups pecans (5 ounces)

1 ripe firm banana

2 tablespoons lemon juice,
   optional

2½–3 cups Vanilla
   Buttercream (page 299)

1 tablespoon walnut extract
   or maple syrup

Some banana cakes are heavy and homey, but this one is worthy of a special dinner—a 2-inch-high cake, layers flecked with hazelnuts, pecans, and chopped chocolate, filled with pecan buttercream, and glazed with chocolate. This cake is an especially good choice in the winter, when other fruits aren't available. The texture is moist, a cross between a cake and a bread.

Use the leftover egg yolks from the cake for making the buttercream filling.

Use an 8-inch round straight-sided layer cake pan.

MAKING THE CAKE

Brush an 8-inch round layer cake pan with melted butter. Line the bottom of the pan with paper; brush with butter again. Chill briefly to set, dust with flour, and knock out excess. Set aside.

Preheat oven to 325 degrees. Adjust oven rack to middle position. Spread the pecans or walnuts on one baking sheet and the hazelnuts on another. Toast for 8–10 minutes each, until brown. Cool. Rub hazelnuts with a clean dish towel to remove skins. Measure ¼ cup pecans and set the remaining aside. Coarsely chop the hazelnuts, the ¼ cup of pecans, and the chocolate; set aside.

In a small bowl, mash the banana with a fork. Combine with egg yolks, maple syrup, vanilla, and sour cream; set aside.

Using the paddle attachment of an electric mixer, beat the butter on medium-high speed until it whitens and holds soft peaks, 3–5 minutes. Beat in brown sugar until well mixed. Add the flour and the egg yolk mixture alternately, beginning and ending with the flour. Before adding the last part of the flour, activate the baking soda by combining it with the boiling water in a small bowl. Beat into batter and then add the rest of the flour. Fold in chopped nuts and chocolate; set aside.

Using the whisk attachment of an electric mixer, beat the egg whites on low speed until frothy. Increase speed to medium and beat until soft peaks form. Increase speed to high and very gradually beat in the granulated sugar, until stiff, glossy peaks form. Whisk one third of the egg whites into the banana mixture to lighten the texture, then fold in the rest.

Decorating the Cake:

2 cups Bitter Chocolate Glaze (page 348)

1 cup ground Praline (page 354) or Nougatine (page 353) or crushed Sugared Almonds (page 353), optional

---

Makes one 8-inch cake, serving 8–10

Pour into prepared pan and bake for 40–45 minutes, until the cake is golden brown and shrinks slightly from the sides of the pan and springs back when lightly touched. Cool completely before assembling. This cake freezes well.

MAKING THE BUTTERCREAM FILLING AND ASSEMBLING THE CAKE

To keep it symmetrical, the cake will be assembled in an 8-inch straight-sided layer cake pan, the same one it was cooked in. Using the pan as a guide, cut a round of paper to fit inside the bottom of the pan and a strip of paper wide enough and long enough to smoothly line the sides of the pan. Brush the pan with melted butter and line with paper. Set aside.

Using a long, thin, serrated knife, cut the cooled cake horizontally into three thin layers. Trim the layers so that they each measure 7½ inches in diameter. Set aside the layer that was originally the bottom of the cake to use on top. Center one layer in the bottom of the pan.

Grate the remaining pecans in a Mouli grater, or chop very fine; set aside. Slice the banana thin and toss with lemon juice; set aside.

If the buttercream is not soft, place it in the metal bowl of an electric mixer and stir it briefly over low heat, stirring constantly, until a few tablespoons have melted. Using the whisk attachment, beat the buttercream at high speed until satiny and smooth. Add the walnut extract (or maple syrup) and the grated pecans and beat until combined.

Fill a pastry bag (No. 2 plain tip) with about one third of the buttercream. (The filling can also be spread with an offset metal spatula or the back of a spoon.) Pipe a border of buttercream to fill in the space between the cake layer and the sides of the pan. Then, starting in the center, pipe an even spiral over the cake layer and out to the sides of the pan. Arrange half the banana slices on the buttercream.

Put on the next cake layer, press down lightly to spread the filling evenly, and again pipe a border and then an even layer of filling. Arrange the other half of the banana slices on top. Put on the reserved bottom of the cake, smooth side up, and press down lightly. Pipe only a border of buttercream around it, between the cake layer and the sides of the pans. Refrigerate for at least 3 hours or freeze for 2 hours, until firm. Refrigerate the remaining buttercream—there should be about one quarter of the original quantity left.

When the cake is firm, unmold onto a foil-covered cardboard round by dipping the pan briefly in hot water or wrapping it in hot towels and then inverting onto the cardboard. Turn the cake upside down so that the smooth bottom is on top again. Peel off paper lining.

Using the whisk attachment of an electric mixer, whip the remaining buttercream at high speed until smooth, heating a bit to soften if necessary. Using a metal spatula, spread a thin layer on top of the cake and smooth the sides if necessary. Chill until the buttercream is firm, about 30 minutes. (See directions for "Frosting a cake," page 23.)

GLAZING THE CAKE

In a heatproof bowl, warm the chocolate glaze over barely simmering water until it is just warm enough to be pourable, but not hot. Hold the cake flat on the palm of your hand over a baking sheet. Pour or ladle the warm glaze over the cake, rotating the cake and letting it run down the sides to make an even coating. Set cake on work surface. With a metal spatula, pick up the glaze and patch any holes on the sides of the cake.

Chill for 10–15 minutes, until the glaze is still a bit sticky but almost set. Using the palm of your hand, press ground praline or nougatine or crushed sugared almonds on the sides. If you are not going to be coating the sides with nuts, chill the cake until the glaze is firm and glaze again. Chill until ready to serve, at least 30 minutes.

Serve with Banana-Honey Ice Cream and Vanilla Sauce flavored with rum.

Poppy Seed Cake

To Prepare Pan:

½ tablespoon butter, melted

1 tablespoon flour

Cake:

⅔ cup milk

2 tablespoons grated or finely chopped orange zest (2 oranges)

¼ cup poppy seeds

1 tablespoon vanilla extract

1½ cups flour

½ tablespoon baking powder

4 ounces unsalted butter (1 stick)

¾ cups granulated sugar in all

4 egg whites

Makes one 8-inch round cake

Used in Orange–Poppy Seed Cake

Dotted with poppy seeds and orange zest, this white cake is attractive and delicious when baked in a decorative mold and served dusted with powdered sugar.

If you're planning on eating the cake plain, use a 2-quart kugelhopf pan or another decorative mold. As a component in the Orange–Poppy Seed Cake, it's baked in an 8-inch round straight-sided layer cake pan.

Preheat oven to 350 degrees. Adjust rack to middle position.

Brush the pan with melted butter. Line the bottom with a round of paper and butter again. Chill briefly to set, dust with flour, knock out excess, and set aside.

In a saucepan, heat the milk and orange zest to scalding. Let cool to room temperature and stir in the poppy seeds and vanilla extract. In a bowl, sift together the flour and baking powder; set aside.

Using the paddle attachment of an electric mixer, beat the butter until it whitens and holds soft peaks, 3–5 minutes. Beat in ½ cup plus 2 tablespoons of the sugar until well mixed. Alternately add the flour mixture and the milk mixture, starting and ending with the flour. Scrape down the sides of the bowl as necessary. Set aside.

Using the whisk attachment of the electric mixer, beat the egg whites on low speed until frothy. Increase speed to medium and beat until soft peaks form. Increase speed to high and very gradually beat in remaining 2 tablespoons of sugar, until very stiff, glossy peaks form. Whisk one third of the egg whites into the batter to lighten texture, then fold in the rest.

Turn into prepared pan and bake 55 minutes, or until the cake is light brown, pulls away from the sides of the pan, and is springy to the touch. Cool completely before turning out of pan.

Keep the cake refrigerated until ready to use. Freezes very well.

Orange–Poppy Seed Cake

1 tablespoon unsalted
  butter, melted

1 Poppy Seed Cake baked
  in an 8-inch round pan
  (page 291)

1 large, very ripe mango,
  optional

1 cup heavy cream

1 cup fresh orange juice
  (3 oranges)

½ cup fresh lemon juice
  (3 lemons)

¼ cup orange liqueur

1 tablespoon granulated
  gelatin (1 envelope)

1½ cups Orange Pastry
  Cream (page 295)

To Decorate:
½ cup White Chocolate
  Glaze (page 349) or
  Bitter Chocolate Glaze
  (page 348), optional

1 White Chocolate Band or
  Chocolate Band (page
  350), optional

**Makes one 4-layer, 8-inch
cake, serving 8–10**

A German-style, soft-textured poppy seed cake is a simple and delicate dessert. In this recipe, the cake is used as a base, divided into four thin layers, and filled with orange pastry cream. When a perfectly ripe mango is available, slice it thin and nestle it in the pastry cream between the layers.

Use an 8-inch foil-covered cardboard round and a pastry bag fitted with a No. 2 plain tip (optional).

PREPARING THE PAN AND SLICING THE CAKE

To keep it symmetrical, the cake is assembled in an 8-inch round straight-sided layer cake pan, the same one it was cooked in. The pan must be lined so that the cake can be turned out easily. Using the pan as a guide, cut a round of paper to fit the bottom of the pan and strips of paper wide enough and long enough to smoothly line the sides of the pan. Brush the pan with melted butter and line with paper. Set aside.

Using a long, serrated knife, slice the poppy seed cake horizontally into four ¼-inch-thick layers. Trim the edges of the cake so that layers are 7½ inches in diameter. Set aside.

MAKING THE FILLING

With a sharp paring knife, peel the mango as thin as possible. Cut the fruit away from the pit in vertical slices about ⅛ inch thick. Set on paper towels to drain.

In an electric mixer, beat the heavy cream on low speed until it thickens enough not to spatter. Increase speed to medium-high and beat until thick and mousselike. Remove from mixer. Whisk a few times by hand until soft peaks form. Refrigerate.

In a bowl, mix together orange juice, lemon juice, and orange liqueur. Place the gelatin in the bottom of a large bowl and pour on ½ cup of the juice mixture. (Set the rest of the juice aside.) If all the gelatin granules do not absorb the juice, or if there are any lumps of gelatin, dribble on a bit more juice or liqueur. Place bowl briefly over gently simmering water and heat until the gelatin dissolves.

Remove from heat and whisk in the orange pastry cream. Whisk in one third of the whipped cream to lighten the texture, then fold in the rest. Set the bowl over ice water, and fold continuously with a rubber spatula until the mixture holds soft peaks, 5–8 minutes. Measure out ½ cup of cream to use for finishing the cake and refrigerate.

ASSEMBLING THE CAKE

Center one layer of cake in the bottom of the prepared pan. Set aside the original bottom of the cake to use on the top. Brush about 3 tablespoons of the reserved juice mixture on the cake layer.

Fill a pastry bag (No. 2 plain tip) half full of orange cream. Pipe a border of orange cream to fill in the space between the cake layer and the sides of the pan. Then, starting in the center, pipe an even spiral over the cake layer all the way to the sides. (The cream can also be spread with an offset metal spatula or the back of a spoon.) If you're using sliced mango, place half the slices on top of the filling.

Place another cake layer on, press down gently to even out the cream, and brush with 3 tablespoons juice. Pipe on cream as directed above. Repeat with third layer, arranging the remaining mango slices on the cream. Brush the cut side of the last layer with 3 tablespoons juice and place on top of the cake, smooth (uncut) side up. Brush top layer with juice and pipe only a border of cream around it, between the cake layer and the sides of the pan. Chill until set, at least 1 hour in freezer, 2 hours in refrigerator.

When cake is set, dip pan briefly in hot water or wrap in hot towels and invert onto a foil-covered 8-inch cardboard round. Turn the cake upside down so that the smooth bottom is on top again. Peel off paper lining.

If reserved orange cream has stiffened, lightly whisk until it is spreadable. Using a metal spatula, frost the top and sides of cake with a thin coating of orange cream. Freeze or refrigerate 15 minutes, or until firm. (See directions for "Frosting a cake," page 23.)

❖ If you don't want to decorate the cake further, it can be served at this point. It will keep refrigerated for two to three days.

Continued on next page

GLAZING THE TOP OF THE CAKE AND WRAPPING
THE CAKE IN A CHOCOLATE BAND

Choose either to wrap the cake in dark chocolate with a
dark chocolate glaze or wrap the cake in white chocolate
with a white chocolate glaze. For easier handling, place the
cake on a serving platter that is larger than the diameter of
the cake. (Once the chocolate band has been put on, you
won't be able to touch the band or it will crack.) Before
glazing, prepare a chocolate band (white or dark chocolate)
as described on page 350 and wrap it around the cake.
Chill until firm.

(If you plan to pipe a chocolate decoration on top of the
glaze, you must have the chocolate that you intend to use
melted and ready in a paper cone before you glaze the
cake. See "Piping chocolate decorations," page 342.)

In a heatproof bowl, warm the chocolate glaze over
barely simmering water until it is just pourable but not hot.

Holding the cake platter flat on your hand, pour or ladle
the glaze over the cake, tilting the platter to distribute the
glaze in a thin, even layer over the top only. The glaze will
run over onto the band but the drips will peel off when you
remove the waxed paper. Pipe on a pulled chocolate decoration if desired. Refrigerate for 30 minutes, until glaze is
set. Peel off wax paper as soon as you remove the cake
from the refrigerator.

Serve with Vanilla Sauce flavored with orange liqueur, or
with Mango Sauce.

Orange Pastry Cream

6 egg yolks

⅔ cup granulated sugar

2 tablespoons flour, sifted

*2 cups fresh orange juice
(6–8 oranges)*

*6–8 tablespoons grated or
finely chopped orange
zest (6–8 oranges)*

*1 vanilla bean, split and
scraped*

Makes 3 cups

Used in Orange–Poppy Seed Cake

Vanilla pastry cream can be made with milk and then flavored with orange. I find, however, that replacing the milk with orange juice gives this pastry cream a much deeper orange taste.

Using the whisk attachment of an electric mixer, or with a wire whisk, beat the egg yolks at high speed with the sugar until the mixture is very thick and pale yellow and forms a ribbon when the beater is lifted from the bowl. Whisk in flour.

In a 2-quart stainless steel saucepan, scald the orange juice, zest, and vanilla bean. Pour about one fourth of the hot orange juice into the egg yolk mixture, whisking continuously. Return to saucepan and combine with remaining orange juice. Cook over medium heat, whisking constantly, until the mixture thickens and bubbles in the center. Let it bubble for a few seconds to cook out the flour taste. Strain into bowl and cover immediately with plastic wrap pressed down on the surface to prevent a skin from forming. Cool.

Keeps refrigerated up to ten days.

Marjolaine

To Prepare Pans:
2 tablespoons unsalted
   butter, melted

Flour

Meringue Layers:
1⅓ cups almonds (6
   ounces)

1 cup hazelnuts (4 ounces)

⅔ cup plus 3 tablespoons
   granulated sugar in all

2 teaspoons flour

6 egg whites

Fillings:
¾ cup heavy cream

2 tablespoons sour cream

4 ounces bittersweet
   chocolate

½ cup orange liqueur

1 cup Buttercream (page
   299)

2 tablespoons grated or
   finely chopped orange
   zest (2 oranges)

6 tablespoons fresh orange
   juice

To Decorate:
½ cup Bitter Chocolate
   Glaze (page 348)

**Makes one 8-inch round
cake, serving 10–12**

Almond-hazelnut meringue layered with chocolate, whipped cream, and orange buttercream make the marjolaine. When cut, the cross-section of several colors is lovely.

At the restaurant, I make this dessert the French way, baking the meringue in four large sheets, sandwiching them together with filling, and then cutting it into squares to serve. The meringue is quite brittle, however, and unless you're really adept, the large sheets can shatter when you handle them. For the home cook, baking the meringue in rounds, as described below, makes the dessert much less difficult to assemble, and the combination of flavors and colors remains the same.

Use four 8-inch flan rings and one 8-inch high-sided springform pan or a 2½-inch-high entremet ring.

MAKING THE MERINGUE LAYERS

Preheat oven to 325 degrees. Adjust oven racks to upper and middle positions.

Spread the almonds and the hazelnuts on separate baking sheets and toast each for 8–10 minutes, until brown. Cool. Rub the hazelnuts in a clean dish towel to remove skins.

Brush the baking sheets with melted butter. Line with paper, butter again, and chill briefly to set. Dust with flour and knock off excess. Set aside.

In a food processor, grind together the nuts, ⅔ cup sugar, and flour until the mixture resembles coarse cornmeal. Do not grind to a paste. Depending on the size of your food processor, you may have to grind the ingredients in two batches.

Using the whisk attachment of an electric mixer, beat the egg whites on low speed until frothy. Increase speed to medium and beat until soft peaks form. Increase speed to high and very gradually beat in the 3 tablespoons sugar, beating until peaks are stiff and glossy. Fold in the nut mixture in two batches.

Place the flan rings on the paper-lined baking sheets. Divide the meringue mixture into four parts and spread thinly in the flan rings, using the back of a spoon or an offset metal spatula. The layers should be no more than ⅜ inch thick. (There may be meringue left over.) Bake for

20–25 minutes, until layers are very crisp and lightly browned. Rotate the baking sheets once during baking so that the layers cook evenly.

When cool, run a sharp knife around the inside edges of the flan rings to release. Remove rings. Peel off meringue layers. Trim the edges of the meringue layers so that they fit into the springform pan by holding them up with one hand and whittling away carefully at the sides with a small, sharp knife. Center one meringue layer in the bottom of the springform pan; set aside.

MAKING THE FILLINGS AND ASSEMBLING THE MARJOLAINE

In an electric mixer, beat the heavy cream with the sour cream until thick enough not to spatter. Increase speed to medium-high and beat until thick and mousselike. Remove from mixer and whisk a few times by hand to form soft peaks. Refrigerate.

Cut the chocolate into 2-inch pieces. In a heatproof bowl, melt chocolate over barely simmering water. (The water should not touch the bottom of the bowl or the chocolate will burn.) Turn off heat and let stand. In a small saucepan, heat ¼ of the orange liqueur over low heat to steaming. Stir into the chocolate. Remove bowl from heat and stir ¼ cup whipped cream into the chocolate. The mixture should be smooth and shiny.

As soon as the chocolate mixture has been made, spread it over the meringue layer to cover the surface. Place another meringue layer on top of the chocolate and press down lightly to spread the filling evenly. Next, spread on an even layer of 1¼ cups whipped cream. Place another meringue layer on top and press down lightly. Refrigerate.

Place the buttercream and orange zest in the metal bowl of an electric mixer with the whisk attached; set aside. Combine the orange juice and remaining ¼ cup orange liqueur in a saucepan and boil until the liquid reduces to about 2 tablespoons and starts to caramelize. Immediately pour the hot liquid into the buttercream and beat on high speed until smooth and shiny. Measure out 3 tablespoons of orange buttercream; set aside.

❖ For a variation, instead of flavoring the buttercream with orange, process praline powder to a paste (page 354) and mix it into the plain buttercream.

Remove springform pan from refrigerator and spread all but the 3 reserved tablespoons of orange buttercream onto the meringue layer. Top with last meringue layer and press down lightly. Spread reserved 3 tablespoons buttercream evenly on top. The cake will not be as high as the sides of the pan. Refrigerate until firm, at least 2 hours.

GLAZING THE MARJOLAINE

Warm the chocolate glaze over barely simmering water until just warm enough to be pourable, but not hot. Pour onto top of the marjolaine, turning the pan to distribute glaze in a thin even layer. Pour off excess. Refrigerate until set, about 30 minutes.

The marjolaine is best after it has set for several hours or overnight in the refrigerator, so that the flavors can come together and the meringue can soften a bit. Keeps refrigerated up to five days.

UNMOLDING AND SERVING THE MARJOLAINE

Unmold by placing hot towels briefly around the pan and then releasing the sides. Smooth sides with a warm knife or metal spatula if necessary. Because the marjolaine is so crisp, you can't slice it by cutting straight down as you would for a softer cake. Instead, heat a knife and rock it back and forth as you cut. Serve in very thin slices with Raspberry Sauce or Strawberry Sauce.

Buttercream

½ cup milk

1 vanilla bean, split and scraped

⅔ cup granulated sugar in all

7 egg yolks

1 pound, 2 ounces unsalted butter (4½ sticks), well softened

Makes 4 cups

Used in Marjolaine

This buttercream was inspired by one I learned to make at the Lenôtre school in France. Most buttercreams are made by pouring hot sugar syrup over beaten egg yolks and then combining with butter, but this one has a base of crème anglaise—egg custard. Don't hesitate to double the recipe and make a big batch of vanilla buttercream to keep in the freezer and flavor as you need it for various recipes.

In a 2-quart stainless steel saucepan, scald the milk, vanilla bean, and ½ cup of the sugar. Meanwhile, in an electric mixer or with a wire whisk, beat egg yolks with remaining sugar until mixture is thick and pale yellow and forms a ribbon when the beater is lifted. Pour about one third of the hot milk onto the egg yolks, whisking constantly. Return mixture to saucepan to combine with remaining milk. Cook over high heat, whisking constantly. Stop whisking briefly as the mixture reaches the boiling point to allow it to bubble. Strain through a fine-mesh strainer back into mixing bowl and beat on medium speed until thick, mousselike, and doubled in volume. Set aside.

Using the paddle attachment of an electric mixer, beat butter on medium-high speed until it whitens and holds soft peaks and makes a slapping sound against the sides of the bowl, 3–5 minutes. Pour the egg yolk mixture down the side of the bowl into the butter in a steady stream, beating continuously on medium speed. The mixture may separate but it will recombine as you continue beating. Beat until the underside of the bowl is cool, and the buttercream is smooth and shiny. The buttercream can be used immediately or it keeps refrigerated up to ten days or frozen up to three months.

RECONSTITUTING FROZEN BUTTERCREAM

Let buttercream soften at room temperature and then beat in an electric mixer at high speed until it holds soft, satiny peaks. Or heat in a metal bowl of the electric mixer over low heat, stirring constantly until a few tablespoons have melted, then beat with the whisk attachment in an electric mixer on high speed until satiny. If the buttercream does not whip up well, it may be too cold; return it to the heat to soften a bit more and whip again. If it starts to separate, beat in a few teaspoons of very soft unsalted butter at high speed, and the mixture will come back together.

Devil's Food Cake

To Prepare Pans:
2 tablespoons butter, melted

2 tablespoons unsweetened cocoa powder

Cake:
4 ounces bittersweet chocolate

6 tablespoons water

6 tablespoons unsweetened cocoa powder

½ pound unsalted butter (2 sticks)

½ cup dark brown sugar

6 eggs, separated

¼ cup sour cream

2 teaspoons baking soda

2 teaspoons boiling water (to infuse baking soda)

1½ cups flour, sifted

3 tablespoons granulated sugar

To Frost Cake:
1 recipe Devil's Food Frosting (page 302)

¼–½ cup unsweetened cocoa powder

Makes three 8-inch layers

This is a very moist devil's food, black with a slight tinge of devilish red. It's adapted from a recipe that Beatrice Keech, one of my stalwart colleagues in the Spago kitchen, brought from her mother's kitchen in South Africa.

The cake itself is a useful and very flavorful substitute for a chocolate génoise.

It can be baked in three 8-inch round straight-sided layer cake pans, or in one layer in an 8-inch round cake pan and sliced into 3 layers after baking. (Oven time needs to be adjusted for baking all the batter in one pan.)

Brush layer cake pans with melted butter. Line the bottom of the pans with a round of baking paper. Brush with butter again, chill briefly to set, dust with cocoa powder, and knock out excess. Set aside.

Preheat oven to 350 degrees. Adjust oven rack to middle position. (If you're baking the cake in 3 pans, adjust oven racks to upper and lower positions.)

Cut chocolate into 2-inch pieces. In a heatproof bowl, melt chocolate over barely simmering water. (The water should not touch the bottom of the bowl or the chocolate will burn.) Turn off heat and let stand over warm water until ready to use.

In a small saucepan, whisk together the water and cocoa powder. Bring to a simmer over medium heat, whisking constantly, until the mixture is smooth and thickened and the whisk leaves an empty trail when it is drawn across the bottom of the pan. Remove from heat. Whisk in melted chocolate; set aside.

Using the paddle attachment of an electric mixer, beat butter until it whitens and holds soft peaks, 3–5 minutes. Beat in brown sugar and combine well. Add egg yolks one at a time, scraping down the sides of the bowl as necessary. Beat in chocolate and combine, then sour cream. Dissolve the baking soda in boiling water, making sure that the baking soda fizzes. Beat in half the flour, add the baking soda, and beat in remaining flour. Set aside.

Using the whisk attachment of an electric mixer, beat egg whites on low speed until frothy. Increase speed to medium and beat until soft peaks form. Increase speed to high and gradually beat in the granulated sugar until stiff, glossy peaks form.

Whisk one third of the egg whites into the chocolate

mixture to lighten texture, then fold in the rest, incorporating well. Pour batter into the single cake pan, or divide batter evenly into the three cake pans. Bake 25 minutes, until cake shrinks slightly from the sides of the pan and springs back when the center is touched. (If the pans are on two oven racks, stagger the placement so that the cakes brown evenly and rotate the positions of the upper and lower cakes halfway during baking.)

When thoroughly cool, remove layers from pans by running a knife around the edges, turning the pan upside down on a work surface, and giving the back of the pan a firm whack. Cool cake completely before using. Freezes very well.

TO ASSEMBLE AND FROST CAKE

With a serrated knife, trim rounded tops of cake layers so they are flat and the layers are no thicker than ½ inch. Place one cake layer on a serving platter or cardboard round, trimmed side up, and spread top with ⅛ inch of frosting. Place second layer on top, press down lightly, and spread with frosting. Top with third cake layer and press down lightly. If the weather is warm, chill or freeze the cake until the frosting firms up, so the cake layers stay securely in place.

Spread frosting on the sides of the cake, chilling as necessary to keep frosting from getting too soft and the cake layers from sliding around. Chill to firm.

Hold the cake flat on your palm for easy handling. Plop the remaining frosting on top of the cake and spread it with a back and forth motion, using a long-bladed spatula held flat against the top of the cake. Allow the frosting to flow over the edges of the top. When the top is smooth, use the spatula to spread the frosting down the sides of the cake in broad, smooth strokes, turning the cake after each stroke. (For a more detailed explanation, see "Frosting a cake," page 23.)

If desired, pipe a decorative shell border on top of cake approximately 1 inch from the edge, using a pastry bag and a No. 3 star tip. Refrigerate until frosting is set, about 30 minutes.

Sift an even coating of unsweetened cocoa powder over the top of the cake.

Continued on next page

The cake will keep up to three days in the refrigerator. Let it stand at room temperature for at least 1 hour before serving so that the cake and frosting soften and the chocolate darkens in color.

Devil's Food Frosting

12 ounces bittersweet chocolate

½ cup plus 1 tablespoon unsweetened cocoa powder

½ cup plus 1 tablespoon water

3 tablespoons corn syrup

6 ounces unsalted butter (1½ sticks)

⅜ cup powdered sugar

2 egg yolks

2 tablespoons Cognac

Makes enough to frost and fill one 8-inch, 3-layer cake

Finished with a thick dusting of cocoa powder on top, the frosting tastes like a chocolate truffle.

This must be made just before frosting the cake; if it is refrigerated more than 30 minutes, the chocolate hardens and the frosting won't come back to a smooth, shiny, spreadable consistency.

Cut chocolate into 2-inch pieces and melt it in a heat-proof bowl over barely simmering water. (The water should not touch the bottom of the bowl or the chocolate will burn.) Turn off heat and let stand over warm water until ready to use.

In a small saucepan, whisk together the cocoa, water, and corn syrup. Simmer over medium heat, whisking constantly, until the mixture is smooth and thickened and the whisk leaves an empty trail behind it when it is drawn across the bottom of the pan. Remove from heat. Whisk in melted chocolate and Cognac; set aside.

Using the whisk attachment of an electric mixer, beat the butter on medium-high speed until it whitens and holds soft peaks, 3–5 minutes. Beat in powdered sugar until well mixed. Add the egg yolks, one at a time, beating well after each addition and scraping down the sides of the bowl as necessary. Remove bowl from mixer and stir in the chocolate mixture by hand. Let frosting sit in a cool place or refrigerate until it becomes a little stiffer than spreading consistency, about 30 minutes. (Watch carefully so that it doesn't harden.)

If you like, you can hasten the setting by stirring the frosting over ice water for a minute or so. You must stir constantly and remove the bowl from the ice water as soon as the frosting begins to set along the sides of the bowl.

You may have as much as ½ cup of frosting left after frosting the cake. It can be stored in the refrigerator or freezer and rewarmed to sandwich cookies together.

FROZEN PARFAITS

A parfait can be called a dessert of frozen, unchurned ice cream, but that would be too prosaic for this exceedingly creamy and delicious dessert. Simply, the following parfaits are flavored custards that are beaten until slightly thickened on an electric mixer. Whipped cream is then folded in and they are frozen in molds until firm. They're marvelous in hot weather, rich but not overpowering, and a perfect frozen dessert if you don't have an ice cream maker. (In the United States, a tall glass of layered ice cream is called a parfait, but these are parfaits in the original French meaning of the word.)

Chocolate, a natural smoother, makes the creamiest parfaits. I add a touch of white chocolate to many of the nonchocolate parfaits—like hazelnut, ginger, and caramel—just enough to create the perfect texture but not so much that the flavor of the chocolate camouflages the basic taste of the parfait.

Parfaits are simple to make, very similar to ice cream. The main difference is that the custard is cooked to a higher temperature than the custard base for ice cream. When you beat the custard in the electric mixer (after it has been heated), it should begin to thicken and become mousselike in 5–6 minutes. If it is still runny at that point, it was not cooked long enough before beating. Leave it in the mixer bowl (if it is a heatproof bowl) and stir it over direct heat for a few seconds to reheat a bit more, and then start beating again. The mixture must be beaten on low speed on an electric mixer for about 10 minutes. If the custard is beaten at too high a speed, it will just get runny and never thicken. The cooked parfait base must be measured before the whipped cream is folded in, because there will always be a slight discrepancy with the exact amount.

For parfaits with layers of more than one flavor, the parfait bases can be made over several days, then combined with the whipped cream when they are to be molded.

A 10-inch flan ring with 1-inch sides is the best mold for the round parfaits, but a springform pan can also be used.

To unmold, heat dish towels in warm water and wring out well. Wrap them around the flan ring or springform pan briefly, and lift off the ring or release sides. Freeze 15 minutes to harden before serving.

To serve, slice thin directly from the freezer and let the slices stand at room temperature for 3–5 minutes, which will allow the parfait to soften and the flavors and textures to improve. These parfaits are delicious with sauces. Parfaits will still be good frozen for seven to ten days. Consider making two parfaits at a time for two different occasions.

Three-Chocolate Parfait with Bitter Chocolate Sauce

To Prepare Mold:
1 tablespoon unsalted butter, melted

Basic Parfait Mixture:
12 egg yolks

½ cup granulated sugar

1½ cups heavy cream

½ cup milk

3 vanilla beans, split and scraped

To Fold into Parfait Mixtures:
1¼ cups heavy cream in all

4 tablespoons sour cream in all

Flavoring for Bittersweet Chocolate Layer:
5 ounces bittersweet chocolate

2½ teaspoons instant coffee

Flavoring for White Chocolate Layer:
5 ounces white chocolate

1 tablespoon lemon juice

1½ teaspoons instant coffee

1 teaspoon freshly ground coffee

Brady Cake was the original name for this three-layered parfait of milk chocolate, bittersweet chocolate, and white chocolate, even though it's not a cake at all. It got that name when I was scheduled to teach a cooking class for my friend Jean Brady. A month in advance of the class, Jean called to ask what recipes I'd be teaching. At that point, I hadn't the slightest idea so I just told her "Brady Cake," and worked out the recipe the night before the class. When Wolfgang Puck tasted it, he decided to make it one of the few desserts that were permanently on the menu at Spago. When it's cut into slices, the three colors make it look like "neapolitan" ice cream.

The easiest way to make this parfait is to make the base mixture for all three layers at the same time, divide it into thirds, and then cook, cool, and flavor each layer separately. The heavy cream is whipped all at once and divided between the layers.

Use a 10 x 4-inch slant-sided French terrine mold (6-cup capacity) or a 12 x 3 x 3-inch straight-sided mold. For other size molds, adjust the quantities accordingly. Prepare a foil-covered cardboard rectangle to unmold the parfait onto.

TO PREPARE MOLD

Cut pieces of parchment paper or wax paper to fit the sides, bottom, and ends of the terrine mold. Using a pastry brush, brush mold with melted butter and line with paper. Set aside in a cool place.

MAKING THE BASIC PARFAIT MIXTURE

Using the whisk attachment of an electric mixer, beat together the egg yolks and the sugar at high speed until the mixture is thick, pale yellow, and forms a ribbon when the beater is lifted from the bowl. In a large saucepan, scald the cream, milk, and vanilla beans. Pour the hot cream gradually into the egg yolks, whisking constantly. Measure the total volume (there should be about 6 cups) and divide equally into three.

❖ At this point the mixture can be refrigerated and the separate layers cooked and flavored as time allows over two days.

Flavoring for Milk
   Chocolate Layer:
*5 ounces milk chocolate
   (preferably Cadbury)*

*2½ tablespoons Irish cream
   liqueur, or 1 tablespoon
   malt (preferably
   Horlicks)*

To Glaze:
*2 cups Bitter Chocolate
   Glaze (page 348)*

Makes 10 servings

WHIPPING THE CREAM

Using the whisk attachment of an electric mixer, beat the heavy cream with the sour cream on low speed until it thickens enough not to spatter. Increase speed to medium-high and beat until thick and mousselike. Remove from mixer and whisk a few strokes by hand, until the cream holds soft peaks. Refrigerate.

FLAVORING THE LAYERS

The process for making all three layers is the same. After each one is poured into the mold, it must be frozen for at least 2 hours to set before the next layer can be added. From the bottom up, the flavors should be bittersweet chocolate, white chocolate, and milk chocolate, so make the layers in that order. The parfait mixture for each layer should measure 2 cups when it is finished.

Cut chocolate into 2-inch pieces. In a heatproof bowl, melt chocolate over barely simmering water. Keep the heat very low for the milk chocolate and white chocolate, because they burn more easily than dark chocolate. (The water should not touch the bottom of the bowl or the chocolate will burn.) When chocolate is melted, turn off heat and let stand until ready to use.

In a saucepan, heat one third of the basic parfait mixture over medium-high heat, whisking constantly, until the mixture just reaches the boiling point. Immediately remove from heat and whisk a few times to stop cooking. Strain through a fine-mesh strainer into the bowl of an electric mixer. Add melted chocolate and the flavorings indicated for each layer. Beat at low speed for 10 minutes, until thick and mousselike and the underside of the bowl is cold. Refrigerate until cold, about 30 minutes.

Remove whipped cream from refrigerator and whisk a few times to remount, if necessary. Measure out one third of the whipped cream (about ⅔ cup) and fold into cold parfait mixture, blending well.

Repeat process for each layer of the parfait. Pour each layer as it is finished into the prepared mold and freeze for 2 hours.

UNMOLDING AND GLAZING THE PARFAIT

When the parfait is completely frozen (6 hours to overnight), remove from freezer and place upside down on the foil-covered cardboard rectangle. Unmold by wrapping a hot towel briefly around the sides of the terrine mold, or by dipping the terrine quickly in a pan of hot water. Too much heat can melt the parfait, so if it doesn't come out of the mold easily at first, try to loosen it by holding the mold and the cardboard together and shaking sharply, or by banging firmly on the bottom and sides. It will come out! Peel off paper lining, smooth the sides of the parfait with a long metal spatula, and freeze again for 15 minutes, until firm.

In a heatproof bowl, warm the chocolate glaze over barely simmering water until it is just warm enough to be pourable, but not hot. Remove the parfait from the freezer. Place on a cooling rack set on a baking sheet. Ladle or pour the glaze evenly over the length of the parfait, allowing the glaze to flow over the top and sides in a thin layer. With a metal spatula, pick up the glaze that dripped off the cake and patch any holes on the sides, if necessary. To prevent drip marks, allow the parfait to sit for a minute or so until the glaze hardens before returning to the freezer.

Freeze until ready to serve, or wrap well and freeze for up to ten days.

Just before serving, cut into ½-inch slices with a heated knife and lay flat on individual plates mirrored with Bitter Chocolate Sauce.

Poppy Seed–Caramel Parfait

To Prepare Pan:
½ tablespoon unsalted butter, melted

1 tablespoon flour

Poppy Seed Cake:
2 tablespoons poppy seeds

⅓ cup milk

1 tablespoon grated or finely chopped orange zest (1 orange)

4 tablespoons unsalted butter (½ stick)

6 tablespoons granulated sugar in all

½ tablespoon vanilla extract

¾ cup flour

¾ teaspoon baking powder

2 egg whites

Parfait Fillings:
7 egg yolks in all

1¾ cups heavy cream in all

6 tablespoons milk in all

6 tablespoons granulated sugar

2 vanilla beans, split and scraped in all

2 tablespoons sour cream

2 ounces white chocolate, melted

3 tablespoons bourbon (preferably Wild Turkey)

2 teaspoons (scant) poppy seeds

A layer of caramel parfait is hidden within a poppy seed parfait smoothed with white chocolate and flavored with whiskey. The dessert is built on a soft layer of poppy seed cake.

You will need a 6 x ½-inch flan ring for the caramel parfait and an 8 x 1-inch flan ring or 2½-inch-high entremet ring set on an 8-inch foil-covered cardboard circle, or an 8-inch springform pan.

MAKING THE POPPY SEED CAKE

Using the quantities of ingredients listed at left, make the cake layer as directed on page 291. Bake for 30–35 minutes, until the cake pulls away from the sides of the pan and springs back when touched lightly. Cool (or freeze until ready to use).

PREPARING THE MOLD

With a long serrated knife, trim the cake layer horizontally to ⅜-inch thickness and trim the edges so that the diameter is about 7½ inches. Center the cake layer, the flat, bottom side up, on the foil-covered cardboard round or the bottom of the springform pan. The ring or the sides of the springform pan will be put on later, after the caramel layer is molded. Set aside.

MAKING AND MOLDING THE CARAMEL LAYER

Using the whisk attachment of an electric mixer, beat 3 of the egg yolks briefly to break them up. In a saucepan, scald ½ cup of the heavy cream and 3 tablespoons of the milk. Keep warm over low heat.

In a small heavy saucepan or an unlined copper pan, heat the sugar and 1 of the vanilla beans over medium heat until the sugar caramelizes, 5–8 minutes. Stir occasionally with a wooden spoon to ensure that the sugar colors evenly. Once one portion of the sugar begins to darken, toss it with the uncooked sugar. This will prevent the sugar from burning in one spot before the entire mixture has liquefied and turned a dark caramel color. As soon as the mixture begins to smoke, set the bottom of the pan in a pan of cold water to stop it from cooking and coloring further. Immediately pour the caramelized sugar into the cream, being careful of spattering. Whisk together to combine well.

To Glaze:
*½ cup Bitter Chocolate
Glaze (page 348),
optional*

Makes 6 servings

Pour about one fourth of the hot cream into the egg yolks, whisking continuously. Return the mixture to the saucepan and whisk into the remaining cream. Cook over medium-high heat, whisking constantly, until the mixture just reaches the boiling point. Immediately remove from heat and whisk a few times to stop the cooking. Strain through a fine-mesh strainer into the bowl of an electric mixer. Beat at low speed for 10 minutes, until thick and mousselike and the underside of the bowl is cold. Refrigerate until cold, about 30 minutes.

Meanwhile, beat ¾ cup of the heavy cream with the sour cream in an electric mixer at low speed until it thickens enough not to spatter. Increase speed to medium-high and beat until thick and mousselike. Remove from mixer and whisk a few strokes by hand, until the cream holds soft peaks. Refrigerate.

Measure out and use no more than 1¼ cups parfait mixture. Measure out ½ cup whipped cream and fold into the cold caramel mixture. Center the 6-inch flan ring on the layer of poppy seed cake. Pour in caramel mixture, filling until it is even with the top of the flan ring. Freeze until firm, about 4 hours.

MAKING THE POPPY SEED LAYER

Cut the white chocolate into 2-inch pieces. In a heatproof bowl, melt chocolate over barely simmering water. Keep the heat low, because white chocolate burns more easily than dark chocolate. (The water should not touch the bottom of the bowl or the chocolate will burn.) Turn off heat and let stand until ready to use.

In a small saucepan, scald the remaining ½ cup cream, 3 tablespoons milk, and the other vanilla bean. Remove from heat, cover, and let stand 30 minutes

Using the whisk attachment of an electric mixer, beat the remaining 4 egg yolks briefly to break up. Reheat cream to scalding. Pour about one fourth of the hot cream into the egg yolks, whisking continuously. Return the mixture to the saucepan and whisk into the remaining cream. Cook over medium-high heat, whisking constantly, until the mixture just reaches the boiling point. Immediately remove from heat and whisk a few times to stop the cooking. Strain through a fine-mesh strainer into the bowl of an electric mixer. Add the bourbon, poppy seeds, and melted white chocolate and beat at low speed for 10 minutes, until mixture is thick and mousselike and the underside of the bowl is cold. Refrigerate until cold, about 30 minutes.

Remove whipped cream from refrigerator and whisk a few times to remount, if necessary. Measure out and use no more than 2½ cups parfait mixture. Fold the remaining whipped cream into cold poppy seed mixture; set aside.

MOLDING THE POPPY SEED LAYER

First, remove the flan ring from the caramel layer by holding a warm towel around it briefly and then slipping off the ring. Be sure the towel is well wrung-out so that it doesn't wet the cake. Return to the freezer to set. If you are using a springform pan, put on the sides. If you are using a flan ring or entrement ring, put the ring around the cake layer and then place the whole assemblage—cardboard round, flan ring, cake, and caramel layer—on a large square of aluminum foil. Fold the foil up, crimping it tight to the sides of the ring, even with the top. This will keep the parfait from leaking out around the bottom edge of the ring before it freezes.

Pour the poppy seed parfait over and around the caramel layer and cake; freeze until firm, at least 2 hours.

GLAZING THE PARFAIT

In a heatproof bowl, warm the chocolate glaze over barely simmering water until it is just warm enough to be pourable, but not hot. Pour the glaze onto the top of the parfait and swirl it around, tilting the pan to make a thin, even layer. Pour off excess. Freeze until ready to serve. Unmold as directed on page 305. Serve with Bitter Chocolate Sauce, Bitter Orange Sauce, or the two sauces swirled together on a plate.

Ginger Parfait

To Prepare Pan:
½ tablespoon butter, melted
1 tablespoon flour

Ginger Cake:
*3 tablespoons unsalted
    butter*
1 tablespoon brown sugar
1 egg yolk
2 egg whites
*1½ tablespoons granulated
    sugar*
¼ cup molasses
1½ teaspoons ground ginger
½ cup flour
*⅛ teaspoon freshly ground
    nutmeg*
⅛ teaspoon ground cloves
*½ teaspoon ground
    cinnamon*
½ teaspoon baking soda
¼ teaspoon instant coffee
1 teaspoon boiling water
2 tablespoons sour cream

Ginger Parfait:
9 ounces fresh ginger root
1¼ cups heavy cream in all
¼ cup milk
3 ounces white chocolate
6 egg yolks

Ginger in a frozen dessert is a delight, cool and hot at the same time. Chopped nougatine folded into the creamy parfait adds crunchiness, and a round of spongy, spicy ginger cake is another contrast.

Use an 8 x 1-inch flan ring or 2½-inch-high entremet ring set on an 8-inch foil-covered cardboard circle, or an 8-inch springform pan.

MAKING THE GINGER CAKE

Using the quantities of ingredients listed at left, make the ginger cake in an 8-inch round paper-lined layer cake pan, following the instructions on page 173. Bake 25 minutes, until the cake pulls away from the sides of the pan and springs back when touched lightly. Cool (or freeze until ready to use).

PREPARING THE MOLD

If you're using a flan ring or entremet ring on a cardboard round for a mold (instead of a springform pan), place the ring on the cardboard and place both on a large square of foil. Fold the foil up, crimping it tight to the sides of the ring, even with the top. This will keep the parfait from leaking out around the bottom edge of the ring before it freezes.

With a long serrated knife, trim the cake layer horizontally to ⅜-inch thickness and trim the edges so that the diameter is about 7½ inches. Center the cake on the foil-covered cardboard circle or the bottom of the springform pan. Set aside.

MAKING THE GINGER PARFAIT

Peel the ginger root with a vegetable peeler and slice it into rounds ¼ inch thick. There should be about 1½ cups. Place the ginger in a saucepan of water, bring it to a boil, and boil for 30 seconds. Drain well.

In a saucepan, scald ¾ cup of the cream with the milk and blanched ginger. Remove from heat, cover, and let stand 30 minutes. Strain, discarding the ginger, and return the cream to the saucepan.

Cut white chocolate into 2-inch pieces. In a heatproof bowl, melt chocolate over barely simmering water. Keep the heat low, because white chocolate burns more easily

2 teaspoons granulated sugar

2 teaspoons molasses

2 tablespoons sour cream

1 cup Nougatine, chopped (page 353)

Makes 6 servings

than dark chocolate. (The water should not touch the bottom of the bowl or the chocolate will burn.) Turn off heat and let stand until ready to use.

Using the whisk attachment of an electric mixer, beat together the egg yolks and sugar until the sugar has dissolved and the mixture is thick and pale yellow; set aside. Reheat cream mixture to scalding. Pour about one fourth of the hot cream into the egg yolks, beating continuously. Return mixture to the saucepan and whisk into remaining cream.

Cook over medium-high heat, whisking constantly, until the mixture just reaches the boiling point. Immediately remove from heat and whisk a few times to stop cooking. Strain into the bowl of an electric mixer. Add the melted chocolate and molasses and beat at low speed for 10 minutes until thick and mousselike and the underside of the bowl is cold. Refrigerate until cold, about 30 minutes.

Using the whisk attachment of an electric mixer, beat the remaining ½ cup heavy cream with the sour cream at low speed until it thickens enough not to spatter. Increase speed to medium-high and beat until thick and mousselike. Remove from mixer and whisk a few strokes by hand until the cream holds soft peaks.

Measure the parfait mixture and use only 3¾ cups. Fold into the cold ginger mixture, blending well. Fold in chopped nougatine. Pour into the prepared mold. Freeze until firm, 2–4 hours.

Unmold as directed on page 305. Serve with Bitter Chocolate Sauce (page 348).

Orange, Hazelnut, and Chocolate Parfait

1 Orange Macaroon Layer
   (page 316)

4 ounces hazelnuts in all

2¾ cups plus 3 tablespoons
   heavy cream in all

½ cup plus 3 tablespoons
   milk in all

1 teaspoon cooking oil

¼ cup plus 1 tablespoon
   granulated sugar in all

2 tablespoons water

2 ounces white chocolate

9 egg yolks in all

1 tablespoon hazelnut
   liqueur

2 tablespoons sour cream

6 ounces bittersweet
   chocolate

2½ teaspoons instant coffee

3 tablespoons orange zest
   (3 oranges) in long
   shreds (do not chop)

¾ cup fresh orange juice
   (3–4 oranges)

⅓ cup orange liqueur

To Decorate:
½ cup Bitter Chocolate
   Glaze (page 348)

Makes 6 servings

Orange, hazelnut, and chocolate are flavors that I love to use together—they're in the Three-Nut Torte, the Hazelnut–Chocolate Sable Cookies, and, in a totally different form, in this frozen parfait.

The three complementary flavors and colors make an interesting cross-section when cut. The hazelnut parfait is hidden in the center, surrounded by the chocolate and orange. If three flavors and a macaroon layer seem like a lot of work, use this recipe only as a guide; improvise by doubling one of the other layers, or perhaps eliminate the macaroon. Do make at least two flavors, though.

You will need a 6 x ½-inch flan ring for the hazelnut layer and an 8 x 1-inch flan ring or 2½-inch-high entremet ring set on an 8-inch foil-covered cardboard round, or an 8-inch springform pan.

Trim the edges of the macaroon, if necessary, so that it measures 7½ inches in diameter. Center macaroon layer, flat side up (the cooked side against the baking sheet), on the foil-covered cardboard round or the bottom of the springform pan. The flan ring or the sides of the springform pan will be put on later, after the hazelnut layer is unmolded. Set aside.

MAKING THE HAZELNUT PARFAIT

Preheat oven to 325 degrees. Spread the hazelnuts on a baking sheet and toast for 8–10 minutes, until brown. Cool. Rub in a clean dish towel to remove skins.

In a food processor, grind to a paste ¾ cup (3 ounces) of the hazelnuts. In a saucepan, scald the ground nuts with 1 cup of the cream and ¼ cup of the milk. Remove from heat, cover, and let stand 30 minutes.

Meanwhile, oil a baking sheet with the cooking oil; set aside. In a small saucepan, heat the ¼ cup sugar and water over high heat. When the water boils, it will throw sugar onto the sides of the pan. At that point, wash down the sides of the pan with a pastry brush, dipping in water as necessary to dissolve sugar. (Alternatively, place a lid on the pan for 30 seconds and the steam condensation will wash the sugar off the sides.) Let the syrup cook to an amber color. Stir in the remaining ¼ cup hazelnuts, and cook, stirring, another 30 seconds, until the hazelnuts turn a golden brown. Pour onto the oiled baking sheet and stir nuts to stop the cooking; spread them out evenly. When the praline is cool, break it into large chunks. Chop coarse and set aside.

Cut white chocolate into 2-inch pieces. In a heatproof bowl melt chocolate over barely simmering water. Keep the heat low, because white chocolate burns more easily than dark chocolate. (The water should not touch the bottom of the bowl or the chocolate will burn.) Turn off heat and let stand until ready to use.

After 30 minutes, strain the cream and hazelnut mixture through a fine-mesh strainer, pressing out as much cream as possible with the back of a spoon. The hazelnuts will absorb some of the cream, but there should be at least ¾ cup left. (If there is less than ¾ cup, add a few tablespoons more cream, but use no more than ¾ cup in making the custard mixture.)

Using the whisk attachment of an electric mixer, beat 3 of the egg yolks briefly to break them up. Reheat cream to scalding. Pour about one fourth of the hot cream into the egg yolks, whisking continuously. Return to the saucepan and whisk into remaining cream. Cook over medium-high heat, whisking constantly, until the mixture just reaches the boiling point. Immediately remove from heat and whisk a few times to stop the cooking. Strain through a fine-mesh strainer into the bowl of an electric mixer. Add the hazelnut liqueur and melted chocolate. Beat at low speed for 10 minutes, until thick and mousselike and the underside of the bowl is cold. Refrigerate until cold, about 30 minutes.

Using the whisk attachment of an electric mixer, beat ¾ cup of the heavy cream with the sour cream at low speed until it thickens enough not to spatter. Increase speed to medium-high and beat until thick and mousselike. Remove from mixer and whisk a few strokes by hand, until the cream holds soft peaks. Refrigerate.

Measure the hazelnut parfait mixture and use only 1½ cups. Fold in ½ cup whipped cream and the praline.

Center the 6-inch flan ring on the macaroon layer. Pour in the hazelnut mixture, filling until it is even with the top of the flan ring. Chill until set, at least 4 hours.

❖ This layer can be made and molded in advance; make

and mold the chocolate and orange layers the next day.

MAKING THE CHOCOLATE LAYER

(Wait until the hazelnut layer has set before making the chocolate layer, because it contains so much chocolate that it firms up much more quickly than the other layers.)

To remove the flan ring from the hazelnut layer, hold a warm towel around the ring briefly and then slip it off. Be sure the towel is well wrung-out so that it doesn't wet the cake. Return to the freezer to set.

Cut the bittersweet chocolate into 2-inch pieces. In a heatproof bowl, melt chocolate over barely simmering water. (The water should not touch the bottom of the bowl or the chocolate will burn.) Turn off heat and let stand until ready to use.

Using the whisk attachment of an electric mixer, beat 3 of the egg yolks briefly to break them up. In a saucepan, scald the remaining ½ cup plus 1 tablespoon heavy cream and 3 tablespoons milk. Pour about half of the hot cream into the egg yolks, whisking continuously. Return to saucepan and whisk into remaining cream. Cook over medium-high heat, whisking constantly, until the mixture just reaches the boiling point.

Immediately remove from heat and whisk a few times to stop the cooking. Strain through a fine-mesh strainer into the bowl of an electric mixer. Add melted chocolate and instant coffee. Beat at low speed for 10 minutes, until thick and mousselike and the underside of the bowl is cold. Do not refrigerate.

Put sides on springform pan. If you're using a flan ring or entrement ring, place the ring around the macaroon layer and place the whole assemblage—cardboard round, meringue layer, hazelnut layer, and flan ring—on a large square of foil. Fold the foil up, crimping it tight to the sides of the ring, even with the top. This will keep the parfait from leaking out the bottom edge of the ring before it freezes.

Remove whipped cream from refrigerator and whisk a few times to remount, if necessary. Measure ½ cup whipped cream and fold into the chocolate mixture. Measure 2 cups chocolate mixture and pour it carefully around —not over—the hazelnut layer. (Alternatively, pipe it in with a pastry bag, No. 4 plain tip.) The chocolate should come to the same height as the hazelnut layer. Freeze. It will set up quickly, so you can make the orange layer immediately.

MAKING THE ORANGE LAYER

In a saucepan, scald ½ cup plus 2 tablespoons heavy cream, ¼ cup milk, and orange zest. Remove from heat, cover, and let stand 30 minutes.

Meanwhile, in a small saucepan, combine the orange juice and liqueur. Boil until the mixture reduces to ¼ cup. Let the bubbles die down to measure accurately. The orange mixture will just start to caramelize and brown. Stir into cream.

In an electric mixer, using the whisk attachment, beat the remaining 3 egg yolks with 1 tablespoon sugar until the sugar has dissolved. Reheat cream to scalding. Pour about half of the hot cream into the egg yolks, whisking continuously. Return to the saucepan and whisk into remaining cream. Cook over medium-high heat, whisking constantly, until the mixture just reaches the boiling point. Immediately remove from heat and whisk a few times to stop the cooking. Strain through a fine-mesh strainer into the bowl of an electric mixer, reserving the orange zest. Beat at low speed for 10 minutes, until the mixture is thick and mousselike and the underside of the bowl is cold.

Rinse the orange zest in running water to remove any clinging bits of cooked egg, drain very well, and stir back into parfait mixture. Refrigerate until cold, about 30 minutes.

Remove whipped cream from refrigerator and whisk a few times to remount, if necessary. Measure 1½ cups parfait mixture and fold in remaining ½ cup whipped cream. Pour over the top of the molded chocolate and hazelnut layers. Freeze until firm, 2–4 hours.

GLAZING THE PARFAIT

Before unmolding, glaze with chocolate glaze as directed for the Poppy Seed–Caramel Parfait (page 307). Then unmold as directed on page 305.

Orange or Lemon Macaroon Layer

To Prepare Pan:

½ tablespoon unsalted butter, melted

Flour for pan

3 tablespoons granulated sugar in all

6 tablespoons powdered sugar

¾ cup plus 1 tablespoon almond meal

2 tablespoons grated or finely chopped orange zest or lemon zest (2 oranges or 3 lemons)

1 tablespoon flour

2 egg whites

1 tablespoon almond extract

Makes one 8-inch meringue layer

Used in Orange, Hazelnut, and Chocolate Parfait

Almond meal and flour make these layers chewy, rather than crunchy.

Use an 8-inch flan ring set on a heavy baking sheet.

Brush the melted butter on the back of a baking sheet. Chill briefly to set. Dust with flour, knock off excess, and set aside. Set an 8-inch flan ring in center of sheet.

Preheat oven to 325 degrees. Adjust oven rack to middle position.

In a food processor, place 2 tablespoons of the granulated sugar, powdered sugar, almond meal, orange or lemon zest, and flour. Process a minute or so until well combined. Sift through a fine-mesh strainer to break up any lumps. If anything remains in the strainer, stir it back into the mixture.

In an electric mixer, beat the egg whites on low speed until frothy. Increase speed to medium and beat until soft peaks form. Increase speed to high and very gradually beat in the remaining 1 tablespoon granulated sugar until stiff, glossy peaks form. Add the almond extract and beat briefly to combine. Fold the almond meal-sugar mixture, one third at a time, into the stiffly beaten egg whites, combining well.

Using a pastry bag (No. 3 plain tip), pipe a border of filling around the edge of the ring. Then, starting in the center, pipe an even spiral all the way to the sides. (Or pour it into the ring and spread with an offset metal spatula or the back of a spoon.)

Bake for 22–24 minutes, until the meringue just starts to color, springs back when touched lightly in the center, and is firm around the edges. It will harden as it cools. If overbaked, the layer will be brittle rather than chewy. If doughy, return briefly to the oven to cook further.

Keeps refrigerated for two days or frozen for one month.

Plain or Coffee Meringue Layers

Plain Meringue Layers:
4 egg whites

11 tablespoons granulated sugar

1 cup plus 2 tablespoons powdered sugar, sifted

Coffee Meringue Layers:
4 egg whites

9 tablespoons granulated sugar

1 cup powdered sugar, sifted

2 teaspoons instant coffee dissolved in 1/2 teaspoon hot water

2 tablespoons freshly ground coffee

Makes three 7-inch meringue layers

Used in Coffee Parfait

Since stiffness is essential when making meringue layers, there is a relatively large amount of sugar in this recipe. Making a perfect meringue layer is really simpler than beating perfect egg whites, because the larger amount of sugar naturally smooths out the egg whites.

Four egg whites will make one extra plain meringue for the Cassis Vacherin, and two extra coffee meringues for the Coffee Parfait. It's good insurance to have an extra in case one cracks. Also, when you're using a free-standing electric mixer (with a beater that doesn't reach the bottom of the bowl), you need a larger volume for the egg whites to beat properly. Extra meringue layers will keep a few days if left at room temperature in a tightly sealed container.

Baking meringues is the process of drying out the moisture in the egg whites, cooking them at very low heat so the sugar won't caramelize and the meringue won't darken.

Preheat oven to 175 degrees. Line 2 heavy baking sheets with paper. Trace three 7-inch circles on the paper-lined baking sheets. Turn the paper over so pencil marks are on reverse side; set aside.

Using the whisk attachment of an electric mixer, beat the egg whites on low speed until frothy. Increase speed to medium and beat until soft peaks form. Increase speed to high and very gradually beat in the granulated sugar, until very stiff, glossy peaks form. Adding the granulated sugar can take up to 5 minutes; the slower the better. (If the sugar is added too fast, it will cause the whites to liquefy.)

When the granulated sugar is incorporated, turn the mixer off and add the powdered sugar (and the ground coffee and instant coffee, for the coffee meringues) all at once. Turn the mixer to low and beat for just four or five turns, until incorporated. Do not overbeat. Remove from mixer and with a rubber spatula fold a couple of times by hand to ensure that the mixture is thoroughly combined.

Using a pastry bag (No. 4 plain tip), pipe the meringue into the circles in an even spiral. The meringue can also be spread with an offset metal spatula or the back of a spoon. Bake for 1½ hours for the plain meringues, or 2 hours for the coffee meringues, in both cases until the circles peel easily off the paper lining without sticking. Plain meringues will be crisp and white all the way through; coffee meringues will be light coffee-color when cooked.

Coffee Parfait

1 Coffee Meringue Layer
   (page 317)

Coffee Parfait:
4 ounces white chocolate

1 cup whole decaffeinated
   coffee beans

1½ cups heavy cream in all

¼ cup milk

6 egg yolks

2 tablespoons granulated
   sugar

2 tablespoons instant coffee

1½ tablespoons coffee
   liqueur

2 tablespoons sour cream

To Decorate:
1½ tablespoons instant
   coffee dissolved in ½
   tablespoon hot water, or
   ½ cup Bitter Chocolate
   Glaze (page 348)

Makes 6 servings

This cool, creamy coffee parfait sits on a crunchy coffee meringue layer and is topped with chocolate glaze. Serve it with Bitter Chocolate Sauce, Coffee Sauce, or both swirled together on a plate.

Use an 8 x 1-inch flan ring or 2½-inch-high entremet ring set on an 8-inch foil-covered cardboard circle, or an 8-inch springform pan.

PREPARING THE MOLD

If you are using a ring set on a cardboard circle (instead of a springform pan), place the ring on the cardboard and then place both on a large square of foil. Fold the foil up, crimping it tight to the sides of the ring, even with the top. This will keep the parfait filling from leaking out around the bottom edge of the ring before it freezes.

Trim the edges of the meringue, if necessary, so that it measures 7½ inches in diameter. (To trim, hold up meringue circle and whittle away gently at the edges with a sharp knife to avoid breaking.) Center meringue smooth side down on the foil-covered cardboard circle or the bottom of the springform pan. Set aside.

MAKING THE PARFAIT

Cut the white chocolate into 2-inch pieces. In a heatproof bowl, melt chocolate over barely simmering water. Keep the heat low because white chocolate burns more easily than dark chocolate. (The water should not touch the bottom of the bowl or the chocolate will burn.) Turn off heat and let stand until ready to use.

With a rolling pin or the back of a saucepan, coarsely crush the coffee beans. In a large saucepan, scald ¾ cup of the heavy cream, milk, and coffee beans. Remove from heat, cover, and let stand 30 minutes. Strain and discard coffee beans. Return cream to saucepan.

Using the whisk attachment of an electric mixer, beat together the egg yolks and sugar until the sugar has dissolved and the mixture is thick and pale yellow; set aside. Reheat cream to scalding. Pour about one fourth of the hot cream into the egg yolks, beating continuously. Return the mixture to the saucepan and whisk into remaining cream. Cook over medium-high heat, whisking constantly, until the mixture just reaches the boiling point. Immediately remove from heat and whisk a few times to stop the cooking. Strain into the bowl of an electric mixer. Add melted chocolate and instant coffee. Beat at low speed for 10 minutes, until the mixture is thick and mousselike and the underside of the bowl is cold. Refrigerate until cold, about 30 minutes.

Using the whisk attachment of an electric mixer, beat the remaining ¾ cup heavy cream with sour cream on low speed until it thickens enough not to spatter. Increase speed to medium-high and beat until thick and mousselike. Remove from mixer and whisk a few strokes by hand until the cream holds soft peaks.

Measure 3¾ cups parfait mixture and fold in the whipped cream and the coffee liqueur. Pour into the prepared mold.

DECORATING THE PARFAIT

There are two ways to decorate the parfait: with swirls of liquid coffee or with a layer of Chocolate Glaze. For the coffee decoration, immediately after the parfait has been poured into the mold, sprinkle the dissolved instant coffee over the entire surface of the parfait. Using the tip of a paring knife, swirl the coffee into freeform curving patterns. Freeze until ready to serve, at least 2 hours.

To glaze with chocolate, freeze parfait until firm, at least 2 hours. In a heatproof bowl, warm the glaze over gently simmering water until it is just warm enough to be pourable but not hot. Pour the glaze onto the top of the parfait, tilting the pan so that it forms a thin, even layer and pour off excess. Freeze until ready to serve. Unmold and serve as directed on page 305.

Cassis Vacherin

2 Plain Meringue Layers
    (page 317)
1 quart Cassis Sherbet
    (page 232)
½ cup heavy cream,
    optional
2 tablespoons sour cream

Makes 6 servings

I've never been very fond of meringue, but it does work well in frozen desserts like this one, where pristine white layers of meringue set off beautifully the dark purple cassis sherbet. The meringue adds sweetness and texture to the tart, smooth sherbet.

Use an 8 x 1-inch flan ring or 2½-inch-high entremet ring set on an 8-inch foil-covered cardboard circle, or an 8-inch springform pan.

If you're using a ring set on a cardboard round, place the ring on the cardboard and place both on a large square of foil. Fold the foil up, crimping it tight to the sides of the ring, even with the top. This will keep the sherbet from leaking out around the bottom edge of the ring.

Trim both meringue layers, if necessary, so they measure 7½ inches in diameter. To trim without breaking, hold up the meringue circle and whittle away gently at the sides with a sharp knife. Center one layer smooth side down in the bottom of the springform pan or on the cardboard circle.

Before piping, let the sherbet firm up in the freezer for at least 1 hour after it comes out of the ice cream machine to ensure that it is creamy, not watery. If the sherbet has been made in advance and is frozen hard, beat it briefly in an electric mixer (using the paddle attachment) or process in a food processor until it is a spreadable consistency but not melted.

Fill a pastry bag (No. 3 plain tip) with sherbet. Work quickly, handling the pastry bag as little as possible to keep the sherbet from melting. If it gets watery when piped, it will melt the meringue.

Pipe a border of sherbet to fill in the space between the meringue layer and the sides of the pan. Then, starting in the center, pipe an even spiral over the meringue layer all the way to the sides of the pan. (An offset metal spatula or the back of a spoon can also be used to spread sherbet.) Center the other meringue layer on the sherbet, press down lightly, and repeat, piping sherbet around the edges and then covering with more sherbet. Smooth the top with a long metal spatula even with the top of the 1-inch flan ring. If you're using a springform pan, smooth the top with the back of a spoon. Freeze until firm, about 2 hours.

DECORATING THE VACHERIN

If you have made the vacherin in a flan ring, you can finish the top with a very thin, smooth layer of whipped cream, which will contrast with the dark cassis color when it is unmolded. If it is made in a springform pan, simply unmold when frozen and serve as directed.

In an electric mixer, whip the heavy cream with sour cream on low speed until it has thickened enough not to spatter. Increase speed to medium-high and beat until thick and mousselike. Remove from mixer and whisk a few strokes by hand, until the cream holds soft peaks.

Using a pastry bag fitted with a No. 3 plain tip, pipe a spiral of whipped cream to cover the top of the frozen vacherin, or spoon on the whipped cream. To make a perfectly smooth top, sweep once across the whipped cream with a 10-inch metal spatula. Don't move the spatula back and forth or the whipped cream will begin to mix with the sherbet. Return to freezer for at least 20 minutes to firm up.

Unmold and cut for serving as directed on page 305. The vacherin keeps frozen, well wrapped, for two to three days.

Finishing Touches

SAUCES

Raspberry Sauce
Rhubarb-Raspberry Sauce
Strawberry Sauce
Blackberry Sauce
Cranberry Sauce
Huckleberry Sauce
Mango Sauce
Apricot Sauce
Ginger Sauce
Kiwi Sauce
Pear Sauce
Caramel
Caramel Sauce
Bitter Orange Sauce
Bitter Chocolate Sauce
Coffee Sauce
Mint Sauce
Vanilla Sauce

DECORATION

Swiss Meringue
Bitter Chocolate Glaze
White Chocolate Glaze
Making a Chocolate Band
Nougatine with Almonds or Coconut
Sugared Almonds
Praline
Candied Walnuts

I take pride in a first-class finish when I serve desserts. A dessert can be served forth at a private table with the finesse and style that is characteristic of a fine restaurant. After all, our first impression of a dish is visual, and it has an enormous influence on how much we enjoy eating it.

Presentation is more than decoration. Perhaps the simplest aspect is the choice of plates and platters on which you serve your desserts. In general, white or very plain plates are the most versatile. Get big enough ones so that individually plated desserts don't look cramped, and so that there's plenty of room for a shining mirror of sauce.

For tarts and cakes, consider the color and style of the dessert as you select a platter. Choose a pottery dish for a homey-looking two-crust pie or hand-formed cookies, an ultramodern porcelain platter for a sleek, chocolate-glazed caramel-walnut tart, or a fluted glass dish for an old-fashioned European Linzer torte.

The taste and appearance of a dessert can be enhanced tremendously by serving it with a beautifully colored, quick-to-make sauce. And by mastering a few simple decorating techniques and tricks, you can add a certain sophistication to desserts that would otherwise be plain-looking—though delicious—just as they come from the oven.

Most important with finishing touches, however, is not to go overboard. Desserts are not just carriers for decoration, in the old wedding-cake school of embellishment; instead, any sauce or decoration should be instrumental in bringing out the basic flavors of a dish. (The best test: if you can't tell what you're eating with your eyes closed, there's something wrong.) Keep it simple, with edible decorations, natural colors, and a delicate touch.

SAUCES

The simplest way to add class to a dessert is to serve it with a sauce. Setting a slice of cake, tart, or parfait in a shallow pool of sauce makes it look much fancier and more "designed" than it would on a bare plate, and sauces are generally so quick to make that the effort on your part is minimal.

A sauce also adds new dimensions to a dessert. For the eye, a contrasting or complementary color is appealing, whether it's shiny blackberry sauce next to a lightly browned Blackberry Custard Tart, or mint custard sauce with a Chocolate-Mint Truffle Cake. A sauce can underline a flavor that's present but not too pronounced—raspberry sauce, for instance, brings out the fresh raspberries in the Raspberry-Caramel Napoleon, and pear sauce emphasizes the subtle pear taste in the Pear and Ginger Brown-Butter Tart.

FRUIT SAUCES

Fruit sauces are simply purées of fresh or frozen fruit, cooked or uncooked, flavored with sugar, liqueur, or fruit juices. A good fruit sauce will be bright-colored, never cloudy, and should pour smoothly without being watery. Many of the sauces are strained before serving, but in some, like strawberry and kiwi, I like the look of the seeds and serve them unstrained.

Because fruit varies widely in quality, it's hard to say exactly how much sugar and flavoring a fruit sauce will need on any given day. Sometimes frozen fruit, which is picked at the height of the season, will be more flavorful than fresh. (If you are using frozen fruit, be sure and defrost it first before puréeing.) Consider these recipes guidelines, and adjust the flavoring to your taste. Sugar syrup rather than granulated sugar is often used in these recipes to both thin down and sweeten the fruit purée.

Sauces are a good opportunity to use overripe or bruised fruit. If you use frozen fruit, use only individually frozen fruit without syrup so you can control how much sugar goes into the sauce.

Fruit sauces will keep up to a week in the refrigerator, and close to indefinitely in the freezer. When it has been too long in the refrigerator, a fruit sauce will ferment, with tiny bubbles appearing on the surface and a carbonated taste developing. Freeze for long storage and defrost as needed. The natural pectin in many fruits will cause sauces to thicken as they stand; if they get too thick, thin with an appropriate liqueur or a little orange juice to the right consistency.

Almost any fruit sauce is delicious spooned over ice cream.

CUSTARD SAUCES

The satisfying, creamy consistency of custard sauces makes them a perfect accompaniment for many desserts. As with fruit sauces, custard sauces (except the Vanilla Mousseline Sauce) should be thin enough to swirl easily on a plate.

For a detailed explanation on making a custard or *crème anglaise,* see page 20.

Custard sauces keep refrigerated for five to seven days; they cannot be frozen. For best all-around flavor, let the sauce come to room temperature before serving. If the sauce thickens during storage, stir in a little cream to thin it out.

Serving sauces: You can take advantage of the decorative qualities of sauces in a number of ways. I like to pool the sauce on the plate and then arrange the dessert on top, which shows off the colors and textures of both to best advantage.

Use slightly oversized plates so that you have plenty of room for sauce. Prepare plates with the sauce before serving, then arrange the dessert on top. When a dessert is warm, try serving it with a chilled sauce for contrast, or vice versa for a cold dessert.

To "mirror" or "mask" a plate with sauce, spoon a tablespoon or so onto the plate, then pick up the plate and tilt it to spread evenly. There should be just enough sauce on the plate to cover it in a thin layer; you should always be able to see the bottom of the plate through the sauce.

For a variation, pool the sauce on one half of the plate only, place a slice of dessert on the edge of the sauce, and leave the other side of the plate bare.

I often dress up plates by using two sauces in contrasting colors. If you're using a custard sauce and a fruit sauce together, spoon some of the heavier custard sauce on one side of the plate and tilt to mask just half the plate. Then spoon the fruit sauce on the other half and tilt until the two sauces run together and meet in the middle. If the sauces are the right consistency, they won't mix when they meet.

You can swirl the two together in a random pattern in the center of the plate. Use the sharp tip of a knife, swirling delicately to keep from mixing them.

Some of my favorite combinations are bitter chocolate sauce and raspberry sauce, raspberry (or any fruit sauce) with vanilla sauce, and green kiwi sauce with a red fruit sauce. Vanilla sauce is very successful paired with almost any fruit sauce, as the creamy custard cuts the acidity of the fruit.

The possibilities for decoration with sauces are unlimited. A beautiful technique is to mask the plate with one sauce, like a chocolate sauce or a raspberry sauce, pipe very thin lines of crème fraîche, sour cream, or a light-colored custard sauce over it, and then "pull" the lines with the tip of a knife to give a marbled effect. (It's the same technique that's used for "Making pulled chocolate decorations," page 343.) The lines can be circular or straight, piped over the whole plate or half the plate. A simple design is to pipe a single line border about an inch from the edge of the plate and then to pull out curves on either side of the line to make a sunburst. Choose a vibrant color contrast for a striking effect. "Pulled" patterns are a bit fragile; don't try to move a decorated plate too far or the pattern will lose its look.

Single sauce

Swirling two sauces together

Making a decorative border

Raspberry Sauce

4 cups raspberries (fresh or frozen without syrup)

½ cup plus 1 tablespoon sugar syrup (page 29)

¼ cup orange juice (1 orange)

2 tablespoons lemon juice (1 lemon)

2 teaspoons raspberry liqueur

Makes 2½ cups

Raspberry sauce is found almost as often in fancy restaurants as ketchup is in coffee shops, because this tasty, bright-colored sauce goes beautifully with both chocolate and fruit desserts.

, Purée all ingredients in a blender or food processor until smooth. Strain through a fine-mesh strainer to remove seeds. Refrigerate. If the sauce thickens during storage, add more lemon or orange juice to thin.

Rhubarb–Raspberry Sauce

1 pound fresh rhubarb

1 cup raspberries (fresh or frozen without syrup)

3/4 cup sugar syrup (page 29)

6 tablespoons fresh orange juice (2 oranges)

Makes 2 cups

The raspberries brighten up the pale pink color of the rhubarb without camouflaging its naturally acidic flavor. Use with any dessert that calls for strawberry or raspberry sauce.

Wash rhubarb and cut into 2-inch pieces. Place rhubarb, raspberries, and sugar syrup in a large enamel or stainless steel saucepan and cook over medium heat until rhubarb is tender, 15–20 minutes. Cool. Stir in orange juice. Purée in a food processor or blender until smooth. Strain through a fine-mesh strainer. Refrigerate. If the sauce thickens during storage, add more orange juice to thin.

Strawberry Sauce

4 cups strawberries (fresh or frozen without syrup)

2–3 tablespoons granulated sugar

2–2 1/2 teaspoons kirsch or cherry brandy

1–2 tablespoons lemon juice

Makes 2 cups

Strawberries are probably the most unpredictable of fruits, sometimes sweet and flavorful, sometimes watery and tasteless. If the strawberries aren't the best, don't hesitate to increase the other flavors to taste.

I never strain strawberry sauce because I like the look and texture of the seeds.

Stem fresh strawberries. Purée all ingredients in a food processor or blender until smooth. Refrigerate.

Blackberry Sauce

6 cups blackberries (fresh or frozen without syrup)

1/2 cup double crème de cassis

Makes 4 cups

The flavor of blackberry purée needs no more help than a splash of crème de cassis to turn it into a beautiful dark purple sauce. Boysenberries, ollalieberries, or loganberries can also be used.

Be sure to use cassis liqueur (preferably the type labeled "double crème de cassis") and not cassis syrup, which is too sweet and does not contain alcohol.

Combine berries and liqueur. Purée briefly in a food processor or blender until smooth. Strain through a fine-mesh strainer. Refrigerate.

Cranberry Sauce

3 cups dry white wine

1 vanilla bean, split and scraped

2–3 tablespoons orange zest (2–3 oranges)

3 cups cranberries, fresh or frozen (12 ounces)

1/3 cup granulated sugar

1 cup orange juice (2–3 oranges)

Makes 2 cups

I never thought of making a cranberry sauce until the people at Ocean Spray Cranberries invited me to participate in their annual "Salute to American Food" in the fall of 1983, and asked me to work out some desserts using cranberries. This sauce turned out well—bright and shiny, with the acidic edge that I love. It's a very workable substitute for raspberry sauce.

In a large stainless steel saucepan, boil the wine with the vanilla bean and orange zest until it reduces to 1½ cups. Add cranberries and continue to boil until the berries pop, 3–5 minutes. Reduce heat, add sugar, and simmer, stirring occasionally, for 5 minutes more, until the mixture has thickened and the spoon leaves an empty trail behind it when drawn across the bottom of the pan. Remove from heat.

Stir in orange juice. Purée in food processor or blender until smooth. Strain through a fine-mesh strainer. Refrigerate. If the sauce thickens during storage, thin it with more orange juice or reduced white wine.

Huckleberry Sauce

4 cups huckleberries
(stemming them is
unnecessary)

1 cup water

6 tablespoons granulated
sugar

1 cinnamon stick

1 cup plain yogurt, crème
fraîche, or sour cream

Makes 2 cups

Yogurt, crème fraîche, or sour cream do turn the sauce a muted purple color, but they smooth out the rough tannic flavor that comes from the huckleberry skins.

Combine huckleberries, water, sugar, and cinnamon stick in a large stainless steel or enamel saucepan. Boil for 8–10 minutes, until berries are cooked and mixture is dark purple, bubbly, and has thickened slightly. (It will continue to thicken as it cools.)

Remove cinnamon stick. Purée in a food processor or blender until smooth. Strain through a fine-mesh strainer to remove skins. Stir in yogurt and add a teaspoon or so more sugar to taste, if necessary. Refrigerate.

Mango Sauce

3½ pounds very ripe
mangoes (4 mangoes)

½–¾ cup lime juice (4–5
limes), to taste

Fresh orange juice, optional

Makes 4 cups

The mangoes must be really ripe and soft to give this sauce the proper taste and yield. The lime juice enhances the sauce by adding the acidic edge that mangoes lack. If the mangoes aren't very flavorful, add some fresh orange juice. Use as a same-colored replacement for Apricot Sauce.

Peel the mangoes as thin as possible and scrape the pulp off the skin. Cut off as much pulp from the large fibrous pits as possible and squeeze the pits in your hand to remove every last bit of pulp. Purée in a food processor or blender with ½ cup lime juice until smooth. Add up to ¼ cup more lime juice, to taste. Strain through a fine-mesh strainer. Add orange juice to taste. Refrigerate.

Apricot Sauce

1 cup dried apricots (5 ounces)

1 cup fresh apricots, pitted and sliced (about 5)

1¾ cups fresh orange juice

½ cup dry white wine

2 tablespoons granulated sugar

3 tablespoons apricot liqueur

Makes 2 cups

The flavor of delicate fresh apricots needs the shot in the arm that dried apricots provide.

Place dried apricots, fresh apricots, orange juice, wine, and sugar in a stainless steel or enamel saucepan and simmer until tender, 15–20 minutes. Purée briefly in a food processor or blender until smooth. Strain through a fine-mesh strainer. Stir in apricot liqueur. Refrigerate. If the sauce thickens during storage, add more orange juice or reduced white wine to thin.

Ginger Sauce

3 ounces fresh ginger root

1 cup heavy cream

1 cup milk

4 egg yolks

3 tablespoons granulated sugar

Makes 2½ cups

Peel ginger with a vegetable peeler and slice into rounds ¼-inch thick. There should be about ½ cup. Put ginger in a saucepan and cover with water, bring to a boil, and boil for 30 seconds. Drain well.

In a large saucepan, scald the cream, milk, and blanched ginger. Remove from heat, cover, and let stand 30 minutes. Strain, discarding the ginger. Return cream to saucepan.

In a bowl, beat together the egg yolks and sugar until the sugar has dissolved. Reheat cream to scalding. Pour about one fourth of the hot cream into the egg yolks, whisking continuously. Return mixture to the saucepan and whisk into remaining cream. Cook over low heat, stirring constantly with a wooden spoon, until the mixture thickens enough to coat the back of the spoon. Strain through a fine-mesh strainer into a bowl. Whisk a few times to release heat. Refrigerate.

Kiwi Sauce

1½ pounds ripe kiwis (about 8 fruit)

¼ cup fresh lime juice (2–3 limes)

3–4 tablespoons sugar syrup (page 29), to taste

Makes 2 cups

Although much overused at the height of *nouvelle cuisine*, kiwi fruit make a very appealing sauce, with a pleasant green color that sets off many different desserts. The kiwi has little acidity, so lime juice adds tang.

Peel kiwis carefully with a knife or vegetable peeler. Purée briefly in a food processor or blender just until smooth. (If the seeds are puréed too long they can give the sauce a brownish color.) Strain through a fine-mesh strainer and reserve seeds. Add lime juice and sugar syrup to taste. Stir 1 tablespoon reserved kiwi seeds back into the sauce; discard the rest of the seeds. Refrigerate.

Pear Sauce

4 Poached Pears (page 24)

4–6 tablespoons pear poaching liquid

2 tablespoons poire Williams (pear brandy)

½ cup lemon juice (3–4 lemons)

Makes 2 cups

It's difficult to give exact proportions for this recipe because the quality and flavor of pears can vary so much. If you need to poach pears for a dessert anyway, poach a few extra and make this sauce.

Purée pears with poaching liquid, pear brandy, and lemon juice in a food processor or blender until smooth. If the sauce is too thick, add pear poaching liquid, poire Williams, or lemon juice, or a combination of all three, to thin. Do not add too much poaching liquid or the sauce will become too sweet. Refrigerate.

Caramel

1 cup heavy cream

4 ounces unsalted butter (1 stick)

1 vanilla bean, split and scraped

¼ cup light corn syrup

2 cups granulated sugar

Makes 3 cups

This buttery, rich-tasting, light amber-colored caramel can be warmed to drizzle over ice cream, thinned with cream for a sauce, or used to flavor buttercream. Caramel makes a beautiful glaze for the top of a cake, or you can spread it between cake layers, sprinkled with nuts. A jar of caramel makes a great gift.

In a small saucepan, heat the cream and butter with the vanilla bean until the butter melts and the mixture is hot. Keep warm over low heat.

In a deep, heavy, 3-quart stainless steel saucepan, heat corn syrup over medium heat just until it bubbles. Sprinkle enough sugar to cover the surface entirely (about ⅓ cup) on top of bubbling corn syrup and stir with a wooden spoon until the sugar is incorporated and the mixture starts to bubble and thin out. The mixture will be opaque and grainy. Stir constantly to prevent it from cooking and coloring while the sugar is being added.

Add the rest of the sugar in batches of the same size, incorporating it all in the same way. The mixture will become stiff. Continue cooking, stirring vigorously, until a thread of syrup dripped from the lifted spoon is runny and straw-colored. Remove from heat immediately.

Add hot cream and butter mixture to sugar in four portions, stirring well to incorporate after each addition. The caramel will spatter so be careful not to burn yourself. Return mixture to high heat and boil 2–3 minutes, stirring gently, until the sugar is completely dissolved and the caramel reduces and becomes thicker and a bit stickier. The thread that drips from the spoon now will be clear rather than cloudy. It should be the pale color of commercial caramels, no darker.

Pour immediately into a heatproof container and stir a few times to release the heat and stop the cooking.

When refrigerated, the finished caramel should be stiff enough that it must be spooned out of the container rather than poured. If it is too stiff to be spooned out, it has been reduced too much. To soften, heat the hard caramel over gently simmering water until it melts, then stir in ¼ cup heavy cream and boil for 1 minute to blend.

Keeps refrigerated up to one month.

Caramel Sauce

2 cups Caramel (page 333)
¾ cup heavy cream
Extra heavy cream to thin

Makes 3 cups

Used sparingly, this sweet, smooth sauce is a lovely addition to many desserts. It should be the same consistency as a custard sauce, thin enough to mask a plate easily with a thin layer, but not watery.

Place ingredients in a saucepan and boil together over medium heat for 2–3 minutes, until combined. Let cool to room temperature. The sauce will seem thin but will thicken as it cools. Refrigerate.

Caramel sauce will solidify in the refrigerator. To use, reheat to boiling to liquefy, adding a little extra cream to thin out if necessary. Keeps refrigerated for two to three weeks.

Bitter Orange Sauce

2 cups heavy cream
6 tablespoons orange zest (6 oranges), chopped
1¼ cups fresh orange juice (5–6 oranges)
4 egg yolks
2 tablespoons granulated sugar
2 tablespoons orange liqueur

Makes 2½ cups

Infusing the orange zest into the cream and caramelizing the orange juice gives this sauce a pale orange color and an intriguing, slightly bitter orange flavor. Use only heavy cream—milk will curdle with the orange juice.

In a large saucepan, scald the heavy cream and the orange zest. Remove from heat, cover, and let stand 30 minutes. Meanwhile, in a small stainless steel or enamel saucepan, boil the orange juice until it has reduced to about 3 tablespoons. The orange juice will just start to caramelize and brown. Stir into cream.

In a bowl, beat together the egg yolks and sugar until the sugar has dissolved. Reheat cream to scalding. Pour about one fourth of the hot cream into the egg yolks, whisking continuously. Return mixture to the saucepan and whisk into remaining cream. Cook over low heat, stirring constantly with a wooden spoon, until the mixture thickens enough to coat the back of the spoon. Strain through a fine-mesh strainer into a bowl. Whisk a few times to release heat. Stir in orange liqueur. Cool. Refrigerate.

For Bitter Chocolate Sauce, see Bitter Chocolate Glaze, p. 348.

Coffee Sauce

1 cup whole decaffeinated
   coffee beans

1 cup heavy cream

1 cup milk

4 egg yolks

¼ cup granulated sugar

1–2 tablespoons coffee
   liqueur, to taste

Makes 2½ cups

A simple coffee sauce can be made by mixing instant coffee into plain Vanilla Sauce, but taking the time to infuse the coffee beans into the cream produces a fuller-flavored sauce.

On the work surface, crush coffee beans lightly with a rolling pin or the bottom of a small pan. In a saucepan, scald the cream, milk, and crushed coffee beans. Remove from heat, cover, and let stand 30 minutes. Strain, discard coffee beans, and return cream to saucepan.

In a bowl, beat together the egg yolks and sugar for a few minutes until the sugar has dissolved and the mixture is thick and pale yellow. Reheat cream to scalding. Pour about one fourth of the hot cream into the egg yolks, whisking continuously. Return mixture to saucepan and whisk into remaining cream. Cook over low heat, stirring constantly with a wooden spoon, until the mixture thickens enough to coat the back of the spoon. Strain through a fine-mesh strainer into a bowl. Whisk a few times to release heat. Stir in coffee liqueur to taste. Refrigerate.

Mint Sauce

2 cups whole mint leaves (3
   bunches), removed from
   stems

4 egg yolks

¼ cup granulated sugar

1 cup heavy cream

1 cup milk

1–2 tablespoons green crème
   de menthe, to taste

Makes 2½ cups

In this sauce, the mint leaves are steeped gently in the finished custard for a few minutes, a technique that gives the sauce just enough fresh mint flavor.

Using green crème de menthe will give the sauce a pale green tint. If the color isn't important to you, peppermint schnapps or white crème de menthe can be substituted.

Roughly chop mint leaves. There should be about 1 cup. Set aside.

In a large bowl, beat together the egg yolks and sugar for a few minutes until the sugar has dissolved and the mixture is thick and pale yellow. In a large saucepan, scald the cream and milk. Pour about one fourth of the hot cream into the egg yolks, whisking continuously. Return to saucepan and whisk into remaining cream. Cook over low heat, stirring constantly with a wooden spoon, until the mixture thickens enough to coat the back of the spoon. Whisk a few times to release heat. Stir in chopped mint and let stand 10 minutes. Strain through a fine-mesh strainer. Stir in crème de menthe to taste. Refrigerate.

Vanilla Sauce

1 cup heavy cream

1 cup milk

2 vanilla beans, split and scraped

4 egg yolks

¼ cup granulated sugar

Makes 2½ cups

Vanilla sauce is a plain custard sauce, appropriate with many desserts and especially good to cut the richness of chocolate. When you're serving it with a dessert that is flavored with an alcohol or liqueur, add up to 4 tablespoons of the same alcohol to flavor the sauce.

In a large saucepan, scald the cream, milk, and vanilla bean. Remove from heat, cover, and let stand 30 minutes.

In a large bowl, beat together the egg yolks and sugar for a few minutes until the sugar has dissolved and the mixture is thick and pale yellow. Reheat cream to scalding. Pour about one fourth of the hot cream into the egg yolks, whisking continuously. Return mixture to the saucepan and whisk into remaining cream. Cook over low heat, stirring constantly with a wooden spoon, until the mixture thickens enough to coat the back of the spoon. Strain through a fine-mesh strainer into a bowl. Whisk a few times to release heat. Cool.

VARIATION: Vanilla Mousseline Sauce can be used in place of Vanilla Sauce if you desire a thicker, sabayon type of sauce that can be spooned out next to a dessert. Using the whisk attachment of an electric mixer, beat 1¼ cups heavy cream until thick and mousselike. Refrigerate. In the metal bowl of an electric mixer, combine 4 egg yolks and 1 vanilla bean, split and scraped, with ¼ cup granulated sugar. Whisk over gently simmering water until the mixture is warm and forms a ribbon when the whisk is lifted. Rotate the bowl as often as necessary to prevent the egg from cooking on the sides. Remove from heat and discard vanilla bean. Beat with the electric mixer at high speed until the underside of the bowl is cool, 3–5 minutes. Fold in the whipped cream.

DECORATION

I believe that food should look as good as it tastes. Unfortunately, desserts often look better than they taste, which has convinced me to take a very conservative approach to decorating. Whenever possible, I prefer decorations that are an integral part of the taste of the dessert itself, like a shining arrangement of fruit on top of a fruit tart. The color and texture of a mousse cake in a perfectly symmetrical mold is lovely on its own, without marzipan roses or a thick coating of too-sweet fondant stuck on as an afterthought. A simple chocolate glaze with a fleck of gold leaf in the center is as elegant a decoration as a parfait could ever need, and a shiny, caramelized lemon tart is much more appetizing to me than one covered with a mound of meringue. My approach cuts down the work involved in dessert making: if I have only limited time, I'd rather spend it making a flavorful, interesting dessert than toiling over some extraneous decoration.

When You Need to Decorate—Fixing Disasters: My father, Larry, who is an amateur carpenter, has always said that there should be a class in how to fix your mistakes. The same is true in dessert making. Knowing a few decorating tricks is useful when a dish comes out of the oven lopsided, when something in the refrigerator falls in the center of your perfect tart, or in any situation when a dessert doesn't look the way you'd like. You name the situation and I've had to face it in a busy restaurant kitchen, so I've discovered some ways to cope with last-minute problems.

If you used good ingredients and made the dessert properly, your disaster is definitely worth fixing. What you want to do is distract the eye so that the problem doesn't look as serious. Fresh fruit, sliced and arranged in a decorative pattern, is a practical and delicious way to conceal a little faux pas. Chopped nuts, ground praline, or nougatine can be pressed onto the smudged side of a cake. Put a border of sliced, toasted almonds onto a tart that's been slightly smashed at the edges. A dusting of powdered sugar or cocoa powder can conceal an ill-placed thumbprint. And the entire top of a cake can be covered with chocolate curls or ruffles for a complete camouflage job.

Powdered Sugar and Cocoa Powder: Dusting lightly with powdered sugar or unsweet-ened cocoa powder is one of the simplest ways to decorate a dessert. Each one is very attractive separately, but never use the two together on the same dessert.

Both powders must be sifted onto desserts to ensure a fine, delicate dusting. Place the sugar or cocoa in a small drum sieve and dust it directly onto the surface of the dessert. If you're dusting onto a dessert that is glazed with chocolate, the glaze must be completely set or it will soak up the sugar or cocoa.

Put powdered sugar on in a thick enough coating so that it looks intentional, not blown on by accident. When sugaring chocolate curls, you can dust the sugar on randomly, but on a symmetrical, carefully arranged dessert you want to put it on in a planned, orderly way—in a border, stripes, or circles. Put powdered sugar on fruit desserts at the last minute because the fruit juices will dissolve the sugar quickly. Dust chocolate desserts the day they are to be served, because powdered sugar beads up with moisture if refrigerated overnight. (Avoid putting powdered sugar on glazed fruits altogether, as it will dissolve immediately.)

Unsweetened cocoa powder adds a very elegant, velvety look to a chocolate dessert, especially when sprinkled randomly over chocolate curls or ruffles. It won't bead up with moisture in the refrigerator as powdered sugar does, so it can be used on desserts that are going to be stored overnight. The bitterness of cocoa powder also cuts the sweetness of a chocolate dessert. Cocoa powder can be sifted on in a thick blanket to cover the top of a cake, like the Devil's Food Cake, Marjolaine, or any of the truffle cakes.

To make a powdered sugar or cocoa powder border, use a template, a pan lid, or cut out a wax paper circle an inch or two smaller in diameter than the top of the dessert. Center it on top and dust the powder over evenly. Lift the circle off carefully to avoid spilling. For a striped pattern, cut strips of wax paper and lay them diagonally across the cake, leaving an equal amount of empty space in between. Dust evenly and remove paper carefully. The same technique can be used for any shape.

Glazing a Fruit Tart: When I was at the Cordon Bleu cooking school in London about ten years ago, the instructors there firmly believed that all fruit tarts should be heavily coated with glaze. We students would have to kneel down, eye level with the tart under consideration, and scan it carefully for any patches of unglazed fruit shining through. That technique didn't set well with me for a number of reasons, the major one being that a thick layer of glaze masks the natural flavor of the fruit and makes it undesirably sweet.

A light glazing, on the other hand, just enough to highlight the natural color of the fruit, is a wonderful addition to a tart. Strong, durable fruit, like strawberries, figs, apples, pears, peaches, apricots, and nectarines, hold up well under a light glazing; I never glaze wild strawberries or raspberries as the subtle flavors would be lost (and the heat of the glaze would destroy the outside of the fruit). When whole strawberries are used on top of a tart, I brush only the tops with glaze, to give them a light shimmer.

Use red currant jelly for red fruit desserts and apricot preserves for yellow or orange fruit. Heat a few tablespoons of jam in a small pan with a few teaspoons of water, a complementary alcohol, or fruit juice. Cook, stirring with a pastry brush, until the glaze starts to bubble. Let it reduce until it is sticky enough that, when lifted with the pastry brush, it dribbles off rather than runs. Brush the warm glaze in a thin layer to cover or to randomly highlight the fruit.

If you're glazing a large tart, you may need to reheat the glaze once and thin it out a bit. The glaze must be warm enough to brush on evenly, but not so hot that it cooks or discolors the fruit.

Sliced Almond Border: This versatile decoration is used for fruit tarts, or to camouflage a broken or lopsided border. Put it on after glazing a fruit tart so that the almonds stick.

Toast 3 ounces (¾ cup) sliced blanched almonds for 8–10 minutes at 325 degrees, until lightly toasted. Cool. Cut out a round of wax paper 1–2 inches smaller in diameter than the tart (or use a pan lid or metal template of the right size). Center the paper round on the tart. Arrange toasted almonds around the exposed border. Dust with powdered sugar. Carefully remove the paper round, lifting straight up to avoid spilling the sugar.

Caramelizing a Dessert: Caramelizing the top of a custard dessert gives it a marvelous, translucent, golden-brown layer of crunchy caramel that cracks when broken with a fork. Caramelized sugar adds texture to a custard, and when used on fruit gives it a shiny glazed look. To caramelize, a layer of sugar is sprinkled on a dessert and then melted under very high direct heat, either under a broiler or with a propane torch. Restaurant-style salamander broilers are perfect. Most home oven broilers will work on something solid, like a fruit tart, broiled apple slices, or an oven-baked custard, but they won't get hot enough to caramelize sugar on a soft custard, such as the crèmes brulées. When the broiler is not hot enough, the sugar will liquefy rather than brown.

Caramelizing a cake with a torch

One of my favorite tools is the propane torch, which is the fastest and most effective way to caramelize anything. Available in hardware stores at very reasonable prices (compared to a number of other kitchen gadgets), torches may seem a bit frightening at first, but they're perfectly safe when used carefully. Their direct, powerful flame is not only hot enough to caramelize perfectly, but it is so localized that there is never any danger of burning the edge of a tart shell, as you can caramelizing under a broiler. A good torch should have a steady flame; if it sputters or goes out when tilted, it's faulty.

To caramelize with the torch, sprinkle the top of a dessert with a thin, even layer of granulated or powdered sugar. Turn the torch on low, light with a match, and adjust the flame to high. Sweep the torch evenly from side to side, stopping just long enough in one place to allow the flame to brown the sugar. If the sugar starts to bubble and burn, just blow it out.

Don't caramelize a dessert more than 30 minutes before serving or the caramel will lose its crispness.

(A torch is also very useful for unmolding refrigerated or frozen desserts, much easier to use than hot towels. For molded desserts, invert the mold onto a cardboard or a platter and heat the bottom and sides briefly with the torch. Shake out. With flan rings, simply heat the sides of the ring and remove.)

Glazing a Dessert with Chocolate: The dessert must be smooth and firm before beginning. Plenty of glaze is necessary to flow freely over the cake. Because the chocolate glaze can be used to glaze any chocolate dessert (and also doubles as Bitter Chocolate Sauce), the excess glaze that runs off can be scraped up, stored, and reused another time.

In a heatproof bowl, warm the chocolate glaze over barely simmering water until it is just warm enough to be pourable, but not hot. The glaze will become thinner as it warms up. To glaze a round cake, place the cake flat on the palm of your hand. Pour or ladle the warm glaze over the cake, tilting the cake, shaking it a bit, and letting the glaze run down the sides to make a thin, even covering. Set the cake down on a flat surface or serving platter. To avoid any drip marks, let the cake sit perfectly still for 3–5 minutes until the glaze sets. Chill 20–30 minutes, until the glaze is completely set. For the smoothest look, glaze cake again in the same manner, and chill until set. To glaze the top only of a dessert, glaze the top before unmolding. Pour or ladle the glaze in the center of the cake. Hold the cake

Glazing a round cake

Glazing a terrine

Glazing the top only

flat on the palm of your hand, rotating and tilting the cake so the glaze spreads in an even, thin layer. Shake off excess.

To glaze most loaf-shaped cakes or parfaits, place the cake on a cooling rack set on a baking sheet. Pour or ladle the warm glaze over the length of it. With a long metal spatula, smooth once over the top of the cake to remove excess glaze, without actually touching the cake itself. Pick up one end of the cooling rack and tap it firmly against the baking sheet to allow the glaze to flow down and cover the sides. Then, with a metal spatula, pick up the glaze that has dripped off the cake and pat it back onto areas that are not covered. Smooth the sides of the cake with the spatula to make sure the glaze is even. Let the cake sit perfectly still for 3–5 minutes, then chill until set.

For frozen desserts such as the Three-Chocolate Parfait or molded mousse desserts like the Chocolate Terrine, simply pour the glaze over the dessert and allow to set before refrigerating. *Do not* smooth the glaze with a spatula or tap the cooling rack on the baking sheet, because the spatula will leave marks in the glaze.

Decorating the Sides of a Dessert with Praline, Nougatine, or Sugared Almonds: Ground praline, nougatine, or sugared almonds can be pressed onto the sides of a glazed dessert for a more decorated look, and to add a crunchy texture. It's also an excellent strategy for camouflaging a dessert with smudged or damaged sides.

After you've given the dessert one or two coats of glaze (depending on your preference), chill it for 10–15 minutes, until the sides are almost set but still a bit sticky. If the cake is round, hold it flat on the palm of your hand; if it is rectangular, let it rest partly on your palm and partly on your forearm. Press the coating onto the sides with the fingers and palm of your hand, stopping it just a fraction of an inch underneath the top edge of the cake. Chill until set.

If a cake is perfectly glazed, a nice variation is to press a narrow border (½ inch to 1 inch wide) around the bottom of the cake.

The nut coating will get soggy, so put it on the cake no more than 24 hours before serving.

Decorating with Gold Leaf: A fleck of brilliant gold leaf looks stunning on a dark chocolate background—and it's edible, too. It turns a simple chocolate-glazed cake into a black-tie dessert. Purchase a little booklet of ultrathin 22-carat gold leaf, the same kind used for illuminating manuscripts, at an art supply or paint store, bookbinder, or framer. The price varies with the price of gold—a packet generally costs $20–$30—and you'll use so little of it that it will probably last a lifetime.

To use, glaze the dessert and refrigerate until completely set and dry. Work in a draft-free area, because the gold is so thin that it will drift around in the slightest breeze. Peel back the separating paper to expose just as much gold leaf as you plan to use. Pick up a small, irregularly shaped bit with the tip of a small sharp knife and delicately lay it flat on the dessert. It can be placed in the center of a chocolate dessert or used as an accent to set off certain letters in a word written on the top. The gold must be laid flat, as it is not attractive if bunched up. If the gold doesn't adhere immediately, blow on it gently and it will stick.

Making a Piping Bag and Piping Chocolate Decorations: A tiny piping bag of wax paper or parchment paper can be used to pipe thin lines of chocolate to decorate the tops of cakes. With an opening much smaller than the smallest tip of a pastry bag, a paper piping bag can be used to make squiggles or "pulled" chocolate patterns and to write.

Cut out a square of parchment paper measuring at least 8 inches on each side, fold in half diagonally and cut into two triangles. (Reserve one triangle for another use.) The edges must be cleanly cut (not frazzled or frayed) so that the piped line will be smooth. Fold the triangle according to the illustration. All three corners of the triangle must meet perfectly when the triangle is folded. The cone must be tight so that the point at the end is completely sealed.

Melt about 2 ounces chocolate. Dark chocolate, milk chocolate, or white chocolate will all show up when piped on a dark chocolate glaze. Strain the melted chocolate through a fine-mesh strainer and fill bag less than half full. Turn the corners of the triangle into the bag and then roll the bag down from the top to close. At this point, the bag can be prepared in advance and kept in a warm place until ready to use.

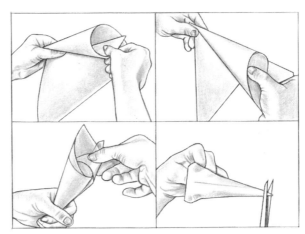

Making a piping bag

When ready to pipe, snip the tip of the bag with scissors. With a small hole, it should pipe a very fine line. Make the opening larger if necessary. For writing or making squiggles, squeeze out a little chocolate. If it is too cold, it will be hard to force out. If it is too warm, the chocolate will spread out when piped and make thick lines. Ideally, you should be able to pipe weblike lines of chocolate that harden as soon as they are piped.

To pipe, use your thumb and index finger to hold the top flap of the bag down and to apply pressure to force the chocolate out of the bag in a steady stream. Rest the top of the bag on the top of your index finger to give you control as you pipe. Keep your arms close to your body, and the bag at about a 60-degree angle to the cake.

The simplest design to pipe is a chocolate squiggle, just back and forth on the top of the cake or crossed, like a tic-tac-toe board, with the ends connected. A looping border is good-looking and easy to do as well.

Pulled Chocolate Designs: These are beautiful designs for topping a cake, professional-looking but easy to do. Pipe immediately after glazing, while the glaze is still warm, so that the lines get a marbled effect when pulled.

Piping thin, straight lines on top of a cake makes the classic "napoleon" decoration. Rather than trying to make each line separate, draw the lines straight across and right off the cake, turning at the end and coming back in the other direction. The line, then, is really continuous, but the connections don't show on the cake because they have fallen on the work surface. As soon as the lines are drawn, drag the tip of a sharp knife through the lines at intervals of 1 to 1½ inches across the cake, pulling them toward you. Drag the knife lightly to avoid cutting into the dessert. Turn the cake around and pull toward you again in the spaces between the first pulled lines.

For a chocolate spiderweb decoration, make a continuous spiral of chocolate, starting at the center of the cake and working toward the outside. With the tip of a sharp knife, pull about 8 lines through the chocolate spiral from the center to the outside, spacing them as if you were marking the cake to be cut into 8 slices. Then, between the lines just marked, pull 8 lines in the opposite direction, starting at the edge of the cake and pulling toward the center.

Spiderweb design

Piping chocolate lines on a cake

Napoleon design

Writing on a Cake: To write, the chocolate must not be too warm or the lines will spread out as they are piped. The glazed surface must be cold and set.

Before starting to write, remember that your penmanship will not look any better on a cake than it does on paper. If you've got poor handwriting, practice with pen and paper before beginning. (You don't have to go overboard, though—in France, pastry chefs fill notebooks and notebooks with writing practice when they do their training.) Besides commemorations of birthdays and the other obvious special occasions, the most usual thing written on the top of a dessert is the dessert's name ("Chocolate terrine") or the major ingredient in the dessert ("Strawberry").

I find that flowing handwriting with lots of squiggles is safest, because it's easiest to cover up any little mistakes. Copy writing styles from various sources, like books, wedding invitations, and writing you see in the pastry shop, or develop your own style. Keep your letters in proportion to each other. Most writing on desserts looks best centered.

Writing on a cake

Making Chocolate Curls, Ruffles, and Cigarettes: All these chocolate shapes make lovely rough-looking toppings for cakes. They're especially nice on mousse cakes, because they add texture and crunch to an otherwise soft dessert.

It takes a lot of practice to work with chocolate in this way, but the final results are impressive. Most important, chocolate work must be done in cool weather. You'll cause yourself a lot of frustration if you try it when the weather's warm.

For all three shapes—curls, ruffles, and cigarettes—the melted chocolate is spread on the back of a 12 x 17-inch warm sheet pan, allowed to firm up, and then scraped off in different ways. To scrape, you will need a flexible, triangular metal paint scraper, preferably with a fairly thin beveled edge (available at hardware stores). For one sheet pan of chocolate, use 8 ounces bittersweet chocolate or 12 ounces white chocolate mixed with 4 teaspoons cooking oil.

Melt chocolate as directed on page 19. Warm the sheet pan in the oven until it is warm but not so hot that you can't touch it. The sheet pan should be about the same temperature as the melted chocolate. If the pan is too cold, the chocolate will cool too fast and lose its shine. Place the sheet pan upside down on the work surface.

Ladle or pour the melted chocolate onto the pan. Using an offset metal spatula, spread the melted chocolate evenly over the back of the pan, covering the entire surface about 1/16 inch thick. If the chocolate is too thin, it is difficult to scrape up; if too thick, the chocolate sheets are not delicate. Refrigerate until the chocolate hardens, about 30 minutes.

When set, remove the pan from the refrigerator and let the chocolate soften to room temperature. If the chocolate melts when you start to scrape it up, it is too warm. Refrigerate until firmer. If the chocolate is difficult to scrape up and cracks, it is too cold and should be allowed to stand longer at room temperature. The chocolate can be warmed and chilled a limitless number of times. Your hands must be *cold* to touch the chocolate without melting it; cool your fingertips with ice. Work quickly, touching the chocolate as little as possible.

Scraping chocolate off a pan is easiest if you brace the pan on the counter against a wall so that it won't slip. Save all the scrapings to melt down and reuse.

For Chocolate Curls: Holding the paint scraper at a 45-degree angle to the pan, scrape the chocolate away from you and lift up each curl with your hands. Pick up short strips. Some of the pieces will bend into curls by themselves and some can be bent into curls with your cold fingertips. If the weather is warm, put the curls onto a sheet pan and keep them refrigerated as you work; if it is cool, you can arrange them directly on the glazed cake. The chocolate glaze must be still sticky so that the curls adhere to it.

Use curls sparingly, covering the cake lightly. Don't overlap the curls too much or there will be an overwhelming amount of chocolate on each slice. Dusting lightly with powdered sugar or cocoa powder, in random or symmetrical patterns, will fill in the gaps.

Chocolate curls

For Chocolate Cigarettes: Chocolate cigarettes are thin sticks of chocolate, pointed and uneven at the ends, *not* wide tubes with round openings at the ends. Cigarettes look wonderful as a border, scattered around a cake, or covering the top of a loaf-shaped cake.

Holding the paint-scraper at a 45-degree angle to the pan, scrape away from you *at an angle* (not straight ahead). The chocolate will roll up, stopping itself from rolling further when the ends close up. Pick up cigarettes with the paint scraper, not with your hands and chill as you scrape them up. Touch them as little as possible, because they are so thin that they melt easily. Arrange the cigarettes on top of the chocolate-glazed dessert while the glaze is still sticky so that the cigarettes adhere to the cake. Dust with cocoa powder or powdered sugar if desired.

Chocolate cigarettes

For Chocolate Ruffles: When the top of a cake is completely covered with ruffles, it looks like a big chocolate flower. Of all the chocolate decorations, this one takes the most practice, but with practice, it is quite simple.

Holding the paint scraper at a 45-degree angle to the pan, scrape up a long strip of chocolate with one hand, using the thumb and forefinger of the other hand to help the chocolate crinkle into ruffles. Don't pinch the chocolate together at the end. Stretch the strip out a bit, turn the ruffle over so the shiny side is up, and arrange it directly on the glazed cake. The glaze must be sticky so the ruffles adhere to it. Scrape up another strip and place it next to the first, so that it looks like one continuous row of ruffles. Cover the cake top with three circles of ruffles, starting at the outside and working in. Place a few extra curls in the center. In the outside row, the ruffles are generally about 2 inches wide, on the inside rows about 2½ inches wide, so they stick up above the outside strip. It will take two 12 x 17-inch sheet pans of chocolate to cover an 8-inch cake with ruffles.

Chocolate ruffles

Swiss Meringue

2 egg whites
*½ cup plus 2 tablespoons
   granulated sugar*
1 teaspoon lemon juice

Makes 1 cup

For the occasional moment when you need to do a quick repair job, this meringue is invaluable. Use it to cover up cracks in a custard tart, to disguise the collapsed edge of a tart shell, or to hide the fact that you didn't have quite enough fruit to cover the top of a tart completely. Heating the egg whites to dissolve the sugar makes a sturdier meringue than the usual uncooked one.

This meringue makes the Lemon-Lime Tart into an unusually good "lemon meringue." It can be caramelized under a preheated broiler, but watch it carefully and be ready to blow out the flames if the meringue ignites. The recipe quantity is for repair jobs. If you want to cover the entire top of a lemon-lime tart, double the recipe.

Place the egg whites, sugar, and lemon juice in the bowl of an electric mixer and whisk together over simmering water until the sugar dissolves, 3–5 minutes, and becomes mousselike. (Don't let the water touch the bottom of the bowl or the egg whites may start to cook.) The only way to tell if the sugar has dissolved is to touch a bit of the mixture to your tongue and see if it still feels grainy.

When the sugar has dissolved, place the bowl on the electric mixer and whip at high speed until the egg whites are thick, stiff, and very white.

For repair jobs, pipe the meringue with a No. 2 star tip. Keep the piping tip as close to the surface of the tart as possible, and don't overlap as you pipe—the meringue shouldn't be thick.

Bitter Chocolate Glaze

8 ounces bittersweet
   chocolate

6 tablespoons unsalted
   butter (3/4 stick)

1 tablespoon plus 1
   teaspoon light corn syrup

3/4 cup heavy cream

6 tablespoons Cognac (or
   an alcohol of your choice)

3 tablespoons unsweetened
   cocoa powder (optional
   if your chocolate is not
   bitter enough)

Makes 2 cups

One of my favorite ways to decorate a dessert is by coating it with a layer of slick, shiny, dark chocolate glaze. There's a very refined quality to the velvety, unadorned chocolate, which is complete in itself.

If you have the time and inclination to decorate a dessert further, though, the essential plainess of a chocolate glaze makes it an excellent background for other chocolate embellishments. Whether a dessert is finished with just a fleck of glowing gold leaf in the center, a chocolate band wrapping the edge, or the top covered with crunchy chocolate ruffles or curls, the glaze is the base. this glaze lends itself perfectly to the bitter chocolate sauce that is called for in several of the recipes.

Cut chocolate into 2-inch pieces. In a heatproof bowl, melt chocolate with butter and corn syrup over barely simmering water. (The water should not touch the bottom of the bowl or the chocolate will burn.) Turn off heat and let mixture stand over warm water until ready to use.

In a small saucepan whisk together the cream, brandy, and cocoa powder. Bring to a simmer over medium heat, whisking constantly until the cocoa powder is dissolved. Scrape into the melted chocolate mixture and stir to combine. Use the sauce while it is still warm.

Chocolate glaze will keep for months stored in the refrigerator. To reuse, reheat glaze in a heatproof bowl set over a pot of barely simmering water.

White Chocolate Glaze

6 ounces white chocolate

¼ cup heavy cream

1 tablespoon light corn syrup

2 tablespoons lemon juice (1 lemon)

Makes enough to glaze the tops of two 8-inch round cakes

When I want a shiny white finish on the top of a cake, I find this white chocolate glaze much preferable to the other possible light-colored icings, like fondant, which is difficult to make. This glaze is a wonderful background for writing with chocolate or making pulled chocolate patterns (page 343).

Because this glaze is on the sticky side, I wouldn't suggest using it to glaze an entire cake. Instead, glaze only the top of a dessert, before it has been unmolded, after the chocolate band is firm.

Cut the chocolate into 2-inch pieces. In a heatproof bowl, melt chocolate over barely simmering water. (The water should not touch the bottom of the bowl or the chocolate will burn.) Turn off heat and let stand until ready to use.

In a saucepan, scald the cream. Stir into the melted chocolate, along with the corn syrup and lemon juice, until mixture is blended and smooth. When a spoonful of the glaze is lifted, it should fall in a steady stream. Thin with a little cream, if necessary.

Reheat over simmering water to use. If the glaze is too thick, it is probably not hot enough, or needs a tablespoon or two more cream. If it is too hot, it will be runny and will be translucent rather than opaque on top of a cake.

Keeps refrigerated up to one month.

Making a Chocolate Band

For a Dark or Milk Chocolate Band:
2 ounces bittersweet or milk chocolate

For a White Chocolate Band:
4 ounces white chocolate
2 teaspoons cooking oil

Wrapping the band around the cake

A chocolate band, in dark chocolate, milk chocolate, or white chocolate, wraps around a cake, giving a smooth, finished look and adding another delectable, crisp layer of chocolate.

The cake you plan to wrap with the band should be entirely prepared, with straight, symmetrical sides.

Cut the chocolate into 2-inch pieces. In a heatproof bowl, melt chocolate (with cooking oil for white chocolate) over barely simmering water. White chocolate and milk chocolate burn quite easily, so watch carefully. The water should not touch the bottom of the bowl or either chocolate will burn. Turn off heat and let stand until ready to use.

Cut out a strip of wax paper as wide as the sides of the cake to be wrapped and long enough to encircle the cake and overlap by at least 2 inches at the ends. The quantities of chocolate given above will make a band 8 inches long by 3 inches wide, or 12 inches long by 1½ inches wide; if you want to make a band that rises higher than the cake (which can be pinched in to enclose the cake), you will need more chocolate. Clear a space in the refrigerator so that the band can be laid out flat for a brief period of time, or chill a work surface on which the band can set.

Lay the wax paper out on a work surface and ladle a line of melted chocolate along the length of it. With a narrow metal spatula, spread the chocolate smooth so that it completely covers the paper in an even layer and flows out slightly over the edges.

Lift the band by the ends and shift its position so that the edges of the band are straight and don't harden with the irregularly shaped overflow still attached. Refrigerate or lay the strip on the chilled work surface until the chocolate loses its shine. The chocolate should be stiff so that the strip will not flop in half, but not so stiff that it will crack when wrapped around a cake.

Set the cake on a serving platter. (Once the band is applied, don't touch the cake or move it from platter to platter.)

Wrap the band, paper side out, around the cake, overlapping the ends. If the band starts to crack when you are handling it, the chocolate is too cold. Let it stand at room temperature until it becomes more pliable. If the band begins to bend and collapse, chill again until firm. At the spot where the outside end overlaps the inside, immediately cut the inside end of the band with scissors and lift out the loose piece. The band will fit the cake perfectly. (If you don't overlap the ends, pinch the ends of the band together toward you and cut them off evenly with a scissors.) If you intentionally made the band a few inches taller than the cake, press the top edge of the chocolate in, randomly, toward the center of the cake. If the band is not firm enough to hold its shape when pressed down, chill again briefly.

A chocolate band can also be applied in two pieces. The first strip must set up on the cake and the wax paper peeled back slightly at either end so that the second strip has chocolate to adhere to.

Leave the paper in place and chill until hard or decorate the top of the cake as desired. Refrigerate until firm and the paper peels off easily. Peel off paper just after removing the cake from the refrigerator; if the chocolate softens, the wax paper cannot be removed smoothly. Once the paper is removed, the band will not melt if the cake is kept out of direct sunlight or high temperatures.

A two-colored band, combining dark chocolate, milk chocolate, or white chocolate, is an unusual, very modern look. It sometimes looks like wood grain; you can also get a striped effect using the following technique.

With a spatula, smear the lighter chocolate (milk chocolate or white chocolate) down the wax paper strip, in a random, freeform design or a more defined striped pattern. Leave empty space for the dark chocolate background to fill in. Pick up the band and shift its position to make a clean edge and refrigerate or allow to harden as directed for the plain chocolate band. When hard, ladle a thin layer of dark chocolate or milk chocolate on the band and spread to completely cover. Refrigerate until set, then place around cake following directions above.

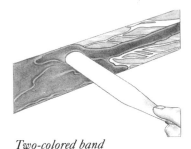

Two-colored band

Chocolate Disks

Disks of chocolate can be used overlapping as a border or can completely cover the top of a cake. Experiment with the thickness of the chocolate until you can get it thick

Continued from previous page

enough that the disks aren't too fragile, but thin enough that they don't become big hunks of chocolate.

Spread a layer of melted chocolate on a piece of wax or parchment paper as directed above. Chill until the chocolate loses its shine but not until it is so firm that it cracks when cut. Cut disks with the wide end of a large pastry-bag tip or a small, plain biscuit cutter and leave in place. Refrigerate until firm. Either peel the disks off the paper or peel off paper and press out disks, whichever is easier. When arranged on a cake, dust lightly with powdered sugar or unsweetened cocoa powder if desired.

Freeform Chocolate Decorations

If a chocolate band cracks, it can always be melted to use again, or you can break it into irregular pieces and freeze them, ready to stick into scoops of ice cream for decoration. You can also crumble the hardened chocolate into fast chocolate chips to stir into ice cream. (If irregular pieces are your goal, spread chocolate on a large piece of wax paper, chill as directed for the chocolate band, and break into pieces when firm.)

Nougatine with Almonds or Coconut

1/2 teaspoon cooking oil

1 1/4 cups granulated sugar

1/4 cup water

4 1/2 ounces raw sliced blanched almonds (1 1/2 cups), or 1 1/2 cups long-shred unsweetened coconut

Makes 2 cups chopped nougatine

Nougatine is candy brittle that is delicious crumbled over ice cream or folded into mousses, ice cream, or parfaits. It can also be ground fine and pressed onto the sides of cakes. When made with corn syrup, nougatine becomes the pliable, golden-brown substance that European-style patissiers sculpt into fountains, baskets, and other marvelous centerpieces.

Oil a metal baking sheet with cooking oil; set aside.

In a saucepan, heat together the sugar and water. When the water boils, it will throw sugar onto the sides of the pan. At that point, wash down the sides with a pastry brush, dipping in water as necessary to dissolve sugar. (Alternatively, place a lid on the pan for 30 seconds and the steam condensation will wash the sugar off the sides.)

Cook until the mixture turns an even light amber color. Stir in the almonds or coconut and cook another 1–2 minutes, until it is a honey color and the almonds or coconut are cooked to a light brown. Pour immediately onto the oiled baking sheet and spread out with a wooden spatula to stop the cooking. When cool, chop by hand into coarse chunks or grind in a food processor to a fine powder.

Store airtight for a few days. Nougatine is good as long as it stays crisp and tastes fresh.

Sugared Almonds

1 cup sliced blanched almonds (not toasted)

6 tablespoons granulated sugar

2 tablespoons water

Makes 1 cup

Much easier to make than praline or nougatine, these sugar-frosted "flakes" can be crushed to press onto the sides of cakes, sprinkled over ice cream, or scattered on a pool of sauce around a dessert. The coating keeps them crunchy longer than plain toasted almonds, but they can't be folded into mousses as a praline can—they'll get soggy.

Preheat oven to 325 degrees. In a bowl, toss almonds with sugar and water until well coated. Spread on a nonstick baking sheet (the nuts will stick to parchment paper or untreated baking sheets), spreading them evenly. Bake for 20 minutes. The finished almonds will be crisp and light brown, and shiny where the sugar has melted. If the almonds are unevenly colored, it may be necessary to turn them over and cook for a few more minutes. Cool. Store airtight as long as they taste fresh and stay crisp.

Praline

1 teaspoon cooking oil

¼ cup plus 1 tablespoon water

1¼ cups granulated sugar

10 ounces (2 cups) whole blanched almonds

Makes 4 cups ground praline

Praline can be very simply described as caramelized nuts, but that hardly does justice to this sweet, crunchy preparation that is one of the most versatile components of dessert making. Ground fine, it can be folded into mousses or ice creams, sprinkled between cake layers or over ice cream, or pressed onto the sides of a cake for decoration.

Praline is traditionally made with hazelnuts or a combination of hazelnuts and almonds, but I prefer using whole blanched almonds only because they are not as oily as hazelnuts and they stay fresh longer when ground. Also, since almonds don't have to be toasted to remove their skins (as hazelnuts do), the praline stays lighter in color and avoids having a burnt taste. (Remember that praline is extremely hot so work carefully while stirring it and pouring it onto the baking sheet.)

Oil a baking sheet with the cooking oil and set aside.

In a heavy 3-quart saucepan, heat water and sugar over high heat. When the water boils, it will throw sugar onto the sides of the pan. At that point, wash down the sides with a pastry brush, dipping in water as necessary to dissolve sugar. (Alternatively, place a lid on the pan for 30 seconds and the steam condensation will wash the sugar off the sides.)

When the entire surface of the mixture is covered with slowly bursting bubbles but has not yet started to color (soft crack stage, 270–290 degrees on a candy thermometer), add all the nuts at once. The mixture will turn white and become very hard to stir. Vigorously break it up with a wooden spoon and stir constantly to remelt the sugar and cook until the mixture colors evenly, at least 5 minutes. If the praline starts to darken in one place, stir energetically to distribute the hot syrup. Be very careful as the mixture is extremely hot. It is done when the sugar has turned an even mahogany color, the nuts start to pop, and the mixture begins to smoke.

Pour quickly onto the oiled baking sheet and stir to stop the caramel from cooking. Remove any white chunks of uncooked sugar. Cool. Break into pieces and grind to a fine meal in a food processor or blender. (The praline will turn into a paste if processed too long.)

Store in an airtight jar at room temperature. Praline is good as long as it stays crunchy and does not taste stale. If you need a very fine powder, strain it again through a fine strainer.

VARIATION: Hazelnut Praline. If you want to make the praline with hazelnuts, use the same quantity as almonds and toast them at 325 degrees for 8–10 minutes, until brown. Cool, rub off the skins with a clean dish towel, and continue as directed above.

Candied Walnuts

½ cup granulated sugar

¼ cup water

Up to 15 perfect walnut halves

Makes up to 15 glazed walnut halves

Candied walnuts make a decorative border on the Caramel-Walnut Tart or any other walnut dessert.

You will need a hatpin, trussing needle, or sharp-pointed paring knife.

In a small heavy saucepan, heat sugar and water over high heat. When the water boils, it will throw sugar onto the sides of the pan. At that point, wash down the sides of the pan with a pastry brush, dipping in water as necessary to dissolve sugar. (Alternatively, place a lid on the pan for 30 seconds and the steam condensation will wash the sugar off the sides.)

When the mixture turns a honey color, remove from heat. Dip pan bottom in cold water, if necessary. Prop up one side of the pan on a folded dish towel so that the caramel is deep. With a hatpin, trussing needle, or sharp tip of a paring knife, stab flat side of walnut half and then dip rounded top side of nut into caramel. Tap off excess caramel on the side of the pan. Using another knife to help, carefully flip nut on its undipped flat side onto a sheet of aluminum foil. Cool.

The candy syrup is extremely hot, so handle the walnuts with utmost care, and do not touch the candied side of the nut until it is cool.

Repeat process with all nuts. Once the sugar has caramelized, it will continue to cook off the heat. If you are not a very fast worker, dip the bottom of the saucepan in a shallow pan of cold water as soon as it has reached a honey color, to stop the cooking. If the caramel in the pan hardens, remelt as needed.

For maximum crispness, use these walnuts the day you candy them.

If there are any specialized ingredients or utensils that you find difficult to locate in your area, check with the following sources. Most have catalogues that will help you to choose the correct item.

American Spoon Foods
411 E. Cake Street
Petoskey, MI 49770

Ingredients only, excellent indigenous American products: maple sugar, preserves, and dried fruit (great dried sour cherries).

Bridge Kitchenware Corporation
214 E. 52nd Street
New York, NY 10022

Fred Bridge is the ultimate in cookware suppliers. He carries an extensive range of domestic and European equipment. He has molds, tart rings, heavy-duty Teflon baking sheets, 4-inch Teflon tart molds (called for in the Individual Apple-Calvados Tarts), and professional whisks, strainers, and pastry bags. Chances are if he doesn't have it, you don't need it.

Dean & Deluca, Inc.
121 Prince Street
New York, NY 10012

Good chocolate and preserves, high-quality fresh fruits, and smallwares.

Gourmet France

in Los Angeles
9373 Remick Avenue
Pacoima, CA 91331

in San Francisco
3095 Kerner Boulevard
San Rafael, CA 94901

in Dallas
10754 North Stemmons Freeway
Dallas, TX 75220

in Houston
2415 Karbach Street #2
Houston, TX 77092

Importers of good European products including chocolates, preserves, almond paste, and flavorings. At the moment, unfortunately, they sell only to the trade. Tell your local gourmet shop about these fine purveyors.

J. B. Prince Company
29 West 38th Street
New York, NY 10018

A mail-order company carrying hard-to-find smallwares such as truffle-dipping tools, lattice cutters, and entrement rings. If by chance Fred Bridge does not have it, J. B. Prince will.

Maid of Scandinavia
3244 Raleigh Avenue
Minneapolis, MN 55416

A full line of pastry ingredients and equipment. They carry an electric krumkake baker that makes it easy to bake the "Italian Ice Cream Cones" and the "Oven Baked Ice Cream Cones."

Marcel Akselrod Company
530 West 25th Street
New York, NY 10001

Marcel and Rachel Akselrod stock perhaps the highest-quality pastry products in the country. They carry excellent almond paste, my favorite brand of chocolate, Valrhona, and a full line of amazing extracts and fruit purées.

Paprikas Weiss Importer
1546 2nd Avenue
New York, NY 10028

Paprikas Weiss does not have an extensive line of pastry ingredients but they have some good ones: flours, good chocolate in small quantities, nuts, and some flavorings.

S. E. Rycoff
761 Terminal Street
Los Angeles, CA 90021

One of the biggest hotel and restaurant supply houses in the country on the East Coast; they own Sexton Company. They can supply everything from pastry brushes to stoves and they sell mail order—good quality, too.

Sûr La Table
84 Pine Street
Seattle, WA 98101

Probably the most extensive line of kitchen gadgets offered in any store. They have everything from wooden ice cream cone molds to a dozen kinds of vegetable peeler.

Tahitian Imports
P.O. Box 67A54
Century City Station
Los Angeles, CA 90067

The best vanilla beans I have ever found.

Torn Ranch Grove
1122 Fourth Street
San Rafael, CA 94901

The best source for dried fruits and nuts.

Williams Sonoma Company
P.O. Box 7456
San Francisco, CA 94120

They offer a good range of cooking equipment, smallwares, and quality chocolates. They don't have everything, but what they have is the best. My ice cream maker, the Ugolini Mini-Gel, is from Williams Sonoma.

INDEX